'This book helps to fill what has long been a glaring gap in the scholarship on Early Buddhism, offering us a detailed textual study of the *Satipaṭṭhāna Sutta*, the foundational Buddhist discourse on meditation practice. With painstaking thoroughness, Ven. Anālayo marshals the *suttas* of the Pāli canon, works of modern scholarship, and the teachings of present-day meditation masters to make the rich implications of this text, so concise in the original, clear to contemporary students of the Dharma. Unlike more popular books on the subject, he is not out to establish the exclusive validity of one particular system of meditation as against others; his aim, rather, is to explore the *sutta* as a wide-ranging and multi-faceted source of guidance which allows for alternative interpretations and approaches to practice. His analysis combines the detached objectivity of the academic scholar with the engaged concern of the practitioner for whom meditation is a way of life rather than just a subject of study. The book should prove to be of value both to scholars of Early Buddhism and to serious meditators alike. Ideally, it will encourage in both types of reader the same wholesome synthesis of scholarship and practice that underlies the author's own treatment of his subject.'

Bhikkhu Bodhi, *scholar and translator*

'Ven. Anālayo has produced a very thorough and comprehensive study of the Buddha's discourse on *satipaṭṭhāna*. It is to be recommended not only for the way in which it examines these instructions in meditation in the context of the early discourses and in relation to the traditional interpretations of the Pāli commentaries, but also for the way in which it encompasses the observations and interpretations of both modern scholars of Buddhism and teachers of meditation. For anyone interested in the theory and practice of *satipaṭṭhāna* meditation this is a most valuable guide.'

Rupert Gethin, *Senior Lecturer on Indian Religions at the University of Bristol*

'*Satipaṭṭhāna: – The Direct Path to Realization* is a gem. Ven. Anālayo has done a superb job of elucidating this core teaching of the Buddha. His clarity of style, nuanced observations, and depth of analysis open many new doors of understanding. I learned a lot from this wonderful book and highly recommend it to both experienced meditators and those just beginning to explore the path.'

Joseph Goldstein, *author of* One Dharma: The Emerging Western Buddhism

'This book explains in detail the full meaning of the entire body of teaching given in this discourse. I believe this commentary by Anālayo on this root text surpasses all previous commentaries in the Theravāda tradition over the past 2,000 years. Anālayo has written an indispensable guide to enable students of the Buddha's teachings to understand this celebrated talk. His book reads like a practice manual for meditators in daily life.

'It is surely destined to become the classic commentary on the *Satipaṭṭhāna*. It will also inspire readers interested in the Buddhist tradition to develop such down-to-earth practices for their own realization.'

Christopher Titmuss, *writer and co-founder of Gaia House meditation centre*

Praise for Anālayo's *Perspectives on Satipaṭṭhāna*, the companion volume to *Satipaṭṭhāna: the Direct Path to Realization*

'In this new book, Anālayo builds on his earlier ground-breaking work, *Satipaṭṭhāna: The Direct Path to Realization*. Here, he enlarges our perspective on this seminal teaching by exploring the practices of mindfulness as presented in both the Pali and Chinese versions of this important discourse. The brilliance of his scholarly research, combined with the depth of his meditative understanding, provides an invaluable guide to the liberating practices of the Buddha's teaching.' – **Joseph Goldstein**, author of *Mindfulness: A Practical Guide to Awakening* and *One Dharma: The Emerging Western Buddhism*, Co-founder, Insight Meditation Society, Barre, Massachusetts, USA

'Anālayo shows that the practical instructions on *Satipaṭṭhāna* from these three traditions are sometimes identical, and sometimes different. The differences are often interesting, adding new perspectives to what we already knew; and affirming, where the traditions speak in one voice, the authenticity of the oral instructions and the likelihood that this was the actual teaching of the historical Buddha. This book will be useful for experienced seekers after truth who want to immerse themselves more deeply, and in more detail, in the core Buddhist practice of *Satipaṭṭhāna*.' – **Kamalashila**, author of *Buddhist Meditation: Tranquillity, Imagination and Insight*, Co-founder, Vajraloka Meditation Centre, Wales, UK

'Anālayo's work is a brilliant treasury of impeccable scholarship and practice, offering a wise, open-minded, and deep understanding of the Buddha's original teachings. His approach makes an inspiring contribution to the modern Dharma world.' – **Jack Kornfield**, author of *The Wise Heart*, founding teacher of the Spirit Rock Center, USA

'Anālayo has offered us a work of great scholarship and wisdom that will be of immense benefit to anyone who wants to seriously study or to establish a practice of mindfulness.' – **Sharon Salzberg**, author of *Lovingkindness*, Co-founder, Insight Meditation Society, Barre, Massachusetts, USA

SATIPAṬṬHĀNA

Anālayo

SATIPAṬṬHĀNA

The Direct Path to Realization

WINDHORSE PUBLICATIONS

Published by Windhorse Publications
169 Mill Road
Cambridge
CB1 3AN
www.windhorsepublications.com

Reprinted 2006, 2008, 2010, 2012, 2014, 2017.

Cover photo Theodor Franz Steffens
Cover design Marlene Eltschig
Printed by Bell & Bain Ltd., Glasgow

British Library Cataloguing in Publication Data:
A catalogue record for this book is available from the British Library

ISBN 9781 899579 54 9

As an act of *Dhammadāna*, Anālayo has waived royalty payments from this book.

CONTENTS

LIST OF FIGURES

Ven. Anālayo was born in 1962 in Germany, was ordained in 1995 in Sri Lanka, and completed his PhD on *satipaṭṭhāna* at the University of Peradeniya in 2000. At present he is mainly engaged in the practice of meditation, and among other things contributes to the *Encyclopaedia of Buddhism*.

ACKNOWLEDGEMENTS

Little of the present work would have come about without the generous support that I received from my parents, K. R. and T. F. Steffens. I am also much indebted to Muni Bhikkhu, Bhikkhu Bodhi, Ñāṇananda Bhikkhu, Guttasīla Bhikkhu, Ñāṇaramita Bhikkhu, Ajahn Vipassī, Dhammajīva Bhikkhu, Brahmāli Bhikkhu, Ānandajoti Bhikkhu, Anagārika Santuṭṭho, Prof. Lily de Silva, Prof. P. D. Premasiri, Godwin Samararatne, Dhammacāri Vishvapani, Michael Drummond, and Andrew Quernmore for suggestions, corrections, inspiration, and criticism. Any shortcomings or misrepresentations are entirely down to my own insufficient level of meditative practice and theoretical understanding.

Jhāyatha, mā pamādattha,
mā pacchā vippaṭisārino ahuvattha!

Meditate, don't be negligent,
lest you may later regret it!

INTRODUCTION

The present work, which is the combined outcome of my Ph.D. research at the University of Peradeniya in Sri Lanka and my own practical experience as a meditating monk, attempts a detailed exploration of the significance and the practice of mindfulness meditation according to its exposition in the *Satipaṭṭhāna Sutta*, and placed within its early Buddhist canonical and philosophical context.

Mindfulness and the proper way of putting it into practice are certainly topics of central relevance for anyone keen to tread the Buddha's path to liberation. Yet for a proper understanding and implementation of mindfulness meditation the original instructions by the Buddha on *satipaṭṭhāna* need to be taken into consideration. In view of this, my inquiry is in particular concerned with the discourses recorded in the four main *Nikāyas* and the historically early parts of the fifth *Nikāya* as centrally important source material.

Satipaṭṭhāna is a matter of practice. In order to ensure that my exploration has practical relevance, I have consulted a selection of modern meditation manuals and related publications. The nature of this selection has been mainly a matter of availability, yet I hope to have included a fairly representative number of meditation teachers. Apart from these, I have also relied on various academic monographs and articles on early Buddhism in order to illustrate the philosophical framework and historical context within which the *Satipaṭṭhāna Sutta* is to be understood. These provide the background information for understanding particular passages or expressions in the discourse.

To help maintain text flow and readability, I have kept the main body of the text as free as possible from direct quotations and tangential observations. Instead, I have made extensive use of footnotes, which provide references of interest and discussions of additional information. The general reader may prefer to focus on the body of the text during a first reading, and only turn to the information in the footnotes during a second reading.

My exposition follows the sequence of the passages in the discourse as closely as possible. At the same time, however, my treatment is not restricted to simple comments, but allows for minor digressions in order to explore relevant points and to provide a background for better understanding the section under discussion.

The first chapter deals with general aspects and terminology in relation to *satipaṭṭhāna*. The next three chapters are concerned with the second paragraph of the *Satipaṭṭhāna Sutta*, the "definition", especially with the implications of *sati* and the role of concentration. In the fifth chapter I turn to a set of general instructions repeated throughout the discourse after each meditation exercise, the "refrain". With the sixth chapter I begin to examine the actual exercises of the "direct path" of mindfulness meditation, concerned with contemplating the body, feelings, mind, and *dhammas*. At the end of this examination of the individual meditation practices I turn to the final paragraph of the discourse and to the implications of *Nibbāna*. By way of conclusion, I try to highlight some key aspects of *satipaṭṭhāna* and to evaluate its importance.

In general, my purpose in the present inquiry is less to prove and establish a particular point of view than to provide suggestions and reflections in the hope of opening up new perspectives in regard to *satipaṭṭhāna*, and in the hope of inspiring the reader to engage in its actual practice.

TRANSLATION OF THE *SATIPAṬṬHĀNA SUTTA*[1]

Thus have I heard. On one occasion the Blessed One was living in the Kuru country at a town of the Kurus named Kammāsadhamma. There he addressed the monks thus: "Monks." "Venerable sir," they replied. The Blessed One said this:

[DIRECT PATH]

"Monks, this is the direct path for the purification of beings, for the surmounting of sorrow and lamentation, for the disappearance of *dukkha* and discontent, for acquiring the true method, for the realization of *Nibbāna*, namely, the four *satipaṭṭhānas*.

[DEFINITION]

"What are the four? Here, monks, in regard to the body a monk abides contemplating the body, diligent, clearly knowing, and mindful, free from desires and discontent in regard to the world. In regard to feelings he abides contemplating feelings, diligent, clearly knowing, and mindful, free from desires and discontent in regard to the world. In regard to the mind he abides contemplating the mind, diligent, clearly knowing, and mindful,

---

1 For my rendering of the *Satipaṭṭhāna Sutta*, I have mostly adopted the translation given in Ñāṇamoli (1995): pp.145–55. In a few instances, however, I have ventured to introduce my own renderings, based on the understanding gained in the progress of my research. In order to facilitate references to particular passages of the discourse, I have inserted a short headline above each section.

free from desires and discontent in regard to the world. In regard to *dhammas* he abides contemplating *dhammas*, diligent, clearly knowing, and mindful, free from desires and discontent in regard to the world.

[BREATHING]

"And how, monks, does he in regard to the body abide contemplating the body? Here, gone to the forest, or to the root of a tree, or to an empty hut, he sits down; having folded his legs crosswise, set his body erect, and established mindfulness in front of him, mindful he breathes in, mindful he breathes out.

"Breathing in long, he knows 'I breathe in long,' breathing out long, he knows 'I breathe out long.' Breathing in short, he knows 'I breathe in short,' breathing out short, he knows 'I breathe out short.' He trains thus: 'I shall breathe in experiencing the whole body,' he trains thus: 'I shall breathe out experiencing the whole body.' He trains thus: 'I shall breathe in calming the bodily formation,' he trains thus: 'I shall breathe out calming the bodily formation.'

"Just as a skilled turner or his apprentice, when making a long turn, knows 'I make a long turn,' or when making a short turn knows 'I make a short turn' so too, breathing in long, he knows 'I breathe in long,'... (continue as above).

[REFRAIN]

"In this way, in regard to the body he abides contemplating the body internally, or he abides contemplating the body externally, or he abides contemplating the body both internally and externally. He abides contemplating the nature of arising in the body, or he abides contemplating the nature of passing away in the body, or he abides contemplating the nature of both arising and passing away in the body. Mindfulness that 'there is a body' is established in him to the extent necessary for bare knowledge and continuous mindfulness. And he abides independent, not clinging to anything in the world.

"That is how in regard to the body he abides contemplating the body.

[POSTURES]

"Again, monks, when walking, he knows 'I am walking'; when standing, he knows 'I am standing'; when sitting, he knows 'I am sitting'; when lying down, he knows 'I am lying down'; or he knows accordingly however his body is disposed.

[REFRAIN]

"In this way, in regard to the body he abides contemplating the body internally ... externally ... both internally and externally. He abides contemplating the nature of arising ... of passing away ... of both arising and passing away in the body. Mindfulness that 'there is a body' is established in him to the extent necessary for bare knowledge and continuous mindfulness. And he abides independent, not clinging to anything in the world. That too is how in regard to the body he abides contemplating the body.

[ACTIVITIES]

"Again, monks, when going forward and returning he acts clearly knowing; when looking ahead and looking away he acts clearly knowing; when flexing and extending his limbs he acts clearly knowing; when wearing his robes and carrying his outer robe and bowl he acts clearly knowing; when eating, drinking, consuming food, and tasting he acts clearly knowing; when defecating and urinating he acts clearly knowing; when walking, standing, sitting, falling asleep, waking up, talking, and keeping silent he acts clearly knowing.

[REFRAIN]

"In this way, in regard to the body he abides contemplating the body internally ... externally ... both internally and externally. He abides contemplating the nature of arising ... of passing away ... of both arising and passing away in the body. Mindfulness that 'there is a body' is established in him to the extent necessary for bare knowledge and continuous mindfulness. And he abides independent, not clinging to anything in the world. That too is how in regard to the body he abides contemplating the body.

[ANATOMICAL PARTS]

"Again, monks, he reviews this same body up from the soles of the feet and down from the top of the hair, enclosed by skin, as full of many kinds of impurity thus: 'in this body there are head-hairs, body-hairs, nails, teeth, skin, flesh, sinews, bones, bone-marrow, kidneys, heart, liver, diaphragm, spleen, lungs, bowels, mesentery, contents of the stomach, faeces, bile, phlegm, pus, blood, sweat, fat, tears, grease, spittle, snot, oil of the joints, and urine.'

"Just as though there were a bag with an opening at both ends full of many sorts of grain, such as hill rice, red rice, beans, peas, millet, and white rice, and a man with good eyes were to open it and review it thus: 'this is hill rice, this is red rice, these are beans, these are peas, this is millet, this is white rice'; so too he reviews this same body.... (continue as above).

[REFRAIN]

"In this way, in regard to the body he abides contemplating the body internally ... externally ... both internally and externally. He abides contemplating the nature of arising ... of passing away ... of both arising and passing away in the body. Mindfulness that 'there is a body' is established in him to the extent necessary for bare knowledge and continuous mindfulness. And he abides independent, not clinging to anything in the world. That too is how in regard to the body he abides contemplating the body.

[ELEMENTS]

"Again, monks, he reviews this same body, however it is placed, however disposed, as consisting of elements thus: 'in this body there are the earth element, the water element, the fire element, and the air element'.

"Just as though a skilled butcher or his apprentice had killed a cow and was seated at a crossroads with it cut up into pieces; so too he reviews this same body.... (continue as above).

[REFRAIN]

"In this way, in regard to the body he abides contemplating the body internally ... externally ... both internally and externally. He abides contemplating the nature of arising ... of passing away ... of both arising and passing away in the body. Mindfulness that 'there is a body' is established in him to the extent necessary for bare knowledge and continuous mindfulness. And he abides independent, not clinging to anything in the world. That too is how in regard to the body he abides contemplating the body.

[CORPSE IN DECAY]

"Again, monks, as though he were to see a corpse thrown aside in a charnel ground – one, two, or three days dead, bloated, livid, and oozing matter ...

being devoured by crows, hawks, vultures, dogs, jackals, or various kinds of worms … a skeleton with flesh and blood, held together with sinews … a fleshless skeleton smeared with blood, held together with sinews … a skeleton without flesh and blood, held together with sinews … disconnected bones scattered in all directions … bones bleached white, the colour of shells … bones heaped up, more than a year old … bones rotten and crumbling to dust – he compares this same body with it thus: 'this body too is of the same nature, it will be like that, it is not exempt from that fate.'[2]

[REFRAIN]

"In this way, in regard to the body he abides contemplating the body internally … externally … both internally and externally. He abides contemplating the nature of arising … of passing away … of both arising and passing away in the body. Mindfulness that 'there is a body' is established in him to the extent necessary for bare knowledge and continuous mindfulness. And he abides independent, not clinging to anything in the world. That too is how in regard to the body he abides contemplating the body.

[FEELINGS]

"And how, monks, does he in regard to feelings abide contemplating feelings?

"Here, when feeling a pleasant feeling, he knows 'I feel a pleasant feeling'; when feeling an unpleasant feeling, he knows 'I feel an unpleasant feeling'; when feeling a neutral feeling, he knows 'I feel a neutral feeling.'

"When feeling a worldly pleasant feeling, he knows 'I feel a worldly pleasant feeling'; when feeling an unworldly pleasant feeling, he knows 'I feel an unworldly pleasant feeling'; when feeling a worldly unpleasant feeling, he knows 'I feel a worldly unpleasant feeling'; when feeling an unworldly unpleasant feeling, he knows 'I feel an unworldly unpleasant feeling'; when feeling a worldly neutral feeling, he knows 'I feel a worldly neutral feeling'; when feeling an unworldly neutral feeling, he knows 'I feel an unworldly neutral feeling.'

---

2 In the actual discourse, each of the individual stages of the corpse in decay is followed by a full version of the "refrain", which, for the sake of convenience, I have abbreviated here and in Fig. 1.1.

[REFRAIN]

"In this way, in regard to feelings he abides contemplating feelings internally ... externally ... internally and externally. He abides contemplating the nature of arising ... of passing away ... of both arising and passing away in feelings. Mindfulness that 'there is feeling' is established in him to the extent necessary for bare knowledge and continuous mindfulness. And he abides independent, not clinging to anything in the world.

"That is how in regard to feelings he abides contemplating feelings.

[MIND]

"And how, monks, does he in regard to the mind abide contemplating the mind?

"Here he knows a lustful mind to be 'lustful', and a mind without lust to be 'without lust'; he knows an angry mind to be 'angry', and a mind without anger to be 'without anger'; he knows a deluded mind to be 'deluded', and a mind without delusion to be 'without delusion'; he knows a contracted mind to be 'contracted', and a distracted mind to be 'distracted'; he knows a great mind to be 'great', and a narrow mind to be 'narrow'; he knows a surpassable mind to be 'surpassable', and an unsurpassable mind to be 'unsurpassable'; he knows a concentrated mind to be 'concentrated', and an unconcentrated mind to be 'unconcentrated'; he knows a liberated mind to be 'liberated', and an unliberated mind to be 'unliberated.'

[REFRAIN]

"In this way, in regard to the mind he abides contemplating the mind internally ... externally ... internally and externally. He abides contemplating the nature of arising ... of passing away ... of both arising and passing away in regard to the mind. Mindfulness that 'there is a mind' is established in him to the extent necessary for bare knowledge and continuous mindfulness. And he abides independent, not clinging to anything in the world.

"That is how in regard to the mind he abides contemplating the mind.

[HINDRANCES]

"And how, monks, does he in regard to *dhammas* abide contemplating *dhammas*? Here in regard to *dhammas* he abides contemplating *dhammas* in terms of the five hindrances. And how does he in regard to *dhammas* abide contemplating *dhammas* in terms of the five hindrances?

"If sensual desire is present in him, he knows 'there is sensual desire in me'; if sensual desire is not present in him, he knows 'there is no sensual desire in me'; and he knows how unarisen sensual desire can arise, how arisen sensual desire can be removed, and how a future arising of the removed sensual desire can be prevented.

"If aversion is present in him, he knows 'there is aversion in me'; if aversion is not present in him, he knows 'there is no aversion in me'; and he knows how unarisen aversion can arise, how arisen aversion can be removed, and how a future arising of the removed aversion can be prevented.

"If sloth-and-torpor is present in him, he knows 'there is sloth-and-torpor in me'; if sloth-and-torpor is not present in him, he knows 'there is no sloth-and-torpor in me'; and he knows how unarisen sloth-and-torpor can arise, how arisen sloth-and-torpor can be removed, and how a future arising of the removed sloth-and-torpor can be prevented.

"If restlessness-and-worry is present in him, he knows 'there is restlessness-and-worry in me'; if restlessness-and-worry is not present in him, he knows 'there is no restlessness-and-worry in me'; and he knows how unarisen restlessness-and-worry can arise, how arisen restlessness-and-worry can be removed, and how a future arising of the removed restlessness-and-worry can be prevented.

"If doubt is present in him, he knows 'there is doubt in me'; if doubt is not present in him, he knows 'there is no doubt in me'; and he knows how unarisen doubt can arise, how arisen doubt can be removed, and how a future arising of the removed doubt can be prevented.

[REFRAIN]

"In this way, in regard to *dhammas* he abides contemplating *dhammas* internally ... externally ... internally and externally. He abides contemplating the nature of arising ... of passing away ... of both arising and passing away in *dhammas*. Mindfulness that 'there are *dhammas*' is established in him to the extent necessary for bare knowledge and continuous mindfulness. And he abides independent, not clinging to anything in the world.

"That is how in regard to *dhammas* he abides contemplating *dhammas* in terms of the five hindrances.

[AGGREGATES]

"Again, monks, in regard to *dhammas* he abides contemplating *dhammas* in terms of the five aggregates of clinging. And how does he in regard to *dhammas* abide contemplating *dhammas* in terms of the five aggregates of clinging?

Here he knows, 'such is material form, such its arising, such its passing away; such is feeling, such its arising, such its passing away; such is cognition, such its arising, such its passing away; such are volitions, such their arising, such their passing away; such is consciousness, such its arising, such its passing away.'

[REFRAIN]

"In this way, in regard to *dhammas* he abides contemplating *dhammas* internally ... externally ... internally and externally. He abides contemplating the nature of arising ... of passing away ... of both arising and passing away in *dhammas*. Mindfulness that 'there are *dhammas*' is established in him to the extent necessary for bare knowledge and continuous mindfulness. And he abides independent, not clinging to anything in the world.

"That is how in regard to *dhammas* he abides contemplating *dhammas* in terms of the five aggregates of clinging.

[SENSE-SPHERES]

"Again, monks, in regard to *dhammas* he abides contemplating *dhammas* in terms of the six internal and external sense-spheres. And how does he in regard to *dhammas* abide contemplating *dhammas* in terms of the six internal and external sense-spheres?

"Here he knows the eye, he knows forms, and he knows the fetter that arises dependent on both, and he also knows how an unarisen fetter can arise, how an arisen fetter can be removed, and how a future arising of the removed fetter can be prevented.

"He knows the ear, he knows sounds, and he knows the fetter that arises dependent on both, and he also knows how an unarisen fetter can arise, how an arisen fetter can be removed, and how a future arising of the removed fetter can be prevented.

"He knows the nose, he knows odours, and he knows the fetter that arises dependent on both, and he also knows how an unarisen fetter can arise, how an arisen fetter can be removed, and how a future arising of the removed fetter can be prevented.

"He knows the tongue, he knows flavours, and he knows the fetter that arises dependent on both, and he also knows how an unarisen fetter can arise, how an arisen fetter can be removed, and how a future arising of the removed fetter can be prevented.

"He knows the body, he knows tangibles, and he knows the fetter that arises dependent on both, and he also knows how an unarisen fetter can arise, how an arisen fetter can be removed, and how a future arising of the removed fetter can be prevented.

"He knows the mind, he knows mind-objects, and he knows the fetter that arises dependent on both, and he also knows how an unarisen fetter can arise, how an arisen fetter can be removed, and how a future arising of the removed fetter can be prevented.

[REFRAIN]

"In this way, in regard to *dhammas* he abides contemplating *dhammas* internally ... externally ... internally and externally. He abides contemplating the nature of arising ... of passing away ... of both arising and passing away in *dhammas*. Mindfulness that 'there are *dhammas*' is established in him to the extent necessary for bare knowledge and continuous mindfulness. And he abides independent, not clinging to anything in the world.

"That is how in regard to *dhammas* he abides contemplating *dhammas* in terms of the six internal and external sense-spheres.

[AWAKENING FACTORS]

"Again, monks, in regard to *dhammas* he abides contemplating *dhammas* in terms of the seven awakening factors. And how does he in regard to *dhammas* abide contemplating *dhammas* in terms of the seven awakening factors?

"Here, if the mindfulness awakening factor is present in him, he knows 'there is the mindfulness awakening factor in me'; if the mindfulness awakening factor is not present in him, he knows 'there is no mindfulness awakening factor in me'; he knows how the unarisen mindfulness awakening factor can arise, and how the arisen mindfulness awakening factor can be perfected by development.

"If the investigation-of-*dhammas* awakening factor is present in him, he knows 'there is the investigation-of-*dhammas* awakening factor in me'; if the investigation-of-*dhammas* awakening factor is not present in him, he knows 'there is no investigation-of-*dhammas* awakening factor in me'; he knows how the unarisen investigation-of-*dhammas* awakening factor can arise, and how the arisen investigation-of-*dhammas* awakening factor can be perfected by development.

"If the energy awakening factor is present in him, he knows 'there is the energy awakening factor in me'; if the energy awakening factor is not present in him, he knows 'there is no energy awakening factor in me'; he knows how the unarisen energy awakening factor can arise, and how the arisen energy awakening factor can be perfected by development.

"If the joy awakening factor is present in him, he knows 'there is the joy awakening factor in me'; if the joy awakening factor is not present in him, he knows 'there is no joy awakening factor in me'; he knows how the unarisen joy awakening factor can arise, and how the arisen joy awakening factor can be perfected by development.

"If the tranquillity awakening factor is present in him, he knows 'there is the tranquillity awakening factor in me'; if the tranquillity awakening factor is not present in him, he knows 'there is no tranquillity awakening factor in me'; he knows how the unarisen tranquillity awakening factor can arise, and how the arisen tranquillity awakening factor can be perfected by development.

"If the concentration awakening factor is present in him, he knows 'there is the concentration awakening factor in me'; if the concentration awakening factor is not present in him, he knows 'there is no concentration awakening factor in me'; he knows how the unarisen concentration awakening factor can arise, and how the arisen concentration awakening factor can be perfected by development.

"If the equanimity awakening factor is present in him, he knows 'there is the equanimity awakening factor in me'; if the equanimity awakening factor is not present in him, he knows 'there is no equanimity awakening factor in me'; he knows how the unarisen equanimity awakening factor can arise, and how the arisen equanimity awakening factor can be perfected by development.

[REFRAIN]

"In this way, in regard to *dhammas* he abides contemplating *dhammas* internally ... externally ... internally and externally. He abides contemplating the nature of arising ... of passing away ... of both arising and passing away in *dhammas*. Mindfulness that 'there are *dhammas*' is established in him to the extent necessary for bare knowledge and continuous mindfulness. And he abides independent, not clinging to anything in the world.

"That is how in regard to *dhammas* he abides contemplating *dhammas* in terms of the seven awakening factors.

[NOBLE TRUTHS]

"Again, monks, in regard to *dhammas* he abides contemplating *dhammas* in terms of the four noble truths. And how does he in regard to *dhammas* abide contemplating *dhammas* in terms of the four noble truths?

"Here he knows as it really is, 'this is *dukkha*'; he knows as it really is, 'this is the arising of *dukkha*'; he knows as it really is, 'this is the cessation of *dukkha*'; he knows as it really is, 'this is the way leading to the cessation of *dukkha*.'

[REFRAIN]

"In this way, in regard to *dhammas* he abides contemplating *dhammas* internally ... externally ... internally and externally. He abides contemplating the nature of arising ... of passing away ... of both arising and passing away in *dhammas*. Mindfulness that 'there are *dhammas*' is established in him to the extent necessary for bare knowledge and continuous mindfulness. And he abides independent, not clinging to anything in the world.

"That is how in regard to *dhammas* he abides contemplating *dhammas* in terms of the four noble truths.

[PREDICTION]

"Monks, if anyone should develop these four *satipaṭṭhānas* in such a way for seven years, one of two fruits could be expected for him: either final knowledge here and now, or, if there is a trace of clinging left, non- returning. Let alone seven years ... six years ... five years ... four years ... three years ... two years ... one year ... seven months ... six months ... five months ... four months ... three months ... two months ... one month ... half a month ... if anyone should develop these four *satipaṭṭhānas* in such a way for seven days, one of two fruits could be expected for him: either final knowledge here and now, or, if there is a trace of clinging left, non-returning. So it was with reference to this that it was said:

[DIRECT PATH]

"Monks, this is the direct path for the purification of beings, for the surmounting of sorrow and lamentation, for the disappearance of *dukkha* and discontent, for acquiring the true method, for the realization of *Nibbāna*, namely, the four *satipaṭṭhānas*."

That is what the Blessed One said. The monks were satisfied and delighted in the Blessed One's words.

I

GENERAL ASPECTS OF THE DIRECT PATH

To begin, I will survey the underlying structure of the *Satipaṭṭhāna Sutta* and consider some general aspects of the four *satipaṭṭhānas*. I will then examine the expressions "direct path" and "*satipaṭṭhāna*".

I.1 OVERVIEW OF THE *SATIPAṬṬHĀNA SUTTA*

Satipaṭṭhāna as the "direct path" to *Nibbāna* has received a detailed treatment in the *Satipaṭṭhāna Sutta* of the *Majjhima Nikāya*.[1] Precisely the same discourse recurs as the *Mahāsatipaṭṭhāna Sutta* of the *Dīgha Nikāya*, the only difference being that this version offers a more extensive treatment of the four noble truths, the last of the *satipaṭṭhāna* contemplations.[2] The topic of *satipaṭṭhāna* has moreover inspired several shorter discourses in the *Saṃyutta Nikāya* and the *Aṅguttara Nikāya*.[3] Apart from the Pāli sources, expositions on *satipaṭṭhāna* are also preserved in Chinese and Sanskrit, with intriguing occasional variations from the Pāli presentations.[4]

---

1 M I 55–63, the tenth discourse of the *Majjhima Nikāya*.

2 D II 305–15. The Burmese edition (sixth *Saṅgāyana*) has added the longer section on the four noble truths to the *Majjhima* version as well; the Sinhalese edition, however, agrees with the PTS edition in presenting only a short statement of the four noble truths.

3 These are the *Satipaṭṭhāna Saṃyutta* at S V 141–92, and the *Satipaṭṭhāna Vagga* at A IV 457–62. In addition, there is also a *Sati Vagga* at A IV 336–47; a *Satipaṭṭhāna Vibhaṅga* at Vibh 193–207; and twice a *Satipaṭṭhāna Kathā* at Kv 155–9 and at Paṭis II 232–5. Shorter discourses with similar titles are the three *Satipaṭṭhāna Suttas* at S IV 360, S IV 363, and A III 142; the three *Sati Suttas* at S II 132, S IV 245, and A IV 336; and the three *Sato Suttas* at S V 142, S V 180, and S V 186.

Most of the discourses in the *Saṃyutta Nikāya* and *Aṅguttara Nikāya* mention only the bare outline of the four *satipaṭṭhānas*, without going into the details of their possible applications. This functional division into four *satipaṭṭhānas* seems to be a direct outcome of the Buddha's awakening,[5] a central aspect of his rediscovery of an ancient path of practice.[6] But the detailed instructions found in the *Mahāsatipaṭṭhāna Sutta* and the *Satipaṭṭhāna Sutta* apparently belong to a later period, when the Buddha's teaching had spread from the Ganges valley to the distant Kammāsadhamma in the Kuru country, where both discourses were spoken.[7]

---

4 According to Schmithausen 1976: p.244, five additional versions are in existence: two complete versions in Chinese (in the *Madhyama Āgama*: Taishō 1, no.26, p.582b, and in the *Ekottara Āgama*: Taishō 2, no.125, p.568a), and three fragmentary versions in Chinese and Sanskrit (these being the *Pañcaviṃśatisāhasrikā Prajñāpāramitā*, the *Śāriputrābhidharma* (Taishō 28, no.1548, p.525a), and the *Śrāvakabhūmi*). An abridged translation of one of the complete Chinese versions, the *Nien-ch'u-ching*, being the ninety-eighth *sūtra* in the Chinese *Madhyama Āgama* can be found in Minh Chau 1991: pp.87–95. A complete translation of this version and also of the other Chinese version from the *Ekottara Āgama*, this being the first *sūtra* in the twelfth chapter (Yi Ru Dao) of the *Ekottara Āgama*, can be found in Nhat Hanh 1990: pp.151–77. A comparison of the *Satipaṭṭhāna Saṃyutta* with its corresponding Chinese version can be found in Choong 2000: pp.215–18, and in Hurvitz 1978: pp.211–29.

5 At S V 178 the Buddha included the four *satipaṭṭhānas* among his insights into things unknown at his time. Cf. also S V 167, which reports how the recently awakened Buddha reflected that the four *satipaṭṭhānas* were the direct path to awakening, whereupon Brahmā Sahampati came down to applaud and approve this reflection (cf. also S V 185). Both cases give only the outline of the four *satipaṭṭhānas* and do not contain the detailed practical examples given in the *Satipaṭṭhāna Sutta* and the *Mahāsatipaṭṭhāna Sutta*.

6 S II 105 refers to *sammā sati* as the rediscovery of an ancient path, traversed by the Buddhas of the past. Similarly A II 29 speaks of *sammā sati* as an ancient practice. In fact D II 35 reports *bodhisatta* Vipassī engaged in *dhammānupassanā* on the five aggregates, which confirms that *satipaṭṭhāna* was an ancient practice, undertaken by previous Buddhas, a practice which however must then have fallen into oblivion until its rediscovery by Gotama Buddha.

7 Lily de Silva (n.d.): p.3, points out that the *Satipaṭṭhāna Sutta* was only delivered once "the *Dhamma* (had) spread from its original seat of Magadha to the outskirts of the Kuru country". Other discourses spoken at Kammāsadhamma in the Kuru country (e.g. D II 55; M I 501; M II 261; S II 92; S II 107; and A V 29) support an association of this location with a relatively evolved stage of development of the early Buddhist community (e.g. M I 502 speaks of many followers from various backgrounds). According to Ps I 227, a uniting feature among the discourses spoken at this particular location is their comparatively advanced nature, owing to the capacity of its inhabitants to receive deep teachings. The location of the Kuru country corresponds to the area of modern Delhi (according to Law 1979: p.18; Malalasekera 1995: vol.I, p.642; and T.W. Rhys Davids 1997: p.27). This same part of India is also associated with the events in the *Bhagavadgītā* (Bhg I.1).

In Fig. 1.1 (below) I have attempted to offer an overview of the structure underlying the detailed exposition of *satipaṭṭhāna* given in the *Satipaṭṭhāna Sutta*, with each of the sections of the discourse represented by a box and arranged from bottom to top.

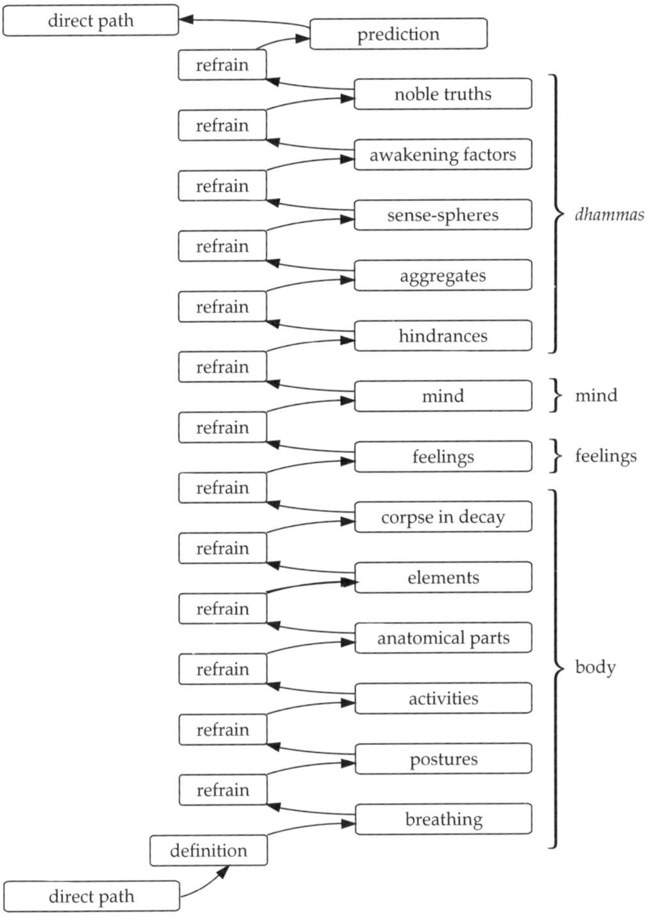

Fig. 1.1 Structure of the *Satipaṭṭhāna Sutta*

The starting and concluding section of the discourse is a passage which states that *satipaṭṭhāna* constitutes the direct path to *Nibbāna*. The next section of the discourse offers a short definition of the most essential aspects of this direct path. This "definition" mentions four *satipaṭṭhānas* for contemplation: body, feelings, mind, and *dhammas*.[8] The "definition" also specifies the mental qualities that are instrumental for *satipaṭṭhāna*: one should be diligent (*ātāpī*), clearly knowing (*sampajāna*), mindful (*sati*), and free from desires and discontent (*vineyya abhijjhādomanassa*).

After this "definition", the discourse describes the four *satipaṭṭhānas* of body, feelings, mind, and *dhammas* in detail. The range of the first *satipaṭṭhāna*, contemplation of the body, proceeds from mindfulness of breathing, postures, and activities, via analyses of the body into its anatomical parts and elements, to contemplating a corpse in decay. The next two *satipaṭṭhānas* are concerned with contemplating feelings and mind. The fourth *satipaṭṭhāna* lists five types of *dhammas* for contemplation: the mental hindrances, the aggregates, the sense-spheres, the awakening factors, and the four noble truths. After the actual meditation practices, the discourse returns to the direct path statement via a prediction about the time within which realization can be expected.

Throughout the discourse, a particular formula follows each individual meditation practice. This *satipaṭṭhāna* "refrain" completes each instruction by repeatedly emphasizing the important aspects of the practice.[9] According to this "refrain", *satipaṭṭhāna* contemplation covers internal and external phenomena, and is concerned with their arising and passing away. The "refrain" also points out that mindfulness should be established merely for the sake of developing bare knowledge and for achieving continuity of awareness. According to the same "refrain", proper *satipaṭṭhāna* contemplation takes place free from any dependence or clinging.

The entire discourse is framed by an introduction, which conveys the occasion of its delivery, and a conclusion, which reports the delighted reaction of the monks after the Buddha's exposition.[10]

By placing the "definition" and the "refrain" at the centre of the above figure, I intend to highlight their central role in the discourse. As the figure shows, the discourse weaves a recurring pattern that systematically alternates between specific meditation instructions

---

8 The implications of the term *dhamma*, which I have left untranslated, are discussed on p.182.

9 The fact that this "refrain" is indispensable to each meditation exercise is shown by the remark concluding each occurrence of the "refrain" (e.g. M I 56): "that is how a monk in regard to the body (feelings, mind, *dhammas*) abides contemplating the body (feelings, mind, *dhammas*)." This remark connects the exposition to the question asked at the outset of each *satipaṭṭhāna* (e.g. M I 56): "how does a monk in regard to the body (etc.) abide contemplating the body (etc.)?"

10 These are the standard introduction and concluding sections in what Manné 1990: p.33, classifies as a typical "sermon".

and the "refrain". Each time, the task of the "refrain" is to direct attention to those aspects of *satipaṭṭhāna* that are essential for proper practice. The same pattern also applies to the start of the discourse, where a general introduction to the topic of *satipaṭṭhāna* through the "direct path" statement is followed by the "definition", which has the role of pointing out its essential characteristics. In this way, both the "definition" and the "refrain" indicate what is essential. Thus, for a proper understanding and implementation of *satipaṭṭhāna*, the information contained in the "definition" and the "refrain" is of particular importance.

1.2 A SURVEY OF THE FOUR *SATIPAṬṬHĀNAS*

On closer inspection, the sequence of the contemplations listed in the *Satipaṭṭhāna Sutta* reveals a progressive pattern (cf. Fig. 1.2 below). Contemplation of the body progresses from the rudimentary experience of bodily postures and activities to contemplating the body's anatomy. The increased sensitivity developed in this way forms the basis for contemplation of feelings, a shift of awareness from the immediately accessible physical aspects of experience to feelings as more refined and subtle objects of awareness.

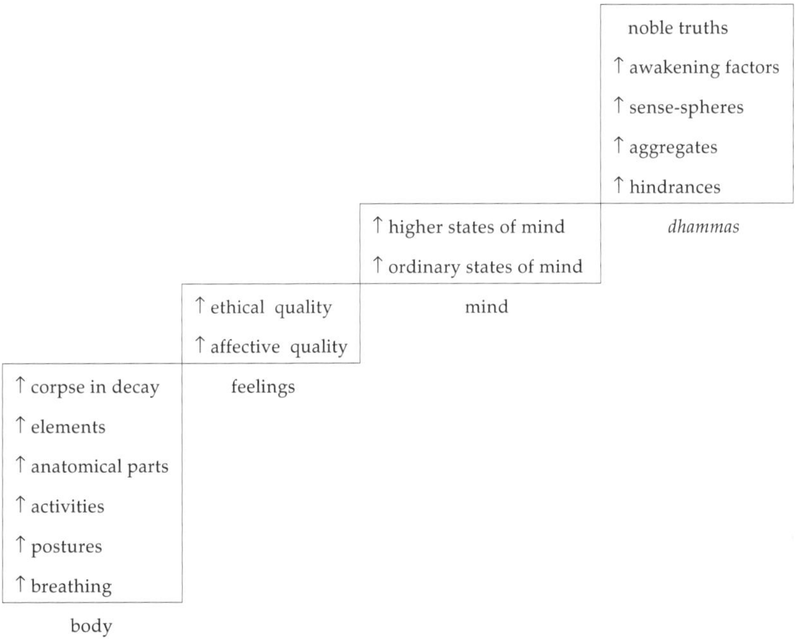

Fig. 1.2 Progression of the *satipaṭṭhāna* contemplations

Contemplation of feeling divides feelings not only according to their affective quality into pleasant, unpleasant, and neutral types, but also distinguishes these according to their worldly or unworldly nature. The latter part of contemplation of feelings thus introduces an ethical distinction of feelings, which serves as a stepping-stone for directing awareness to the ethical distinction between wholesome and unwholesome states of mind, mentioned at the start of the next *satipaṭṭhāna*, contemplation of the mind.

Contemplation of the mind proceeds from the presence or absence of four unwholesome states of mind (lust, anger, delusion, and distraction), to contemplating the presence or absence of four higher states of mind. The concern with higher states of mind in the latter part of the contemplation of the mind naturally lends itself to a detailed investigation of those factors which particularly obstruct deeper levels of concentration. These are the hindrances, the first object of contemplation of *dhammas*.

After covering the hindrances to meditation practice, contemplation of *dhammas* progresses to two analyses of subjective experience: the five aggregates and the six sense-spheres. These analyses are followed by the awakening factors, the next contemplation of *dhammas*. The culmination of *satipaṭṭhāna* practice is reached with the contemplation of the four noble truths, full understanding of which coincides with realization.

Considered in this way, the sequence of the *satipaṭṭhāna* contemplations leads progressively from grosser to more subtle levels.[11] This linear progression is not without practical relevance, since the body contemplations recommend themselves as a foundational exercise for building up a basis of *sati*, while the final contemplation of the four noble truths covers the experience of *Nibbāna* (the third noble truth concerning the cessation of *dukkha*) and thus corresponds to the culmination of any successful implementation of *satipaṭṭhāna*.

At the same time, however, this progressive pattern does not

---

11 The *Mahāprajñāpāramitāśāstra* offers the following explanation for this pattern: having investigated the body, the meditator searches for the cause of attachment to it, which is found to be pleasant feeling. Investigating feelings the question "who experiences feelings?" arises, leading to contemplation of the mind. This in turn forms a basis for an inquiry into the causes and conditions of mind, being the focus of contemplation of *dhammas* (in Lamotte 1970: pp.1158, 1162, 1167). On the progressive pattern underlying the sequence of the *satipaṭṭhāna* contemplations cf. also Ariyadhamma 1994: p.6; Gethin 1992: p.47; Guenther 1991: p.219; Khemacari 1985: p.38; King 1992: p.67; and Meier 1978: p.16.

prescribe the only possible way of practising *satipaṭṭhāna*. To take the progression of the meditation exercises in the *Satipaṭṭhāna Sutta* as indicating a necessary sequence would severely limit the range of one's practice, since only those experiences or phenomena that fit into this preconceived pattern would be proper objects of awareness. Yet a central characteristic of *satipaṭṭhāna* is awareness of phenomena as they are, and as they occur. Although such awareness will naturally proceed from the gross to the subtle, in actual practice it will quite probably vary from the sequence depicted in the discourse.

A flexible and comprehensive development of *satipaṭṭhāna* should encompass all aspects of experience, in whatever sequence they occur. All *satipaṭṭhānas* can be of continual relevance throughout one's progress along the path. The practice of contemplating the body, for example, is not something to be left behind and discarded at some more advanced point in one's progress. Much rather, it continues to be a relevant practice even for an *arahant*.[12] Understood in this way, the meditation exercises listed in the *Satipaṭṭhāna Sutta* can be seen as mutually supportive. The sequence in which they are practised may be altered in order to meet the needs of each individual meditator.

Not only do the four *satipaṭṭhānas* support each other, but they could even be integrated within a single meditation practice. This is documented in the *Ānāpānasati Sutta*, which describes how mindfulness of breathing can be developed in such a way that it encompasses all four *satipaṭṭhānas*.[13] This exposition demonstrates the possibility of comprehensively combining all four *satipaṭṭhānas* within the practice of a single meditation.

I.3 THE RELEVANCE OF EACH *SATIPAṬṬHĀNA* FOR REALIZATION

According to the *Ānāpānasati Sutta*, it is possible to develop a variety of different aspects of *satipaṭṭhāna* contemplation with a single meditation object and in due course cover all four *satipaṭṭhānas*. This raises the question how far a single *satipaṭṭhāna*, or even a single meditation exercise, can be taken as a complete practice in its own right.

---

12 Cf. e.g. S V 326, which reports that the Buddha himself, after his awakening, still continued to practise mindfulness of breathing.

13 M III 83.

Several discourses relate the practice of a single *satipaṭṭhāna* directly to realization.[14] Similarly, the commentaries assign to each single *satipaṭṭhāna* meditation the capacity to lead to full awakening.[15] This may well be why a high percentage of present-day meditation teachers focus on the use of a single meditation technique, on the ground that a single-minded and thorough perfection of one meditation technique can cover all aspects of *satipaṭṭhāna*, and thus be sufficient to gain realization.[16]

Indeed, the development of awareness with any particular meditation technique will automatically result in a marked increase in one's general level of awareness, thereby enhancing one's capacity to be mindful in regard to situations that do not form part of one's primary object of meditation. In this way, even those aspects of *satipaṭṭhāna* that have not deliberately been made the object of contemplation to some extent still receive mindful attention as a by-product of the primary practice. Yet the exposition in the *Ānāpānasati Sutta* does not necessarily imply that by being aware of the breath one automatically covers all aspects of *satipaṭṭhāna*. What the Buddha demonstrated here was how a thorough development of *sati* can lead from the breath to a broad range of objects, encompassing different aspects of subjective reality. Clearly, such a broad range of aspects was the outcome of a deliberate development, otherwise the Buddha would not have needed to deliver a whole discourse on how to achieve this.

In fact, several meditation teachers and scholars place a strong emphasis on covering all four *satipaṭṭhānas* in one's practice.[17] According to them, although one particular meditation practice can

---

14 S V 158; S V 181; S V 182; and S IV 363.

15 Ps I 249 allows for full awakening based on breath-awareness, Ps I 252 based on awareness of the four postures, Ps I 270 based on clearly knowing bodily activities, Ps I 274 based on the cemetery contemplations, Ps I 277 based on contemplation of feelings, Ps I 280 based on contemplation of the mind etc.

16 Cf. e.g. Dhammadharo 1997: p.54, who assembles all four *satipaṭṭhānas* under one single practice. Goenka 1994b: p.2, proposes the same, explaining that since the "body" is to be experienced via "feelings", which at the same time are related to the "mind" by being "mental objects", by observing bodily sensation one can cover all four *satipaṭṭhānas*. Sunlun 1993: p.110 takes a similar position regarding the touch-sensation. Taungpulu 1993: p.189, also includes all four *satipaṭṭhānas* under the single practice of body contemplation.

17 e.g. Ñāṇapoṇika 1992: p.58, recommends practice of all four *satipaṭṭhānas*. He suggests focusing on a few selected contemplations, and to give attention to the other contemplations whenever an opportunity arises in the course of practice. Soma 1981: p.xxii, takes a similar position.

serve as the primary object of attention, the other aspects of *satipaṭṭhāna* should be deliberately contemplated too, even if only in a secondary manner. This approach can claim some support from the concluding part of the *Satipaṭṭhāna Sutta*, the "prediction" of realization. This passage stipulates the development of all four *satipaṭṭhānas* for contemplation to lead to the realization of the higher two stages of awakening: non-returning and arahantship.[18] The fact that all four *satipaṭṭhānas* are mentioned suggests that it is the comprehensive practice of all four which is particularly capable of leading to high levels of realization. The same is also indicated by a statement in the *Satipaṭṭhāna Saṃyutta*, which relates the realization of arahantship to "complete" practice of the four *satipaṭṭhānas*, while partial practice corresponds to lesser levels of realization.[19]

In a passage in the *Ānāpāna Saṃyutta*, the Buddha compared the four *satipaṭṭhānas* to chariots coming from four directions, each driving through and thereby scattering a heap of dust lying at the centre of a crossroads.[20] This simile suggests that each *satipaṭṭhāna* is in itself capable of overcoming unwholesome states, just as any of the chariots is able to scatter the heap of dust. At the same time this simile also illustrates the cooperative effect of all four *satipaṭṭhānas*, since, with chariots coming from all directions, the heap of dust will be scattered even more.

Thus any single meditation practice from the *satipaṭṭhāna* scheme is capable of leading to deep insight, especially if developed according to the key instructions given in the "definition" and "refrain" of the discourse. Nevertheless, an attempt to cover all four *satipaṭṭhānas* in one's practice does more justice to the distinct character of the various meditations described in the *Satipaṭṭhāna Sutta* and thereby ensures speedy progress and a balanced and comprehensive development.[21]

---

18 M I 62: "if anyone should develop these four *satipaṭṭhānas* ... one of two fruits could be expected for him: either final knowledge here and now, or, if there is a trace of clinging left, non-returning." Pradhan 1986: p.340, points out that the practice of all *satipaṭṭhānas* is required for being able to gain such high levels of realization.

19 S V 175.

20 S V 325.

21 Debes 1994: p.190, aptly sums up: "it may be possible to gain realization with one single exercise, but that one who has practised all of them should still not realize awakening would seem to be impossible." (My translation)

1.4 THE CHARACTER OF EACH *SATIPAṬṬHĀNA*

The need for such comprehensive development is related to the fact that each *satipaṭṭhāna* has a different character and can thereby serve a slightly different purpose. This is documented in the *Nettippakaraṇa* and the commentaries, which illustrate the particular character of each *satipaṭṭhāna* with a set of correlations (cf. Fig. 1.3 below).

According to the commentaries, each of the four *satipaṭṭhānas* corresponds to a particular aggregate: the aggregates of material form (*rūpa*), feeling (*vedanā*), and consciousness (*viññāṇa*) match the first three *satipaṭṭhānas*, while the aggregates of cognition (*saññā*) and volitions (*saṅkhārā*) correspond to the contemplation of *dhammas*.[22]

On closer inspection, this correlation appears a little forced, since the third *satipaṭṭhāna*, contemplation of the mind, corresponds to all mental aggregates and not only to consciousness. Moreover, the fourth *satipaṭṭhāna*, contemplation of *dhammas*, includes the entire set of the five aggregates as one of its meditations, and thus has a wider range than just the two aggregates of cognition (*saññā*) and volition (*saṅkhārā*).

Nevertheless, what the commentaries might intend to indicate is that all aspects of one's subjective experience are to be investigated with the aid of the four *satipaṭṭhānas*. Understood in this way, the division into four *satipaṭṭhānas* represents an analytical approach similar to a division of subjective experience into the five aggregates. Both attempt to dissolve the illusion of the observer's substantiality.[23] By turning awareness to different facets of one's subjective experience, these aspects will be experienced simply as objects, and the notion of compactness, the sense of a solid "I", will begin to disintegrate. In this way, the more subjective experience can be seen "objectively", the more the "I"-dentification diminishes.[24] This correlates well with the Buddha's instruction to investigate thoroughly each aggregate to the point where no more "I" can be found.[25]

In addition to the aggregate correlation, the commentaries recommend each of the four *satipaṭṭhānas* for a specific type of character or

---

22 Ps I 281.

23 Cf. also Fryba 1989: p.258, who proposes employing the four *satipaṭṭhānas* as labelling categories for such analytical dissolution of subjective experience by classifying experiences of warmth, movement, trembling, itching, pressure, lightness, etc. under "body"; being pleased, amused, bored, sad, etc. under "feelings"; being concentrated, scattered, tense, greedy, hate-filled, etc. under "mind"; and experiencing thinking, wishing, planning, intending, etc. under "*dhammas*".

inclination. According to them, body and feeling contemplation should be the main field of practice for those who tend towards craving, while meditators given to intellectual speculation should place more emphasis on contemplating mind or *dhammas*.[26] Understood in this way, practice of the first two *satipaṭṭhānas* suits those with a more affective inclination, while the last two are recommended for those of a more cognitive orientation. In both cases, those whose character is to think and react quickly can profitably centre their practice on the relatively subtler contemplations of feelings or *dhammas*, while those whose mental faculties are more circumspect and measured will have better results if they base their practice on the grosser objects of body or mind. Although these recommendations are expressed in terms of character type, they could also be applied to one's momentary disposition: one could choose that *satipaṭṭhāna* that best corresponds to one's state of mind, so that when one feels sluggish and desirous, for example, contemplation of the body would be the appropriate practice to be undertaken.

	body	feelings	mind	*dhammas*
aggregate	material form	feeling	consciousness	cognition + volition
character	slow craver	quick craver	slow theorizer	quick theorizer
insight	absence of beauty	unsatisfactoriness	impermanence	absence of self

Fig. 1.3 Correlations for the four *satipaṭṭhānas*

The *Nettippakaraṇa* and the *Visuddhimagga* also set the four *satipaṭṭhānas* in opposition to the four distortions (*vipallāsas*), which are to "mis-take" what is unattractive, unsatisfactory, impermanent, and not-self, for being attractive, satisfactory, permanent, and a self.[27]

---

24 Ñāṇananda 1993: p.48, aptly expresses this by speaking of *satipaṭṭhāna* as "an objective approach to understand the subjective in one's experience". Ñāṇaponika 1992: p.75, comments: "the whole discourse on the foundations of mindfulness may be regarded as a comprehensive ... instruction for the realization of ... *anattā*." Of a similar opinion are Schönwerth 1968: p.193; and Story 1975: p.viii.

25 S IV 197.

26 Ps I 239.

27 Nett 83; cf. also Ps I 239 and Vism 678. Concerning these four *vipallāsas* it is noteworthy that they are listed only once in the four *Nikāyas*, at A II 52. The term as such occurs also at Vin III 7 in the sense of "disturbance" and at Sn 299 in the sense of "change"; and is referred to as *catubbipallāsā* at Th 1143. The four *vipallāsas* become prominent particularly in Paṭis and the later Pāli literature. The same four mistaken notions form part of a definition of ignorance in Patañjali's *Yoga Sūtra* (at II.5).

According to them, contemplation of the body has the potential to reveal in particular the absence of bodily beauty; observation of the true nature of feelings can counter one's incessant search for fleeting pleasures; awareness of the ceaseless succession of states of mind can disclose the impermanent nature of all subjective experience; and contemplation of *dhammas* can reveal that the notion of a substantial and permanent self is nothing but an illusion. This presentation brings to light the main theme that underlies each of the four *satipaṭṭhānas* and indicates which of them is particularly appropriate for dispelling the illusion of beauty, happiness, permanence, or self.[28] Although the corresponding insights are certainly not restricted to one *satipaṭṭhāna* alone, nevertheless this particular correlation indicates which *satipaṭṭhāna* is particularly suitable in order to correct a specific distortion (*vipallāsa*). This correlation, too, may be fruitfully applied in accordance with one's general character disposition, or else can be used in order to counteract the momentary manifestation of any particular distortion.

In the end, however, all four *satipaṭṭhānas* partake of the same essence. Each of them leads to realization, like different gateways leading to the same city.[29] As the commentaries point out, the fourfold division is only functional and can be compared to a weaver splitting a piece of bamboo into four parts to weave a basket.[30]

So much for a preliminary survey of the four *satipaṭṭhānas*. By way of providing some background to the title I have chosen for this work, I will now turn to the two key expressions "direct path" and "*satipaṭṭhāna*".

---

28 Nett 123 also associates each *satipaṭṭhāna* with a corresponding type of realization, relating contemplation of body and feelings to the desireless liberation, contemplation of the mind to the empty liberation, and contemplation of *dhammas* to the signless liberation. (One would, however, have expected the last two to be the other way round.)

29 Ps I 239 points out that all four *satipaṭṭhānas* partake of the same essence, Ps I 240 adds that it is only by way of differing objects that they are distinguished. Than Daing 1970: p.59, illustratively compares the similarity of all four *satipaṭṭhānas* in leading to the same goal to four staircases leading up to the platform of a pagoda.

30 Vibh-a 222. Bodhi 1993: p.279, explains: "the four foundations of mindfulness have a single essence, which consists of mindful contemplation of phenomena. They are differentiated in so far as this mindful contemplation is to be applied to four objects."

I.5 THE EXPRESSION "DIRECT PATH"

The first section of the *Satipaṭṭhāna Sutta* proper introduces the four *satipaṭṭhānas* as the "direct path" to realization. The passage reads:

> **Monks, this is the direct path for the purification of beings, for the surmounting of sorrow and lamentation, for the disappearance of *dukkha* and discontent, for acquiring the true method, for the realization of *Nibbāna*, namely, the four *satipaṭṭhānas*.**[31]

The qualification of being a "direct path" occurs in the discourses almost exclusively as an attribute of *satipaṭṭhāna*, thus it conveys a considerable degree of emphasis.[32] Such emphasis is indeed warranted, since practice of the "direct path" of *satipaṭṭhāna* is an indispensable requirement for liberation.[33] As a set of verses in the *Satipaṭṭhāna Saṃyutta* point out, *satipaṭṭhāna* is the "direct path" for crossing the flood in past, present, and future times.[34]

"Direct path" is a translation of the Pāli expression *ekāyano maggo*, made up of the parts *eka*, "one", *ayana*, "going", and *magga*, "path". The commentarial tradition has preserved five alternative explanations for understanding this particular expression. According to them, a path qualified as *ekāyano* could be understood as a "direct" path in the sense of leading straight to the goal; as a path to be travelled by oneself "alone"; as a path taught by the "One" (the Buddha); as a path that is found "only" in Buddhism; or as a path which leads to "one" goal, namely to *Nibbāna*.[35] My rendering of *ekāyano* as "direct path" follows the first of these explanations.[36] A more

---

31 M I 55. On this passage cf. also Janakabhivaṃsa 1985: pp.37–44.

32 *Ekāyano* occurs in relation to *satipaṭṭhāna* at D II 290; M I 55; S V 141; S V 167; and S V 185. In contrast at A III 314, a passage otherwise resembling the "direct path" statement does not have the *ekāyano* specification. The same absence of *ekāyano* can be seen at A III 329 in relation to the practice of recollecting the Buddha. Khantipālo 1981: p.29; and Ñāṇaponika 1973: p.12; draw attention to the emphatic implications of the term *ekāyano* in ancient India (various examples of which are discussed in Gethin 1992: p.61).

33 According to A V 195, whosoever have escaped, are escaping, or will escape from this world, all of them do so by way of well developing the four *satipaṭṭhānas*.

34 S V 167 and S V 186.

35 Ps I 229: *ekamaggo na dvedhāpathabhūto … ekena ayitabbo … ekassa ayano … ekasmiṃ ayano … ekaṃ ayati*. These alternatives are discussed by Gethin 1992: pp.60–3.

36 "Direct path" as a way of translating *ekāyano* is also used by Ñāṇatiloka 1910: p.91 n.7 ("der direkte Weg"); and by Ñāṇamoli 1995: p.145. Translating *ekāyano* as "direct path" has the advantage of avoiding the slightly dogmatic nuance conveyed by the translation "the only path", noted e.g. by Conze 1962: p.51 n.++.

commonly used translation of *ekāyano* is "the only path", corresponding to the fourth of the five explanations found in the commentaries.

In order to assess the meaning of a particular Pāli term, its different occurrences in the discourses need to be taken into account. In the present case, in addition to occurring in several discourses in relation to *satipaṭṭhāna*, *ekāyano* also comes up once in a different context. This is in a simile in the *Mahāsīhanāda Sutta*, which describes a man walking along a path leading to a pit, such that one can anticipate him falling into the pit.[37] This path is qualified as *ekāyano*. In this context *ekāyano* seems to express straightness of direction rather than exclusion. To say that this path leads "directly" to the pit would be more fitting than saying that it is "the only" path leading to the pit.

Of related interest is also the *Tevijja Sutta*, which reports two Brahmin students arguing about whose teacher taught the only correct path to union with Brahmā. Although in this context an exclusive expression like "the only path" might be expected, the qualification *ekāyano* is conspicuously absent.[38] The same absence recurs in a verse from the *Dhammapada*, which presents the noble eightfold path as "the only path".[39] These two instances suggest that the discourses did not avail themselves of the qualification *ekāyano* in order to convey exclusiveness.

Thus *ekāyano*, conveying a sense of directness rather than exclusiveness, draws attention to *satipaṭṭhāna* as the aspect of the noble eightfold path most "directly" responsible for uncovering a vision of things as they truly are. That is, *satipaṭṭhāna* is the "direct path", because it leads "directly" to the realization of *Nibbāna*.[40]

This way of understanding also fits well with the final passage of the *Satipaṭṭhāna Sutta*. Having stated that *satipaṭṭhāna* practice can lead to the two higher stages of realization within a maximum of seven years, the discourse closes with the declaration: "because of this, it has been said – this is the direct path". This passage highlights

---

37 M I 75, the same is then repeated for a path leading in the direction of a tree, a mansion, and a pond. Cf. also Ñāṇamoli 1995: p.1188 n.135.

38 D I 235.

39 Dhp 274. Ñāṇavīra 1987: p.371, points out that to speak of the "only path" would be applicable only to the entire noble eightfold path, not to *satipaṭṭhāna* alone, which after all is just one of its factors.

40 Gethin 1992: p.64, commenting on *ekāyano*, explains: "what is basically being said is that the four *satipaṭṭhānas* represent a path that leads straight and directly all the way to the final goal."

the directness of *satipaṭṭhāna*, in the sense of its potential to lead to the highest stages of realization within a limited period of time.

I.6 THE TERM *SATIPAṬṬHĀNA*

The term *satipaṭṭhāna* can be explained as a compound of *sati*, "mindfulness" or "awareness", and *upaṭṭhāna*, with the u of the latter term dropped by vowel elision.[41] The Pāli term *upaṭṭhāna* literally means "placing near",[42] and in the present context refers to a particular way of "being present" and "attending" to something with mindfulness. In the discourses, the corresponding verb *upaṭṭhahati* often denotes various nuances of "being present",[43] or else "attending".[44] Understood in this way, "*satipaṭṭhāna*" means that *sati* "stands by", in the sense of being present; *sati* is "ready at hand", in the sense of attending to the current situation. *Satipaṭṭhāna* can then be translated as "presence of mindfulness" or as "attending with mindfulness".[45]

The commentaries, however, derive *satipaṭṭhāna* from the word "foundation" or "cause" (*paṭṭhāna*).[46] This seems unlikely, since in the discourses contained in the Pāli canon the corresponding verb *paṭṭhahati* never occurs together with *sati*. Moreover, the noun *paṭṭhāna* is not found at all in the early discourses, but comes into use only in the historically later *Abhidhamma* and the commentaries.[47] In contrast, the discourses frequently relate *sati* to the verb *upaṭṭhahati*, indicating that "presence" (*upaṭṭhāna*) is the etymologically correct

---

41 Cf. also Bodhi 2000: p.1504 and p.1915 n.122; and Ñāṇapoṇika 1992: p.10.

42 Maurice Walshe 1987: p.589 n.629.

43 Occurrences of *upaṭṭhahati* which correspond to "being present" are, for example, a watchdog being present at D I 166; the messengers of death being ever present (in the sense of being ready) for someone of advanced age at Dhp 235; meal time "has come" at Sn 130; a seat being present (in the sense of being put up) under a tree at Sn 708. Cf. also It 36, which relates *upaṭṭhahati* to mental factors (the presence of shame and fear of wrong-doing), thereby forming a close parallel to its use in the *satipaṭṭhāna* context.

44 *Upaṭṭhahati* in the sense of "attending" can be found, for example, at D II 271, where *devas* have to attend on Sakka; or at D III 189 in the sense of waiting on one's teacher; or in the sense of looking after one's parents at A I 151 and Sn 262; or as ministering to the monastic community at A I 279. The same nuance also underlies the recurrent noun "attendant", *upaṭṭhāka* (e.g. at S III 95).

45 C.A.F. Rhys Davids 1978: p.256, speaks of the "four presences of mindfulness".

46 e.g. Ps I 238 and Vism 678. However, on this derivation one would expect a doubling of the consonant, the resulting term being *satippaṭṭhāna*.

47 C.A.F. Rhys Davids 1979: p.xv. By distinguishing between the early discourses on the one hand and the historically later *Abhidhamma* and commentaries on the other I follow Ñāṇamoli 1991: p.xli, who distinguishes between these three as the three main layers of the Pāli tradition.

derivation.[48] In fact, the equivalent Sanskrit term is *smṛtyupasthāna*, which shows that *upasthāna*, or its Pāli equivalent *upaṭṭhāna*, is the correct choice for the compound.[49]

The problem with the commentarial explanation is that, instead of understanding *satipaṭṭhāna* as a particular attitude of being aware, *satipaṭṭhāna* becomes a "foundation" of mindfulness, the "cause" for the establishment of *sati*. This moves emphasis from the activity to the object. Yet these four *satipaṭṭhānas* are not the only possible cause or foundation for mindfulness, since in the *Saḷāyatanavibhaṅga Sutta* the Buddha spoke of three other *satipaṭṭhānas*, none of which corresponds to the four *satipaṭṭhānas* usually mentioned.[50] The three *satipaṭṭhānas* described by the Buddha on this occasion were his maintenance of mindfulness and equanimity as a teacher in regard to three different situations: none of the pupils paid attention, some paid attention and some not, and all paid attention. The fact that the Buddha nevertheless defined these three as *satipaṭṭhānas* shows that to speak of "*satipaṭṭhāna*" is less a question of the nature of the object that is chosen than of "attending" to whatever situation with a balanced attitude and with mindfulness being "present".

---

48 e.g. at M III 23, where *upaṭṭhita sati* is contrasted with *muṭṭhassati*, loss of mindfulness; or at M III 85, where *upaṭṭhita sati* is the result of practising *satipaṭṭhāna*; cf. also S IV 119: *upaṭṭhitāya satiyā*; or A II 244: *sati sūpaṭṭhitā hoti*; or the causative form *satiṃ upaṭṭhāpessanti* at A IV 22. As a matter of fact, the *Satipaṭṭhāna Sutta* itself speaks of *satiṃ upaṭṭhapetvā*, "having established mindfulness", and of *sati paccupaṭṭhitā*, "mindfulness is established" (both at M I 56). Paṭis I 177 also relates *sati* to *upaṭṭhāna*.

49 Cf. e.g. Edgerton 1998: p.614.

50 M III 221.

II

THE "DEFINITION" PART OF THE *SATIPAṬṬHĀNA SUTTA*

This chapter and the next two are devoted to an examination of the "definition" part of the *Satipaṭṭhāna Sutta*. This "definition", which occurs also in other discourses as the standard way of defining right mindfulness (*sammā sati*), describes essential aspects of *satipaṭṭhāna* practice and therefore forms a key to understanding how the meditation techniques listed in the *Satipaṭṭhāna Sutta* are to be undertaken. The passage in question reads:

> **Here, monks, in regard to the body a monk abides contemplating the body, diligent, clearly knowing, and mindful, free from desires and discontent in regard to the world.**
>
> **In regard to feelings he abides contemplating feelings, diligent, clearly knowing, and mindful, free from desires and discontent in regard to the world.**
>
> **In regard to the mind he abides contemplating the mind, diligent, clearly knowing, and mindful, free from desires and discontent in regard to the world.**
>
> **In regard to *dhammas* he abides contemplating *dhammas*, diligent, clearly knowing, and mindful, free from desires and discontent in regard to the world.**[1]

In this chapter I will first take a look at the expression "contemplating" (*anupassī*) and consider why the objects of this contemplation

---

1 M I 56.

are mentioned twice (for example, in regard to the body, one is to contemplate the body). I will then explore the significance of the first two qualities mentioned in the "definition": "diligent" (*ātāpī*) and "clearly knowing" (*sampajāna*). The remaining qualities, mindfulness and the absence of desires and discontent, will be the subjects of Chapters III and IV.

II.1 CONTEMPLATION

The "definition" of right mindfulness is concerned with "contemplating". The corresponding Pāli verb *anupassati* can be derived from the verb "to see", *passati*, and the emphatic prefix *anu*, so that *anupassati* means "to repeatedly look at", that is, "to contemplate" or "to closely observe".[2] The discourses often speak of contemplation in order to describe a particular way of meditation, an examination of the observed object from a particular viewpoint. In the case of the body, for example, such observation can involve contemplating the body as impermanent (*aniccānupassī, vayānupassī*), and therefore as something which does not yield lasting satisfaction (*dukkhānupassī*); or as unattractive (*asubhānupassī*) and not-self (*anattānupassī*), and therefore as something to let go of (*paṭinissaggānupassī*).[3]

These various forms of contemplation emphasize how the object is to be perceived. That is, as used in the discourses "contemplation" implies that particular features of the object are to be given prominence, such as its impermanence, or its selfless nature. In the present context, however, the feature to be contemplated appears to be the same as the object of contemplation. Literally translated, one "contemplates body in body", or "feelings in feelings", etc.[4] This slightly peculiar expression requires further consideration.

---

2 T.W. Rhys Davids 1993: p.38. Cf. also Upali Karunaratne 1989: p.484, who translates *anupassati* as "observing or seeing properly"; Ñāṇārāma 1997: p.11, who speaks of "special modes of attention ... cognitive evaluations"; and Vajirañāṇa 1946: p.47, who has "analytical reflection" as a translation. According to Sasaki 1992: p.16, "*anu*" has a particularly emphatic function in Pāli. Another relevant nuance of *anu* is "along with", which in the present context could be taken to point to the process character of all experience, revealed during contemplation. According to Vism 642, "*anu*"-*passati* implies observation of an object repeatedly and in diverse ways, that is, from different angles.

3 Cf. e.g. S IV 211; A III 142; and A V 359.

4 Hamilton 1996: p.173, translates: "body qua body"; Ñāṇamoli 1995: p.145: "body as a body"; Ṭhānissaro 1993: p.97: "body in and of itself".

Taking the first *satipaṭṭhāna* as an example, the instructions are: "in regard to the body abide contemplating the body". Here, the first instance of "body" can be understood in the light of the *satipaṭṭhāna* "refrain". The "refrain" explains that to contemplate the body applies to internal and external bodies.[5] According to the commentaries, "internal" and "external" here represent one's own and another person's body.[6] On this understanding, the first instance of "body" (in the locative case) could be translated as "where one's own or another's body is concerned", or "in regard to one's own or another's body", delineating the compass of this *satipaṭṭhāna*.

For the second instance of "body", the *Satipaṭṭhāna Sutta* offers detailed specifications: to contemplate "body" can be undertaken by contemplating the breath, or the postures of the body, or activities of the body, or the anatomical constitution of the body, or the four elementary qualities of the body, or the decomposition of the body after death. Thus the second occurrence of "body" stands for a particular aspect from the general area of contemplation, a "sub-body" in the "overall body", so to speak.[7]

The *satipaṭṭhāna* "refrain" also contains additional information about the significance of "contemplation" in the present context. The same term is used, with the specification that the "arising" and the "passing away" of phenomena is the focus of contemplation.[8] That is, to speak of contemplation in the present context refers to directing awareness to the body and in particular to a specific feature of it, namely its impermanent nature.

In drawing from other parts of the *Satipaṭṭhāna Sutta*, one can thus expand the somewhat puzzling instruction: "in the body abide contemplating the body" to read: "in regard to your own body or the bodies of others, direct awareness to its (or their) impermanent

---

5 M I 56: "he abides contemplating *dhammas* internally ... externally ... internally and externally."

6 Ps I 249. A more detailed discussion of this commentarial explanation can be found on page 95.

7 This suggestion can claim support from M III 83, where the Buddha spoke of the process of breathing as a "body among bodies". A similar position is also taken by several modern meditation teachers; cf. e.g. Buddhadāsa 1976: p.64; Maha Boowa 1994: p.101; and Ñāṇasaṃvara 1974: p.41.

8 M I 56: "he abides contemplating the nature of arising ... of passing away ... of both arising and passing away." Such contemplation of impermanence can then lead on to an understanding of the other two characteristics of conditioned existence, *dukkha* and *anattā*. Cf. Paṭis II 232 and Ps I 243. Ps I 242 moreover speaks of overcoming the wrong notion of substantiality.

nature evident in different aspects of the body, such as the process of breathing, or its postures and activities, or its anatomical constitution, or its elementary qualities, or its decay at death."

According to the commentaries, the repetition of the object of contemplation also indicates emphasis, implying that the object of contemplation should be considered simply as perceived by the senses, and in particular without taking it to be "I" or "mine".[9] In this way the repetition – body in body – underlines the importance of direct experience, as opposed to mere intellectual reflection.[10] One should let the body speak for itself, so to say, disclosing its true nature to the scrutiny of the meditator.

II.2 THE SIGNIFICANCE OF BEING DILIGENT (*ĀTĀPĪ*)

According to the "definition", the practice of *satipaṭṭhāna* requires the establishment of four particular mental qualities (cf. Fig. 2.1 below), which can be taken to represent the mental faculties of energy, wisdom, mindfulness, and concentration.[11]

diligent (*ātāpī*)
clearly knowing (*sampajāna*)
mindful (*sati*)
free from desires and discontent (*vineyya abhijjhādomanassa*)

Fig. 2.1: Key characteristics of *satipaṭṭhāna*

---

9 Ps I 242; also Debvedi 1990: p.23; and Ñāṇamoli 1982b: p.206 n.17. Here it needs to be pointed out that although the discourses do use repetition in order to express emphasis, this is usually done by repeating the same phrase without case variations. In contrast, in the present instance the repetition occurs in a different case. Ps I 241 also offers another explanation, suggesting that the repetition implies that each area of contemplation should be kept separate from the other areas (cf. also Ñāṇapoṇika 1992: p.33; and Sīlananda 1990: p.20). This commentarial suggestion is questionable, since in the *Ānāpānasati Sutta* (M III 83) the Buddha clearly showed that an object of body contemplation, the breath, can be used to contemplate feelings, mind, and *dhammas*, rather than keeping breath contemplation restricted to the area of body contemplation only.

10 Lily de Silva (n.d.): p.6.

11 Nett 82 correlates *ātāpī* with energy (*viriya*), *sampajāna* with wisdom (*paññā*), and *vineyya loke abhijjhādomanassa* with concentration (*samādhi*). Paṭis II 15 further expands the correlation with all five faculties.

The first of these four is the quality of diligence. The term diligent (*ātāpī*) is related to the word *tapas*, which connotes self-mortification and ascetic practices. The use of such vocabulary is surprising, since the Buddha did not consider self-mortification to be conducive to the realization of *Nibbāna*.[12] To better understand the Buddha's position, the historical context should be considered.

A substantial number of wandering ascetics in ancient India regarded self-mortification as the model path to purification. Jain and Ājīvika ascetics considered death by ritual suicide to be the ideal expression of successful realization.[13] Commonly accepted means for spiritual development were prolonged fasting, exposure to extremes of temperature, and the adoption of particularly painful postures.[14] Although the Buddha did not categorically reject such practices in their entirety,[15] he openly criticized the belief that self-mortification was necessary for realization.[16]

Before his awakening, the Buddha himself had been influenced by the belief that spiritual purification requires self-mortification.[17] Based on this mistaken belief, he had pursued ascetic practices to considerable extremes, without being able to realize awakening in this way.[18] He found ultimately that awakening does not depend on mere asceticism, but requires mental development, in particular the development of *sati*.[19]

Therefore, the form of "asceticism" the Buddha later taught was predominantly a mental one, characterized by a firm opposition to unwholesome thoughts and tendencies.[20] In an intriguing statement found in the discourses, the cultivation of the awakening factors is

---

12 Cf. S I 103 and S V 421.

13 Basham 1951: p.88.

14 Bronkhorst 1993: pp.31–6, and 51.

15 At D I 161 and at S IV 330 the Buddha rejected the false report that he was categorically against all austerities. At A V 191 the Buddha explained that he was neither in favour of nor against austerities, since what really mattered was whether any particular austerity or practice led to an increase of either wholesome or unwholesome states of mind.

16 At A II 200. Cf. also M I 81, where the Buddha, after listing the ascetic practices he had performed previous to awakening, concluded that these had not led him to realization because of the absence of wisdom.

17 M II 93.

18 The *bodhisatta*'s ascetic practices are described in detail at M I 77–81 and at M I 242–6. Mil 285 explains that none of the previous Buddhas ever practised austerities, Gotama being the only case, owing to his immature knowledge at the time.

19 Cf. S I 103, where the recently awakened Buddha congratulated himself on having left asceticism behind and having gained awakening through mindfulness instead.

referred to as the highest form of exertion.[21] Such subtler forms of "austerity" did not easily receive recognition by contemporary ascetics, and on several occasions the Buddha and his followers were ridiculed for their seemingly easy-going attitude.[22]

Another point worth considering is that in ancient India there were a variety of deterministic and fatalistic teachings.[23] In contrast, the Buddha emphasized commitment and effort as essential requirements for achieving realization. According to him, only by way of desire, effort, and personal commitment can desirelessness be realized.[24] Effort, as an expression of wholesome desire, leads along the path until with full realization all desire will be abandoned.[25] In this context, the Buddha at times reinterpreted expressions commonly used within ascetic circles to express his own position.[26]

---

20 This can be gathered from his humorous reply to the accusation of being a *tapassī* himself at Vin I 235; Vin III 3; A IV 175; and A IV 184; where he pointed out that his form of self-mortification was to "mortify" what is unwholesome. Cf. also Collins 1982: p.235; and Horner 1979: p.97.

21 D III 106. The association of the awakening factors with "exertion" (*padhāna*) occurs also at D III 226; A II 16; and A II 74. S I 54 even goes so far as to associate them with "austerity": *bojjhaṅgatapasā* (however, Bodhi 2000: p.390 n.168, suggests the reading *bojjhā tapasā* instead).

22 D III 130 speaks of other ascetics accusing the Buddha's disciples of living a life devoted to indulgence in pleasure. At M I 249 the Buddha faced criticism because he sometimes slept during the day. The same topic comes up again at S I 107, where Māra poked fun at the Buddha for being still asleep at sunrise (after a night spent in walking meditation), cf. also S I 110. At Vin IV 91 the Buddha was derisively called a "shaven-headed householder" by an Ājīvika ascetic, presumably because of the abundance of food received by Buddhist monks. Cf. further Basham 1951: p.137; and Chakravarti 1996: p.51.

23 Compare e.g. Makkhali Gosāla's view (at D I 53 or at S III 210) that there is no power or energy (to take decisions or influence one's destiny in any way), a view which the Buddha strongly censured (e.g. at A I 286); or Pūraṇa Kassapa's view (at D I 52) that there is neither evil nor good. (S III 69 seems to confuse these two teachers, putting Gosāla's view into Kassapa's mouth.)

24 Cf. e.g. M II 174; Dhp 280; It 27; and Th 1165. Cf. also Pande 1957: p.519; and C.A.F. Rhys Davids 1898: p.50.

25 At S V 272, Ānanda countered the proposal that to overcome desire using desire would be a task without end with the argument that the desire for realization will automatically subside once realization is gained. Similarly, according to A II 145 it is on the basis of "craving" (for the destruction of the influxes) that craving (in general) will be overcome. Cf. also Sn 365, where the Buddha spoke approvingly of someone longing to attain *Nibbāna*. The importance of "desire" as an aspect of the path leading to realization is also exemplified in the canonical presentation of the four roads to power (*iddhipāda*), one of which is desire (*chanda*). Cf. also Burford 1994: p.48; Katz 1979: p.58; and Matthews 1975: p.156. A helpful distinction between various types of desire in this context can be found in Collins 1998: pp.186–8.

26 A typical instance of such reinterpretation is Dhp 184, where patience is identified as the highest austerity. Cf. also Kloppenborg 1990: p.53.

The quality of being diligent (*ātāpī*) in the *satipaṭṭhāna* context appears to be one such instance.

A different example of rather forceful vocabulary can be found in those passages in which the Buddha described his firm resolution prior to awakening: "let my flesh and blood dry up, I will not give up",[27] or "I will not change my posture unless realization has been gained".[28] Concerning the resolve to refrain from changing posture, it needs to be kept in mind that the Buddha was able to achieve deep meditative absorption, so he could sit for long periods of time in the same posture without pain.[29] Thus what these expressions point to is not so much the endurance of a painful sitting posture as a strong and unwavering commitment.[30] Similar expressions are used by some of his disciples on the brink of realization.[31] Since the breakthrough to realization can only take place in a balanced state of mind, it might be best not to take these expressions too literally.

In a similar way, the expression "diligent" (*ātāpī*) might not have carried the same literal connotations for the Buddha as it did for his more ascetically-inclined contemporaries. In fact, in the *Kāyagatāsati Sutta* diligent (*ātāpī*) comes up in relation to experiencing the bliss of absorption.[32] Similarly, in a passage from the *Indriya Saṃyutta* the quality of diligence is combined with pleasant feelings, mental and physical.[33] In these instances, "diligent" has clearly lost any relation to self-mortification and its concomitant physical pain.

Since both deficiency of effort and excessive tension can obstruct one's progress,[34] the quality of "diligence" is best understood as a

---

27 A I 50.
28 M I 219.
29 M I 94. This ability of the Buddha to sit without moving for seven days is also documented at Vin I 1; Ud 1–3; Ud 10; and Ud 32. Thī 44 and Thī 174 each report the same for a realized nun. It is telling if one contrasts the Buddha's experience of sitting without moving for seven days experiencing only bliss with a description of sitting "with determination" in Maha Boowa 1997: p.256: "sitting ... for many hours ... the painful feelings quickly spread to all parts of the body ... even the backs of the hands and feet feel as if they are on fire ... inside the body it seems as if ... bones ... are about to break apart and separate ... the body ... as if it were burning in a mass of flames externally ... internally as if it was being beaten by hammers and stabbed with sharp steel daggers ... the whole body is in agony."
30 In fact at M I 481 the Buddha used the expression "let my blood dry up" etc. in order to admonish monks who were unwilling to give up eating in the evening. As 146 glosses this expression with "firm and steadfast effort".
31 e.g. at Th 223; Th 313; and Th 514.
32 M III 92.
33 S V 213.

balanced but sustained application of energy.[35] Such balanced endeavour avoids, on the one hand, passive submission to "destiny", a higher will, or personal idiosyncrasies, and on the other, excessive effort, self-assertive striving, and self-inflicted suffering in the name of a higher goal.

The Buddha once compared the balanced effort needed for proper progress to the tuning of a lute, whose strings should be neither too tight nor too loose.[36] This comparison of mental cultivation to the tuning of a musical instrument illustrates the well-adjusted effort and sensitivity required for the development of the mind.[37] The notion of a "middle path" of wise balance, avoiding the extremes of excessive and insufficient effort, has of course been one of the Buddha's central teachings since the time of his first discourse.[38] It was this balanced "middle path" approach, avoiding the two extremes of stagnation and excessive striving, which had enabled him to gain awakening.[39]

The practical implications of being "diligent" can best be illustrated with two maxims from the discourses, both of which use the word diligent (*ātāpī*): "right now is the time to practise diligently",

---

34 Cf. e.g. M III 159, where both are listed as possible obstructions to developing a concentrated mind. The need for an intelligent maintenance of balance in meditation practice is also reflected at M II 223, according to which the path to freedom from *dukkha* at times requires the application of effort, while at other times it just requires equanimous observation.

35 Other translations of *ātāpī* reflect similar shades of meaning, it being variously rendered as "conscientious", as "active", or as the input of energy that "revives the decreasing morale" (Hamilton 1996: p.173; Katz 1989: p.155; and Pandey 1988: p.37). The nuance of continuity can be seen at A III 38 and A IV 266, which associate *ātāpī* with being continuously active. Another relevant instance is at M III 187, where *ātāpī* occurs in what might refer to spending a night in meditation (following Ñāṇapoṇika 1977: p.346, for *bhaddekaratta*). Similarly Dhīravaṃsa 1989: p.97, understands *ātāpī* as "perseverance"; and Ñāṇārāma 1990: p.3, as "unbroken continuity".

36 Vin I 182 and A III 375; (also Th 638–9); and in the *satipaṭṭhāna* subcommentary, Ps-pṭ I 384, in order to illustrate the need for balanced energy in *satipaṭṭhāna* contemplation. The need for balance is also stressed by Kor 1985: p.23.

37 Khantipālo 1986: p.28; and Vimalaraṃsi 1997: p.49, warn against the dangers of overstraining or forcing meditation and the emotional disturbances and hardening of the mind that may ensue. Mann 1992: p.120, based on comparing the common character type in ancient Indian and the typical modern "western" mind, warns against indiscriminately applying to "hate" type meditators instructions developed mainly for the "craving" type. Cf. also W.S. Karunaratne 1988a: p.70.

38 S V 421.

39 At S I 1 the Buddha pointed out that by avoiding stagnation and excessive striving he had been able to "cross the flood". Cf. also Sn 8–13, which similarly recommend neither going too far nor lagging behind.

and "you yourself have to practise with diligence."[40] Similar connotations underlie the occurrence of the quality of "diligence" in those passages that describe the serious commitment of a monk who retires into seclusion for intensive practice after having received a brief instruction from the Buddha.[41]

Applying these nuances to *satipaṭṭhāna*, to be "diligent" then amounts to keeping up one's contemplation with balanced but dedicated continuity, returning to the object of meditation as soon as it is lost.[42]

II.3 CLEARLY KNOWING (*SAMPAJĀNA*)

The second of the four mental qualities mentioned in the "definition" is *sampajāna*, a present participle of the verb *sampajānāti*. *Sampajānāti* can be divided into *pajānāti* (he or she knows) and the prefix *saṃ* (together), which often serves an intensifying function in Pāli compounds.[43] Thus *sam-pajānāti* stands for an intensified form of knowing, for "clearly knowing".[44]

The range of meaning of "clearly knowing" (*sampajāna*) can be conveniently illustrated by briefly surveying some of its occurrences in the discourses. In a discourse found in the *Dīgha Nikāya*, clearly knowing stands for consciously experiencing one's own life as an embryo in a womb, including the event of being born.[45] In the *Majjhima Nikāya* one finds clearly knowing representing the presence of deliberateness, when one "deliberately" speaks a falsehood.[46] In a passage from the *Saṃyutta Nikāya*, clearly knowing refers to awareness of the impermanent nature of feelings and thoughts.[47] A discourse in the *Aṅguttara Nikāya* recommends clear

---

40 M III 187 and Dhp 276.

41 e.g. at S II 21; S III 74–9; S IV 37; S IV 64; S IV 76; and A IV 299. T.W. Rhys Davids 1997: p.242, and Singh 1967: p.127, relate *tapas* in a secondary sense to retirement into solitude in the forest, which parallels the use of *ātāpī* together with "dwelling alone and secluded" in the standard description of such a monk's going into seclusion for intensive practice.

42 Jotika 1986: p.29 n.15. This parallels the commentarial understanding of the related term *appamāda* as undistracted mindfulness, *satiyā avippavāso* (e.g. Sv I 104 or Dhp-a IV 26).

43 T.W. Rhys Davids 1993: pp.655 and 690.

44 The *Satipaṭṭhāna* subcommentary, Ps-pṭ I 354, explains *sampajāna* as "knowing in every way and in detail". Guenther 1991: p.85, speaks of "analytical appreciative understanding"; Ñāṇārāma 1990: p.4, of "investigative intelligence"; and van Zeyst 1967a: p.331, of "deliberate, discriminative knowledge".

45 D III 103 and D III 231.

knowledge (*sampajañña*) for overcoming unwholesomeness and establishing wholesomeness.[48] Finally, the *Itivuttaka* relates clearly knowing to following the advice of a good friend.[49]

A common denominator suggested by these examples selected from all five *Nikāyas* is the ability to fully grasp or comprehend what is taking place. Such clear knowledge can in turn lead to the development of wisdom (*paññā*). According to the *Abhidhamma*, clear knowledge does in fact already represent the presence of wisdom.[50] Considered from an etymological viewpoint, this suggestion is convincing, since *paññā* and *(sam-)pajānāti* are closely related. But a close examination of the above examples suggests that clearly knowing (*sampajāna*) does not necessarily imply the presence of wisdom (*paññā*). When one utters a falsehood, for example, one might clearly know one's speech to be a lie, but one does not speak the falsehood "with wisdom". Similarly, while it is remarkable enough to be clearly aware of one's embryonic development in the womb, to do so does not require wisdom. Thus, though clear knowing might lead to the development of wisdom, in itself it only connotes "to clearly know" what is happening.

In the *satipaṭṭhāna* instructions, the presence of such clear knowledge is alluded to by the frequently recurring expression "he knows" (*pajānāti*), which is found in most of the practical instructions. Similar to clearly knowing, the expression "he knows" (*pajānāti*) at times refers to rather basic forms of knowing, while in other instances it connotes more sophisticated types of understanding. In the context of *satipaṭṭhāna*, the range of what a meditator "knows" includes, for example, identifying a long breath as long, or recognizing one's physical posture.[51] But with the later *satipaṭṭhāna* contemplations, the meditator's task of knowing evolves until it comes to include the presence of discriminative understanding,

---

46 M I 286 and M I 414. Furthermore A II 158 distinguishes between the threefold action being done either *sampajāna* or else *asampajāna*, a context which also merits rendition as "deliberateness".

47 S V 180.

48 A I 13.

49 It 10.

50 e.g. Dhs 16 and Vibh 250. *Sampajañña* is also related to wisdom by Ayya Kheminda (n.d.): p.30; Buddhadāsa 1989: p.98; Debvedi 1990: p.22; Dhammasudhi 1968: p.67; Ñāṇapoṇika 1992: p.46; and Swearer 1967: p.153.

51 M I 56: "breathing in long, he knows 'I breathe in long'"; M I 57: "he knows accordingly however his body is disposed."

such as when one is to understand the arising of a fetter in dependence on a sense door and its respective object.[52] This evolution culminates in knowing the four noble truths "as they actually are", a penetrative type of deep understanding for which again the expression "he knows" is used.[53] Thus both the expression "he knows" (*pajānāti*) and the quality of "clearly knowing" (*sampajāna*) can range from basic forms of knowing to deep discriminative understanding.

II.4 MINDFULNESS AND CLEAR KNOWLEDGE

Clearly knowing, apart from being listed in the "definition" part of the *Satipaṭṭhāna Sutta*, is mentioned again under the first *satipaṭṭhāna*, with regard to a set of bodily activities.[54] Expositions of the gradual path of training usually refer to such clear knowing in regard to bodily activities with the compound *satisampajañña*, "mindfulness and clear knowledge".[55] On further perusing the discourses one finds that this combination of mindfulness with clear knowledge (or clearly knowing) is employed in a wide variety of contexts, paralleling the above documented flexible usage of clearly knowing on its own.

The Buddha, for instance, taught his disciples, went to sleep, endured an illness, relinquished his life-principle, and prepared for death – each time endowed with mindfulness and clear knowledge.[56] Even in his previous life he was already in possession of mindfulness and clear knowledge when he arose in heaven, stayed there, passed away from there, and entered his mother's womb.[57]

Mindfulness and clear knowledge also contribute towards improving one's ethical conduct and overcoming sensuality.[58] In the

---

52 e.g. M I 61: "he knows the eye, he knows forms, and he knows the fetter that arises dependent on both."

53 M I 62: "he knows as it really is, 'this is *dukkha*' ... 'this is the arising of *dukkha*' ... 'this is the cessation of *dukkha*' ...'this is the way leading to the cessation of *dukkha*.'"

54 M I 57: "when going forward and returning he acts clearly knowing; when looking ahead and looking away he acts clearly knowing...." I will consider this exercise in more detail on page 141.

55 e.g. at D I 70.

56 Maintaining equanimity towards attentive or non-attentive disciples at M III 221; going to sleep at M I 249; enduring illness and pain at D II 99; D II 128; S I 27; S I 110; and Ud 82; giving up his life principle at D II 106; S V 262; A IV 311; and Ud 64; lying down to die at D II 137. The presence of both at the time of death is recommended to the monks in general at S IV 211.

57 M III 119 (parts of this also at D II 108).

58 A II 195 and S I 31.

context of meditation, mindfulness and clear knowledge can refer to contemplating feelings and thoughts; they can mark a high level of equanimity in the context of perceptual training; or they can take part in overcoming sloth-and-torpor.[59] Mindfulness and clear knowledge become particularly prominent during the third meditative absorption (*jhāna*), where the presence of both is required to avoid a relapse into the intense joy (*pīti*) experienced during the second absorption.[60]

This broad variety of occurrences demonstrates that the combination of mindfulness with clear knowledge is often used in a general manner to refer to awareness and knowledge, without being restricted to its specific use as clearly knowing bodily activities in the gradual path scheme or in the *satipaṭṭhāna* context of body contemplation.

Such cooperation of mindfulness with clear knowledge, which according to the "definition" is required for all *satipaṭṭhāna* contemplations, points to the need to combine mindful observation of phenomena with an intelligent processing of the observed data. Thus "to clearly know" can be taken to represent the "illuminating" or "awakening" aspect of contemplation. Understood in this way, clear knowledge has the task of processing the input gathered by mindful observation, and thereby leads to the arising of wisdom.[61]

These qualities of clear knowledge and mindfulness thus remind one of the development of "knowledge" and "vision" of reality (*yathābhūtañāṇadassana*). According to the Buddha, to both "know" and "see" are necessary conditions for the realization of *Nibbāna*.[62] It might not be too far-fetched to relate such growth of knowledge (*ñāṇa*) to the quality of clearly knowing (*sampajāna*), and the accompanying aspect of "vision" (*dassana*) to the activity of watching represented by mindfulness (*sati*).

---

59 Contemplating feelings and thoughts at A IV 168; (cf. also A II 45); perceptual training at D III 250 and D III 113; and overcoming sloth-and-torpor e.g. at D I 71.

60 e.g. at D II 313; cf. also the comment at Vism 163; Guenther 1991: p.124; and Gunaratana 1996: p.92.

61 The interaction between *sati* and wisdom is described at Ps I 243, according to which wisdom contemplates what has become an object of awareness. Cf. also Vibh-a 311, which distinguishes between *sati* with and without wisdom, showing that wisdom is not an automatic result of the presence of *sati*, but needs to be deliberately developed. On the importance of combining *sati* with *sampajañña* cf. Chah 1996: p.6; and Mahasi 1981: p.94.

62 S III 152 and S V 434.

More remains to be said about this quality of clear knowledge.[63] In order to do this, however, some additional ground has to be covered, such as examining in more detail the implications of *sati*, which I will do in Chapter III.

---

63 I will consider *sampajañña* again when discussing the practice of mental labelling (page 113) and when investigating clearly knowing in regard to bodily activities as one of the body contemplations (page 141).

III

SATI

In this chapter I continue to investigate the "definition" part of the *Satipaṭṭhāna Sutta*. As a way of providing some background for *sati*, the third quality mentioned in the "definition", I briefly survey the general approach to knowledge in early Buddhism. In order to evaluate *sati* as a mental quality, the main task of the present chapter, I go on to explore its typical characteristics from different angles, and also contrast it with concentration (*samādhi*).

III.1 THE EARLY BUDDHIST APPROACH TO KNOWLEDGE

The philosophical setting of ancient India was influenced by three main approaches to the acquisition of knowledge.[1] The Brahmins relied mainly on ancient sayings, handed down by oral transmission, as authoritative sources of knowledge; while in the *Upaniṣads* one finds philosophical reasoning used as a central tool for developing knowledge. In addition to these two, a substantial number of the wandering ascetics and contemplatives of that time considered extrasensory perception and intuitive knowledge, gained through meditative experiences, as important means for the acquisition of knowledge. These three approaches can be summarized as: oral tradition, logical reasoning, and direct intuition.

When questioned on his own epistemological position, the Buddha placed himself in the third category, i.e. among those who

1 Following Jayatilleke 1980: p.63.

emphasized the development of direct, personal knowledge.[2] Although he did not completely reject oral tradition or logical reasoning as ways of acquiring knowledge, he was keenly aware of their limitations. The problem with oral tradition is that material committed to memory might be wrongly remembered. Moreover, even material that has been well remembered might be false and misleading. Similarly, logical reasoning might seem convincing, but then turn out to be unsound. Moreover, even sound reasoning might prove false and misleading if it is based on false premises. On the other hand, what has not been well remembered or what does not appear to be perfectly well reasoned might turn out to be true.[3]

Similar reservations hold true for direct knowledge gained in meditation. In fact, according to the Buddha's penetrating analysis in the *Brahmajāla Sutta*, sole reliance on direct extrasensory knowledge had caused a considerable number of mistaken views among contemporary practitioners.[4] The Buddha once illustrated the dangers of relying entirely on one's own direct experience with the help of a parable. In this parable, a king had several blind men each touch a different part of an elephant.[5] When questioned on the nature of the elephant, each blind man gave an entirely different account as the only right and true description of an elephant. Although what was experienced by each of the blind men was empirically true, yet their personal direct experience had revealed only part of the picture. The mistake each made was to wrongly conclude that his direct knowledge gained through personal experience was the only truth, so that anyone disagreeing must be mistaken.[6]

This parable goes to show that even direct personal experience might reveal only a part of the picture and therefore should not be grasped dogmatically as an absolute ground for knowledge. That is,

---

2 M II 211.

3 M I 520 and M II 171.

4 A survey of the sixty-two grounds for formulating views, presented in the *Brahmajāla Sutta* (D I 12–39), reveals that "direct" meditative experiences are the most frequent cause for formulating a view, while speculative thought assumes only a subordinate role: forty-nine instances appear to be based purely or at least in part on meditative experiences [nos 1–3, 5–7, 9–11, 17, 19–22, 23–5, 27, 29–41, 43–9, 51–7, 59–62]; against only thirteen instances based on pure reasoning [nos 4, 8, 12–16, 18, 26, 28, 42, 50, 58] (correlations made with the help of the commentary). Cf. also Bodhi 1992a: p.6.

5 Ud 68.

6 Ud 67; cf. also D II 282. Another illustration of such a wrong conclusion can be found at M III 210, where direct supernormal knowledge led to various wrong assumptions about the working mechanism of karma.

emphasis on direct experience need not entail a complete rejection of oral tradition and reasoning as auxiliary sources of knowledge. Nevertheless, direct experience constitutes the central epistemological tool in early Buddhism. According to a passage in the *Saḷāyatana Saṃyutta*, it is in particular the practice of *satipaṭṭhāna* that can lead to an undistorted direct experience of things as they truly are, independent of oral tradition and reasoning.[7] Thus, clearly, *satipaṭṭhāna* is an empirical tool of central importance in the pragmatic theory of knowledge in early Buddhism.

Applying the epistemological position of early Buddhism to actual practice, oral tradition and reasoning, in the sense of some degree of knowledge and reflection about the *Dhamma*, form the supporting conditions for a direct experience of reality through the practice of *satipaṭṭhāna*.[8]

III.2 *SATI*

The noun *sati* is related to the verb *sarati*, to remember.[9] *Sati* in the sense of "memory" occurs on several occasions in the discourses,[10] and also in the standard definitions of *sati* given in the *Abhidhamma* and the commentaries.[11] This remembrance aspect of *sati* is personified by the Buddha's disciple most eminent in *sati*, Ānanda, who is credited with the almost incredible feat of recalling all the discourses spoken by the Buddha.[12]

The connotation of *sati* as memory becomes particularly prominent with the recollections (*anussati*). The discourses often list a set of six recollections: recollection of the Buddha, of the *Dhamma*, of

---

7 At S IV 139 the Buddha proposed contemplation of the mind in relation to sense experience as a method of arriving at final knowledge independent of faith, personal preferences, oral tradition, reasoning, and acceptance of a view.

8 This brings to mind the threefold distinction between wisdom based on reflecting, on learning, and on mental development (a threefold presentation which in the discourses occurs only at D III 219).

9 Cf. Bodhi 1993: p.86; Gethin 1992: p.36; Guenther 1991: p.67; and Ñāṇamoli 1995: p.1188 n.136. The Sanskrit equivalent of *sati* is *smṛti*, also connoting memory and mental retention, cf. Monier-Williams 1995: p.1271; and C.A.F. Rhys Davids 1978: p.80.

10 e.g. *sati pamuṭṭhā* at M I 329 meaning "forgotten"; or *sati udapādi* at D I 180 as "remembering"; cf. also A IV 192, which uses the term *asati* when describing a monk pretending to have forgotten an offence for which he was being reproved.

11 Cf. Dhs 11; Vibh 250; Pp 25; As 121; Mil 77; and Vism 162.

12 Vin II 287 reports Ānanda calling to mind and reciting the discourses spoken by the Buddha during the first council. Whether or not this account of the first council corre-

the *Saṅgha*, of one's ethical conduct, of one's liberality, and of heavenly beings (*devas*).[13] Another kind of recollection, usually occurring in the context of the "higher knowledges" gained through deep concentration, is the recollection of one's past lives (*pubbenivāsānussati*). In regard to all these, it is *sati* that fulfils the function of recollecting.[14] This recollective function of *sati* can even lead to awakening, documented in the *Theragāthā* with the case of a monk who gained realization based on recollecting the qualities of the Buddha.[15]

This connotation of *sati* as memory appears also in its formal definition in the discourses, which relates *sati* to the ability of calling to mind what has been done or said long ago.[16] A closer examination of this definition, however, reveals that *sati* is not really defined as memory, but as that which facilitates and enables memory. What this definition of *sati* points to is that, if *sati* is present, memory will be able to function well.[17]

Understanding *sati* in this way facilitates relating it to the context of *satipaṭṭhāna*, where it is not concerned with recalling past events, but functions as awareness of the present moment.[18] In the context of *satipaṭṭhāna* meditation, it is due to the presence of *sati* that one is

---

sponds to historical truth, the fact that the *Vinaya* attributes the recital of the discourses to Ānanda must be reflecting his outstanding powers of memory (to which he himself refers at Th 1024). Ānanda's eminence in *sati* comes in for the Buddha's praise at A I 24. Nevertheless, according to Vin I 298 he also had lapses of *sati*, such as when he once set out to collect alms forgetting to put on all his robes.

13 e.g. at A III 284. On the six recollections cf. also Vism 197–228; and Devendra 1985: pp.25–45.

14 A II 183 points out that recollection of past lives is to be undertaken through *sati*. Similarly A V 336 speaks of directing *sati* to the Buddha in order to recollect him. Nid II 262 clearly understands all recollections as activities of *sati*. Vism 197 sums up: "it is through *sati* that one recollects."

15 Th 217–8. Th-a II 82 explains that based on recollecting the Buddha the monk then developed deep concentration which enabled him to recall past Buddhas, with the result that he realized that even Buddhas are impermanent. This in turn led to his awakening.

16 e.g. at M I 356.

17 The passage at M I 356 could then be rendered as: "he is mindful, being endowed with highest discriminative mindfulness (so that) things said or done long ago are recalled and remembered." Ñāṇamoli 1995: p.1252 n.560, explains: "keen attentiveness to the present forms the basis for an accurate memory of the past." Ñāṇananda 1984: p.28, points out: "mindfulness and memory ... the keenness of the one naturally leads to the clarity of the other."

18 Ñāṇaponika 1992: p.9; Ñāṇavīra 1987: p.382; and T.W. Rhys Davids 1966: vol.II, p.322. Griffith 1992: p.111, explains: "the basic meaning of *smṛti* and derivatives in Buddhist technical discourse ... has to do with observation and attention, not with awareness of past objects."

able to remember what is otherwise only too easily forgotten: the present moment.

Sati as present moment awareness is similarly reflected in the presentations of the *Paṭisambhidāmagga* and the *Visuddhimagga*, according to which the characteristic quality of *sati* is "presence" (*upaṭṭhāna*), whether as a faculty (*indriya*), as an awakening factor (*bojjhaṅga*), as a factor of the noble eightfold path, or at the moment of realization.[19]

Thus mindfulness being present (*upaṭṭhitasati*) can be understood to imply presence of mind, in so far as it is directly opposed to absent-mindedness (*muṭṭhassati*); presence of mind in the sense that, endowed with *sati*, one is wide awake in regard to the present moment.[20] Owing to such presence of mind, whatever one does or says will be clearly apprehended by the mind, and thus can be more easily remembered later on.[21]

Sati is required not only to fully take in the moment to be remembered, but also to bring this moment back to mind at a later time. To "re-collect", then, becomes just a particular instance of a state of mind characterized by "collectedness" and the absence of distraction.[22] This twofold character of *sati* can also be found in some verses in the *Sutta Nipāta*, which instruct the listener to set out with *sati*, subsequent to an instruction given by the Buddha.[23] In these instances *sati* seems to combine both present moment awareness and remembering what the Buddha had taught.

The kind of mental state in which memory functions well can be characterized by a certain degree of breadth, in contrast to a narrow focus. It is this breadth that enables the mind to make the necessary connections between information received in the present moment and information to be remembered from the past. This quality becomes evident on those occasions when one tries to recall a particular instance or fact, but where the more one applies one's mind, the less one is able to remember it. But if the issue in question is laid aside for a while and the mind is in a state of relaxed receptivity, the

---

19 Paṭis I 16; Paṭis I 116; and Vism 510.

20 Cf. S I 44, where *sati* is related to wakefulness. A related nuance occurs at Vism 464, which relates *sati* to strong cognition (*thirasaññā*).

21 The opposite case is documented at Vin II 261, where a nun failed to memorize the training rules for lack of *sati*.

22 Ñāṇananda 1993: p.47.

23 Sn 1053; Sn 1066; and Sn 1085.

information one was trying to remember will suddenly spring to mind.

The suggestion that the mental state in which *sati* is well-established can be characterized as having "breadth" instead of a narrow focus finds support in some discourses which relate the absence of *sati* to a narrow state of mind (*parittacetasa*), while its presence leads to a broad and even "boundless" state of mind (*appamāṇacetasa*).[24] Based on this nuance of "breadth of mind", *sati* can be understood to represent the ability to simultaneously maintain in one's mind the various elements and facets of a particular situation.[25] This can be applied to both the faculty of memory and to awareness of the present moment.

III.3 THE ROLE AND POSITION OF *SATI*

More understanding about *sati* can be gained by considering its role and position among some of the central categories of early Buddhism (cf. Fig. 3.1 below). *Sati* not only forms part of the noble eightfold path – as right mindfulness (*sammā sati*) – but also occupies a central position among the faculties (*indriya*) and powers (*bala*), and constitutes the first member of the awakening factors (*bojjhaṅga*). In these contexts, the functions of *sati* cover both present moment awareness and memory.[26]

---

24 S IV 119. M I 266; S IV 186; S IV 189; and S IV 199 make the same statement in relation to *kāyasati*. Similarly Sn 150–1 refers to the practice of radiating *mettā* in all directions as a form of *sati*, so here too *sati* represents an "immeasurable" state of mind.

25 Piatigorski 1984: p.150. Cf. also Newman 1996: p.28, who distinguishes between two levels of attention, primary and secondary: "I may be thinking about tomorrow and still be aware that now I am thinking about tomorrow ... my first level awareness is on tomorrow but my second level awareness is on what is happening now (i.e. that now I am thinking about tomorrow)."

26 Definitions of *sati* as a faculty mention both the practice of *satipaṭṭhāna* (S V 196 and S V 200) and memory (S V 198), the latter being also the definition of *sati* as a power (A III 11). As an awakening factor, *sati* again covers both aspects, since at M III 85 the presence of undistracted mindfulness as the outcome of *satipaṭṭhāna* practice forms *sati* as an awakening factor (the same definition is found several times at S V 331–9); whereas the awakening factor *sati* functions as memory at S V 67, since here it is concerned with recollecting and considering the teaching.

faculties + powers	noble eightfold path	awakening factors
confidence	right view	***sati***
energy	right thought	investigation-of-*dhammas*
sati	right speech	energy
concentration	right action	joy
wisdom	right livelihood	tranquillity
	right effort	concentration
	sammā sati	equanimity
	right concentration	

Fig. 3.1 The position of *sati* among important categories

Among the faculties (*indriya*) and powers (*bala*), *sati* occupies the middle position. Here *sati* has the function of balancing and monitoring the other faculties and powers, by becoming aware of excesses or deficiencies. A monitoring function similar to its position among the faculties and powers can be found in the noble eightfold path, where *sati* occupies the middle position in the three-factored path section directly concerned with mental training. The monitoring quality of *sati* is however not restricted to right effort and right concentration only, since according to the *Mahācattārīsaka Sutta* the presence of right mindfulness is also a requirement for the other path factors.[27]

In regard to its two neighbours in the noble eightfold path, *sati* performs additional functions. In support of right effort *sati* performs a protective role by preventing the arising of unwholesome states of mind in the context of sense-restraint, which in fact constitutes an aspect of right effort. In relation to right concentration, well-established *sati* acts as an important foundation for the development of deeper levels of mental calm, a topic to which I will return later on.

This position of *sati* in between the two mental qualities of energy (or effort) and concentration recurs also among the faculties and

27 M III 73 defines right mindfulness as the presence of awareness when overcoming wrong thought, wrong speech, wrong action, and wrong livelihood, and when establishing their counterparts.

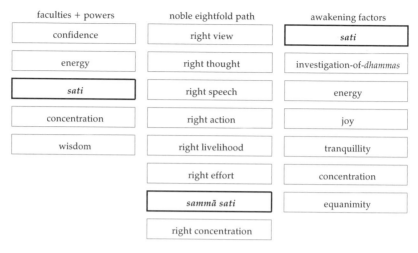

powers. The "definition" part of the *Satipaṭṭhāna Sutta* also combines *sati* with these two qualities, which are here represented by being diligent (*ātāpī*) and by the absence of desires and discontent (*abhijjhādomanassa*). The placement of *sati* between energy and concentration in all these contexts mirrors a natural progression in the development of *sati*, since in the early stages of practice a considerable degree of energy is required to counter distraction, while well-established *sati* in turn leads to an increasingly concentrated and calm state of mind.

In contrast to its middle position among the faculties and powers, and in the final section of the noble eightfold path, in the list of the awakening factors *sati* assumes the starting position. Here *sati* constitutes the foundation for those factors that bring about realization.

Since in relation to the faculties, powers, and factors of the noble eightfold path *sati* is clearly distinguished from associated factors like energy, wisdom, and concentration, *sati* has to be something clearly different from them in order to merit separate listing.[28] Similarly, since *sati* is differentiated from the awakening factor "investigation-of-*dhammas*", the task of investigating *dhammas* cannot be identical with the activity of awareness, otherwise there would have been no need to introduce it as a separate term. In this case, however, the activity of *sati* is closely related to "investigation-of-*dhammas*", since according to the *Ānāpānasati Sutta* the awakening factors arise sequentially, with "investigation-of-*dhammas*" arising consequent on the presence of *sati*.[29]

Coming back to right mindfulness as a factor of the noble eightfold path, it is noteworthy that the term *sati* is repeated within the definition of right mindfulness (*sammā sati*).[30] This repetition is not merely accidental, but rather points to a qualitative distinction between "right" mindfulness (*sammā sati*) as a path factor and mindfulness as

---

28 This is highlighted in the *Paṭisambhidāmagga*, according to which a clear appreciation of this difference constitutes "discriminative understanding" (*dhammapaṭisambhidañāṇa*), cf. Paṭis I 88 and Paṭis I 90.

29 M III 85; cf also S V 68.

30 D II 313: "he abides contemplating the body ... feelings ... the mind ... *dhammas*, diligent, clearly knowing and mindful, free from desires and discontent in regard to the world – this is called right mindfulness." An alternative definition of "right mindfulness" can be found in the *Atthasālinī*, which simply speaks of remembering properly (As 124). The definition of right mindfulness in the Chinese *Āgamas* also does not mention the four *satipaṭṭhānas*: "he is mindful, widely mindful, keeping in mind, not forgetful, this is called right mindfulness," (translation by Minh Chau 1991: p.97; cf. also Choong 2000: p.210).

a general mental factor. In fact, numerous discourses mention "wrong" mindfulness (*micchā sati*), which suggests that certain forms of *sati* can be quite different from right mindfulness.[31] According to this definition, *sati* requires the support of being diligent (*ātāpī*) and of clearly knowing (*sampajāna*). It is this combination of mental qualities, supported by a state of mind free from desires and discontent, and directed towards the body, feelings, the mind, and *dhammas*, which becomes the path factor of right mindfulness.

In the *Maṇibhadda Sutta* the Buddha pointed out that *sati* on its own, despite its manifold advantages, might not suffice for eradicating ill will.[32] This passage indicates that additional factors are needed in combination with *sati*, such as being diligent and clearly knowing in the case of developing *satipaṭṭhāna*.

Thus, in order to constitute "right mindfulness", *sati* has to cooperate with various other mental qualities. However, for the purpose of clearly defining *sati*, which is my present task, I will consider *sati* in isolation from these other mental factors in order to discern its most essential features.

---

31 "*Micchā sati*" at D II 353; D III 254; D III 287; D III 290; D III 291; M I 42; M I 118; M III 77; M III 140; S II 168; S III 109; S V 1; S V 12; S V 13; S V 16; S V 18–20; S V 23; S V 383; A II 220–9; A III 141; A IV 237; and A V 212–48 (A III 328 also has a wrong form of *anussati*). This substantial number of references to "wrong" types of *sati* to some extent disagrees with the commentarial presentation of *sati* as an exclusively wholesome mental factor (e.g. As 250). This presentation of the commentaries causes, in fact, a practical difficulty: how to reconcile *sati* as a wholesome factor with *satipaṭṭhāna* in relation to the hindrances, if wholesome and unwholesome mental qualities cannot coexist in the same state of mind? The commentaries attempt to resolve this contradiction by presenting *satipaṭṭhāna* of a defiled state of mind as a quick alternation between mind-moments associated with *sati* and those under the influence of defilements (e.g. at Ps-pṭ I 373). This explanation is however not convincing, since with either the defilement or else *sati* being absent, *satipaṭṭhāna* contemplation of the presence of a defilement in one's mind becomes impossible (cf. e.g. the instructions for contemplating the hindrances, which clearly refer to such a hindrance being present at the time of *satipaṭṭhāna* practice, M I 60: "he knows 'there is ... in me'"). Cf. furthermore Gethin 1992: pp.40–3; and Ñāṇapoṇika 1985: pp.68–72. According to the Sarvāstivāda tradition, *sati* is an indeterminate mental factor, cf. Stcherbatsky 1994: p.101.

32 At S I 208 Maṇibhadda proposed: "being mindful one is always blessed, being mindful one dwells happily, being mindful one lives better each day, and one is free from ill-will." The Buddha then repeated the first three lines, but corrected the fourth line to read: "yet one is not free from ill-will". Thus the central point in the Buddha's answer was to emphasize that *sati* alone might not suffice for eradicating ill will. This does, however, not mean that *sati* is incapable of preventing the arising of ill will, since its presence goes a long way in helping one to remain calm when confronted with the anger of others, as documented at S I 162; S I 221; S I 222; and S I 223.

III.4 *SATI* IMAGERY

The significance and various nuances of the term *sati* are illustrated by a considerable number of images and similes in the discourses. If these images and similes are examined and their implications drawn out, additional insights can be gained into how the Buddha and his contemporaries understood the term *sati*.

A simile in the *Dvedhāvitakka Sutta* describes a cowherd who had to watch closely over his cows to prevent them straying into fields where the crop was ripe. But once the crop was harvested, he was able to relax, sit under a tree, and watch over them from a distance. To express this comparatively relaxed and distant manner of observation, *sati* is used.[33] The disposition suggested by this simile is a calm and detached type of observation.

Another simile supporting this quality of detached observation occurs in a verse in the *Theragāthā*, which compares the practice of *satipaṭṭhāna* to climbing an elevated platform or tower.[34] Connotations of aloofness and uninvolved detachment are confirmed by the context of this passage, which contrasts the tower image to being carried away by the stream of desire. Detachment comes up again in the *Dantabhūmi Sutta*, which compares *satipaṭṭhāna* to the taming of a wild elephant. Just as a recently captured elephant has to be gradually weaned of his forest habits, so too *satipaṭṭhāna* can gradually wean a monk from memories and intentions related to the household life.[35]

Another simile compares *sati* to the probe of a surgeon.[36] Like the surgeon's probe, whose function is to provide information about the wound for subsequent treatment, so too the "probe" *sati* can be used to carefully gather information, thereby preparing the ground for subsequent action. This ground-preparing quality is conveyed again by another simile, relating *sati* to the goad and the ploughshare of a farmer.[37] Just as a farmer has first to plough the ground in

---

33 M I 117 speaks in this context of practising mindfulness (*sati karaṇīyaṃ*), while earlier he had actively to protect the crop by closely watching over the cows (*rakkheyya*). This, however, does not imply that *sati* cannot also take part in holding back a cow about to stray into ripe crops, which in fact it does at Th 446, but only that the more relaxed observation described above brings out a characteristic feature of bare and receptive *sati*.

34 Th 765.

35 M III 136.

36 M II 260.

order to be able to sow, so too *sati* fulfils an important preparatory role for the arising of wisdom.[38]

This role of *sati* in support of the arising of wisdom occurs again in another simile, which associates the parts of an elephant's body with mental qualities and factors. Here *sati* is compared to the elephant's neck, the natural support for its head, which in the same simile represents wisdom.[39] The choice of the elephant's neck is of additional significance, since it is a characteristic of both elephants and Buddhas to look around by turning with the whole body instead of only with the head.[40] The elephant's neck, then, represents the quality of giving full attention to a matter at hand as a feature of *sati*.

Although the "elephant look" is a specific characteristic of the Buddha, to give continuous and full attention to a matter at hand is a characteristic common to all *arahants*.[41] This is illustrated in another simile, which compares *sati* to the single spoke of a chariot.[42] In this simile, the rolling chariot represents the bodily activities of an *arahant*, all of which take place with the support of a single spoke – *sati*.

---

37 S I 172 and Sn 77. This simile might have suggested itself since with the help of the goad the farmer ensures the continuity of the ploughing, keeping the ox "on track", while the ploughshare penetrates the surface of the earth, turns up its hidden parts, and thereby prepares it for seeds to be grown and planted. Similarly, continuity of *sati* keeps the mind "on track" with regard to the meditation object, so that *sati* can penetrate the surface appearance of phenomena, turn up their hidden aspects (the three characteristics), and enable the seeds of wisdom to grow. The fact that ploughshare and goad are mentioned together in the above simile points moreover to the need to combine clarity of direction with balanced effort in developing *sati*, since the farmer has to execute two tasks at the same time: with the goad in one hand he has to ensure the straightness of the furrow by keeping the oxen moving in a straight line, while with the other hand he has to exert just the right amount of pressure on the ploughshare, so that it neither gets stuck because he has pushed it too deeply into the ground or only scratches over the surface for lack of pressure.

38 Spk I 253 and Pj II 147 explain the import of this simile to be that wisdom understands phenomena only when they are known through *sati*.

39 A III 346. The same imagery occurs again at Th 695; and is at Th 1090 even transferred from an elephant to the Buddha himself.

40 M II 137 depicts the Buddha turning his whole body whenever looking back. This "elephant look" of the Buddha is again documented at D II 122; while M I 337 reports the same for the Buddha Kakusandha.

41 According to Mil 266, *arahants* never lose their *sati*.

42 S IV 292. The whole simile originally comes up at Ud 76, where it is only the commentary, Ud-a 370, which relates the single spoke to *sati*. Though the image of a single spoke might appear strange, as long as this spoke is strong enough (viz. the *arahant*'s presence of *sati*), it is capable of providing the required connection between hub and rim to form a wheel.

The supportive role of *sati* in the development of wisdom comes up again in a verse from the *Sutta Nipāta*, where *sati* keeps the streams in this world in check, so that the faculty of wisdom can cut them off.[43] This verse points in particular to the role of *sati* in relation to restraint at the sense doors (*indriya saṃvara*) as a basis for the development of wisdom.

What the similes of the "surgeon's probe", the "ploughshare", the "elephant's neck", and "keeping the streams in check" have in common is that they illustrate the preparatory role of *sati* for insight. According to these similes, *sati* is the mental quality that enables wisdom to arise.[44]

Another simile, found in the *Saṃyutta Nikāya*, compares *sati* to a careful charioteer.[45] This brings to mind the monitoring and steering quality of *sati* in relation to other mental factors, such as the faculties and the powers. The qualities evoked by this simile are careful and balanced supervision. A similar nuance can be found in another simile, which compares mindfulness in relation to the body to carrying a bowl full of oil on one's head, vividly illustrating the balancing quality of *sati*.[46]

The quality of careful supervision occurs again in yet another simile, in which *sati* is personified by the gatekeeper of a town.[47] The simile portrays messengers arriving at the town gate with an urgent message to be delivered to the king. The function of the gatekeeper is to inform them of the shortest route to the king. The gatekeeper image occurs again elsewhere in relation to the defence of a town. This town has energy (*viriya*) as its troops and wisdom (*paññā*) as its fortification, while the function of the gatekeeper *sati* is to recognize the genuine citizens of the town and to allow them to enter the gates.[48] Both of these similes associate *sati* with having a clear over-

---

43 Sn 1035; on this verse cf. also Ñāṇananda 1984: p.29.

44 The relation of *sati* to wisdom is also alluded to at Vism 464, according to which the characteristic function of *sati* is absence of confusion (*asammoharasa*).

45 S V 6. A variation on the same imagery occurs at S I 33, where the *Dhamma* itself becomes the charioteer, with the consequence that *sati* is relegated to being the chariot's upholstery. The image of *sati* as upholstery illustrates how established *sati* in a way "cushions" the practitioner against the impact of the "potholes" of life, since the presence of awareness counters the tendency towards those mental reactions and proliferations that ordinarily tend to arise in relation to the vicissitudes of life.

46 S V 170. I will examine this simile in more detail on page 122.

47 S IV 194.

48 A IV 110.

view of the situation.[49]

The second simile moreover brings out the restraining function of bare *sati*, a function which is of particular relevance in relation to restraint at the sense doors (*indriya saṁvara*). This brings to mind the above-mentioned passage where *sati* was to keep the streams in this world in check. Just as the presence of the gatekeeper prevents those not entitled from entering the town, so too the presence of well-established *sati* prevents the arising of unwholesome associations and reactions at the sense doors. The same protective role of *sati* also underlies other passages, which introduce *sati* as the one factor that guards the mind,[50] or as a mental quality able to exert a controlling influence on thoughts and intentions.[51]

A discourse in the *Aṅguttara Nikāya* compares the practice of *satipaṭṭhāna* to a cowherd's skill in knowing the proper pasture for his cows.[52] The image of a proper pasture occurs again in the *Mahāgopālaka Sutta*, throwing into relief the importance of *satipaṭṭhāna* contemplation for growth and development on the path to deliverance.[53] Another discourse employs the same image to describe the situation of a monkey who has to avoid straying into regions visited by hunters.[54] Just as the monkey, wishing to be safe, has to keep to its proper pasture, so too practitioners of the path should keep to their proper pasture, which is *satipaṭṭhāna*. Since one of the above passages explains sensual pleasures to be an improper "pasture", this set of images depicting *satipaṭṭhāna* as one's proper pasture points to the restraining role of bare awareness in regard to sense-input.[55]

---

49 Cf. also Chah 1997: p.10: "that which 'looks over' the various factors which arise in meditation is '*sati*'."

50 D III 269 and A V 30.

51 A IV 385. Cf. also the similar formulation at A IV 339 and A V 107. Th 359 and 446 also refer to the controlling influence of *sati* on the mind.

52 A V 352.

53 M I 221.

54 S V 148, where the Buddha related a parable in which a monkey was caught by a hunter because he had left the jungle (his "pasture") and entered a region visited by men. The need to keep to one's proper pasture comes up again at S V 146 in a parallel simile depicting a quail which in this way can avoid getting caught by a falcon.

55 S V 149. However, the commentaries to M I 221 and A V 352 (Ps II 262 and Mp V 95) explain lack of skill in "pasture" to imply lack of understanding the difference between mundane and supramundane *satipaṭṭhāna*.

This stabilizing function of established mindfulness in regard to distraction by way of the six sense doors is exemplified in another simile by a strong post, to which six different wild animals are bound.[56] No matter how much each animal might struggle to get off on its own, the "strong post" *sati* will remain stable and unshaken. Such a stabilizing function of *sati* is of particular relevance during the initial stages of *satipaṭṭhāna* practice, given that without a firm foundation in balanced awareness one only too easily succumbs to sensual distraction. This danger is illustrated in the *Cātumā Sutta*, which describes a monk who goes begging alms without having established *sati* and therefore without restraint at the sense doors. Encountering a scantily clad woman on his tour causes sensual desire to arise in his mind, so that he eventually decides to give up his practice and to disrobe.[57]

III.5 CHARACTERISTICS AND FUNCTIONS OF *SATI*

A close examination of the instructions in the *Satipaṭṭhāna Sutta* reveals that the meditator is never instructed to interfere actively with what happens in the mind. If a mental hindrance arises, for example, the task of *satipaṭṭhāna* contemplation is to know that the hindrance is present, to know what has led to its arising, and to know what will lead to its disappearance. A more active intervention is no longer the domain of *satipaṭṭhāna*, but belongs rather to the province of right effort (*sammā vāyāma*).

The need to distinguish clearly between a first stage of observation and a second stage of taking action is, according to the Buddha, an essential feature of his way of teaching.[58] The simple reason for this approach is that only the preliminary step of calmly assessing a situation without immediately reacting enables one to undertake the appropriate action.

Thus, although *sati* furnishes the necessary information for a wise deployment of right effort, and will monitor the countermeasures by noting if these are excessive or deficient, *sati* nevertheless

---

56 S IV 198. Since this simile is concerned with mindfulness of the body in particular, I will discuss it in more detail on page 123.

57 M I 462. In fact at D II 141 the Buddha particularly emphasized the need to keep to *sati* for monks who were coming in contact with women.

58 At It 33 the Buddha distinguished between two successive aspects of his teaching, the first of which was to recognize evil as evil, while the second was to get free from such evil.

remains an aloof quality of uninvolved, detached observation. *Sati* can interact with other, much more active factors of the mind, yet by itself it does not interfere.[59]

Uninvolved and detached receptivity as one of the crucial characteristics of *sati* forms an important aspect in the teachings of several modern meditation teachers and scholars.[60] They emphasize that the purpose of *sati* is solely to make things conscious, not to eliminate them. *Sati* silently observes, like a spectator at a play, without in any way interfering. Some refer to this non-reactive feature of *sati* as "choiceless" awareness.[61] "Choiceless" in the sense that with such awareness one remains impartially aware, without reacting with likes or dislikes. Such silent and non-reactive observation can at times suffice to curb unwholesomeness, so that an application of *sati* can have quite active consequences. Yet *sati*'s activity is confined to detached observation. That is, *sati* does not change experience, it deepens it.

This non-interfering quality of *sati* is required to enable one clearly to observe the building up of reactions and their underlying motives. As soon as one becomes in any way involved in a reaction, the detached observational vantage point is immediately lost. The detached receptivity of *sati* enables one to step back from the situation at hand and thereby to become an unbiased observer of one's subjective involvement and of the entire situation.[62] This detached distance allows for a more objective perspective, a characteristic illustrated in the above-mentioned simile of climbing a tower.

This detached but receptive stance of *satipaṭṭhāna* constitutes a "middle path", since it avoids the two extremes of suppression and reaction.[63] The receptivity of *sati*, in the absence of both suppression and reaction, allows personal shortcomings and unjustified reactions to unfold before the watchful stance of the meditator, without

---

59 An example for the coexistence of *sati* with intense effort is furnished by the *bodhisatta*'s ascetic practices (at M I 242), where even during excessive striving he was able to maintain his mindfulness.

60 Lily de Silva (n.d.): p.5; Fraile 1993: p.99; Naeb 1993: p.158; Swearer 1971: p.107; and van Zeyst 1989: pp.9 and 12. This receptive and not interfering quality of *sati* is also echoed at Nid II 262, which relates *sati* to peacefulness.

61 The expression "choiceless awareness" is used by Brown 1986b: p.167; Engler 1983: p.32; Epstein 1984: p.196; Goldstein 1985: p.19; Kornfield 1977: p.12; Levine 1989: p.28; and Sujīva 2000: p.102.

62 Dhīramvaṃsa 1988: p.31.

63 This is to some extent paralleled at A I 295, which presents *satipaṭṭhāna* as a middle path, aloof from both indulgence in sensuality and self-mortification.

being suppressed by the affective investment inherent in one's self-image. Maintaining the presence of *sati* in this way is closely related to the ability to tolerate a high degree of "cognitive dissonance", since the witnessing of one's own shortcomings ordinarily leads to unconscious attempts at reducing the resulting feeling of discomfort by avoiding or even altering the perceived information.[64]

This shift towards a more objective and uninvolved perspective introduces an important element of sobriety into self-observation. The element of "sobriety" inherent in the presence of *sati* comes up in an entertaining canonical description of a particular celestial realm, whose divine inhabitants get so "intoxicated" with sensual indulgence that they lose all *sati*. As a consequence of being without *sati*, they fall from their elevated celestial position and are reborn in a lower realm.[65] The reverse case is also documented in another discourse, in which negligent monks, reborn in an inferior celestial realm, on regaining their *sati* are at once able to ascend to a higher realm.[66] Both these instances point to the edifying power of *sati* and its wholesome repercussions.

Sati as a mental quality is closely related to attention (*manasikāra*), a basic function which, according to the *Abhidhammic* analysis, is present in any kind of mental state.[67] This basic faculty of ordinary attention characterizes the initial split seconds of bare cognizing of an object, before one begins to recognize, identify, and conceptualize. *Sati* can be understood as a further development and temporal extension of this type of attention, thereby adding clarity and depth to the usually much too short fraction of time occupied by bare attention in the perceptual process.[68] The resemblance in function between *sati* and attention is also reflected in the fact that wise attention (*yoniso manasikāra*) parallels several aspects of *satipaṭṭhāna* contemplation, such as directing attention to antidotes for the hindrances, becoming aware of the impermanent nature of the

---

64 Cf. Festinger 1957: p.134.

65 D I 19 and D III 31.

66 D II 272.

67 Abhidh-s 7. The discourses assign a similarly important role to attention (*manasikāra*) by including it in the definition of "name" (*nāma*), e.g. at M I 53. On the relation of *sati* to attention cf. Bullen 1991: p.17; Gunaratana 1992: p.150; and Ñāṇapoṇika 1950: p.3.

68 Ñāṇapoṇika 1986b: p.2. This "bare" quality of *sati* is alluded to at Vism 464, which considers being directly face-to-face with an object as a characteristic manifestation of *sati*.

aggregates or of the sense-spheres, establishing the awakening factors, and contemplating the four noble truths.[69]

This "bare attention" aspect of *sati* has an intriguing potential, since it is capable of leading to a "de-automatization" of mental mechanisms.[70] Through bare *sati* one is able to see things just as they are, unadulterated by habitual reactions and projections. By bringing the perceptual process into the full light of awareness, one becomes conscious of automatic and habitual responses to perceptual data. Full awareness of these automatic responses is the necessary preliminary step to changing detrimental mental habits.

Sati as bare attention is particularly relevant to restraint at the sense doors (*indriya saṃvara*).[71] In this aspect of the gradual path, the practitioner is encouraged to retain bare *sati* in regard to all sense-input. Through the simple presence of undisrupted and bare mindfulness, the mind is "restrained" from amplifying and proliferating the received information in various ways. This guardianship role of *sati* in relation to sense-input is alluded to in those similes that declare *satipaṭṭhāna* to be the proper "pasture" for a meditator and which compare *sati* to the gatekeeper of a town.

According to the discourses, the purpose of restraining the senses is to avoid the arising of desires (*abhijjhā*) and discontent (*domanassa*). Such freedom from desires and discontent is also an aspect of *satipaṭṭhāna* contemplation, mentioned in the "definition" part of the discourse.[72] Thus the absence of reactions under the influence of desires and discontent is a common feature of both *satipaṭṭhāna* and sense-restraint. This goes to show that there is a considerable degree of overlap between these two activities.

To sum up, *sati* entails an alert but receptive equanimous observation.[73] Viewed from the context of actual practice, a predominantly receptive *sati* is then enlivened by the quality of being diligent

---

69 Wise attention (*yoniso manasikāra*) is applied to antidotes for the hindrances at S V 105, can lead to realization by giving attention to the impermanent nature of the aggregates at S III 52 and of the sense-spheres at S IV 142, establishes the awakening factors at S V 94, and consists in contemplating the four noble truths at M I 9. Cf. also A V 115, where wise attention functions as "nutriment" for mindfulness and clear knowledge, which in turn act as nutriment for *satipaṭṭhāna*.

70 Deikman 1966: p.329; Engler 1983: p.59; Goleman 1980: p.27; and 1975: p.46; and van Nuys 1971: p.127.

71 The standard definition of sense-restraint, found e.g. at M I 273, speaks of avoiding being carried away by one's evaluations and reactions to what is perceived through the senses. Cf. also Debvedi 1998: p.18; and page 225 infra.

72 M I 56: "free from desires and discontent in regard to the world."

(*ātāpī*), and supported by a foundation in concentration (*samādhi*). To the interrelation of *sati* with concentration I will now turn in more detail.

III.6 *SATI* AND CONCENTRATION (*SAMĀDHI*)

The continuous presence of well-established *sati* is a requirement for absorption (*jhāna*).[74] Without the support of *sati*, as the *Visuddhimagga* points out, concentration cannot reach the level of absorption.[75] Even on emerging from an experience of deep concentration *sati* is required when one reviews the constituent factors of one's experience.[76] Thus *sati* is relevant for attaining, for remaining in, and for emerging from deep concentration.[77]

Sati becomes particularly prominent when the third level of absorption (*jhāna*) is reached.[78] With the attainment of the fourth absorption, when the mind has reached such a degree of proficiency that it can be directed towards the development of supernormal powers, *sati* also reaches a high degree of purity, because of its association with deep equanimity.[79]

Several discourses testify to the important role of *satipaṭṭhāna* as a basis for the development of absorption and for the subsequent

73 Modern scholars and meditation teachers offer several alternative summaries of the essential aspects of *sati*. Ayya Khema 1991: p.182, distinguishes two applications of *sati*: the mundane application, helping one to be aware of what one is doing, and the supramundane application of penetrating to the real nature of things. Dhammasudhi 1969: p.77, describes four aspects of *sati*: awareness of surroundings, of one's reactions to these surroundings, of one's own conditioning, and of stillness ("pure awareness"). Hecker 1999: p.11, mentions vigilance, self-control, depth, and steadiness. Ñāṇaponika 1986b: p.5, enumerates four "sources of power" in *sati*: tidying up by naming, non-coercive procedure, stopping and slowing down, and directness of vision.

74 M III 25–8 documents that this need applies to each stage in the ascending series of meditative absorptions, since it lists *sati* among the mental factors of the four absorptions of the form sphere and of the first three immaterial attainments. The fourth immaterial attainment and the attainment of cessation, both being states of mind not amenable to factor analysis, are still related to *sati* on emergence (M III 28). Presence of *sati* in all *jhānas* is also documented at Dhs 55 and at Paṭis I 35.

75 Vism 514.

76 Described e.g. at M III 25.

77 Cf. D III 279; Paṭis II 16; and Vism 129.

78 The standard descriptions of the third *jhāna* (e.g. at D II 313) explicitly mention the presence of *sati* and of clearly knowing.

79 The standard descriptions of the fourth *jhāna* (e.g. at D II 313) speak of "purity of mindfulness due to equanimity", which then can be used to develop supernatural powers (e.g. at M I 357). That here *sati* is indeed purified by the presence of equanimity can be gathered from M III 26 and Vibh 261; cf. also As 178 and Vism 167.

attainment of supernormal powers.[80] The role of *satipaṭṭhāna* in supporting the development of concentration is also reflected in the standard expositions of the gradual path, where the preliminary steps that lead up to the attainment of absorption include mindfulness and clear knowledge (*satisampajañña*) in relation to bodily activities, and the task of recognizing the hindrances and supervising their removal, an aspect of the fourth *satipaṭṭhāna*, contemplation of *dhammas*.

The progression from *satipaṭṭhāna* to absorption is described in the *Dantabhūmi Sutta* with an intermediate step. In this intermediate step, contemplation of the body, feelings, mind, and *dhammas* continues with the specific qualification that one should avoid having any thoughts.[81] In the instruction for this transitional stage, the mental qualities of diligence and clear knowledge are conspicuously absent. Their absence suggests that at this point the contemplation is no longer *satipaṭṭhāna* proper, but only a transitional stage. This thought-free transitional stage still partakes of the same receptive observational quality and of the same object as *satipaṭṭhāna*, but at the same time it marks a clear shift from insight to calm. It is subsequent to this shift of emphasis from *satipaṭṭhāna* proper to a state of calm awareness that the development of absorption can take place.

On considering these instances it is indubitably clear that *sati* has a crucial role to fulfil in the realm of *samatha*. This might be why the *Cūḷavedalla Sutta* speaks of *satipaṭṭhāna* as the "cause" of concentration (*samādhinimitta*).[82] The relation between *satipaṭṭhāna* and the development of deep concentration is exemplified by the monk

---

80 The concentrative attainments possible through *satipaṭṭhāna* practice are documented on several occasions, such as D II 216; S V 151; S V 299; S V 303; and A IV 300. According to Ledi 1985: p.59, one should embark on the development of absorption only when one is able to maintain *satipaṭṭhāna* contemplation uninterruptedly for one or two hours daily.

81 M III 136. Whereas the PTS edition speaks of thoughts in relation to the objects of *satipaṭṭhāna* (*kāyūpasaṃhitaṃ vitakkaṃ* etc.), the Burmese and the Sinhalese editions speak of sensual thoughts instead (*kāmūpasaṃhitaṃ vitakkaṃ*). Judging from the dynamics of the discourse, this seems to be the less probable reading, since this passage follows on the removal of the five hindrances and leads on to absorption, and that straightaway into the second *jhāna*. The corresponding Chinese version (T'iao Yü Ti Ching, *Madhyama Āgama* no. 198), however, supports the reading of the Burmese and Sinhalese editions. In addition, it also mentions the attainment of the first *jhāna*, which in all the Pāli editions is missing.

82 M I 301. Ps II 363 takes this to refer to the moment of realization, which, however, as

Anuruddha, foremost among the Buddha's disciples in the supernormal ability of seeing beings in other realms of existence,[83] an ability based on a high degree of proficiency in concentration. Whenever asked about his abilities, Anuruddha invariably explained that his skills were the outcome of his practice of *satipaṭṭhāna*.[84]

On the other hand, however, to consider *satipaṭṭhāna* purely as a concentration exercise goes too far and misses the important difference between what can become a basis for the development of concentration and what belongs to the realm of calmness meditation proper.[85] In fact, the characteristic functions of *sati* and concentration (*samādhi*) are quite distinct. While concentration corresponds to an enhancement of the selective function of the mind, by way of restricting the breadth of attention, *sati* on its own represents an enhancement of the recollective function, by way of expanding the breadth of attention.[86] These two modes of mental functioning correspond to two different cortical control mechanisms in the brain.[87] This difference, however, does not imply that the two are incompatible, since during absorption attainment both are present. But during absorption *sati* becomes mainly presence of the mind, when it to some extent loses its natural breadth owing to the strong focusing power of concentration.

The difference between these two becomes evident from the vocabulary employed in a passage from the *Satipaṭṭhāna Saṃyutta*.

---

the commentary also admits, is difficult to reconcile with the fact that the discourse speaks of developing and making much of this *samādhinimitta*. The supportive role of *satipaṭṭhāna* for the development of right concentration is also echoed at A V 212, according to which right mindfulness gives rise to right concentration.

83 A I 23.

84 S V 294–306; cf. also Malalasekera 1995: vol.I, p.88.

85 Cf. e.g. Schmithausen 1973: p.179, who suggests that *satipaṭṭhāna* was originally purely a concentration exercise.

86 Cf. also Bullen 1982: p.44; Delmonte 1991: pp.48–50; Goleman 1977a: p.298; Shapiro 1980: pp.15–19; and Speeth 1982: pp.146 and 151. Gunaratana 1992: p.165, aptly sums up: "concentration is exclusive. It settles down on one item and ignores everything else. Mindfulness is inclusive. It stands back from the focus of attention and watches with a broad focus."

87 Brown 1977: p.243: "two major cortical control mechanisms ... involved in selecting and processing information ... a frontal system associated with restrictive processing and a posterior-temporal system associated with more wide-range processing of information. The brain may be likened to a camera that can use either a wide-angle lens or a zoom lens. Or, in cognitive terms, attention can be directed to the more dominant details in a stimulus field or to the entire field."

In this passage the Buddha recommended that, if one is being distracted or sluggish while practising *satipaṭṭhāna*, one should temporarily change one's practice and develop a calm (*samatha*) object of meditation, in order to cultivate internal joy and serenity.[88]

This he termed a "directed" form of meditation (*paṇidhāya bhāvanā*). Once, however, the mind has been calmed, one can return to an "undirected" mode of meditation (*appaṇidhāya bhāvanā*), namely the practice of *satipaṭṭhāna*. The distinction drawn in this discourse between "directed" and "undirected" forms of meditation suggests that, considered on their own, these two modes of meditation are clearly different. At the same time, however, the whole discourse is concerned with their skilful interrelation, clearly demonstrating that whatever the degree of their difference, the two can be interrelated and support each other.[89]

The characteristic quality of concentration is to "direct" and apply the mind, focusing on a single object to the exclusion of everything else. Thus the development of concentration promotes a shift from the common structure of experience as a subject-object duality towards an experience of unity.[90] Concentration, however, thereby excludes a broader awareness of circumstances and of their interrelations.[91] This awareness of circumstances and interrelations is, however, essential in order to become aware of those characteristics of experience whose understanding leads to awakening. In this context, the broadly receptive quality of *sati* is particularly important.

These two rather distinct qualities of concentration and mindfulness are combined to some extent in the descriptions of insight meditation by those meditation teachers who emphasize the "dry insight" approach, dispensing with the formal development of mental calm. They sometimes describe *sati* as "attacking" its object in a

---

88 S V 156.

89 At the beginning of this passage the Buddha spoke in praise of being well established in the four *satipaṭṭhānas*. Thus the reason for his exposition about "directed" and "undirected" modes of meditation appears to be that he wanted to show how *samatha* can act as a support for the practice of *satipaṭṭhāna*.

90 Kamalashila 1994: p.96; Kyaw Min 1980: p.96; and Ruth Walshe 1971: p.104. Cf. also page 262.

91 Cf. Brown 1986b: p.180, who in a comparison of Rorschach tests done with different meditators describes in his conclusion the "unproductivity and relative paucity of associative process which characterizes the samādhi state", while "the Rorschachs of the insight group ... are primarily characterized by increased productivity and richness of associative elaborations."

way that is comparable to a stone hitting a wall.[92] These forceful terms probably represent the need for a considerable degree of effort during contemplation, such prodigious effort being required to compensate for the comparatively low degree of concentration developed when following the "dry insight" approach to awakening. In fact, some of these same meditation teachers consider the bare and equanimous qualities of *sati* as a more evolved stage of practice, presumably when the more forceful stage of "attacking" an object has fulfilled its role and has provided a basis of mental stability.[93]

The above way of considering *sati* may be related to the commentarial definition of *sati* as "non-floating" and therefore as "plunging into its object".[94] Certainly the absence of "floating", in the sense of distraction, is a characteristic of *sati*. However "to plunge" into an object appears to be more characteristic of concentration, particularly during the progress towards absorption. According to modern scholarship, it seems that this aspect of the commentarial understanding of *sati* arose because of a misreading or misinterpretation of a particular term.[95] In fact, "attacking" an object or "plunging into" an object do not correspond to the characteristic features of *sati* in itself, but represent *sati* in a secondary role, acting in combination with effort or concentration.

Thus although it plays an important part in the development of absorption, considered on its own *sati* is a mental quality distinct from concentration. Indeed, the reason even the attainment of high levels of absorption by itself is insufficient for liberating insight is quite probably related to the inhibition of the passive observational

---

92 Mahasi 1990: p.23: "the knowing mind … as in the case of a stone hitting a wall"; which Sīlananda 1990: p.21, identifies: "like the stone hitting the wall … that hitting of the object is mindfulness". Paṇḍita (n.d.): p.6, goes further, when he describes *satipaṭṭhāna* as implying to "attack the object without hesitation … with violence, speed or great force … with excessive haste or hurry", which he then compares to soldiers defeating an enemy troop in a sudden attack.

93 Such more advanced stages of *satipaṭṭhāna* practice are sometimes referred to as "*vipassanā jhānas*", an expression not found in the discourses, the *Abhidhamma*, or the commentaries. Cf. Mahasi 1981: p.98; and a detailed exposition in Paṇḍita 1993: pp.180–205, cf. esp. p.199: "non-thinking, bare attention is called the second *vipassanā jhāna*".

94 This is the term *apilāpanatā*, found at Dhs 11 (detailed expo at As 147); Vibh 250; Pp 25; Nett 54; Mil 37; and Vism 464. On the term cf. also Guenther 1991: p.68 n.2; Horner 1969: p.50 n.5; Ñāṇamoli 1962: p.28 n.83/3; and C.A.F. Rhys Davids 1922: p.14 n.3.

95 Gethin 1992: pp.38–40, suggests that the commentarial reading of *apilāpeti* should rather be *apilapati* (or *abhilapati*), which instead of describing *sati* as "plunging into", would come to mean "reminding someone of something". Cf. also Cox 1992: pp.79–82.

qualities of awareness by the strong focusing power of absorption concentration. This, however, does not detract from the fact that the development of concentration fulfils an important role in the context of insight meditation, a topic I will discuss in more detail in Chapter IV.

IV

THE RELEVANCE OF CONCENTRATION

This chapter is devoted to the expression "free from desires and discontent in regard to the world" and its implications. Since the freedom from desires and discontent envisaged in this final part of the "definition" points to the development of mental composure when practising *satipaṭṭhāna*, in this chapter I investigate the role of concentration in the context of insight meditation, and try to ascertain the degree of concentration needed for realization. Thereafter I examine the general contribution of concentration to the development of insight and their interrelatedness.

IV.1 FREEDOM FROM DESIRES AND DISCONTENT

The "definition" part of the *Satipaṭṭhāna Sutta* concludes with the expression "free from desires and discontent in regard to the world".[1] According to the *Nettippakaraṇa*, to be "free from desires and discontent" represents the faculty of concentration.[2] This suggestion finds support in some discourses, which slightly vary the "definition", replacing "free from desires and discontent" with references to a concentrated mind or to experiencing happiness.[3] These passages

---

1 M I 56. A IV 430 explains "world" as referring to the pleasures of the five senses. This squares well with A IV 458, where *satipaṭṭhāna* leads to their abandoning. Vibh 195 takes "world" in the *satipaṭṭhāna* context to represent the five aggregates.

2 Nett 82.

3 S V 144 and S V 157.

indicate that freedom from desires and discontent represents mental calm and contentment.

The commentaries go further and identify this part of the "definition" with the removal of the five hindrances.[4] This is sometimes understood to imply that the five hindrances have to be removed prior to embarking on *satipaṭṭhāna* contemplation.[5] Therefore this expression requires a detailed examination in order to see how far such a stipulation is justified.

The Pāli term rendered "free" is *vineyya*, from the verb *vineti* (to remove). Although *vineyya* is best translated as "having removed", this does not necessarily imply that desires and discontent must be removed before undertaking the practice of *satipaṭṭhāna*; it can also mean that this activity takes place simultaneously with the practice.[6]

---

4 Ps I 244.

5 e.g. by Kheminda 1990: p.109.

6 Generally speaking, the form *vineyya* can be either a gerund: "having removed" (this is how the commentary understands it, cf. Ps I 244: *vinayitvā*), or else 3rd sing. potential: "one should remove" (as e.g. at Sn 590; cf. also Woodward 1980: vol.IV, p.142 n.3). However, in the present context to take *vineyya* as a potential form is not acceptable, as then the sentence would have two finite verbs in different moods (*viharati* + *vineyya*). Usually the gerund form does imply an action preceding the action of the main verb, which in the present case would mean that the removal has to be completed prior to the practice of *satipaṭṭhāna*. However, in some cases the gerund can also represent an action occurring concurrently with the action denoted by the main verb. An example of a concurrent action expressed by the gerund is the standard description of the practice of loving kindness in the discourses (e.g. at M I 38) where the "abiding" (*viharati*) and the "pervading" (*pharitvā*) are simultaneous activities, together describing the act of radiating loving kindness. The same type of construction occurs in relation to the attainment of absorption (e.g. at D I 37), where the "abiding" (*viharati*) and the "attaining" (*upasampajja*) also take place simultaneously. In fact, several translators have rendered *vineyya* in such a way that it represents the outcome of *satipaṭṭhāna* practice. Cf. e.g. Dhammiko 1961: p.182: "um weltliches Begehren und Bekümmern zu überwinden"; Gethin 1992: p.29: "he ... overcomes both desire for and discontent with the world"; Hamilton 1996: p.173: "in order to remove [himself] from the covetousness and misery in the world"; Hare 1955: vol.IV, p.199: "overcoming the hankering and dejection common in this world"; Hurvitz 1978: p.212: "putting off envy and ill disposition toward the world"; Jotika 1986: p.1: "keeping away covetousness and mental pain"; Lamotte 1970: p.1122: "au point de controler dans le monde la convoitise et la tristesse"; Lin Li Kouang 1949: p.119: "qu'il surmonte le déplaisir que la convoitise cause dans le monde"; C.A.F. Rhys Davids 1978: p.257: "overcoming both the hankering and the dejection common in the world"; Schmidt 1989: p.38: "alle weltlichen Wünsche und Sorgen vergessend"; Sīlananda 1990: p.177: "removing covetousness and grief in the world"; Solé-Leris 1999: p.116: "desechando la codicia y la aflicción de lo mundano"; Talamo 1998: p.556: "rimovendo bramosia e malcontento riguardo al mondo"; Ṭhānissaro 1996: p.83: "putting aside greed and distress with reference to the world"; Woodward 1979: vol.V, p.261: "restraining the dejection in the world that arises from coveting".

This way of understanding concurs with the general picture provided in the discourses. In a passage from the *Aṅguttara Nikāya*, for example, the practice of *satipaṭṭhāna* does not require, but rather results in, overcoming the hindrances.[7] Similarly, according to a discourse in the *Satipaṭṭhāna Saṃyutta*, lack of skill in the practice of *satipaṭṭhāna* prevents the practitioner from developing concentration and overcoming mental defilements.[8] This statement would be meaningless if the development of concentration and the absence of mental defilements were prerequisites for the practice of *satipaṭṭhāna*.

Desires (*abhijjhā*) and discontent (*domanassa*), the two mental qualities whose removal is stipulated in the "definition", occur again in relation to the last four steps in the sixteen-step scheme for mindfulness of breathing described in the *Ānāpānasati Sutta*. According to the Buddha's explanation, by this stage of practice freedom from desires and discontent has been achieved.[9] This explanation suggests that the same was not yet the case for the previous twelve steps, which the Buddha nevertheless described as corresponding to the first three *satipaṭṭhānas*.[10] The disappearance of discontent on its own occurs also in the "direct path" passage of the *Satipaṭṭhāna Sutta*, where its removal is a goal of *satipaṭṭhāna* practice.[11] All these passages clearly demonstrate that a complete "removal" of desires and discontent is not a prerequisite for *satipaṭṭhāna*, but comes about as a result of successful practice.[12]

The mental qualities to be removed are desires (*abhijjhā*) and discontent (*domanassa*). The commentaries identify these with the entire set of the five hindrances.[13] As a matter of fact, in several

---

7 A IV 458.
8 S V 150.
9 M III 84.
10 This would however only apply for the preliminary stages of practice, since for the first three *satipaṭṭhānas* to lead to awakening, freedom from desire and discontent is a requirement, indicated at M III 86 by qualifying the arising of the awakening factor of equanimity in relation to each of the four *satipaṭṭhānas* with the same expression as the one used at M III 84 in relation to the final four steps of mindfulness of breathing.
11 M I 55: "this is the direct path ... for the disappearance of ... discontent ... namely, the four *satipaṭṭhānas*."
12 Ps I 244 understands a successful removal of desires and discontent to be an outcome of the practice. Cf. also Debvedi 1990: p.22; Khemacari 1985: p.18; Ñāṇasaṃvara 1961: p.8, Ñāṇuttara 1990: p.280; and Yubodh 1985: p.9.
13 Ps I 244.

discourses "desires" (*abhijjhā*) do replace the more usual sensual desire (*kāmacchanda*) as the first of the hindrances.[14] It is difficult to understand, however, why discontent (*domanassa*) should correspond to the hindrance of aversion (*byāpāda*). In the discourses, discontent (*domanassa*) stands for any kind of mental dejection, which would not necessarily be related to aversion, and certainly not be synonymous with it.[15] Besides, even if one were to accept the questionable equating of discontent with aversion, one would still have to account for the remaining three hindrances.[16]

If it really were essential to remove the five hindrances before undertaking the practice of *satipaṭṭhāna*, several of the meditation practices described in the *Satipaṭṭhāna Sutta* would be rendered superfluous. These are the contemplation of unwholesome feelings and of unwholesome states of mind (worldly feelings, mind affected by lust or anger), and in particular awareness of the presence of just these five hindrances as the first contemplation of *dhammas*. These *satipaṭṭhāna* instructions clearly suggest that unwholesome states of mind, whether they be desires, discontent, or any of the hindrances, need not prevent one from practising *satipaṭṭhāna*, since they can profitably be turned into objects of mindful contemplation.

In the light of these considerations, it seems quite probable that the Buddha did not envisage the removal of the five hindrances as a necessary precondition for the practice of *satipaṭṭhāna*. In fact, if he intended to stipulate their removal as a requirement for undertaking *satipaṭṭhana*, one might wonder why he did not explicitly mention the hindrances, as he invariably did when describing the development of absorption (*jhāna*).

14 At D I 72; D I 207; D III 49; M I 181; M I 269; M I 274; M I 347; M II 162; M II 226; M III 3; M III 35; M III 135; A II 210; A III 92; A III 100; A IV 437; A V 207; and It 118. In its general usage in the discourses, *abhijjhā* represents one of the ten unwholesome ways of acting (e.g. at D III 269). In this context it means covetousness, in the sense of the wish to own the possessions of others (cf. e.g. M I 287). Cf. also van Zeyst 1961b: p.91.

15 D II 306 defines *domanassa* as mental pain and unpleasantness. M III 218 then distinguishes between the types of *domanassa* owing to sensual discontent and those owing to spiritual dissatisfaction. According to M I 304, these latter types of *domanassa* are not at all related to the underlying tendency to irritation.

16 It is a typical tendency of the commentaries to associate a key term (in the present context *abhijjhā*) with a whole set or standard category as part of their attempt to clarify the teachings, but at times this is done without sufficient consideration of the context.

The two mental qualities of desires and discontent, which the Buddha did mention in the *satipaṭṭhāna* "definition", often occur in the discourses in relation to sense-restraint, a stage in the gradual path scheme prior to formal meditation.[17] At this stage, the meditator guards the sense doors in order to prevent sense impressions from leading to desires and discontent. Judging from these contexts, the expression "desires and discontent" refers in a general way to "likes" and "dislikes" in regard to what has been perceived.

According to the presentation in the *Ānāpānasati Sutta*, the absence of such desires and discontent constitutes an important factor in carrying out the comparatively subtle and sophisticated meditations listed for contemplation of *dhammas*. This relates the absence of desires and discontent to an advanced stage of *satipaṭṭhāna*. Thus, *vineyya* as the completed action of "having removed" desires and discontent represents more advanced levels of *satipaṭṭhāna*. The discourses often refer to such advanced stages of *satipaṭṭhāna* contemplation as "well-established" (*supatiṭṭhita*).[18] At these more advanced stages of *satipaṭṭhāna*, impartial awareness is so firmly established (*supatiṭṭhita*) that one is effortlessly able to maintain dispassionate observation, without reacting with desires and discontent.

Conversely, *vineyya* as a simultaneous action, as the act of "removing" taking place in the present, indicates a purpose of the initial stages of *satipaṭṭhāna* practice. During these initial stages the task is to build up a degree of inner equipoise within which desires and discontent are held at bay. These initial stages of *satipaṭṭhāna* parallel sense-restraint, which combines bare *sati* with deliberate effort in order to avoid or counterbalance desires and discontent. Although sense-restraint precedes proper meditation practice in the gradual path scheme, this does not imply that sense-restraint is completed at an exact point in time, only after which one moves on to formal practice.[19] In actual practice the two overlap to a considerable degree, so

---

17 The standard definition, e.g. at M I 273, speaks of guarding the sense doors in order to avoid the flowing in of desires and discontent.

18 e.g. at D II 83; D III 101; M I 339; S III 93; S V 154; S V 160; S V 184; S V 301; S V 302; A III 155; A III 386; and A V 195. Of particular interest in this context is S III 93, which states that during this advanced level of well-established *satipaṭṭhāna* practice unwholesome thoughts will no longer be able to arise.

19 Cf. e.g. A V 114, where *satipaṭṭhāna* depends on sense-restraint, which in turn depends on mindfulness and clear knowledge (one of the body contemplations). This suggests some degree of interrelation between sense-restraint and *satipaṭṭhāna* in actual practice, rather than a one-sided dependency of the former on the latter.

that sense-restraint can be considered part of *satipaṭṭhāna* practice, particularly at those stages when desires and discontent have not yet been completely removed.

Although the initial stages of *satipaṭṭhāna* practice may not require the prior establishment of a high level of concentration, or the complete removal of unwholesome states of mind, these are necessary for the advanced stages of the practice that are to lead up to realization. This necessity will occupy me during most of the remainder of this chapter, in which I will investigate in more detail the relationship of concentration to the progress towards realization. As a preparation for this investigation, I will first attempt to clarify the implications of the relevant terms: concentration (*samādhi*), right concentration (*sammā samādhi*), and absorption (*jhāna*).

IV.2 CONCENTRATION, RIGHT CONCENTRATION, AND ABSORPTION

The noun *samādhi* is related to the verb *samādahati*, "to put together" or "to collect", such as when one collects wood to kindle a fire.[20] *Samādhi* thus stands for "collecting" oneself, in the sense of composure or unification of the mind.[21]

The discourses use the term "concentration" (*samādhi*) in a surprisingly broad manner, relating it to walking meditation, for example, or to observing the arising and passing away of feelings and cognitions, or to contemplating the arising and passing away of the five aggregates.[22] In a passage from the *Aṅguttara Nikāya*, even the four *satipaṭṭhānas* are treated as a form of concentration.[23] These occurrences demonstrate that, as used in the discourses, the term "concentration" (*samādhi*) is not restricted to the development of

20 e.g. at Vin IV 115.

21 At M I 301 *samādhi* is defined as unification of the mind (*cittassekaggatā*).

22 A III 30 speaks of *samādhi* gained through walking meditation. Although walking meditation can be employed to develop mental calm, it would not be the appropriate posture for deeper states of concentration. A II 45 refers to contemplating the arising and disappearance of feelings, cognitions, and thoughts, and to contemplating the impermanent nature of the five aggregates, as forms of *samādhi*. This breadth of meaning of *samādhi* is also documented at D III 222, which speaks of four different ways of developing *samādhi*, distinguished according to their results: *samādhi* leading to pleasant abiding (the *jhānas*), to knowledge and vision (through development of clarity of cognition), to mindfulness and clear knowledge (by contemplating the arising and passing away of feelings, cognitions, and thoughts), and to the destruction of the influxes (by contemplating the arising and passing away of the five aggregates).

23 A IV 300.

calm (*samatha*) only, but can also refer to the realm of insight meditation (*vipassanā*).

Turning to "right concentration" (*sammā samādhi*), here one finds time and again that the discourses equate right concentration with the four absorptions (*jhānas*).[24] This is of considerable importance, since "right" concentration is a prerequisite for awakening. Taking this definition literally, the development of "right" concentration requires the ability to attain all four absorptions. However, several discourses allow for full awakening based "only" on the ability to attain the first absorption.[25] This suggests that even the first absorption may be sufficient, in terms of concentrative ability, to enable the breakthrough to full awakening.[26]

Interestingly, in the *Mahācattārīsaka Sutta* and several other discourses another definition of right concentration can be found that does not mention the absorptions at all.[27] The importance of the *Mahācattārīsaka Sutta* to the present discussion is further highlighted in the preamble to this discourse, which states the topic to be a teaching on right concentration.[28] The definition of right concentration given here speaks of unification of the mind (*cittassekaggatā*) in interdependence with the other seven path factors.[29] That is, in order for unification of the mind to become "right" concentration it needs to be contextualized within the noble eightfold path scheme.[30] Definitions of right concentration that do not mention absorption

---

24 e.g. at D II 313: "he enters upon and remains in the first *jhāna* ... the second *jhāna* ... the third *jhāna* ... the fourth *jhāna* ... this is called right concentration."

25 A IV 422 speaks of realizing the destruction of the influxes based on the first *jhāna*; cf. also M I 350; M I 435; and A V 343.

26 All four *jhānas* are needed only for the approach to realization by way of the threefold higher knowledge (*tevijjā*), cf. e.g. M I 357. In fact S I 191 reports that, of a substantial congregation of *arahants*, two out of each three had neither the threefold higher knowledge (*tevijjā*), nor supernormal knowledges (*abhiññā*) nor immaterial attainments. If all *arahants* possessed the ability to attain the fourth *jhāna*, one would expect a much higher percentage of them to have used this in order to develop one or the other of these attainments. However, Perera 1968: p.210, considers attainment of all four *jhānas* a necessary condition for awakening.

27 D II 217; M III 7; and S V 21. Cf. also D III 252 and A IV 40. Other ways of defining right concentration can also be found at e.g. M III 289, where a penetrative understanding of the six senses constitutes right concentration; or at S I 48, where rightly concentrating is a result of establishing *sati*; or at A III 27, which lists what is probably a form of insight meditation as an alternative way to develop right concentration.

28 M III 71: "monks, I will teach you noble right concentration."

attainment can also be found in the *Abhidhamma* and the commentaries.[31]

Thus the decisive factor that qualifies concentration as "right" is not just a question of the depth of concentration achieved, but is concerned with the purpose for which concentration is employed. In particular, the presence of the path factor right view is indispensable.[32] By way of contrast, the Buddha's former teachers, Āḷāra Kālāma and Uddaka Rāmaputta, despite their deep concentration attainments, were not endowed with "right" concentration because of the absence of right view.[33] This goes to show that the ability to attain absorption in itself does not yet constitute the fulfilment of the path factor of right concentration.

A similar nuance underlies the qualification *sammā*, "right", which literally means "togetherness", or "to be connected in one".[34] Thus to speak of the four absorptions or of unification of the mind as "right" concentration does not simply mean that these are "right" and all else is "wrong", but points to the need to incorporate the development of concentration into the noble eightfold path.

Such a stipulation is not without practical relevance, since although the experience of absorption is a powerful tool to diminish

---

29 M III 71: "right view, right intention, right speech, right action, right livelihood, right effort, and right mindfulness. Unification of the mind equipped with these seven factors is called noble right concentration." Judging from other discourses, to speak of "unification of the mind" need not necessarily imply absorption attainment, since e.g. A II 14 relates unification of the mind to walking and standing, or at A III 174 unification of the mind occurs while listening to the *Dhamma*.

30 Cf. also Ba Khin 1994: p.69: "right concentration cannot be achieved unless there is right effort and right mindfulness"; Buddhadāsa 1976: p.36: "'a wholesome mind steadily fixed on an object' … the term 'wholesome' is much more important than 'steadily fixed' … the motives for practising concentration must be pure … must be based on insight and right view"; and Weeraratne 1990: p.45: "right concentration … is the one pointedness of mind achieved through cultivating the preceding seven stages of the path," (as a translation of M III 71).

31 Vibh 107 defines right concentration simply as "steadfastness of the mind" (in the *Abhidhamma* exposition; the *Suttanta* exposition at Vibh 106, however, enumerates the four *jhānas*). Vism 510 also defines right concentration as "unification of the mind".

32 A III 423 points out that without purifying view it is not possible to develop right concentration.

33 Cf. M I 164 for the *bodhisatta*'s encounters with Āḷāra Kālāma and Uddaka Rāmaputta.

34 Cf. Monier-Williams 1995: p.1181, who translates the corresponding Sanskrit term *samyak* with "complete", "entire", and "whole". T.W. Rhys Davids 1993: p.655, has "towards one point". Cf. also Gruber 1999: p.190, who comments on the inappropriateness of translating *sammā* as "right".

craving and attachment in regard to the five senses, it all too easily lends itself to stimulating craving for and attachment to these sublime "mind door" experiences. But only concentration untainted by craving can act as a full-fledged path factor of the noble eightfold path leading to the eradication of *dukkha*. It is this quality, and not just the depth of concentration achieved, that turns a concentrative attainment into right concentration.

To sum up: to speak of "right" concentration is not simply a question of being able to attain absorption, since the decisive criterion for describing concentration as "right" is whether it is developed in conjunction with the other factors of the noble eightfold path.

The word *jhāna* (absorption) is derived from the verb *jhāyati* "to meditate".[35] Although *jhāna* usually refers to the attainment of deep absorption, the word occasionally retains its original meaning of meditation. The *Gopakamoggallāna Sutta*, for example, mentions a form of *jhāna* in which the hindrances still obsess the mind.[36] Such "*jhāna*" does not qualify as a meditative absorption, since it is the absence of the hindrances that characterizes true absorption.

In order to assess the practical implications of such a true state of absorption, a brief examination of the first absorption is required at this point. The problem with understanding the first absorption is that two of its mental factors, initial mental application (*vitakka*) and sustained mental application (*vicāra*),[37] have been differently interpreted. As *vitakka*, initial mental application, is etymologically related to *takka*, which denotes thought and logical reasoning, several scholars conclude that conceptual thought continues in the first

---

35 The relation between these two words appears on several occasions, e.g. at D II 239; D II 265; M I 243; Dhp 372; Sn 1009; and Thī 401.

36 M III 14 speaks of being under the influence of the five hindrances as a type of *jhāna* of which the Buddha did not approve. Another example is the injunction "not to neglect *jhāna*" (*anirākatajjhāna*), which at M I 33 and It 39 occurs together with "being devoted to mental calm" and "being endowed with insight", probably including both in the general sense of "meditation". Similarly, the frequent exhortation *jhāyatha bhikkhave* (e.g. at M I 46) is better rendered "meditate monks" than "attain absorption monks". Another example is the expression "not lacking *jhāna*" (*arittajjhāno*), which at A I 39–43 is combined with several meditation practices that do not in themselves yield absorption attainment, such as *satipaṭṭhāna*, contemplation of impermanence, or the six recollections. The most common use of *jhāna* in the discourses, however, refers to absorption, this kind of usage being easily recognizable by the circumstance that absorption *jhāna* is usually classified as "first", "second", etc. (except for A V 133, where "*jhāna*" is at first used unspecified, but at the conclusion of the discourse this *jhāna* is shown to be the first level of absorption).

stage of absorption.[38] Some discourses appear at first sight to support this, since they refer to the second absorption as the "cessation of wholesome intentions", or as a state of "noble silence".[39]

This point is of considerable relevance to an understanding of the nature of absorption. The issue at stake, simply stated, is whether the first absorption is a deep state of concentration, achieved only after a prolonged period of practice and seclusion, or a stage of relaxed happy reflection within easy reach of anyone and without much need for meditative proficiency.

The latter assumption stands in contradiction to the commentarial presentation, which describes in detail the stages of development prior to absorption.[40] These sources indicate that to attain the first absorption a considerable amount of meditative development is required. Although references to this preliminary development appear only obliquely in the discourses, in one instance at least, the *Upakkilesa Sutta*, the Buddha gave a detailed account of his own struggle to attain the first absorption.[41] This passage leaves no doubt that the Buddha himself encountered considerable difficulty when he attempted to attain the first absorption, even though in his early youth he had already once experienced it.[42]

---

37 The standard definitions, e.g. at D I 73, speak of the first *jhāna* as "with initial and sustained mental application" (*savitakkaṃ savicāraṃ*). Several discourses also mention a level of absorption without initial but with sustained mental application (D III 219; D III 274; M III 162; S IV 360; S IV 363; and A IV 300). The resulting fivefold form of presenting the four *jhānas* became more prominent in the *Abhidhamma* (explained in detail at As 179). Stuart-Fox 1989: p.92, points out that some of the above quoted occurrences are missing from the corresponding Chinese editions.

38 Barnes 1981: p.257; Bucknell 1993: p.397; Kalupahana 1994: p.35; Ott 1912: p.348; and Stuart-Fox 1989: p.94.

39 M II 28 associates the second *jhāna* with the cessation of "wholesome intentions", while S II 273 speaks of the second *jhāna* as "noble silence"; the same expression occurs also at Th 650 and 999. (Commentary Th-a II 274 identifies this as second *jhāna*, but Th-a III 102 even speaks of the fourth *jhāna*.)

40 Cf. e.g. Vism 125 on the development of the counterpart sign; and Vism 285 on the development of absorption based on the concentrative sign gained through in- and out-breathing.

41 M III 162, where only after having consecutively overcome a whole series of mental obstructions (cf. in detail page 199, footnote 73) he was able to attain the first *jhāna*. Cf. also A IV 439, which reports his struggle to overcome sensuality in order to be able to develop *jhāna*.

42 M I 246. Possibly his ability to enter the first *jhāna* so easily at this particular moment during his early youth was related to *samatha* practice undertaken in a previous life, an ability lost during his adolescence and later sensual indulgence as a young man, so that he had to develop it anew.

The *Upakkilesa Sutta* is addressed to Anuruddha and a group of monks who were evidently in similar difficulties. On another occasion the Buddha also had to assist Moggallāna to attain the first absorption.[43] It is noteworthy that Anuruddha and Moggallāna, who both later excelled all other disciples with their concentrative powers,[44] needed the Buddha's personal intervention to attain "merely" the first absorption. These examples suggest that the attainment of the first absorption requires a considerable degree of meditative proficiency.

According to the discourses, one who has entered the first absorption is no longer able to speak.[45] This would not apply if the first absorption were merely a state of calm mental reflection. Not only speech, but also hearing does not occur during the deeper stages of absorption; in fact, sound is a major obstacle to attaining the first absorption.[46] The experience of the first absorption is an "unworldly" experience;[47] it constitutes another world in the psychological and the cosmological sense.[48] To attain the first absorption is to reach a

---

43 S IV 263.

44 Cf. A I 23.

45 S IV 217; same at S IV 220–3. Kv 200 uses this passage to oppose the (wrong) view that the *jhāna* factors initial and sustained mental application refer to vocal activity. This view arose because of their definition as verbal formations at M I 301.

46 A V 135. According to Brahmavaṃso 1999: p.29, "while in any *jhāna* it is impossible to ... hear a sound from outside or produce any thought." Kv 572 also refutes the view that it is possible to hear sound during *jhāna* attainment. At Vin III 109, some monks accused Moggallāna to have falsely claimed attainment, because he had stated that while being in the "imperturbable concentration" (i.e. fourth *jhāna* or an immaterial attainment) he had heard sounds. The fact that this led the monks to accuse him of false claims shows that the impossibility of hearing sound during deep absorption was generally accepted among the monks. However, the Buddha exonerated Moggallāna, explaining that it was possible to hear sound even during such a deep level of *jhāna*, if the attainment was impure (*aparisuddho*). Sp II 513 explains that because he had not fully overcome the obstructions to absorption, Moggallāna's attainment was not stable and thus the hearing took place in a moment of instability of the concentration.

47 A IV 430 refers to a monk having attained the first *jhāna* as having reached the end of the world ("world" being identified with the five sense-pleasures in the same discourse). Another example of the distinct character of the *jhānic* experience is the kind of cognition operating during the first *jhāna*, which D I 182 calls a "subtle but real" cognition (*sukhumasaccasaññā*). This expression indicates the attenuated form of cognition that takes place during absorption, different from the way in which the ordinary world is cognized.

48 These are the elements of materiality and immateriality (D III 215), corresponding to the material and immaterial realms of existence (S V 56), and different from the element of sensuality or the sensual realm.

"superbly extraordinary state".[49] Already the first absorption "blindfolds" Māra, since on entering this state one goes beyond the range of Māra's vision.[50]

These passages support an understanding of the first absorption as a deeply absorbed state of mind, beyond mere reflection and conceptual thought. It is therefore reasonable to suppose that, as absorption-factors, initial mental application (*vitakka*) and sustained mental application (*vicāra*) do not imply full-fledged thinking activity. Rather, they refer to the initial and sustained application of attention. Such application of attention can also take place in the domain of thought or verbal communication, when initial mental application directs the mind towards what is to be thought or said, while sustained mental application maintains the coherence of a particular sequence of thoughts or words. In the context of absorption, however, this same activity is nothing more than an intentional deployment of attention, directed towards the object of concentration.

To translate *vitakka* as "initial mental application" finds support in the *Mahācattārīsaka Sutta*, which includes "application of the mind" (*cetaso abhiniropanā*) in a list of synonyms for "right thought" along with *vitakka*.[51] To understand *vitakka* as initial application of the mind can moreover claim support from the *Abhidhamma* and the commentaries, and from numerous modern meditation teachers and scholars.[52]

This way of understanding can also be applied to the above-mentioned passages, which at first sight seemed to suggest that conceptual thought continues in the first stage of absorption, since they spoke of the "cessation of wholesome intentions" on attaining the second absorption, a state of "noble silence". Although initial mental application as a factor of the first absorption is different from discursive thought, initial mental application is nonetheless in this context a kind of "intention" and thereby involves a very subtle degree of deliberate mental activity. Only on entering the second absorption, when this last vestige of mental activity is abandoned and concen-

49 M I 521.
50 M I 159 and M I 174.
51 M III 73.
52 "Application of the mind" (*cetaso abhiniropanā*) occurs at Vibh 257 and at Vism 142 in a definition of *vitakka*. Similar understandings of *vitakka* can be found in Ayya Khema 1991: p.115; Bodhi 2000: p.52, and 1993: p.82; Chah 1992: p.53; Cousins 1992: p.153; Eden 1984: p.89; Goenka 1999: p.93; Ledi 1986a: p.52; Pa Auk 1999: p.17; C.A.F. Rhys Davids 1922: p.8 n.1; Shwe 1979: p.238 n.1; Stcherbatsky 1994: p.104; and Sujīva 1996: p.10.

tration has become fully stable,[53] does the mind reach a state of complete inner stillness ("noble silence"), leaving behind even these subtle "wholesome intentions".

Based on the passages considered so far, it seems reasonable to suppose that "absorption" (*jhāna*) refers to profound experiences of deep concentration achieved after having developed a considerable degree of meditative proficiency.

IV.3 ABSORPTION AND REALIZATION

Countless discourses recommend the development of concentration as an essential factor for "knowing things as they really are".[54] Concentration is a requirement for full awakening,[55] and this concentration has to be "right" concentration.[56] These specifications recommend absorption concentration as a requisite for full awakening. However, the question might be asked if the same is also required for stream-entry. Although, owing to the powerful impact of experiencing *Nibbāna* at stream-entry, the concentrative unification of one's mind (*cittassekaggatā*) will momentarily reach a level comparable to absorption, how far does this require the previous development of absorption with a calmness object of meditation?[57]

The qualities listed in the discourses as essential for the realization of stream-entry do not stipulate the ability to attain absorption.[58] Nor are such abilities mentioned in the descriptions of the qualities

---

53 Indicated in the standard descriptions of the second *jhāna* (e.g. at D I 74) by qualifying the joy and happiness experienced to be "born of concentration" (*samādhija*), and by the expression "singleness of mind" (*cetasa ekodibhāva*).

54 e.g. at S IV 80.

55 A III 426 points out that without *samādhi* it is impossible to gain realization.

56 A III 19; A III 200; A III 360; A IV 99; A IV 336; A V 4–6; and A V 314 explain that without right concentration it is not possible to gain liberation. A III 423 stresses again that right concentration is required to be able to eradicate the fetters and realize *Nibbāna*. It is interesting to note that in most of these cases the absence of right concentration is due to a lack of ethical conduct, so that in the reverse case (cf. e.g. A III 20) one gets a statement indicating that the "rightness" of concentration is the outcome of ethical conduct (viz. factors three, four, and five of the noble eightfold path). This brings to mind the alternative definition discussed above of right concentration as unification of the mind in interrelation with the other path factors. (This is further supported by the use of the Pāli word *upanisā* in the instances under discussion at present, which echoes the expression *sa-upanisā* used in the definition of right concentration as unification of the mind at M III 71.)

57 The distinction drawn here is concerned with what the commentaries refer to as "supramundane" and as "mundane" concentration (cf. the definition given at Vism 85).

that are characteristic of a stream-enterer subsequent to realization.[59]

According to the discourses, what is a necessary condition for being able to gain stream-entry is a state of mind completely free from the five hindrances.[60] Although a convenient way to remove the hindrances is the development of absorption, this is not the only way to do so. According to a discourse in the *Itivuttaka*, the hindrances can also be removed and the mind become concentrated even during walking meditation, a posture not suitable for attaining absorption.[61] In fact, another passage shows that the hindrances can be temporarily absent even outside the context of formal meditation, such as when one is listening to the *Dhamma*.[62]

This alternative is corroborated by a fair number of the attainments of stream-entry recorded in the discourses where the person in question might not even have meditated regularly in this life, much less be able to attain absorption.[63] Yet these reports invariably

---

58 S V 410 lists the need to associate with worthy men, to listen to the *Dhamma*, to develop wise attention (*yoniso manasikāra*), and to undertake practice in accordance with the *Dhamma* as requirements for the realization of stream-entry. (S II 18 explains practice in accordance with the *Dhamma* to refer in particular to overcoming ignorance through developing dispassion.) On requirements for stream-entry cf. also M I 323.

59 One would expect this ability to be mentioned among the four characteristic qualities of a stream-enterer, which however are confined to perfect confidence in the Buddha, *Dhamma*, and *Saṅgha*, together with firm ethical conduct. At S V 357 the Buddha mentioned these four as defining characteristics of a stream-enterer.

60 e.g. A III 63. Cf. also M I 323, which mentions several qualities needed for stream-entry, among them not being obsessed by the hindrances.

61 It 118.

62 S V 95.

63 D I 110 and D I 148 feature rich Brahmins, whose busy lifestyle as administrators of a royal domain would not be particularly conducive to the development of *jhāna*, yet each of them realized stream-entry while hearing a discourse of the Buddha. M I 380 and A IV 186 report the stream-entries of stout followers of the Jains during a discourse of the Buddha. (Considering that the leader of the Jains, according to S IV 298, even doubted the existence of the second *jhāna*, one may well suppose that *jhānic* abilities are improbable in the case of his followers. This impression is borne out by the account given in Tatia 1951: pp.281–93.) At A IV 213 a drunken layman, sobered up through the impact of meeting the Buddha for the first time, realized stream-entry during a gradual discourse given at that same first meeting. Ud 49 has a leper, described as a poor, pitiable, and wretched person, similarly realizing stream-entry during a discourse of the Buddha. This leper had actually mistaken the crowd listening to the Buddha for a free distribution of food and had only approached in hope of getting a meal. Finally, according to Vin II 192, several hired killers, one of whom even had the mission of killing the Buddha, all became stream-enterers instead of completing their mission after hearing a gradual discourse by the Buddha. In all these cases it is not very probable that those realizing stream-entry were involved in the regular practice of meditation or in the possession of *jhānic* attainments.

mention the removal of the hindrances previous to the arising of insight.[64] In all these instances, the hindrances were removed as a result of attentively listening to the gradual instructions given by the Buddha.

In fact, a substantial number of well-known modern meditation teachers base their teachings on the dispensability of absorption abilities for the realization of stream-entry.[65] According to them, for the mind to become momentarily "absorbed" in the experience of *Nibbāna* at stream-entry, the ability to attain mundane absorption is not a necessary requirement.

The issue at question becomes even clearer when the next stage of awakening is considered, that of once-returning. Once-returners are so called because they will be reborn only once again in "this world" (i.e. the *kāmaloka*).[66] On the other hand, those who have developed the ability to attain absorption at will, and have not lost this ability, are not going to return to "this world" in their next life.[67] They will be reborn in a higher heavenly sphere (i.e. the *rūpaloka* or the *arūpaloka*). This certainly does not imply that a stream-enterer or a once-returner cannot have absorption attainments. But if they were all absorption attainers, the very concept of a "once-returner" would be superfluous, since not a single once-returner would ever return to "this world".

According to the discourses, the difference between the realizations of "once-returning" and "non-returning" is related to differing

64 All above quoted instances explicitly mention the mind being free from the hindrances.

65 Cf. Visuddhacara 1996: who gives a convenient overview of statements by several well-known meditation teachers on the issue.

66 e.g. at M I 226. The fact that once-returners do return to "this world" is documented e.g. at A III 348 and A V 138, where once-returners are reborn in the Tusita heaven, a lower celestial realm of the sensual sphere, far inferior to those planes of existence corresponding to absorption attainment. Similarly, according to A IV 380 the more advanced types of stream-enterers will be reborn as human beings, a level of rebirth even further removed from the planes of existence gained through absorption abilities.

67 According to A II 126, one who has developed the first *jhāna* will be reborn in the Brahmā world. A worldling (*puthujjana*) will then after some time be reborn in lower realms again, while a noble one (*ariya*) will proceed from there to final *Nibbāna*. (This passage refers not only to someone who is absorbed in the actual attainment at the time of death, but to anyone who possesses the ability to attain *jhāna*.) A similar passage can be found at A I 267 concerning immaterial attainments and rebirth, and at A II 129 regarding the divine abodes and rebirth.

levels of concentrative ability. Several passages point out that the once-returner, in contrast to the non-returner, has not yet fulfilled the development of concentration.[68] Judging from this, the attainment of absorption might be of relevance for the realization of non-returning. In fact, several discourses relate progress towards the higher two stages of the path, non-returning and arahantship, to having had the experience of the first or higher absorptions.[69] The reason for this could be that the insightful contemplation of meditative absorption fulfils an important role in overcoming and completely eradicating the last traces of desire, and thereby facilitates the breakthrough to non-returning or full awakening.[70]

The concluding passage of the *Satipaṭṭhāna Sutta*, the "prediction", appears at first sight to contradict this, since it predicts the realization of full awakening or non-returning for successful *satipaṭṭhāna* practice without making any additional stipulations.[71] This could be taken to imply that absorption abilities can be dispensed with even for the higher stages of awakening. However, such assumptions need to be weighed against other evidence in the discourses, where the need for at least the first absorption is clearly and explicitly stated.[72] Although absorption abilities are not directly mentioned in the *Satipaṭṭhāna Sutta*, the general picture provided by the discourses suggests that the ability to attain at least the first absorption is required for the higher two stages of awakening. Otherwise it would be difficult to understand why the Buddha mentioned absorption in the standard expositions of the noble eightfold path leading to full awakening.

---

68 According to A IV 380 the once-returner, in contrast to the non-returner, has not perfected/completed *samādhi*. A similar passage can be found at A I 232 and 233. Cf. also Dhammavuddho 1994: p.29; and Ñāṇavīra 1987: p.372.

69 e.g. M I 350 and A V 343 describe how a monk, based on attainment of the first or a higher *jhāna*, is able to reach the destruction of the influxes or non-returning. More explicit is M I 434–5, which clearly stipulates the attainment of *jhāna* as a necessity for the two higher stages of awakening. Similarly A IV 422 mentions *jhānic* abilities as a necessary condition for gaining non-returning or full awakening.

70 At A II 128 the insightful contemplation of absorption leads to non-returning (rebirth in the Suddhāvāsa heaven). Compare also M I 91 where Mahānāma, who according to the commentary (Ps II 61) was a once-returner, was advised by the Buddha to develop *jhāna* for further progress on the path.

71 M I 62: "if anyone should develop these four *satipaṭṭhānas* ... one of two fruits could be expected for him: either final knowledge here and now, or, if there is a trace of clinging left, non-returning."

72 M I 434 states that there is a path of practice which needs be undertaken in order to be able to overcome the five lower fetters, and this path of practice is *jhāna* attainment.

When considering the concluding passage of the *Satipaṭṭhāna Sutta*, one needs to take into account that this passage is concerned with the fruits of the practice, not with the need for a particular level of concentration as a prerequisite for realization. The fact that it mentions only the higher two fruits of realization highlights the potential of proper practice. The same holds true for a group of twenty discourses in the *Bojjhaṅga Saṃyutta*, which relate a broad range of meditation practices to these two higher realizations.[73] These instances, too, do not bear any relation to the presence or absence of absorption abilities, but rather call attention to the potential of the respective meditation practices. Moreover, the *Madhyama Āgama* and the *Ekottara Āgama* both mention absorption attainment as part of their expositions on *satipaṭṭhāna*.[74] This suggests that for *satipaṭṭhāna* to unfold its full potential of leading to non-returning or full awakening, the development of absorption is required.

Another term relevant to the present topic is "purification of mind" (*cittavisuddhi*). This expression occurs in the *Rathavinīta Sutta*, which enumerates a series of seven successive stages of purification.[75] The discourse compares each stage of purification to a single chariot in a relay of chariots connecting two locations. In this sequence, purification of mind occupies the second position between the preceding purification of ethical conduct and the

73 S V 129–33.

74 In the *Madhyama Āgama* as part of the body contemplations, and in the *Ekottara Āgama* as part of the contemplations of *dhammas* (in Minh Chau 1991: pp.89 and 90; and Nhat Hanh 1990: p.154 and 176).

75 M I 149. This particular "path" scheme forms the underlying structure of the *Visuddhimagga*. It has been compared to other religious traditions by Brown (1986a) who relates it to path descriptions in the *Mahāmudra* and the *Yoga Sūtras*, and by Cousins (1989) who compares it to St Teresa's "Interior Castle". Concerning this path scheme it may be worthwhile to point out that, even though it has a normative role for the commentaries and most modern *vipassanā* schools, this set of seven purifications occurs only once again in the discourses, at D III 288, where it forms part of a nine-stage scheme. This passage does not fit too well with Buddhaghosa's presentation of the seven-stage model, since it adds two additional stages at the end of a progression of stages where, according to Buddhaghosa, with the seventh stage the peak of purification has already been reached (cf. Vism 672). Judging from its usage at M I 195 and M I 203, the term used for the seventh purification, "knowledge and vision", is indeed only a stage leading up to, but not yet identical with, realization. This impression is confirmed by the *Rathavinīta Sutta* itself, which qualifies the purification by "knowledge and vision" as "with clinging" and therefore as falling short of the final goal (M I 148). Thus it seems as if Buddhaghosa's interpretation of the seventh stage of purification were to some degree at variance with the implications of the same term in the discourses.

subsequent purification of view. The fact that purification of mind precedes purification of view is sometimes taken to imply that absorption is a necessary basis for realization.[76]

In this discourse, however, the question leading to the chariot simile was not at all concerned with the conditions necessary for realization. Rather, the topic discussed in the *Rathavinīta Sutta* was the aim of living the life of a monk or nun in the early Buddhist monastic community. The point was that each purification, though a necessary step on the path, falls short of the final goal. To illustrate this, the chariot simile was introduced. The need to move beyond different stages of purification in order to reach the final goal is in fact a recurrent theme in the discourses.[77]

Although the chariot simile in the *Rathavinīta Sutta* does imply a conditional relationship between the various stages mentioned, to take this as stipulating that absorption must be attained before turning to the development of insight pushes this simile too far. Such a literal interpretation needs to regard the establishment of ethical conduct, concentration, and wisdom as a matter of strict linear sequence, whereas in practical reality these three have a symbiotic character, each enhancing and supporting the other. This is illustrated in the *Soṇadaṇḍa Sutta*, which compares the mutual interrelatedness of ethical conduct and wisdom to two hands washing each other.[78]

Besides, according to two discourses in the *Aṅguttara Nikāya* it is impossible to purify concentration (viz. purification of the mind) without having first purified right view (viz. purification of view).[79] This statement proposes exactly the reverse sequence to the *Rathavinīta Sutta*, where purification of the mind preceded purification of view.

On further perusing the discourses one finds that they depict a variety of approaches to final realization. Two passages in the *Aṅguttara Nikāya*, for example, describe a practitioner who is able to gain deep wisdom, though lacking proficiency in concentration.[80]

---

76 Possibly based on A II 195, where purity of mind is related to attaining the four *jhānas*. The ability to attain absorption as a necessary basis for realization is maintained by e.g. Kheminda 1980: p.14.

77 Cf. e.g. M I 197 and M I 204.

78 D I 124. Cf. also Chah 1998: p.9; and Goleman 1980: p.6.

79 A III 15 and A III 423.

80 A II 92–4 and A V 99.

Another discourse in the same *Nikāya* speaks of two alternative approaches to full realization: the pleasant approach by way of absorption, and the much less pleasant approach by way of contemplating the repulsiveness of the body.[81] In addition, the *Yuganaddha Sutta* (in the same *Aṅguttara Nikāya*) states that realization can be gained by developing either concentration or insight first and then developing the other, or both can be developed together.[82] This discourse clearly shows that although some practitioners will build up concentration first and then turn to insight, others can follow the reverse procedure. It would do little justice to these passages if one were to limit the approach to realization to only one of these sequences, presuming that the development of concentration invariably has to precede the development of insight.

IV.4 THE CONTRIBUTION OF ABSORPTION TO THE PROGRESS OF INSIGHT

Nevertheless, in many discourses the Buddha pointed out that the cultivation of absorption is particularly conducive to realization.[83] The development of deep concentration leads to a high degree of mastery over the mind.[84] Not only does absorption attainment entail the temporary removal of the hindrances, it also makes it much more difficult for them to invade the mind on later occasions.[85] On emerging from deep concentration the mind is "malleable", "workable", and "steady",[86] so that one can easily direct it to seeing things "as they truly are". Not only that; when things are seen as they truly

81 A II 150.
82 A II 157; cf. also Tatia 1992: p.89.
83 e.g. D III 131; M I 454; or S V 308. The importance given to absorption in early Buddhism is documented by Griffith 1983: p.57, and C.A.F. Rhys Davids 1927a: p.696, both giving an overview of occurrences of the term *jhāna* in the Pāli *Nikāyas*.
84 A IV 34.
85 M I 463 explains that the mind of one who has had *jhānic* experiences will no longer be overwhelmed by the hindrances. On the other hand, it needs to be pointed out that if sensual desire or aversion should nevertheless manage to invade the mind, they can manifest with surprising vehemence, owing to the increased ability of the mind to remain undistractedly with a single object, even an unwholesome one. Examples of this can be found in several Jātaka tales (e.g. no. 66 at Ja I 305, no. 251 at Ja II 271, and no. 431 at Ja III 496), which report previous lives of the *bodhisatta* as an ascetic. In spite of being able to attain deep levels of concentration and possessed of supernormal powers, in each case this ascetic was nevertheless completely overwhelmed by sensual desire on unexpectedly seeing a sparsely-dressed woman.
86 This is the standard qualification of the mental condition on emerging from the fourth *jhāna* (e.g. at D I 75).

are by a calm and malleable mind, this vision affects the deeper layers of the mind. Such a vision goes far beyond a superficial intellectual appreciation, because, owing to the receptivity and malleability of the mind, insights will be able to penetrate into the deeper regions of the mind and thereby bring about inner change.

The advantages of developing absorption concentration are not only that it provides a stable and receptive state of mind for the practice of insight meditation. The experience of absorption is one of intense pleasure and happiness, brought about by purely mental means, which thereby automatically eclipses any pleasure arising in dependence on material objects. Thus absorption functions as a powerful antidote to sensual desires by divesting them of their former attraction.[87] In fact, according to the *Cūḷadukkhakkhandha Sutta* wisdom alone does not suffice to overcome sensuality, but needs the powerful support available through the experience of absorption.[88] The Buddha himself, during his own quest for awakening, overcame the obstruction caused by sensual desires only by developing absorption.[89]

---

87 At M I 504 the Buddha related his lack of interest in sensual pleasures to his ability to experience far superior types of pleasure; cf. also A III 207 and A IV 411. A I 61 explains that the purpose of *samatha* is to overcome lust. Conze 1960: p.110, explains: "it is the inevitable result of the habitual practice of trance that the things of our commonsense world appear delusive, deceptive, remote, and dreamlike." Cf. also Debes 1994: pp.164–8; and van Zeyst 1970: p.39.

88 M I 91.

89 M I 92; cf. also S IV 97 and A IV 439. A IV 56 stresses the importance of overcoming sensual desires for him to have been able to gain realization. The Buddha's attainment of absorption might have taken place based on mindfulness of breathing, which according to S V 317 he practised frequently in the time before his awakening. His gradual progress through the various levels of absorption is described at M III 162 and A IV 440, clearly showing that by then he no longer had access to the *jhānic* experience of his early youth. His encounter with Āḷāra Kālāma and Uddaka Rāmaputta would have to be placed after this gradual progress, since without having developed the four *jhānas* he would not have been able to reach any of the immaterial attainments. (The need for this is documented at D III 265, where the four *jhānas* precede the immaterial attainments in a sequence of successive stages of development.) Ps IV 209, however, assumes that the Buddha developed the four *jhānas* only during the first watch of the night of his awakening. This makes little sense in view of the fact that his pre-awakening development of *samatha* included also the practice of the "roads to power" (the *iddhipādas*, cf. A III 82) and developing the concentrative ability to know various aspects of the *deva* realms (A IV 302), in addition to attaining the four *jhānas* after overcoming a whole set of mental obstructions (M III 157; cf. also A IV 440, which clearly shows that he had to overcome various obstacles in order to gain each *jhāna*) and also gaining the four immaterial attainments (A IV 444). The broad range and gradual progression of the Buddha's development of *samatha* does not fit well into a single night.

Deep concentration promotes inner stability and integration.[90] In this way, the experience of deep concentration fulfils an important role in fortifying the ability to withstand the destabilizing effect of those experiences that might be encountered during advanced stages of insight meditation.[91] Without a calm and integrated mind, able to withstand the impact of such experiences, a practitioner might lose the balanced stance of observation and become overwhelmed by fear, anxiety, or depression. The development of mental calm thus builds up a healthy degree of self-integration as a supportive basis for the development of insight.[92]

Clearly, there are substantial advantages to be gained when the development of insight is supported and counterbalanced by the development of *samatha*. The experience of higher forms of happiness and the concomitant degree of personal integration are benefits that show that the development of *samatha* makes its own substantial contribution to progress along the path. This importance is expressed vividly in the discourses with the statement that one who has respect for the Buddha and his teaching will automatically hold concentration in high regard.[93] On the other hand, one who looks down on the development of concentration thereby only approves of those who have an unsteady mind.[94]

Nevertheless, it needs to be said that the Buddha was also keenly aware of potential shortcomings of deep states of concentration. The attainment of absorption can turn into an obstacle on the path to

90 According to Alexander 1931: p.139, "the absorption scale corresponds to the chronological path of a well-conducted analysis." Cf. also Conze 1956: p.20.

91 Ayya Khema 1991: p.140; and Epstein 1986: pp.150–5.

92 Engler 1986: p.17, aptly sums up the need for a well integrated personality as a basis for developing insight meditation: "you have to be somebody before you can be nobody." Epstein 1995: p.133, (commenting on the insight knowledges) explains: "experiences such as these require an ego, in the psychoanalytic sense, that is capable of holding and integrating what would ordinarily be violently destabilizing. One is challenged to experience terror without fear and delight without attachment. The work of meditation, in one sense, is the work of developing an ego that is flexible, clear and balanced enough to enable one to have such experiences." The supportive role of non-sensual inner happiness in case of hardship is documented at Th 351 and Th 436.

93 A IV 123.

94 A II 31. Cf. also S II 225, where lack of respect for the development of concentration is one of the causes of the disappearance of the true *Dhamma*. According to Thate 1996: p.93: "those who think that *samādhi* is not necessary are the ones who have not yet reached *samādhi*. That's why they cannot see the merit of *samādhi*. Those who have attained *samādhi* will never speak against it."

realization if such attainment becomes a cause for pride or an object of attachment. The satisfaction and pleasure experienced during absorption, though facilitating the relinquishment of worldly pleasures, can make it more difficult to arouse the dissatisfaction and disenchantment required for the complete relinquishment of everything that leads up to realization.[95]

The *Māra Saṃyutta* even reports a casualty of concentration meditation: a monk committed suicide because he had several times failed to stabilize his concentrative attainment.[96] On another occasion, when a monk was mourning his loss of concentration owing to physical illness, the Buddha dryly commented that such a reaction is characteristic of those who consider concentration the essence of their life and practice.[97] He then instructed the monk to contemplate the impermanent nature of the five aggregates instead.

IV.5 CALM AND INSIGHT

The central point that emerges when considering the relationship between calm and insight is the need for balance. Since a concentrated mind supports the development of insight, and the presence of wisdom in turn facilitates the development of deeper levels of concentration, calm (*samatha*) and insight (*vipassanā*) are at their best when developed in skilful cooperation.[98]

Considered from this perspective, the controversy over the necessity or dispensability of absorption abilities for gaining a particular

95 At A II 165 the Buddha compared attachment to the gratification and bliss experienced during absorption to grasping a branch full of resin, because owing to such attachment one will lose the inspiration to aim at the complete giving up of all aspects of one's personality and experience. At M I 194 the Buddha then illustrated such attachment using the example of someone who took the inner bark of a tree in mistake for the heartwood he was searching for. Cf. also M III 226, which refers to such attachment to *jhāna* experiences as "getting stuck internally". Buddhadāsa 1993: p.121, even goes so far as to suggest that "deep concentration is a major obstacle to insight practice".

96 According to S I 120, the monk Godhika committed suicide because on six successive occasions he had attained and lost "temporary liberation of the mind", which according to Spk I 182 refers to a "mundane" attainment, i.e. some concentrative attainment. The commentary explains that his repeated loss of the attainment was because of illness. According to a statement made by the Buddha after the event, Godhika died as an *arahant*. The commentary suggests that his realization took place at the moment of death (cf. also the similar commentarial explanations of the suicide cases of Channa at M III 266 or S IV 59, and of Vakkali at S III 123).

97 S III 125.

98 Nett 43 explains that both *samatha* and *vipassanā* need to be developed, since *samatha*

level of realization is to some extent based on a misleading premise. This controversy takes for granted that the whole purpose of calmness meditation is to gain the ability to enter absorption as a stepping-stone for the development of insight, a sort of preliminary duty that either needs or does not need to be fulfilled. The discourses offer a different perspective. Here calm and insight are two complementary aspects of mental development. The question of practising only insight meditation does not arise, since the important function of calmness meditation, as a practice in its own right, is never reduced to its auxiliary role in relation to insight meditation.

This need for both calm and insight on the path to realization leads me on to another issue. Some scholars have understood these two aspects of meditation to represent two different paths, possibly even leading to two different goals. They assume that the path of *samatha* proceeds via the ascending series of absorptions to the attainment of the cessation of cognition and feeling (*saññāvedayitanirodha*) and thence to the cessation of passion. In contrast to this, the path of insight, at times mistakenly understood to be a process of pure intellectual reflection, supposedly leads to a qualitatively different goal, the cessation of ignorance.[99]

A passage from the *Aṅguttara Nikāya* does indeed relate the practice of *samatha* to the destruction of passion and the practice of *vipassanā* to the destruction of ignorance.[100] The distinction between the two is expressed by the expressions "freedom of the mind" (*cetovimutti*) and "freedom by wisdom" (*paññāvimutti*) respectively. However, these two expressions are not simply equivalent in value relative to realization. While "freedom by wisdom" (*paññāvimutti*) refers to the realization of *Nibbāna*, "freedom of the mind" (*cetovimutti*), unless further specified as "unshakeable" (*akuppa*), does not imply the same. "Freedom of the mind" can also connote temporary

---

counters craving, while *vipassanā* counters ignorance. According to A I 61, the development of both *samatha* and *vipassanā* is required to gain knowledge (*vijjā*). A I 100 stipulates the same two as requirements for overcoming lust, anger, and delusion. Awareness of their cooperative effect also underlies Th 584, which recommends practising both *samatha* and *vipassanā* at the right time. On the need to balance both cf. Cousins 1984: p.65; Gethin 1992: p.345; and Maha Boowa 1994: p.86.

99 Cf. de la Vallée Poussin 1936: p.193; Gombrich 1996: p.110; Griffith 1981: p.618, and 1986: p.14; Pande 1957: p.538; Schmithausen 1981: pp.214–17; and Vetter 1988: p.xxi. Kv 225 confutes a somewhat similar "wrong view", involving two types of cessation (*nirodha*).

100 A I 61.

experiences of mental freedom, such as the attainment of the fourth absorption, or the development of the divine abodes (*brahmavihāra*).[101] Thus this passage is presenting not two different approaches to realization but two aspects of the meditative path, one of which is not sufficient by itself to bring realization.[102]

Another relevant discourse is the *Susīma Sutta*, which reports various monks declaring realization.[103] Since these monks at the same time denied having attained supernatural powers, this passage has sometimes been understood to imply that full awakening can be attained merely by intellectual reflection.[104] In reality, however, the monks' declaration that they were only "freed by wisdom" indicates that they were not in possession of the immaterial meditative attainments. It does not mean that they gained realization without meditating at all, by a purely intellectual approach.[105]

A similar problem is sometimes seen in regard to the *Kosambi Sutta*, where a monk declared that he had personal realization of dependent co-arising (*paṭicca samuppāda*), although he was not an *arahant*.[106] This passage becomes intelligible if one follows the commentarial explanation, according to which the monk in question was "only" a once-returner.[107] The point here is that personal realization of the principle of dependent co-arising is not a characteristic of full awakening only, but is already a feature of stream-entry.

---

101 Cf. e.g. M I 296; see further Lily de Silva 1978: p.120.

102 In fact, Vism 702 explains that the attainment of the cessation of cognition and feeling (*saññāvedayitanirodha*) cannot be reached by *samatha* alone, but requires insight of the non-returner's level at least. Although this is not directly stated in the discourses, at M III 44, after all eight preceding concentrative attainments have been distinguished according to whether they are attained by the unworthy person or by the worthy person (*sappurisa*), once the attainment of the cessation of cognition and feeling comes up the unworthy person is no longer mentioned, thereby indicating that this attainment is the sole domain of the worthy person (a term which on other occasions is used on a par with "noble", cf. e.g. M I 300). This clearly shows that the attainment of the cessation of cognition and feeling is not merely the outcome of concentrative mastery, but also requires the development of insight, a fact that is hinted at in the standard descriptions with the expression, "having seen with wisdom, the influxes are destroyed" (e.g. at M I 160). Cf. also A III 194, which appears to relate the cessation of cognition and feeling to arahantship and non-returning in particular.

103 S II 121.

104 Gombrich 1996: p.126.

105 In this context it is telling that A IV 452 lists different types of *arahants* "freed by wisdom", all of them, however, able to attain *jhāna*.

106 S II 115. Cf. de la Vallée Poussin 1936: p.218; and Gombrich 1996: p.128.

107 Spk II 122.

Instead of perceiving these passages as expressing an "underlying tension" between two different paths to realization, they simply describe different aspects of what is basically one approach.[108] As a matter of fact, full awakening requires a purification of both the cognitive and the affective aspect of the mind. Although on theoretical examination these two aspects of the path might appear different, in actual practice they tend to converge and supplement each other.

This is neatly summarized in the *Paṭisambhidāmagga*, which emphasizes the importance of appreciating the essential similarity between calm and insight meditation in terms of their function.[109] A practitioner might develop one or the other aspect to a higher degree at different times, but in the final stages of practice both calm and insight need to be combined in order to reach the final aim – full awakening – the destruction of both passion and ignorance.

---

108 Critical assessments of the "two paths theory" can be found in Gethin 1997b: p.221; Swearer 1972: pp.369–71; and Keown 1992: pp.77–9, who concludes (p 82): "two types of meditation technique ... exist precisely because final perfection can only be achieved when both dimensions of psychic functioning, the emotional and the intellectual, are purified."

109 Paṭis I 21. On the interrelation of both in the Sarvāstivāda tradition cf. Cox 1994: p.83.

V

THE *SATIPAṬṬHĀNA* "REFRAIN"

Having examined the "definition" of the *Satipaṭṭhāna Sutta* at some length, I shall now look at a part of the discourse which could be called the "modus operandi" of *satipaṭṭhāna*.[1] This part, which I refer to as the "refrain", occurs after each of the meditation exercises described in the discourse and presents four key aspects of *satipaṭṭhāna* (cf. Fig. 5.1 below).[2] The task of this "refrain" is to direct attention to those aspects that are essential for the proper practice of each exercise. Thus an understanding of the implications of the "refrain" forms a necessary background to the meditation techniques described in the *Satipaṭṭhāna Sutta*, which I will begin to examine in Chapter VI. In the case of the first *satipaṭṭhāna*, the "refrain" reads:

> **In this way, in regard to the body he abides contemplating the body internally, or he abides contemplating the body externally, or he abides contemplating the body both internally and externally.**
>
> **He abides contemplating the nature of arising in the body, or he abides contemplating the nature of passing away in the body, or he abides contemplating the nature of both arising and passing away in the body.**
>
> **Mindfulness that "there is a body" is established in him to the extent necessary for bare knowledge and continuous mindfulness.**
>
> **And he abides independent, not clinging to anything in the world.**[3]

---

1 This expression is suggested by W.S. Karunaratne 1979: p.117.

2 Ṭhānissaro 1996: p.79, alternatively speaks of a basic pattern of three stages underlying the "refrain".

internal/external
(*ajjhatta/bahiddhā*)

arising/passing away
(*samudaya/vaya*)

bare knowledge + continuous mindfulness
(*ñāṇamattāya paṭissatimattāya*)

independent, without clinging
(*anissito ca viharati, na ca kiñci loke upādiyati*)

Fig. 5.1: Key aspects of the *satipaṭṭhāna* refrain

The "refrain" indicates that the scope of *satipaṭṭhāna* practice includes internal and external phenomena, and that it is in particular their nature to arise and pass away which should be given attention. By including both internal and external phenomena, the "refrain" broadens the contemplative perspective. By mentioning contemplation of their impermanent nature, the "refrain" moreover directs awareness to the temporal axis of experience, that is, to the passage of time. Thus, with these instructions, the "refrain" expands the scope of each *satipaṭṭhāna* exercise along its spatial and temporal axes. As the discourses explicitly point out, these two aspects are required for a proper undertaking of *satipaṭṭhāna*.[4] The "refrain" also describes the proper attitude to be adopted during contemplation: observation should be undertaken merely for the purpose of establishing awareness and understanding, and should remain free from clinging.

With the "refrain", the practice of *satipaṭṭhāna* turns towards the general characteristics of the contemplated phenomena.[5] At this stage of practice, awareness of the specific content of experience gives way to an understanding of the general nature and character of the *satipaṭṭhāna* under contemplation.

This shift of awareness from the individual content of a particular experience to its general features is of central importance for the

3 M I 56. For the other *satipaṭṭhānas*, each instance of "body" in the above instruction should be replaced with "feelings", "mind", or "*dhammas*".

4 Cf. S V 294, according to which to contemplate both internally and externally is the proper way to undertake *satipaṭṭhāna*.

5 This can to some extent be inferred from the way the "refrain" is worded, since attention now shifts from a particular instance (such as, for example, "a worldly pleasant feeling") back to the general area (such as "feelings").

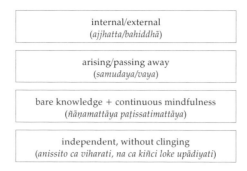

development of insight.[6] Here the task of *sati* is to penetrate beyond the surface appearance of the object under observation and to lay bare the characteristics it shares with all conditioned phenomena. This move of *sati* towards the more general characteristics of experience brings about insight into the impermanent, unsatisfactory, and selfless nature of reality. Such a more panoramic kind of awareness emerges at an advanced stage of *satipaṭṭhāna*, once the meditator is able to maintain awareness effortlessly. At this stage, when *sati* has become well-established, whatever occurs at any sense door automatically becomes part of the contemplation.[7]

It is noteworthy that two of the most popular contemporary *vipassanā* schools of the Theravāda tradition both recognize the importance of developing such bare awareness of whatever arises at any sense door as an advanced stage of insight meditation. To judge from writings of Mahasi Sayadaw and U Ba Khin, their particular meditation techniques are apparently mainly expedient means for beginners, who are not yet able to practise such bare awareness at all sense doors.[8]

V.1 INTERNAL AND EXTERNAL CONTEMPLATION

The two expressions used in the first part of the "refrain" are "internal" (*ajjhatta*) and its complementary opposite "external" (*bahiddhā*). The significance of these two terms is not further explained in the *Satipaṭṭhāna Sutta*. The *Abhidhamma* and the commentaries associate internal with the personal and external with corresponding

---

6 On the importance of shifting from content to general process cf. Brown 1986a: p.233; Goldstein 1994: p.50; and Kornfield 1977: p.19. According to Engler 1986: p.28, one of the reasons western meditators tend to progress more slowly than their eastern counterparts is "the tendency to become absorbed in the content of awareness rather than continuing to attend to its process ... become preoccupied with individual thoughts, images, memories, sensations etc., rather than keeping their attention focused on the essential characteristics of all psycho-physical events, whatever the content ... a tendency to confuse meditation with psychotherapy and to analyse mental content instead of simply observing it." On the same problem cf. also Walsh 1981: p.76. The need to contemplate the general characteristics of *anicca*, *dukkha*, and *anattā* when cultivating *satipaṭṭhāna* is also noted in the *Abhidharmakośabhāṣyam* (in Pruden 1988: p.925).

7 Jumnien 1993: p.279, aptly describes this stage of practice: "at some point the mind becomes so clear and balanced that whatever arises is seen and left untouched with no interference. One ceases to focus on any particular content and all is seen as simply mind and matter, an empty process arising and passing away of its own ... a perfect balance of mind with no reactions ... there is no longer any doing...."

phenomena in other human beings.[9] Modern meditation teachers have proposed several alternative interpretations. In order to explore the possible implications of internal and external *satipaṭṭhāna* comprehensively, I will at first consider the *Abhidhammic* and commentarial interpretation. Then I will survey some alternative interpretations.

According to the *Abhidhamma* and the commentarial interpretation, "internal" and "external" *satipaṭṭhāna* encompasses phenomena arising in oneself and in others. In this way, proper practice of *satipaṭṭhāna* would also include awareness of the subjective experience of others. Although this may be quite feasible in the case of observing another person's body, to directly experience another's feelings or states of mind seems at first sight to require psychic powers.[10] This would, of course, significantly limit the possibility of carrying out "external" *satipaṭṭhāna*.

Yet in the *Satipaṭṭhāna Saṃyutta* the Buddha introduced these three modes of attention – internal, external, and both – separately as a "threefold way of developing *satipaṭṭhāna*".[11] This passage certifies that each of the three constitutes a relevant aspect of *satipaṭṭhāna* practice. The same can be inferred from the fact that the *Vibhaṅga*, a

---

8 Cf. Mahasi 1990: pp.17 and 21: "the actual method of practice in *vipassanā* meditation is to ... observe ... the successive occurrences of seeing, hearing, and so on, at the six sense doors. However, it will not be possible for a beginner to follow these on all successive incidents as they occur, because his mindfulness, concentration and knowledge are still very weak.... A simpler and easier form of the exercise for a beginner is this: With every breath there occurs in the abdomen a rising–falling movement. A beginner should start with the exercise of noting this movement." Mahasi 1992: p.75: "we used to instruct the yogi whose powers of concentration have strengthened to extend this method of meditation to noting all that happens at his six sense doors." Ba Khin 1985: p.94: "in fact one can develop the understanding of *anicca* through any of the six organs of sense. In practice, however, we have found that ... the feeling by contact of touch ... is more tangible than other types of feeling and therefore a beginner in *Vipassanā* meditation can come to the understanding of *anicca* more easily through bodily feelings.... This is the main reason we have chosen the body feelings as a medium for the quick understanding of *anicca*. It is open to anyone to try other means, but my suggestion is that one should have oneself well established in the understanding of *anicca* through bodily feelings before an attempt is made through other types of feeling."

9 Dhs 187; same at Vibh 2–10 for each aggregate. Cf. also Vism 473.

10 This is, in fact, implied by the presentation at D II 216, where internal *satipaṭṭhāna* contemplation leads to concentration, which then enables one to undertake external contemplation. Cf. also S II 127, where contemplation of the states of mind of others forms part of a list of deep concentrative attainments, which suggests that here too such contemplation is understood as an exercise of psychic powers. Cf. also Ṭhānissaro 1996: p.76.

comparatively early part of the Pāli *Abhidhamma*, shifts the distinction between internal and external from the "refrain" to the "definition" part of the *Satipaṭṭhāna Sutta*,[12] thereby incorporating internal and external contemplation into what constitutes "right" mindfulness. Both this *Abhidhammic* modification and the above quoted discourse point to the importance of applying *sati* both internally and externally. In fact, the *Vibhaṅga* makes a special point of stating that an external application of *sati*, just as much as an internal application, can lead to realization.[13] Similarly, a discourse in the *Bojjhaṅga Saṃyutta* points out that both internal and external *sati* can act as an awakening factor.[14]

In order to do justice to this evident importance, a practicable solution is possibly to develop awareness of another's feelings and mental condition by carefully observing their outer manifestations. Feelings and states of mind do affect the outer appearance of a person by influencing their facial expression, tone of voice, and physical posture.[15]

This suggestion finds support in several discourses that list four means of knowing another person's state of mind: based on what one sees, based on what one hears, by considering and further reflecting on what one has heard, and lastly with the help of mind reading.[16] Apart from mind reading, these means do not require

---

11 S V 143. Similarly S V 294; S V 297; and A III 450 treat these three modes as distinct contemplations. Several discourses apply the distinction between the internal and the external individually to feelings, to the hindrances, to the awakening factors, and to the aggregates (cf. e.g. M III 16; S IV 205; and S V 110). These passages suggest that the application of "internal" and "external" to all *satipaṭṭhānas* in the "refrain" is not merely a case of meaningless repetition, but has to have some significance in each case. Cf. also Gethin 1992: p.54.

12 Vibh 193 (this occurs in the *Suttanta* exposition). On the dating of Vibh cf. Frauwallner 1971: vol.15, p.106; and Warder 1982: p.xxx.

13 Vibh 228. In fact, the *satipaṭṭhāna* commentary explicitly applies "external" to each *satipaṭṭhāna* technique, to the breath at Ps I 249, to the postures at Ps I 252, to bodily activities at Ps I 270, to the bodily parts at Ps I 271, to the elements at Ps I 272, to the cemetery contemplations at Ps I 273, to feelings at Ps I 279, to the mind at Ps I 280, to the hindrances at Ps I 286, to the aggregates at Ps I 287, to the sense-spheres at Ps I 289, to the awakening factors at Ps I 300, and to the four noble truths at Ps I 301.

14 S V 110.

15 Khemacari 1985: p.26.

16 D III 103 and A I 171. Cf. also M I 318, which recommends investigating by way of seeing and hearing for monks without telepathic powers in order to be able to assess the Buddha's mental purity; or else M II 172, where observing the bodily and verbal conduct of a monk forms the basis for assessing whether his mind is under the influence of greed, anger, or delusion.

psychic powers, only awareness and some degree of common sense. Understood in this way, an "external" application of awareness in relation to the various practices detailed in the *Satipaṭṭhāna Sutta* becomes a practicable possibility.

Thus external *satipaṭṭhāna* could be undertaken by directing awareness towards another person's posture, facial expression, and tone of voice, as indicators of their feelings or state of mind. Undertaking external awareness of another in this way would to some extent resemble the way a psychoanalyst observes a patient, closely examining behaviour and related symptoms in order to assess their state of mind. Thus an external application of awareness would be a practice particularly suitable in daily life, since most of the phenomena to be observed will probably not occur while one is seated in formal meditation.

Such "external" contemplation of the behaviour and mental reactions of others can then lead to an increasingly deeper appreciation of the character traits of the person in question. Helpful information for such appreciation can be found in the commentaries, which offer descriptions of different human character-types and their corresponding behaviour patterns.[17] According to these descriptions, characteristic mental dispositions of anger or greed can be inferred by observing, for example, a particular monk's eating habits and way of wearing his robes. Differences in character even show up in the different ways a simple task such a sweeping is performed.

According to the instructions in the "refrain", "internal" contemplation precedes its "external" counterpart. This indicates that the first step of internal contemplation serves as a basis for understanding similar phenomena in others during the second step, external contemplation. Indeed, to be aware of one's own feelings and reactions enables one to understand the feelings and reactions of others more easily.[18]

---

17 Ehara 1995: pp.58–61; and Vism 101–10. Cf. also Mann 1992: pp.19–51.

18 Mann 1992: p.112, speaks of realizing "that the forces at work within other people are the same as the forces that motivate our own behaviour". Similarly, insights gained during external contemplation will in turn also support internal contemplation. For example, it is comparatively easy to uncover the underlying motives of particular reactions in someone else, while the same motives might pass undetected if one is the actor oneself. Cf. also Bullen 1982: p.32; Khemacari 1985: p.23; and Ñāṇapoṇika 1992: p.58, who explains that "many things permit of better understanding when observed in others, or in external objects, than in oneself".

For a balanced development of awareness, this shift from the internal to the external is of considerable importance. Awareness applied only internally can lead to self-centredness. One can become excessively concerned with what happens with and within oneself while at the same time remaining unaware of how one's action and behaviour affect others. Practising both internal and external *satipaṭṭhāna* can prevent such lopsidedness and achieve a skilful balance between introversion and extroversion.[19]

The third step of this aspect in the "refrain" instructs the meditator to observe "both internally and externally". The commentaries explain that, since one cannot contemplate an object both internally and externally simultaneously, the instruction implies that one should alternate between these two modes.[20] This commentarial presentation does not really add anything new to the previous two stages of practice, since to contemplate either internally or externally already entails alternating between these two modes. The *Vibhaṅga* offers a more convincing perspective, since its presentation of contemplating both internally and externally points to an understanding of the contemplated object as such, without considering it as part of one's own subjective experience, or that of others.[21] Practised in this way, *satipaṭṭhāna* contemplation shifts towards an increasingly "objective" and detached stance, from which the observed phenomena are experienced as such, independent of whether they occur in oneself or in others.

The *Abhidhammic* and commentarial interpretation of "internal" and "external" as referring to oneself and others tallies with several other passages in the early discourses. In the *Sāmagāma Sutta*, for example, the same two terms are used when countering various unwholesome qualities and unskilful forms of behaviour, whether these occur in oneself (*ajjhatta*) or in others (*bahiddhā*).[22] And in the *Janavasabha Sutta*, in a context directly related to *satipaṭṭhāna*, "external" explicitly refers to the bodies, feelings, etc. of others.[23] This

---

19 Cf. also Ñāṇapoṇika 1951: p.35.

20 Ps I 249.

21 This is implicit in the way the respective contemplations are formulated at Vibh 195, according to which internally one understands: "I feel a pleasant feeling", externally one understands: "he or she feels a pleasant feeling", internally and externally one understands: "a pleasant feeling". The same recurs at Vibh 197 for mind and at Vibh 199–201 for *dhammas*.

22 M II 246.

23 D II 216.

passage carries considerable weight in relation to the present discussion, since it is the only discourse to provide additional information on the nature of "external" *satipaṭṭhāna*.

V.2 ALTERNATIVE INTERPRETATIONS OF INTERNAL AND EXTERNAL CONTEMPLATION

Modern meditation teachers have proposed various alternative interpretations of internal and external *satipaṭṭhāna*. Some take "internal" and "external" to mean quite literally what is spatially internal and external. They suggest that external bodily feelings, for example, are those observed at skin level (*bahiddhā*), while internal bodily feelings are those occurring deeper within the body (*ajjhatta*).[24]

"Internal" (*ajjhatta*) occurs in the *Satipaṭṭhāna Sutta* itself in a clearly spatial sense, referring to the six internal senses in contrast to their external objects. However, the Pāli term used in this context for the external sense objects is not *bahiddhā*, but *bāhira*.[25] In contrast, "internal" (*ajjhatta*) and "external" (*bahiddhā*) as qualities mentioned in the "refrain" do not seem to convey such a spatial distinction. In the case of contemplating the sense-spheres, for example, such a spatial understanding of "internal" and "external" does not yield a meaningful way of practice, since according to the "refrain" the entire sense-sphere, consisting of internal sense and external object, has to be contemplated internally and then externally. The difficulty involved in taking "internal" and "external" to represent a spatial distinction extends to most of the *satipaṭṭhāna* contemplations. Neither states of mind nor such *dhammas* as the hindrances or the awakening factors fit easily into a distinction between spatially internal and external occurrences, unless one were to adopt the commentarial interpretation and take "external" to refer to states of mind, hindrances, or awakening factors occurring in other persons.

Other teachers suggest that the distinction between internal and external contemplation hints at the difference between apparent and ultimate truth.[26] It is certainly true that as practice progresses

---

24 Goenka 1999: p.54; Solé-Leris 1992: p.82; and Thate 1996: p.44. This way of understanding "internal" and "external" could be supported with Th 172, where "internal" and "external" are both used with regard to the speaker's own body, so that here too they seem to be referring to the inner and outer parts of the same body.

25 M I 61: *ajjhattikabāhiresu āyatanesu*.

26 Dhammadharo 1993: pp.263–6; and Ñāṇasaṃvara 1961: p.27.

one comes to see phenomena more and more in their true nature. Yet it is highly improbable that a distinction between apparent and ultimate truth corresponds to the original sense of "internal" and "external" in the *Satipaṭṭhāna Sutta*, firstly because neither of the two terms ever has this implication in the discourses, and secondly simply because the distinction between these two levels of truth is a late development, belonging to the post-canonical period.[27]

Another interpretation proposes to distinguish between internal mental and external physical objects, so that in the case of feelings, for example, one distinguishes mental feelings (*ajjhatta*) from physical feelings (*bahiddhā*), and in the case of mind one distinguishes between purely mental experience (*ajjhatta*) and states of mind related to sensory experiences (*bahiddhā*).[28]

This way of understanding "internal" and "external" can claim for support a passage in the *Iddhipāda Saṃyutta*, which relates internal contraction to sloth-and-torpor, while its externally distracted counterpart is sensual distraction by way of the five senses.[29] Another relevant passage occurs in the *Bojjhaṅga Saṃyutta*, which differentiates the hindrances sensual desire, aversion, and doubt into internal and external occurrences.[30] This passage could refer to the arising of

---

27 Cf. Jayatilleke 1980: pp.361–8; Kalupahana 1992: p.107; Karunadasa 1996: p.35; and W.S. Karunaratne 1988a: p.90. The term *paramattha* occurs at Sn 68; Sn 219; and Th 748. Elsewhere related terms occur, like *paramañāṇa* at A III 354, *paramapaññā* and *parama ariyasacca* at M III 245, *paramasacca* at M I 480, M II 173, and A II 115, and *uttamattha* at Dhp 403. All these instances are references only to *Nibbāna*. The presumption that the one-hundred-and-twenty-one types of mental states, fifty-two types of mental factors, and twenty-eight types of matter listed in the Abhidh-s can be considered "*paramattha*", in the sense of being ultimately real, is a late development not found in the early discourses. For an exposition of this later conception of *paramattha* cf. Bodhi 1993: pp.6 and 25; and Ledi 1999b: p.99.

28 Dhammadharo 1987: pp.20 and 25, and Maha Boowa 1994: p.101, relate the distinction between internal and external to mental and physical feelings respectively, and to mind only (internal) and mind with an external object in the case of mind. Fessel 1999: p.105, understands "internal" to refer to internal mental experience and introversion, while "external" represents external influences and object-directed activities. Tiwari 1992: p.82, also relates "internal" to mental and "external" to physical feelings. Similarly, the *Mahāprajñāpāramitāśāstra* considers internal feelings and states of mind to be those related to mind door events, while the corresponding external counterparts are those related to the other five senses (in Lamotte 1970: pp.1173–5). Ñāṇasaṃvara 1974: pp.28 and 71 applies this way of understanding to mindfulness of breathing, in the sense that the breath is "external", while awareness of the breath is "internal". This, however, does not yield meaningful alternative forms of practice, since the presence of both breath and awareness is required for "internal" and for "external" contemplation.

29 S V 279.

30 S V 110. However, it should be noted that the same discourse does not apply this

these hindrances owing to mind door events (*ajjhatta*), or owing to a sense door input (*bahiddhā*).

On the other hand, the qualification "internal" occurs in the *Satipaṭṭhāna Sutta* also as part of the main instruction for contemplating the hindrances and the awakening factors. This usage does not seem to be related to the distinction between experiences by way of the mind door and that of the five sense doors, but appears to emphasize the sense that a hindrance or an awakening factor is present "within me", paralleling the commentarial understanding of "internal" as referring to oneself.[31]

Elsewhere in the discourses, *ajjhatta* on its own does indeed denote what is internal in the sense of being a predominantly mental type of experience. A typical example of such usage is the second *jhāna*, which the standard descriptions qualify as a state of "internal" serenity.[32] Internal in the sense of "mental" occurs also in the *Uddesavibhaṅga Sutta*, which contrasts an "internally stuck" state of mind with consciousness being "externally distracted". Yet in this discourse, "external", which according to the above interpretation should stand only for the five physical senses, refers to all six senses.[33] Similarly, in other discourses "internal" stands not only for pure mind door events, but is at times related to all six senses.[34]

These passages suggest that to understand "internal" and "external" as respective references to mind door and five sense door events is not always appropriate. The same holds true in relation to several of the *satipaṭṭhāna* contemplations. Among the six sense-spheres, for example, a distinction can easily be made between the mind door and the physical sense doors. Yet it is difficult to conceive of a meaningful contemplation that treats the entire set

---

distinction to sloth-and-torpor or to restlessness-and-worry, although both these hindrances could also arise owing to either mind door or five sense door experiences.

31 M I 60: "he knows 'there is aversion in me'" (*atthi me ajjhattaṃ*); or M I 61: "he knows 'there is the mindfulness awakening factor in me'" (*atthi me ajjhattaṃ*). These instructions do not seem to apply only to hindrances or awakening factors arising in relation to mind door events.

32 e.g. at D I 74. Other examples are "internal" calm of the mind at M I 213, or "internal" happiness (referring to *jhāna*) at M III 233.

33 M III 225: "seeing a visible object ... cognizing a mental object ... consciousness is distracted externally." The phrase "internally stuck state of mind", however, does indeed imply mental experience, namely attachment to the pleasure of *jhāna*.

34 e.g. M I 346 relates internal happiness to all six senses; or S IV 139 speaks of internal lust, anger, and delusion in relation to all six senses; or S V 74 relates an internally steady mind to all six senses.

of six sense-spheres first internally, from a purely mental viewpoint, and then externally, from the perspective of the five sense doors.

In summary, although alternative ways of understanding internal and external *satipaṭṭhāna* have their practical value, to understand "internal" as referring to oneself and "external" as referring to others offers a practicable form of contemplation which can moreover claim support from the discourses, the *Abhidhamma*, and the commentaries.

In the end, whichever interpretation one may adopt, once contemplation is practised both internally and externally it entails a shift towards a comprehensive type of practice.[35] At this stage even the boundary between "I" and "other" or "internal" and "external" is left behind, leading to a comprehensive vision of phenomena as such, independent of any sense of ownership. Such a more wide-ranging view involves either a contemplation of oneself and others, or a contemplation of any internal phenomenon together with its external counterpart. Thus each of the ways of understanding "internal" and "external" discussed above ultimately leads to a more comprehensive appreciation of the phenomena under observation.[36] Based on such a comprehensive view of phenomena, *satipaṭṭhāna* practice then proceeds to the next aspect mentioned in the "refrain": awareness of their impermanent nature.

V.3 IMPERMANENCE

The "refrain" instructs the meditator to contemplate "the nature of arising", "the nature of passing away", and "the nature of both arising and passing away".[37] Paralleling the instruction on internal and external contemplation, the three parts of this instruction represent a temporal progression which leads from observing the arising

---

35 This is suggested by several verses in the *Sutta Nipāta*, where "internal" and "external" occur together in the sense of "whatever there is", expressing a sense of comprehensiveness, cf. Sn 516; Sn 521; Sn 527; and Sn 738. The need for such comprehensiveness is not only a characteristic of *satipaṭṭhāna* practice, but also features in a contemplation of emptiness described at M III 112, which similarly proceeds from "internal" to "external" and culminates in contemplation undertaken "both internally and externally".

36 A similar shift towards comprehensiveness features in the standard descriptions on how to develop insight with regard to the five aggregates, where after a detailed examination of a single aggregate, the insight gained is applied to all possible instances of it (cf. e.g. M I 138).

aspect of phenomena to focusing on their disappearance, and culminates in a comprehensive vision of impermanence as such.

According to the discourses, not seeing the arising and passing away of phenomena is simply ignorance, while to regard all phenomena as impermanent leads to knowledge and understanding.[38] Insight into the impermanence of the five aggregates or of the six sense-spheres is "right view", and thereby leads directly on to realization.[39] Thus the direct experience of impermanence represents indeed the "power" aspect of meditative wisdom.[40] These passages clearly show the central importance of developing a direct experience of the impermanent nature of all phenomena, as envisaged in this part of the *satipaṭṭhāna* "refrain". The same is reflected in the commentarial scheme of the insight knowledges, which details key experiences to be encountered during the path to realization, where the stage of apprehending the arising and passing away of phenomena is of central importance.[41]

The other two characteristics of conditioned existence – *dukkha* (unsatisfactoriness) and *anattā* (absence of a self) – become evident as a consequence of a direct experience and thereby realistic appreciation of the truth of impermanence. The discourses frequently point to this relationship between the three characteristics by presenting a progressive pattern that leads from awareness of impermanence (*aniccasaññā*) via acknowledging the unsatisfactory nature of what is impermanent (*anicce dukkhasaññā*) to appreciating the selfless nature of what is unsatisfactory (*dukkhe anattasaññā*).[42] The same pattern features prominently in the *Anattalakkhaṇa Sutta*, in which the Buddha instructed his first disciples to become clearly aware of the impermanent nature of each aspect of subjective

---

37 This way of translating the compound is supported by its use at S III 171, where it clearly refers to the "nature of arising and passing away". Cf. also Ñāṇatiloka 1910: p.95 n.1, who translates *samudayadhamma* as "the law of arising" (das Enstehungsgesetz); and Ñāṇamoli 1994: p.53, who translates *vayadhamma* "having the nature of fall".

38 S III 171 and S IV 50.

39 S III 51 and S IV 142.

40 A III 2. Impermanence as the key aspect of insight is also emphasized by Fleischman 1986: p.11; Ledi 1999a: p.151; Ñāṇaponika 1992: p.60; Solé-Leris 1992: p.82; and Than Daing 1970: p.62.

41 According to Ledi (n.d): p.233, insight into arising and passing away is the key aspect of the insight knowledges and relevant for the progress to all four stages of awakening. Excellent expositions on the insight knowledges can be found in Mahasi 1994: pp.8–36; and Ñāṇārāma 1993: pp.19–62.

experience, expounded in terms of the five aggregates. Based on this, he then led them to the conclusion that whatever is impermanent cannot yield lasting satisfaction and therefore does not qualify to be considered as "I", "mine", or "my self".[43] This understanding, after being applied to all possible instances of each aggregate, was powerful enough to result in the full awakening of the first five monk disciples of the Buddha.

The underlying pattern of the Buddha's instruction in this discourse shows that insight into impermanence serves as an important foundation for realizing *dukkha* and *anattā*. The inner dynamic of this pattern proceeds from clear awareness of impermanence to a growing degree of disenchantment (which corresponds to *dukkhasaññā*),[44] which in turn progressively reduces the "I"-making and "my"-making embedded in one's mind (this being the equivalent to *anattasaññā*).[45]

The importance of developing insight into the arising and passing away of phenomena is highlighted in the *Vibhaṅga Sutta* of the *Saṃyutta Nikāya*, according to which this insight marks the distinction between mere establishment of *satipaṭṭhāna* and its complete and full "development" (*bhāvanā*).[46] This passage underlines the importance of the "refrain" for a proper development of *satipaṭṭhāna*. Mere awareness of the various objects listed under the four *satipaṭṭhānas* might not suffice for the task of developing penetrative

---

42 At D III 243; D III 251; D III 290; D III 291; S V 132; S V 345; A I 41; A III 85; A III 277; A III 334; A III 452; A IV 46; A IV 52; A IV 148; A IV 387; A IV 465; A V 105; and A V 309. (Literally translated, the pattern runs: "cognition of impermanence, cognition of unsatisfactoriness in the impermanent, cognition of not-self in the unsatisfactory".) This pattern is also reflected in the statement "what is impermanent that is unsatisfactory, what is unsatisfactory that is not-self", e.g. at S III 22; S III 45; S III 82; S IV 1; and S IV 153. Cf. also Bodhi 2000: p.844. Ñāṇananda 1986: p.103, explains: "in '*sukha*' and '*attā*' we have the affective and conative reactions to the illusion of permanence."

43 S III 67.

44 A III 443 and A III 447 relate awareness of impermanence to disenchantment in general, while A IV 51 relates it in particular to being disinterested in worldly gains.

45 Awareness of the empty nature of what is unsatisfactory leads, according to A IV 53, to overcoming all notions of I or mine. Cf. also A IV 353; A IV 358; and Ud 37; according to which insight into not-self, being based on awareness of impermanence, leads to the eradication of all conceit and therewith to realization.

46 S V 183 explains the shift from mere *satipaṭṭhāna* to a "development" (*bhāvanā*) of *satipaṭṭhāna* to consist in contemplation of the nature of arising and passing away. This discourse is, however, missing from the Chinese *Āgamas*, cf. Akanuma 1990: p.247.

insight. What is additionally required is to move on to a comprehensive and equanimous vision of impermanence.[47]

Direct experience of the fact that everything changes, if applied to all aspects of one's personality, can powerfully alter the habit patterns of one's mind.[48] This may well be why awareness of impermanence assumes a particularly prominent role in regard to the contemplation of the five aggregates where, in addition to being mentioned in the "refrain", it has become part of the main instruction.[49]

Continuity in developing awareness of impermanence is essential if it is really to affect one's mental condition.[50] Sustained contemplation of impermanence leads to a shift in one's normal way of experiencing reality, which hitherto tacitly assumed the temporal stability of the perceiver and the perceived objects. Once both are experienced as changing processes, all notions of stable existence and substantiality vanish, thereby radically reshaping one's paradigm of experience.

Contemplation of impermanence has to be comprehensive, for if any aspect of experience is still taken to be permanent, awakening will be impossible.[51] A comprehensive realization of impermanence is a distinctive feature of stream-entry. This is the case to such an extent that a stream-enterer is incapable of believing any phenomenon to be permanent.[52] Understanding of impermanence reaches perfection with the realization of full awakening.[53] For *arahants*,

---

47 In fact, M I 62 speaks of the need to "develop" *satipaṭṭhāna* in order for it to lead to highest realization: "if anyone should develop these four *satipaṭṭhānas* ... one of two fruits could be expected for him"; an expression that is reminiscent of the reference to "development" (*bhāvanā*) at S V 183. It is noteworthy that, in contrast to the emphasis the Pāli texts place on contemplation of impermanence, the *Madhyama Āgama* version of the *satipaṭṭhāna* "refrain" does not mention it at all. The *Ekottara Āgama* version, however, has preserved it at least in relation to contemplation of feelings, mind, and *dhammas* (cf. Minh Chau 1991: p.88; and Nhat Hanh 1990: pp.173, 175 and 177). The injunction to contemplate "arising" and "disappearing" in relation to all four *satipaṭṭhānas* occurs also in the *Saṃyukta Āgama* equivalent of the *Samudaya Sutta* (S V 184), cf. the translation in Hurvitz 1978: p.215.

48 Goenka 1994a: p.112.

49 M I 61: "such is material form ... feeling ... cognition ... volitions ... consciousness, such its arising, such its passing away." Cf. further page 213.

50 Continuity in contemplating impermanence is mentioned at A IV 13 and A IV 145; cf. also Th 111.

51 A III 441.

52 A III 439.

53 A IV 224 and A V 174.

awareness of the impermanent nature of all sensory input is a natural feature of their experience.[54]

Apart from encouraging awareness of impermanence, this part of the "refrain" can also, according to the commentarial view, be taken to refer to the factors (*dhammas*) that condition the arising and the disappearance of the observed phenomena.[55] These factors are treated in the *Samudaya Sutta*, which relates the "arising" and "disappearing" of each *satipaṭṭhāna* to its respective condition, these being nutriment in the case of body, contact for feelings, name-and-form for mind, and attention for *dhammas*.[56]

Within the framework of early Buddhist philosophy, both impermanence and conditionality are of outstanding importance. In the course of the Buddha's own approach to awakening, recollection of his past lives and the sight of other beings passing away and being reborn vividly brought home to him the truths of impermanence and conditionality on a personal and universal scale.[57] The same two aspects contributed to the realization of the previous Buddha, Vipassī, when after a detailed examination of dependent co-arising (*paṭicca samuppāda*), *satipaṭṭhāna* contemplation of the impermanent nature of the five aggregates led to his awakening.[58] I will therefore consider this additional perspective on this part of the *satipaṭṭhāna*

---

54 Cf. A III 377; A IV 404; A III 379; and Th 643.

55 Ps I 249.

56 S V 184. (However, this passage does not fully fit with the "refrain", since the term used here is "disappearing", *atthagama*, not "passing away", *vaya*, as in the *Satipaṭṭhāna Sutta*.)

57 M I 22; M I 248; and A IV 176. S II 10 and S II 104 document his realization of dependent co-arising. The importance of the first two higher knowledges as exemplifications of impermanence and causality is noted by Demieville 1954: p.294; and Werner 1991: p.13; cf. also Lopez 1992: p.35. In addition to the above passages, the discourses document the growth of the Buddha's wisdom from a variety of angles, involving a contemplation of the enjoyment, the inherent disadvantage, and the escape in relation to the elements (S II 170), the aggregates (S III 27; S III 29; and S III 59), the sense-spheres (S IV 7–10 and S V 206), feeling (S IV 233), the faculties (S V 204), the "world" (A I 258), and the four noble truths (S V 423). Each of these discourses directly relates the respective insight to the Buddha's attainment of full awakening, which suggests that each of these insights can be considered a particular aspect of his comprehensive realization.

58 D II 31–5, where a detailed investigation of the conditional links leading from *dukkha* up to the reciprocal relationship between consciousness and name-and-form led on to his practice of the *satipaṭṭhāna* contemplation of the five aggregates, resulting in realization. A practical example of how impermanence and conditionality can be interrelated in the context of contemplation can also be found at S IV 211, which relates the conditioned arising of the three types of feelings to the impermanent nature of the body; (same at S IV 215 in regard to contact).

"refrain" by surveying the Buddha's teaching on conditionality within its philosophical and historical context.

V.4 DEPENDENT CO-ARISING (*PAṬICCA SAMUPPĀDA*)

At the time of the Buddha, a variety of philosophical positions on causality were current in India.[59] Some teachings claimed that the universe was controlled by an external power, either an omnipotent god or a principle inherent in nature. Some took man to be the independent doer and enjoyer of action. Some favoured determinism, while others completely rejected any kind of causality.[60] Despite their differences, all these positions concurred in recognizing an absolute principle, formulated in terms of the existence (or absence) of a single or first cause.

The Buddha, on the other hand, proposed dependent co-arising (*paṭicca samuppāda*) as his "middle way" explanation of causality. His conception of dependent co-arising was so decisive a departure from existing conceptions of causality that he came to reject all of the four prevalent ways of formulating causality.[61]

The discourses often describe dependent co-arising (*paṭicca samuppāda*) with a model of twelve sequential links. This sequence traces the conditioned arising of *dukkha* back to ignorance (*avijjā*). According to the *Paṭisambhidāmagga*, these twelve links extend over three consecutive individual lifetimes.[62] The twelve links applied to three lifetimes probably assumed increasing importance in the historical development of Buddhist thought, as a way of explaining

---

59 Cf. Kalupahana 1975: p.125.

60 See esp. Pūraṇa Kassapa and Makkhali Gosāla at D I 52. Cf. also Bodhi 1989: p.7.

61 A typical example can be found at S II 19, where the Buddha was asked whether *dukkha* was caused by oneself, by others, by both, or by neither (i.e. arisen by chance). After the Buddha had denied all four alternatives his interlocutor, surprised that all four ways of stating the causality of *dukkha* had been rejected, wondered whether the Buddha was simply unable to see or admit the existence of *dukkha*. A similar dialogue in relation to *sukha dukkha* occurs at S II 22. The novelty of the Buddha's position can also be seen in the fact that the term *paṭicca samuppāda* was apparently invented by him in order to express his understanding of causality, cf. Kalupahana 1999: p.283. However C.A.F. Rhys Davids, in one of her imaginative interpretations of the Pāli canon, suggests that it was not the Buddha, but rather Assaji, who was responsible for the early Buddhist theory of causation (1927b: p.202).

62 Paṭis I 52. Bodhi 2000: p.741 n.50, points out that the scheme of four temporal modes (past cause, present result, present cause, future result) underlying the three-lifetime presentation has a predecessor at S II 24.

rebirth without an eternally surviving agent.[63] Although the sequence of twelve links occurs frequently in the discourses, substantial variants can also be found. Some of these start with the third link, consciousness, which moreover stands in a reciprocal relationship with the next link, name-and-form.[64] These and other variations suggest that the mode of explanation based on three lifetimes is not the only possible way of approaching an understanding of dependent co-arising.

In fact, the twelve links are but a particularly frequent application of the general structural principle of dependent co-arising.[65] In the *Paccaya Sutta* of the *Saṃyutta Nikāya*, the Buddha introduced this important distinction between the general principle and its application. This discourse speaks of the twelve links as dependently originated phenomena, while "*paṭicca samuppāda*" refers to the relation between them, that is, to the principle.[66]

This distinction between the principle and the twelve links as one of its applications is of considerable practical relevance, since a full understanding of causality is to be gained with stream-entry.[67] The distinction between principle and application suggests that such an

---

63 Jayatilleke 1980: p.450.

64 At D II 57, the first two links, ignorance and formations, as well as the six-sense-spheres link are missing, and consciousness is presented in a reciprocal relationship with name-and-form. The same reciprocal relationship between consciousness and name-and-form occurs at D II 32; S II 104; and S II 113. Sn 724–65 relates each of the links separately and independently to *dukkha*. (On these variations of the standard twelve-link formula cf. also Bucknell 1999: pp.314–41.) S II 31 leads from ignorance to birth but then on to joy, concentration, and realization. A different course from craving onwards is also taken at S II 108. Furthermore at D II 63 consciousness is shown to condition name-and-form at conception, during the embryonic stage, and also during life, a presentation which does not seem to be confined to rebirth within the context of the three-life application only. Or at S III 96 formations, as a result of ignorance, are not a past experience, but arise in the present moment. Cf. also W.S. Karunaratne 1988b: p.30.

65 Collins 1982: p.106 points out that "it is crucially important to distinguish between the general idea of conditionality and the twelve-fold series". Cf. also W.S. Karunaratne 1988b: p.33; and Ñāṇavīra 1987: p.31. Reat 1987: p.21: explains: "*paṭicca samuppāda* ... the term may properly be applied to any set of results dependent upon necessary and sufficient conditions."

66 S II 26. This same distinction can be deduced from the standard way in which the "twelve link" application of dependent co-arising is often introduced in the discourses, where after a formulation of the principle ("when this is that comes to be ...") the twelve links are introduced with the Pāli expression "that is to say" (*yadidaṃ*), showing that the twelve links are an exemplification of the principle just stated (cf. e.g. S II 28).

67 A III 439 explains that a quality of a stream-enterer is that he or she has understood causality and the causal origin of phenomena.

understanding of causality need not necessarily require a personal experience of the twelve links. That is, even without developing the ability to recollect past lives and thereby directly experiencing those factors of the twelve links that supposedly pertain to a past life, one can still personally realize the principle of dependent co-arising.

Compared to the entire set of twelve links, the basic principle of dependent co-arising is more easily amenable to direct contemplation. A discourse in the *Nidāna Saṃyutta*, for example, applies "dependent co-arising" to the conditioned relation between contact and feeling.[68] Such direct application of the principle to subjective experience occurs also in the *Vibhaṅga*, which relates dependent co-arising to single mind-moments.[69]

Another example of a direct application of the principle of conditionality can be found in the *Indriyabhāvanā Sutta*, which qualifies pleasure and displeasure arising at any of the six sense doors as dependently arisen (*paṭicca samuppanna*), a usage that is not related to past or future lives.[70] The same holds true for the *Madhupiṇḍika Sutta*'s detailed analysis of the perceptual process.[71] This discourse depicts the "arising" (*uppāda*) of consciousness "in dependence" (*paṭicca*) on sense organ and sense object, with contact being the coming "together" (*saṃ*) of the three. This passage reveals a deeper significance of each part of the term *paṭicca sam-uppāda*, "dependent" "co-" "arising", without any need for different lifetimes or for the whole set of twelve links. Thus realization of dependent co-arising can take place simply by witnessing the operation of

---

68 S II 96, a contemplation which then leads to realization. Similarly, at S II 92 the Buddha illustrated the depth and importance of dependent co-arising with the help of only the final five links (from craving onwards), a presentation more easily amenable to direct experience than the complete set of twelve links. That the entire set of twelve links is not necessarily intended for contemplation is also suggested by S II 81, where the Buddha recommended "thinking over" (*parivīmaṃsati*) the twelve links, using a type of terminology that points to a form of intellectual consideration. This suggests that a direct experience of the principle, gained through meditation, can then be applied to the twelve links by way of intellectual reflection, considering that the same principle operated in the past and will operate in the future, without any need to experience directly those past or future operations.

69 Vibh 164–92. On this passage cf. also Bodhi 1998: p.46 n.4; and Gethin 1997a: p.195. According to Buddhadāsa 1992: p.98, "the entire series of Dependent Origination operates ... in a flash.... The ... twelve conditions ... may all arise, exercise their function and pass away, so fast that we are completely unaware of it."

70 M III 299.

71 M I 111.

conditionality in the present moment, within one's own subjective experience.

V.5 THE PRINCIPLE OF DEPENDENT CO-ARISING AND ITS PRACTICAL APPLICATION

To speak of dependent co-arising is to speak of specific conditions related to specific events. Such "specific conditionality" (*idappaccayatā*) can be illustrated in the following manner:

When A is → B comes to be. With the arising of A → B arises.

When A is not → B does not come to be. With the cessation of A → B ceases.[72]

The operation of dependent co-arising is not confined to a strictly linear sequence of events in time. Rather, dependent co-arising stands for the conditional interrelation of phenomena, constituting a web of interwoven events, where each event is related to other events by way of both cause and effect.[73] Each conditioning factor is at the same time itself conditioned, which thereby excludes the possibility of a transcendent, independent cause.[74]

Within these interwoven patterns, the centrally important specific condition, from the viewpoint of subjective experience, is volition. It is the mental volition of the present moment that decisively influences future activities and events.[75] Volition itself is under the influence of other conditions such as one's habits, character traits, and past experiences, which influence the way one experiences a

---

72 e.g. at M III 63: "when this exists, that comes to be; with the arising of this, that arises. When this does not exist, that does not come to be; with the cessation of this, that ceases." On specific conditionality cf. also Bodhi 1995: pp.2 and 9; and Ñāṇamoli 1980: p.161.

73 The complexity of the conditional interrelation of phenomena is illustrated in the *Paṭṭhāna* of the Pāli *Abhidhamma* from a variety of angles with altogether twenty-four types of conditions. Thus, for example, the conditioning influence exercised by A on B (A → B) could, from a temporal perspective, take place not only with A arising earlier than B (*purejātapaccaya*), but also if both arise simultaneously (*sahajātapaccaya*), or even when A arises later than B (*pacchājātapaccaya*). It could be the presence of A (*atthipaccaya*), but also its absence (*natthipaccaya*), that conditions B. Moreover A could be the active cause (*kammapaccaya*), or it could exert its conditioning influence while being itself a resultant effect (*vipākapaccaya*), or else A could be both cause and effect, when A and B are related to each other by way of mutuality condition (*aññamaññapaccaya*).

74 Tilakaratne 1993: p.41.

75 A III 415 explains that volition is the factor responsible for the undertaking of activities by way of body, speech, or mind.

particular situation. Nevertheless, inasmuch as each volition involves a decision between alternatives, one's volitional decision in the present moment is to a considerable degree amenable to personal intervention and control. Each decision in turn shapes the habits, character traits, experiences, and perceptual mechanisms that form the context of future decisions. It is precisely for this reason that systematic training of the mind is imperative.

In the *Satipaṭṭhāna Sutta*, a more specific application of conditionality to the practice of meditation becomes apparent during most of the contemplations of *dhammas*. Here one finds that the meditator's task in relation to the five hindrances is to observe the conditions for their arising and removal.[76] Regarding the six sense-spheres, contemplation should disclose how the process of perception can cause the arising of mental fetters at the sense doors.[77] In the case of the awakening factors, the task is to recognize the conditions for their arising and further development.[78] Coming to the four noble truths, this last contemplation of *dhammas* is in itself a statement of conditionality, namely of the conditions for *dukkha* and its eradication. In this way, the principle of dependent co-arising underlies a range of applications in the fourth *satipaṭṭhāna*.[79]

The development of a meditative realization of dependent co-arising could be alluded to in the "direct path" passage of the *Satipaṭṭhāna Sutta*, since it lists the acquiring of "method" (*ñāya*) as one of the goals of *satipaṭṭhāna*.[80] The same term, "method", occurs often in the discourses as a quality of those who have realized stream-entry or higher stages of awakening.[81] Several instances speak of "noble method" as an outcome of the realization of stream-

---

76 M I 60: "he knows how unarisen sensual desire can arise, how arisen sensual desire can be removed, and how a future arising of the removed sensual desire can be prevented."

77 M I 61: "he knows the eye, he knows forms, and he knows the fetter that arises dependent on both, and he also knows how an unarisen fetter can arise, how an arisen fetter can be removed, and how a future arising of the removed fetter can be prevented."

78 M I 62: "he knows how the unarisen mindfulness awakening factor can arise, and how the arisen mindfulness awakening factor can be perfected by development."

79 According to the *Mahāprajñāpāramitāśāstra*, conditionality is indeed the distinctive characteristic of contemplation of *dhammas*, cf. Lamotte 1970: p.1169.

80 M I 55: "this is the direct path ... for acquiring the true method ... namely, the four *satipaṭṭhānas*."

81 The standard recollection of the community of noble disciples (e.g. at A II 56) speaks of them being in possession of the right method (*ñāyapaṭipanno*).

entry.[82] In these contexts, "noble method" implies the realization of dependent co-arising.[83] The relevance of dependent co-arising for progress to realization is confirmed in several other passages, according to which one who knows dependent co-arising is standing at the threshold of the deathless.[84] Although the expression "method" is not further specified as noble in the *Satipaṭṭhāna Sutta*, it does not seem too far-fetched to presume that its occurrence indicates a direct realization of the principle or "method" of dependent co-arising to be one of the purposes of *satipaṭṭhāna* practice.

V.6 MERE AWARENESS AND CLINGING TO NOTHING

As the "refrain" stipulates, awareness of the body, feelings, mind, and *dhammas* should take place merely for the sake of knowledge and continued mindfulness.[85] This instruction points to the need to observe objectively, without getting lost in associations and reactions. According to the commentaries, this refers in particular to avoiding any form of identification.[86] Freedom from identification then enables one to regard any aspect of one's subjective experience

---

82 S II 68; S II 71; S V 389; and A V 184 mention "noble method" as a quality of stream-entry.

83 S V 388; cf. also A V 184. "Noble method" also comes up at A II 36, where it is further explained to be of a wholesome nature (*kusaladhammatā*), a reference that could also be alluding to dependent co-arising, since the commentary Mp III 74 relates this reference to the path of insight. T.W. Rhys Davids 1993: p.394, confirms that dependent co-arising is referred to as noble method. However, the term "method" can elsewhere assume different implications, since at M I 522 it comes to include attainment of the four *jhānas* and the three higher knowledges, while at M II 182 it is related to overcoming the ten unwholesome paths of action (cf. also M II 197, where it is not further specified but distinguished according to whether it is being developed by a householder or by a monk).

84 S II 43; S II 45; S II 59; S II 79; and S II 80; each relates an understanding of dependent co-arising to "standing at the threshold of the deathless". A temporal succession with understanding of dependent co-arising preceding realization of *Nibbāna* seems also to be implied by the Buddha's statement at S II 124, where he explained that "knowledge of the stability of the *Dhamma*" (*dhammaṭṭhitiñāṇa*) precedes realization, since at S II 60 such "knowledge of the stability of the *Dhamma*" refers to dependent co-arising. This is further supported by S II 25, which identifies specific conditionality as the "stableness of the *Dhamma*" (*dhammaṭṭhitatā*). Cf. also Choong 1999: p.50.

85 M I 56: "mindfulness that 'there is a body' is established in him to the extent necessary for bare knowledge and continuous mindfulness." I take the prefix *paṭi* added to *sati* in the present context in its temporal nuance of "again" or "re-", in the sense of pointing to the absence of lapses in the presence of *sati*, viz. its continuity.

86 Ps I 250; cf. also Ariyadhamma 1995: p.5; Debes 1994: p.130; Dhammiko 1961: p.189; and Ṭhānissaro 1993: p.101.

as a mere phenomenon, free from any type of self-image or attachment.

The way this instruction is phrased suggests the use of mental labelling. Mindfulness is established that "there is body" (feelings, mind, *dhammas*). The Pāli particle *iti* used here indicates direct speech, which in the present context suggests a form of mental noting. This is in fact not the only instance of this kind of recommendation in the *Satipaṭṭhāna Sutta*. Most of the instructions in the discourse use direct speech to formulate what is to be known.[87]

This way of presentation shows that concepts, especially when used as labelling tools for the purpose of mental noting, can be skilfully employed within the context of *satipaṭṭhāna*.[88] Thus the practice of *satipaṭṭhāna* does not require a complete relinquishment of all forms of verbal knowledge.[89] In fact, concepts are intrinsically related to cognition (*saññā*), since the ability to recognize and understand relies on a subtle level of mental verbalization and thereby on the use of concepts. The skilful use of labelling during *satipaṭṭhāna* contemplation can help to strengthen clear recognition and understanding. At the same time, labelling introduces a healthy degree of inner detachment, since the act of apostrophizing one's moods and emotions diminishes one's identification with them.

According to the Buddha's survey of wrong views in the *Brahmajāla Sutta*, misinterpretations of reality can often be based on meditative experiences, not only on theoretical speculation.[90] To prevent such misinterpretations, a firm acquaintance with the *Dhamma* is an important factor for proper progress along the meditative path. In one instance, the Buddha compared such sound knowledge of the

---

87 e.g. M I 56: "he knows 'I breathe in long'"; M I 56: "he knows 'I am walking'"; M I 59: "he knows 'I feel a pleasant feeling'"; M I 59: "he knows a lustful mind to be 'lustful'"; M I 60: "he knows 'there is sensual desire in me'"; M I 61: "he knows 'there is the mindfulness awakening factor in me'"; M I 62: "he knows as it really is, 'this is *dukkha*'".

88 On labelling cf. Fryba 1989: pp.130–2; Mangalo 1988: p.34; and Ñāṇapoṇika 1986b: p.13.

89 Earle 1984: p.398; and Tilakaratne 1993: p.103. Epstein 1995: p.94, warns against simply "casting off ... mental activity and thinking" since "people with this misconception abandon the ego skills necessary for successful meditation". He explains (p 99) that "those with this misunderstanding ... tend to overvalue the idea of the 'empty mind' free of thoughts. In this case, thought itself is identified with ego, and such persons seem to be cultivating a kind of intellectual vacuity, in which the absence of critical thought is seen as an ultimate achievement." Ñāṇananda 1985: p.60, speaks of "rallying the concepts for the higher purpose of developing wisdom whereby concepts themselves are transcended".

90 D I 12–39, cf. in detail page 45, footnote 4 and page 181, footnote 34.

Dhamma to the armoury of swords and spears used to defend a fortress.[91] Clearly, for the Buddha the mere absence of concepts does not constitute the final goal of meditation practice.[92] Concepts are not the problem, the problem is how concepts are used. An *arahant* still employs concepts, yet without being bound by them.[93]

On the other hand, *satipaṭṭhāna* has to be clearly distinguished from mere intellectual reflection. What this part of the "refrain" indicates is the extent to which concepts and labels are appropriate within the context of insight meditation. This should be kept to an absolute minimum, only "to the extent necessary for bare knowledge and continuous mindfulness".[94] Labelling is not an end in itself, only a means to an end. Once knowledge and awareness are well established, labelling can be dispensed with.

The inability of a purely theoretical approach to result in awakening is a recurrent theme in the discourses.[95] To spend one's time intellectually considering the *Dhamma* and thereby neglecting actual practice clearly meets with the Buddha's disapproval. According to him, one who acts thus cannot be considered a practitioner of the *Dhamma*, but merely as someone caught up in thinking.[96]

---

91 At A IV 110, because endowed with knowledge of the *Dhamma* the disciple will be able to overcome what is unwholesome and develop what is wholesome. Th 1027 recommends knowledge of the discourses as the basis for living the holy life. Similarly, M I 294 lists knowledge of the discourses and related discussions as two of five factors required for right view to lead to realization. (The others are ethical conduct and the practice of *samatha* and *vipassanā*.)

92 In fact, even the fourth immaterial attainment (*nevasaññānāsaññāyatana*), a deep meditative experience as far removed from concepts as possible within the realm of mundane experience, still falls short of realization. Cf. Hamilton 1996: p.60.

93 According to It 53, *arahants*, because of their penetrative understanding of concepts and verbal expressions, are able to use them freely, without in any way falling prey to them. Cf. also Ñāṇananda 1986: p.103: "to believe that by merely demolishing concepts or theories one can rise above them is to stop at the fringe of the problem".

94 M I 56. Kalupahana 1992: p.74, explains that the concepts used for *satipaṭṭhāna* "are to be pursued only to the point where they produce knowledge (*ñāṇa-matta*), and not beyond, for ... conceptions carried beyond their limits can lead to substantialist metaphysics".

95 At S I 136 the Buddha described his realization as beyond the reach of mere theoretical inquiry. Cf. also Dhp 19; Dhp 20; Dhp 258; and Dhp 259; which emphasize that what really matters is the practice of the *Dhamma*. At A V 162, excessive emphasis on a theoretical understanding of the *Dhamma* even led some monks to mistakenly claim realization. Cf. also W.S. Karunaratne 1988a: p.83.

96 A III 87. The same description, however, comes up at A III 178 in a recommendation to reflect on the *Dhamma*, demonstrating that the Buddha did not categorically reject such theoretical inquiry, but that his criticism was directed against neglect of the practice.

Sati as such is mere awareness of phenomena, without letting the mind stray into thoughts and associations.[97] According to the *satipaṭṭhāna* "definition", *sati* operates in combination with clearly knowing (*sampajāna*). The same presence of knowledge also underlies the expression "he knows" (*pajānāti*), which occurs frequently in the individual *satipaṭṭhāna* contemplations. Thus to "know", or to contemplate "clearly knowing", can be taken to represent the conceptual input needed for taking clear cognizance of the observed phenomena, based on mindful observation.[98]

This (re-)cognizing aspect inherent in the quality of clearly knowing or in the expression "he knows" can be further developed and strengthened through the practice of mental noting. It is this "knowing" quality of the mind that brings about understanding. Thus, while *satipaṭṭhāna* meditation takes place in a silently watchful state of mind, free from intellectualization, it can nevertheless make appropriate use of concepts to the extent needed to further knowledge and awareness.

The fact that contemplation undertaken in this manner has the sole purpose of enhancing mindfulness and understanding points to an important shift away from goal-oriented practice. At this comparatively advanced stage, *satipaṭṭhāna* is practised for its own sake. With this shift in attitude, the goal and the act of meditation begin to merge into one, since awareness and understanding are cultivated for the sake of developing ever more awareness and understanding. The practice of *satipaṭṭhāna* becomes an "effortless effort", so to speak, divested of goal-orientation and expectation.

It is precisely this way of contemplating that in turn enables one to proceed independently, "without clinging to anything in the world" of experience, as stipulated in the final part of the "refrain".[99] In several discourses, the stipulation "to abide independently" occurs immediately before realization takes place.[100] This suggests that with this part of the "refrain", *satipaṭṭhāna* contemplation gradually

97 Cf. Chapter III.

98 This suggestion is supported to some extent by the commentary, Ps I 250, which relates this part of the "refrain" to mindfulness and clearly knowing.

99 M I 56: "he abides independent, not clinging to anything in the world."

100 D II 68; M I 251; M III 244; S II 82; S IV 23; S IV 24; S IV 65; S IV 67; S IV 168; and A IV 88. Similarly M III 266 relates the absence of dependencies to overcoming *dukkha*. Cf. also A V 325, which points out that an advanced meditator can meditate without "depending" on the material or the immaterial elements, or on any aspect of perceptual experience, a description which Spk V 79 relates to the experience of *Nibbāna*.

builds up to the constellation of mental qualities required for the event of awakening. According to the commentaries, "to abide independently" refers to the absence of dependency through craving and speculative views, while to avoid "clinging to anything in the world" stands for not identifying with any of the five aggregates.[101]

By letting go of all dependencies and cravings during this advanced level of practice, a deepening realization of the empty nature of all phenomena dawns on the meditator. With this state of independence and equipoise, characterized by the absence of any sense of "I" or "mine", the direct path of *satipaṭṭhāna* gradually approaches its culmination. It is in this balanced state of mind, free from "I"-making or "my"-making, that the realization of *Nibbāna* can take place.

---

101 Ps I 250.

VI

THE BODY

VI.1 THE BODY CONTEMPLATIONS

Starting with this chapter, I will consider the actual meditation practices described in the *Satipaṭṭhāna Sutta*. The practices listed under the first *satipaṭṭhāna*, contemplation of the body, comprise awareness of breathing, awareness of bodily postures, clear knowledge in regard to bodily activities, analysis of the body into its anatomical parts, analysis of the body into its elementary qualities, and contemplation of a dead body in nine consecutive stages of decay. I will examine each of these meditation practices in turn, after an introductory assessment of body contemplation in general.

The sequence of the body contemplations is progressive, beginning with the more obvious and basic aspects of the body and continuing towards a more detailed and analytical understanding of the nature of the body. This pattern becomes all the more evident if one transposes mindfulness of breathing from the first position to the third, after awareness of postures and clear knowledge in regard to bodily activities, a position it assumes in the Chinese *Madhyama Āgama* and in two other versions of *satipaṭṭhāna* (cf. Fig. 6.1 below).[1] Through this shift in position, awareness of the body's postures and

1 For the *Madhyama Āgama* version cf. Minh Chau 1991: p.88; and Nhat Hanh 1990: p.138. The other versions are (according to Schmithausen 1976: p.250) the *Pañcaviṃśatisāhasrikā Prajñāpāramitā* and the *Śāriputrābhidharma*. In contrast, the two *Satipaṭṭhāna Suttas* (D II 291 and M I 56) and the *Kāyagatāsati Sutta* (M III 89) place mindfulness of breathing at the outset of the body contemplations.

clear knowledge of activities would precede mindfulness of breathing, rather than following it as they do in the Pāli versions.

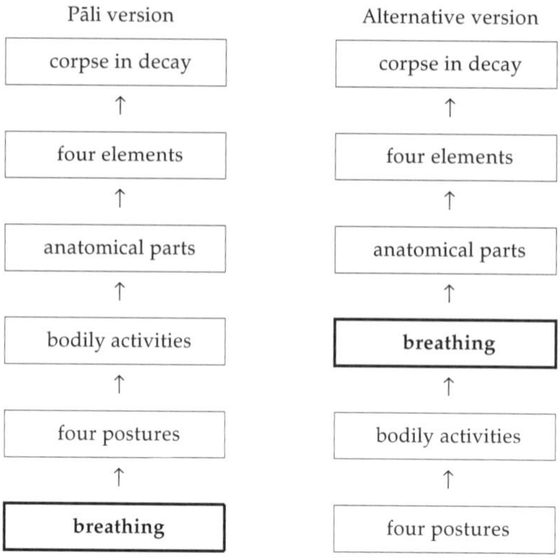

Fig. 6.1 The body contemplations

Awareness of the four postures and clear knowledge of activities can be characterized as simpler and more rudimentary forms of contemplation than the other body contemplations. Taking into consideration their more elementary character, it seems reasonable to place them at the beginning of a cultivation of *satipaṭṭhāna*, as convenient ways to build up a foundation in *sati*. This, however, does not imply that in actual practice mindfulness of breathing need always be preceded by awareness of postures and clear knowledge of activities, since mindfulness of the breath can also be followed by mindfulness of one's postures and activities.

Awareness of postures and clear knowledge of activities are predominantly concerned with the body in action. In comparison, the remaining exercises examine the body in a more static manner, analysing it into its constituent components from anatomical, material, and temporal perspectives (by focusing on its disintegration after death). In this context, mindfulness of breathing has a transitional role, since although it is traditionally carried out in the stable sitting posture, it is still concerned with an active aspect of the body, namely the process of breathing. When it is shifted to the third position, mindfulness of breathing becomes the first in a series of practices conducted mainly in the sitting posture. In fact, the proper sitting posture is described in detail only in the instructions for mindfulness of breathing. Since awareness of the four postures and clear knowledge in regard to bodily activities are forms of contemplation that take place in different postures, it makes sense to introduce the sitting posture only when it becomes relevant. This is the case for mindfulness of breathing and the remaining exercises, whose comparative subtlety requires a fairly stable posture, thereby facilitating the development of deeper degrees of concentration. By shifting mindfulness of breathing to the third position, the description of the sitting posture also moves to the most convenient position within the body contemplations.

The body contemplations begin with an emphasis on "knowing" (*pajānāti, sampajānakāri*) in the two exercises concerned with bodily postures and activities and in the first two steps of mindfulness of breathing. Subsequent exercises introduce slightly different methods of contemplation. The third and fourth steps of mindfulness of breathing are concerned with "training" (*sikkhati*), the two bodily analyses with "considering" (*paccavekkhati*),[2] and the contemplation of a corpse in decay with "comparing" (*upasaṃharati*). This change in the choice of verbs underscores a progression from comparatively simple acts of observation to more sophisticated forms of analysis. Here again mindfulness of breathing assumes a transitional role, with its first steps partaking of the character of the two contemplations of postures and of activities, while its third and fourth steps can be grouped together with the other three contemplations.

Except for awareness of the four postures and clear knowledge in regard to activities, each of the other body contemplations is illustrated by a simile. These similes compare mindfulness of breathing to a turner at his lathe, contemplation of the anatomical parts to examining a bag full of grains, and contemplation of the four elements to butchering a cow. The last exercise employs mental images of a body in various stages of decay. Although these stages of decay cannot be reckoned as similes, the use of mental imagery here parallels the similes given in the other three exercises. These similes and mental images point to an additional degree of affinity between mindfulness of breathing and the final three body contemplations, and

2 Ps-pṭ I 365 explains "considering" to refer to repeated analytical observation.

thereby further support the idea of presenting them together by shifting mindfulness of breathing to the third position in the sequence of the body contemplations.

The instruction for contemplating the anatomical parts employs the word "impure" (*asuci*), which betrays a certain degree of evaluation inherent in this type of practice.[3] In a passage from the *Aṅguttara Nikāya*, contemplation of the anatomical parts and of a corpse in decay come under the "recollection" (*anussati*) category.[4] This evokes *sati*'s connotations of memory and shows that these two contemplations imply to some extent a form of practice which is not confined to bare awareness only.

The breadth of "body contemplation" as a *satipaṭṭhāna* becomes even more extensive in the Chinese version found in the *Madhyama Āgama*, which adds several meditations to those described in the Pāli discourses. Surprisingly, at least at first sight, the *Madhyama Āgama* counts the development of the four absorptions as body contemplations.[5] However, the positioning of the four absorptions under body contemplation has a parallel in the *Kāyagatāsati Sutta* of the Pāli canon, which also directs awareness to the effect these absorptions have on the physical body.[6] Thus it is not too far-fetched to take the physical bliss experienced during absorption as an object of contemplation of the body. Nevertheless, several of the additional contemplations in the *Madhyama Āgama* do not fit well into "body contemplation", but seem rather to be the outcome of a progressive assimilation of other practices under this heading.[7]

---

3 M I 57: "he reviews this same body ... as full of many kinds of impurity."

4 A III 323.

5 Minh Chau 1991: p.89; and Nhat Hanh 1990: p.154. These are the sixth, seventh, eighth, and ninth of the body contemplations in this version, which describe the physical effect of each of the four *jhānas* with the help of the same set of similes found in the Pāli discourses (kneading soap powder into a lump, a lake fed by water from within, lotuses submerged in water, and a man dressed all in white).

6 M III 92.

7 e.g. various ways of dealing with unwholesome thoughts are listed as the third and the fourth of the body contemplations in this version. (Pāli parallels to these exercises are the first and the last of the antidotes to unwholesome thoughts mentioned at M I 120.) Or else the tenth and the eleventh of the body contemplations in this version are concerned with developing a "brilliant perception" and with "well remembering the contemplated image". These could correspond to clarity of cognition (*āloka-saññā*) and to the sign of concentration (*samādhi-nimitta*) found elsewhere in the Pāli discourses. Cf. Minh Chau 1991: pp.88–90; and Nhat Hanh 1990: pp.153–6.

The Chinese *Ekottara Āgama* version, on the other hand, contains only four body contemplations in total: awareness of the anatomical parts, of the four elements, of a rotting corpse, and a contemplation of the various bodily orifices together with the impure liquids discharged by them.[8] An even more abridged version can be found in the Pāli *Vibhaṅga*, which lists only contemplation of the anatomical constitution under this *satipaṭṭhāna*.[9] The reasons for these "omissions" are open to conjecture, but what remains as the unanimously accepted core of the contemplation of the body in all the different versions is a thorough investigation of its anatomical constitution. This gives a considerable degree of emphasis to this exercise,[10] even though it does involve some degree of evaluation and therefore seems different from the typical *satipaṭṭhāna* approach to contemplation.

VI.2 PURPOSE AND BENEFITS OF CONTEMPLATION OF THE BODY

Although contemplating the nature of the body highlights its less attractive features, the purpose of this exercise is not to demonize the body. While it is certainly true that at times the discourses describe the human body in rather negative terms,[11] some of these instances occur in a particular context in which the point being made is that the speakers in question have overcome all attachment to their

---

8 Nhat Than 1990: p.169.

9 Vibh 193. The commentary Vibh-a 252 further expands this to some extent by relating the anatomical parts to the four elements. Bronkhorst 1985: p.311, on the basis of this passage from the *Vibhaṅga* suggests that possibly the analysis into anatomical parts constitutes the most ancient and original approach to contemplating the body. Cf. also Lin Li-Kouang 1949: pp.122–7, who takes the entire *Satipaṭṭhāna Sutta* to be an elaboration of the more original *Kāyagatāsati Sutta*. A similar suggestion can be found in Schmidt 1989: p.41 n.3.

10 This emphasis can also be found in the fact that *kāyagatāsati* (mindfulness of the body), a word which in *sutta* usage is synonymous with *kāyānupassanā* (contemplation of the body), came to connote only the contemplation of the anatomical parts in the commentaries; cf. also Bodhi 2000: p.1453 n.366; and Upali Karunaratne 1999a: p.168. This shift in meaning underlines the importance of contemplating the anatomical parts as 'the' body contemplation.

11 Cf. e.g. M I 500; M I 510; S I 131; A IV 377; A IV 386; Sn 197–9; Sn 205; Th 279; Th 453; Th 567–9; Th 1150–3; Thī 19; Thī 82–3; Thī 140; and Thī 466–71. These passages indicate that a somewhat negative attitude towards the body is not only a product of the commentarial writings (as suggested by Hamilton 1995b: p.61). Conversely, however, Heiler 1922: p.18, who speaks of a "vehement loathing of the body" (my translation of "ungestümer Ekel an allem Leiblichen") as the aim of body contemplation, goes too far.

body.[12] In contrast, the *Kāyagatāsati Sutta* takes the physical bliss of absorption attainment as an object for body contemplation. This passage clearly demonstrates that contemplation of the body is not necessarily linked to repugnance and loathing.

The purpose of contemplating the nature of the body is to bring its unattractive aspects to the forefront of one's attention, thereby placing the attractive aspects previously emphasized in a more balanced context. The aim is a balanced and detached attitude towards the body. With such a balanced attitude, one sees the body merely as a product of conditions, a product with which one need not identify.[13]

The discourses illustrate the practice and benefits of contemplating the body with a variety of similes. One of these similes depicts a man carrying a bowl brimming with oil on his head through a crowd watching a beautiful girl singing and dancing.[14] He is followed by another man with a drawn sword, ready to cut off his head if even one drop of oil is spilled. To preserve his life, the man carrying the oil has to apply his full attention to each step and movement, without allowing the commotion around the girl to distract him.

The careful behaviour of the man carrying the oil exemplifies the circumspect behaviour of a practitioner well established in present moment awareness of the body. The image of carrying an object on the head in particular points to the balance and centredness that accompany bodily activities carried out with *sati*. Another important aspect of this simile is that it relates sustained awareness of the body's activities to sense-restraint. In this way it vividly illustrates the importance of developing awareness grounded in the body, since in the situation depicted in this simile restraint of the senses through being grounded in the body constitutes the means to preserve one's life in the midst of commotion and danger.

12 e.g. Vijayā at S I 131; Sāriputta at A IV 377; and Khemā at Thī 140; each stating that they feel ashamed and disgusted by their own body. However, this particular expression arose owing to the circumstances of each case, since Sāriputta was defending himself against the accusation of having physically shown lack of respect to another monk (cf. Mp IV 171), while the nuns Vijayā and Khemā were trying to discourage someone who was attempting to seduce them. In fact, the same expression occurs again at Vin III 68 and S V 320, where a number of monks engaged in contemplating the unattractive nature of the body with such fervour that they committed suicide, which is certainly not the appropriate way of carrying out this practice.

13 At S II 64 the Buddha pointed out that the body is neither one's own nor does it belong to another, but is simply the product of conditions.

14 S V 170.

Sense-restraint comes up again in another simile, which compares mindfulness of the body to a strong post to which six different wild animals are bound.[15] Since the animals are firmly bound to the post, however much they might struggle to escape, they have sooner or later to sit or lie down next to the post. Similarly, mindfulness of the body can become a strong post for tethering the six senses.

This simile compares the mental agitation of searching for sensual gratification to wild animals struggling to go into different directions. Once the post of body mindfulness is firmly established, however, the senses will invariably have to calm down, just as the animals will come to lie down next to the post to which they are bound. This simile points to the benefit of being anchored or grounded in the experience of the present moment through mindfulness of the body.[16] Lacking such grounding in body awareness, attachment and clinging can easily arise.[17]

A similar connotation underlies a set of similes in the *Kāyagatāsati Sutta*, which present mindfulness of the body as a crucial factor for withstanding Māra, the personification of mental defilements.[18] Just as a heavy stone ball can penetrate a mound of wet clay, or just as fire can be produced from dry wood, or just as an empty jug can be filled with water, so too will Māra find an opportunity to overpower those who are not well established in mindfulness of the body. But just as a light ball of string cannot penetrate a door panel made of heartwood, or just as fire cannot be produced from wet wood, or just as a full jug cannot take more water, so too will Māra be unable to overpower those who develop und cultivate mindfulness of the body.

The *Kāyagatāsati Sutta* contains the same sequence of body contemplations as the *Satipaṭṭhāna Sutta*. There is, however, a notable difference in the *Kāyagatāsati Sutta*'s version of the "refrain", which relates body contemplation to the overcoming of worldly thoughts and the development of concentration.[19] This points to another

---

15 S IV 198.

16 Fryba 1989: p.111, fittingly speaks of "strategies of reality anchoring". Tart 1994: p.44, explains: "instead of every thought carrying you away, you have an anchor in the here and now through your body". Cf. also Nett 13, which points out that mindfulness of the body protects against sensory distraction.

17 According to M I 266, neglecting mindfulness of the body leads to delighting in feelings and therewith to attachment.

18 M III 95.

19 M III 89.

important benefit of body contemplation: overcoming sensual infatuation through a proper assessment of the nature of the body. Such waning of sensual infatuation facilitates the development of concentration unhindered by sensual distractions. The *Kāyagatāsati Sutta* illustrates this with another set of similes: just as drinking water will flow out if a jug is tipped over, or just as water in a pond will flow out if the embankment is broken, or just as a skilled driver is able to drive a chariot wherever he likes, so too mindfulness of the body will lead easily to the development of deep concentration.[20]

Thus contemplation of the body can become a basis for the development of *samatha*, or it can lead to an application of *sati* to feelings and mental phenomena, as described in the *Satipaṭṭhāna Sutta*.[21] The fact that a firm grounding of awareness in the body provides an important basis for the development of both calm and insight may be why, of the four *satipaṭṭhānas*, body contemplation has received the most extensive and detailed treatment in the discourses and commentaries.[22] This emphasis on the body contemplations continues today in the *vipassanā* schools of the Theravāda tradition, where mindfulness of the body occupies a central position as a foundational *satipaṭṭhāna* practice.

The discourses repeatedly emphasize the great value of mindfulness of the body.[23] According to them, those who do not practise mindfulness of the body do not "partake of the deathless".[24] Mindfulness of the body is a source of joy,[25] and can truly be considered one's best friend.[26] A verse from the *Theragāthā* even reports a monk

20 M III 96.

21 The importance of a foundation in body contemplation for the practice of *samatha* or *vipassanā* is stressed by Ledi 1983: p.38, who compares attempts to practise either without a previous grounding in awareness of the body to driving an ox-cart yoked to an untamed bullock without a nose-rope. The importance of the body contemplations for the development of *samatha* is also reflected at Ps I 301, which points out that mindfulness of breathing, of the anatomical parts, and of the bodily decomposition after death are *satipaṭṭhāna* contemplations particularly suitable for the development of concentration.

22 e.g. in the *Majjhima Nikāya* aspects of body contemplation are separately expounded as independent discourses (*Ānāpānasati Sutta*, M III 78; *Kāyagatāsati Sutta*, M III 88). Similarly the *satipaṭṭhāna* commentaries devote as much space to the body contemplations as to the remaining three *satipaṭṭhānas*: Ps I 247–74 against Ps I 274–301 (each 27 pages).

23 e.g. at M III 94–9; A I 43; and Dhp 293.

24 A I 45.

25 A I 43. Cf. also D III 272 and S II 220.

reflecting that if he were granted only one wish, it would be that the whole world might enjoy unbroken mindfulness of the body.[27]

Although meditation practices for contemplating the body appear to have had ancient origins and were already known in ascetic and contemplative circles contemporary with the Buddha,[28] the commentaries point out that his analytical and comprehensive approach was a distinctively new feature.[29]

VI.3 MINDFULNESS OF BREATHING

In ancient times, and still today, mindfulness of breathing might well be the most widely used method of body contemplation. The Buddha himself frequently engaged in mindfulness of breathing,[30] which he called a "noble" and "divine" way of practice.[31] According to his own statement, even his awakening took place based on mindfulness of breathing.[32]

The discourses present mindfulness of breathing in a variety of ways. The *Satipaṭṭhāna Sutta* describes four steps of the practice, to which the *Ānāpānasati Sutta* adds another twelve, thereby forming a scheme of altogether sixteen steps. Elsewhere the discourses speak of mindfulness of breathing as a cognition (*saññā*), and as a concentration practice.[33] These various presentations demonstrate the multi-functional character of the process of breathing as a meditation object. This much is also documented in the range of its possible benefits, which include both penetrative insight and deep concentration.[34]

---

26 Th 1035. (This statement was made by Ānanda after the passing away of the Buddha.)

27 Th 468.

28 Lin Li-Kouang 1949: p.124; and Schmithausen 1976: p.254. The impression that contemplation of the body was known in ancient India is also to some extent supported by the introductory part to the *Kāyagatāsati Sutta*, M III 88, where the monks spoke in praise of the Buddha's way of presenting body contemplation in such a manner that it would have manifold benefits. If the act of contemplating the body were in itself an innovation, it would most likely have merited their explicit praise.

29 Ps I 247 and Ps-pṭ I 348 maintain that other dispensations do not teach body contemplation as completely as the Buddha.

30 S V 326.

31 S V 326.

32 S V 317.

33 As a four-step *satipaṭṭhāna* in the *(Mahā-)Satipaṭṭhāna Suttas* at D II 291 and M I 59; as a sixteen-step practice in the *Ānāpānasati Sutta* at M III 79; as a *saññā* e.g. at A V 111; and as *ānāpānasatisamādhi* in the *Ānāpāna Saṃyutta* (e.g. at S V 317); cf. Vajirañāṇa 1975: p.227.

As a meditation practice, mindfulness of breathing has a peaceful character and leads to stability of both posture and mind.[35] The mental stability brought about through mindfulness of breathing acts in particular as an antidote to distraction and discursive thought.[36] Awareness of the breath can also become a stabilizing factor at the time of death, ensuring that even one's last breath will be a mindful one.[37]

According to the *Satipaṭṭhāna Sutta*, the practice of mindfulness of breathing should be undertaken in the following way:

> **Here, gone to the forest, or to the root of a tree, or to an empty hut, he sits down; having folded his legs crosswise, set his body erect, and established mindfulness in front of him, mindful he breathes in, mindful he breathes out.**
>
> **Breathing in long, he knows "I breathe in long," breathing out long, he knows "I breathe out long." Breathing in short, he knows "I breathe in short", breathing out short, he knows "I breathe out short." He trains thus: "I shall breathe in experiencing the whole body," he trains thus: "I shall breathe out experiencing the whole body." He trains thus: "I shall breathe in calming the bodily formation," he trains thus: "I shall breathe out calming the bodily formation".**[38]

The instructions for mindfulness of breathing include the appropriate external environment and the suitable physical posture. The three kinds of places recommended for practice are a forest, the root of a tree, and an empty hut. In the discourses, these three usually indicate suitable conditions for the practice of formal meditation,[39] representing the appropriate degree of seclusion required for mindfulness of breathing (or other meditation practices).[40] According to modern meditation teachers, however, mindfulness of breathing

---

34 S V 317–19 list the overcoming of worldly intentions, of aversion and attraction, attaining the four *jhānas* and immaterial attainments, and realization as potential benefits of mindfulness of breathing.

35 S V 321 and S V 316.

36 A III 449; Ud 37; and It 80. The *Abhidharmakośabhāṣyam* explains that mindfulness of breathing is particularly suitable for countering discursive thought because the breath is a bland meditation object, devoid of colour or outer form, and therefore does not in itself stimulate the imaginative tendency of the mind (in Pruden 1988: p.917).

37 M I 426.

38 M I 56.

can be developed in any situation, even while, for example, standing in a queue or sitting in a waiting-room.[41]

As well as describing the external environment, the *Satipaṭṭhāna Sutta* also specifies the proper sitting posture: the back should be kept straight and the legs crossed.[42] In the discourses, this description of the appropriate posture for meditation occurs not only in relation to mindfulness of breathing, but also in the context of several other meditation practices.[43] Although this does not imply that meditation should be confined to the sitting posture only, these occurrences nevertheless clearly underline the importance of formal sitting for cultivating the mind.

---

39 From these three, the root of a tree stands in a particularly close relation to the practice of meditation; so much so that at M II 118 the mere sight of secluded trees led a king to associate them with the practice of meditation and thereby reminded him of the Buddha. Similarly, the space occupied by the root of a tree can act as a standard for measuring the area a meditator is able to pervade or suffuse with his or her practice (cf. M III 146). The root of a tree as a dwelling place constitutes also one of the four basic monastic requisites of a Buddhist monk or nun (together with almsfood, cast-off cloth for robes, and cow urine as medicine) and thus conveys nuances of contentment with the most minimal necessities of life. The "forest" and the "root of a tree" form part of the standard expression for introducing formal meditation (e.g. at D I 71). The "root of a tree" and the "empty hut" come up in the Buddha's emphatic exhortation to meditate (e.g. at M I 46). In addition to forming part of the introduction to mindfulness of breathing, the same three types of place occur in relation to various other meditation practices: at M I 297 in relation to reflection on emptiness; at M I 323 in relation to overcoming the hindrances; at M I 333 in relation to the attainment of cessation; at M I 335 in relation to the divine abodes; at M I 336 in relation to unattractiveness of the body, awareness of repulsiveness in food, disenchantment with the whole world, and contemplation of impermanence; and at A V 109 in relation to the aggregates, to the sense-spheres, to various bodily illnesses, and to recollection of *Nibbāna*.

40 Cf. Ps I 247. Ps I 248 stresses that it is not easy to develop mindfulness of breathing in the presence of noise and distractions. Similarly Vibh 244 speaks of a forest and the root of a tree as solitary and silent places and therefore appropriate for retirement into meditative seclusion.

41 Gunaratana 1981: p.10; and Khantipālo 1986: p.11.

42 The expression "having folded his legs crosswise" is not further explained in the discourses. The commentaries take it as representing the lotus posture (e.g. Sv I 209), but in view of modern practical experience it seems reasonable to include any cross-legged sitting posture in which the back is kept straight and which can be maintained for a reasonably long time without causing pain.

43 The description of the sitting posture occurs in relation to overcoming the hindrances and developing absorption as part of the standard expositions of the gradual path, e.g. at D I 71; in the context of practising the divine abodes (*brahmavihāras*) at D III 49 and A I 183; in relation to contemplation of the five aggregates at M I 421; in the context of recollecting realization or levels of insight gained at A I 184; Ud 46; Ud 60; and Ud 77; in relation to mindfulness of the body at Ud 27 and Ud 77; and in the context of meditation in general at Ud 43.

Once the posture is set up, mindfulness is to be established "in front". The injunction "in front" (*parimukhaṃ*) can be understood literally or figuratively.[44] Following the more literal understanding, "in front" indicates the nostril area as the most appropriate for attention to the in- and out-breaths. Alternatively, "in front" understood more figuratively suggests a firm establishment of *sati*, *sati* being mentally "in front" in the sense of meditative composure and attentiveness.[45]

Both the *Abhidhamma* and the commentaries take "in front" (*parimukhaṃ*) to indicate a precise anatomical location.[46] In the discourses, however, the specification "in front" occurs in a variety of contexts, such as, for example, in relation to overcoming the hindrances or to developing the divine abodes (*brahmavihāra*).[47]

---

44 This ambiguity arises because *mukha* can assume a variety of meanings, among them "mouth" and "face", and also "front" and "top", cf. T.W. Rhys Davids 1993: pp.533–4.

45 Paṭis I 176 explains *sati* qualified as *parimukhaṃ* to mean that it "provides" a "way out" (of forgetfulness). Fessel 1999: p.79, suggests understanding the term in contrast to the Sanskrit *bahir mukha* (averting one's face), *parimukhaṃ* then implying presence of mind directed to the immediate environment. T.W. Rhys Davids (1993) has: "to surround oneself with watchfulness of mind" (p 672), and "to set one's mindfulness alert" (p 431). The corresponding passage from the Chinese *Āgamas* reads: "with thoughts well controlled, not going astray" (in Minh Chau 1991: p.99). In fact, in several discourses the expression "mindfulness established in front" was used by people who were apparently quite unfamiliar with meditation in order to describe the Buddha seated in meditation (a Brahmin searching for his ox at S I 170, a woodworker at S I 179, and some Brahmin students at S I 180). It is difficult to imagine that these people should have been able to know, from merely seeing the Buddha seated, that he was directing awareness to his nostrils. The more probable explanation for these instances is that "mindfulness established in front" was used by them just to express the visible fact that the Buddha was sitting in meditative composure.

46 Vibh 252 explains it to refer to the nose tip or the upper lip; same at Paṭis I 171; and in Ehara 1995: p.157. Vism 283 further explains that the nose tip is the appropriate point of observation for meditators with a longer nose, while the upper lip fulfils the same function for those who have a shorter nose.

47 D III 49; M I 274; and A IV 437 relate mindfulness established "in front" to overcoming the hindrances; A I 183 to the divine abodes. Other occurrences of the expression "establishing mindfulness in front" occur in the context of forming the determination not to change one's posture until realization is gained (at M I 219), in relation to developing a mind set on the welfare of both oneself and others (at M II 139), when directing the mind to the reflective understanding that the defilements have been eradicated from one's mind (at A I 184), or as part of the description of a monk well versed in meditation (at A III 320). It may also be worth while to point out that the qualification "in front" appears to be more than simply part of a stereotype formula, since in several passages in the *Udāna* it is missing from otherwise identical descriptions of meditators sitting down cross-legged (Ud 21; Ud 42; Ud 43; Ud 46; Ud 60; Ud 71; and Ud 77).

Although overcoming the hindrances can occur with the aid of mindfulness of breathing, this is not necessarily the case. In fact, the standard instructions for overcoming the hindrances do not mention the breath.[48] Similarly, the discourses do not relate the development of the divine abodes in any way to awareness of the breath.[49] Apart from awareness of the breath, however, to direct mindfulness to the nostril area makes little sense, whether in relation to overcoming the hindrances or to developing the divine abodes. Thus, at least in these contexts, the figurative sense of "in front" as a firm establishment of *sati* is the more meaningful alternative.

Therefore, although to understand "in front" to indicate the nostril area makes sense in relation to mindfulness of breathing, alternative ways of practice, based on a more figurative understanding of the term, cannot be categorically excluded. In fact, several modern teachers have developed successful approaches to mindfulness of breathing independent of the nostril area. Some, for example, advise their pupils to experience the breath in the chest area, others suggest observing the air element at the abdomen, while still others recommend directing awareness to the act of breathing itself, without focusing on any specific location.[50]

---

48 According to the standard expositions (e.g. D III 49; M I 274; M III 3; or S V 105) the antidotes for each respective hindrance are: attending to the unattractiveness of the body, loving kindness, clarity of cognition, mental calm, and being unperplexed about wholesome states. Particularly interesting in this context is M I 421, where Rāhula sat down to establish mindfulness "in front" in order to contemplate the aggregates, but was only at a later point given instructions in mindfulness of breathing. This suggests that he had not previously received instructions in mindfulness of breathing, so it is not very probable that he was directing awareness to his nostrils during the contemplation of the aggregates that he had been taught previously.

49 The instructions describe a form of radiation (e.g. at M II 207) that does not seem to be in any way related to mindfulness of breathing.

50 Dhammadharo 1987: p.16, and Maha Boowa 1983: pp.14–16, instruct one to fix attention at the nose at first, but to shift to the chest or solar plexus area later on. Kamalashila 1994: p.168, proposes to counter slackness of energy by observing the breath higher up in the body (e.g. the nose), while in case of excess energy one can calm down by using a spot lower down (e.g. the abdomen). Brahmavaṃso 1999: p.17, suggests not locating the breath anywhere physically. On the other hand, Kassapa 1966: p.242, sharply criticizes the Mahasi tradition for observing the movement of the breath at the abdomen. However, in order to avoid contradiction with the commentarial explanation, the Mahasi tradition has always taken care to present their main meditation practice as a contemplation of the air element (as one of the elements mentioned in the instructions for meditating on the four elements), not as a form of mindfulness of breathing.

Having described the appropriate environment and posture, the *Satipaṭṭhāna Sutta* instructs the meditator to breathe in and out mindfully.[51] Next, the meditator should become aware of the length of each breath as "long" or "short". The point here is to be aware of long and short breaths, not consciously to control the length of the breath. Nevertheless, the progression from knowing longer breaths to knowing shorter breaths reflects the fact that the breath naturally becomes shorter and finer with continued contemplation, owing to increasing mental and physical calmness.[52]

The discourse compares this progress to a skilled turner who attends to his lathe with full awareness of making a long turn or a short turn.[53] The simile of the turner suggests increasing degrees of refinement and subtlety in practising mindfulness of breathing.[54] Just as a turner makes progressively finer and more delicate cuts on the lathe, contemplation proceeds from long and comparatively gross breaths to shorter and subtler breaths. The *Paṭisambhidāmagga* compares this progressive refinement of mindfulness of breathing to the progressively fainter sound of a gong after it has been struck.[55]

The third and fourth steps introduce a different verb to describe the process of contemplation: in place of "he knows" (*pajānāti*), the text now uses the expression "he trains" (*sikkhati*).[56] In the *Ānāpānasati Sutta*, this "training" covers altogether fourteen steps, in addition to the first two steps concerned with "knowing". The use of the word "training" indicates some degree of additional effort on the part of the meditator, owing to an increased degree of difficulty in these steps.[57] Such training seems to entail a shift to a broader kind

---

51 According to Chit Tin 1989: p.44, this instruction refers in particular to clearly distinguishing between the in-breath and the out-breath.

52 The relation of shorter breaths to the development of some degree of concentration is noted by Dhammadharo 1996: p.19; Dhīravaṃsa 1989: p.46; Goenka 1999: p.29; and Khantipālo 1981: p.30.

53 D II 291 and M I 56.

54 Ariyadhamma 1995: p.3, moreover explains the simile of the turner to indicate fixity of attention.

55 Paṭis I 185 in commenting on the third step of mindfulness of breathing.

56 According to Buddhadāsa 1976: p.63, the first two steps are preliminaries, and the real practice starts with this "training".

57 In fact at S V 326, which documents the Buddha's own practice of mindfulness of breathing, all occurrences of "he trains" are replaced by "I know". This indicates that, unlike the ordinary practitioner who has to make an effort in order to proceed through the sixteen steps, the Buddha, with his meditative expertise, was able to do so effortlessly.

of awareness, which also includes phenomena other than the breath itself.

In the scheme described in the *Ānāpānasati Sutta*, awareness moves through sixteen steps, which proceed from the bodily phenomena of breathing to feelings, mental events, and the development of insight. Considering the range of these sixteen steps it becomes evident that mindfulness of breathing is not limited to changes in the process of breathing, but covers related aspects of subjective experience. Undertaken in this way, mindfulness of breathing becomes a skilful tool for self-observation.[58]

The third and fourth steps of mindfulness of breathing, alike in both the *Ānāpānasati Sutta* and the *Satipaṭṭhāna Sutta*, are concerned with experiencing the "whole body" (*sabbakāya*) and with calming the "bodily formation" (*kāyasaṅkhāra*). In the present context, the "whole body" can be taken literally to refer to the whole physical body. Understood in this way, the instruction points to a broadening of awareness, a shift from the breath alone to its effect on the entire body.[59] According to the commentaries, however, the "whole body" should be understood to refer, more figuratively, to the "body" of the breath. By understanding the "whole body" as the whole breath-body the instruction then indicates full awareness of the beginning, middle, and end stages of each breath.[60] This interpretation can claim support from the same *Ānāpānasati Sutta*, since the Buddha here identified the breath as a "body" (*kāya*) among bodies.[61] An argument against this interpretation, however, could be that the cultivation of full awareness of the length of the breath was the task of the previous two steps, knowing a long or a short breath, which already required the meditator to be aware of each breath

---

58 Cf. also Kor 1993: p.35; van Zeyst 1981: p.94; and Vimalo 1987: p.158. Shapiro 1984: p.588, suggests that from a psychological perspective awareness of the breath teaches one to be self conscious. Observation of the breath is indeed an appropriate vehicle for such self-observation, because emotional changes are reflected in the breath, such as when one yawns out of boredom, sighs in grief, or snorts in anger. Moreover, since breathing is a process that can take place either involuntarily or deliberately, it stands in a distinctive conditional position in regard to body and mind, and therefore offers a convenient opportunity to contemplate the conditional interrelationship between physical and mental phenomena. Cf. also Govinda 1991: pp.27 and 110.

59 Buddhadāsa 1989: p.38; Debes 1994: p.105; Goenka 1999: p.29; Kor 1993: p.38; and Solé-Leris 1992: p.80.

60 Vism 273.

61 At M III 83.

from beginning to end.[62] One would therefore expect this next step in the progression to introduce a distinctly new feature for contemplation, such as, for example, a shift of awareness to include the whole physical body.

The next step of training is the calming of the "bodily formation" (*kāyasaṅkhāra*). Elsewhere the discourses define the "bodily formation" as in-breathing and out-breathing.[63] This dovetails with the second interpretation above, according to which "whole body" refers to the whole length of the breath.[64] The *Paṭisambhidāmagga* and the *Vimuttimagga* indicate that this fourth step of mindfulness of breathing also refers to maintenance of a calm and stable posture, in the sense of calming any inclination to move.[65] Thus the instruction to calm the bodily formations also implies an increase in general bodily calmness, an understanding that fits with the first interpretation mentioned above, taking "body" to refer to the anatomical body. In the end, both interpretations overlap, since a calming of the breath naturally leads to increased bodily tranquillity and vice versa.[66]

Such calming of breath and body can then either become the basis for developing awareness of the inner constitution of the body, as in the subsequent *satipaṭṭhāna* exercises, or else lead to an awareness of feelings and mental processes, as in the sixteen steps.[67] In both cases this constitutes a natural progression in which the establishment of a basis in bodily calmness enables awareness to proceed to subtler

62 Nhat Hanh 1990: p.42.

63 At M I 301 and S IV 293 (cf. also Ñāṇamoli 1982a: p.6 n.1).

64 The calming of the bodily formation (in the sense of in- and out-breathing) reaches its culmination with the attainment of the fourth absorption (cf. D III 270 and A V 31), because during this attainment the breath completely ceases (cf. S IV 217). Pa Auk 1995: p.15, explains: "with the attainment of the fourth *jhāna* the breath completely stops. This completes the fourth stage in the development of *ānāpānasati*, calming the breath body." Such complete calming, however, does not form part of the sixteen steps, since it would be difficult to reconcile with the subsequent progression towards experiencing joy (*pīti*) and happiness (*sukha*); mental qualities that have been left behind with the attainment of the fourth *jhāna*. In fact, once the breath has completely ceased, it is impossible to carry out the instruction to breathe in (and out) while calming the bodily formations.

65 Paṭis I 184; Ehara 1995: p.161.

66 According to Vism 274, calming body and mind leads in turn to calming the breath. Cf. also Jayatilleke 1948: p.217, who suggests that breathing may be taken as one concrete instance of bodily formations in the general sense of bodily reflexes. In fact "bodily formation" occurs at times as bodily action in general (e.g. at A I 122; or at A II 231–6), a usage that is not restricted to the breath. Cf. also Schumann 1957: p.29.

67 M III 82. Cf. also Kor 1993: p.38.

aspects of contemplation. I will now consider these subtler aspects by briefly digressing from the *Satipaṭṭhāna Sutta* and examining further the scheme of sixteen steps described in the *Ānāpānasati Sutta*.

VI.4 THE *ĀNĀPĀNASATI SUTTA*

Subsequent to the first four steps of mindfulness of breathing, the *Ānāpānasati Sutta*'s contemplation scheme directs awareness to the experience of joy (*pīti*) and happiness (*sukha*). Since these two are factors of absorption, their occurrence in this part of the sixteen steps has led the *Visuddhimagga* to the assumption that this progression refers exclusively to absorption experience.[68] Possibly because of this assumption, even the first four steps of mindfulness of breathing in the *Satipaṭṭhāna Sutta* have at times been identified as being no more than a concentration practice.[69]

Here it needs to be noted that the occurrence of joy (*pīti*) and happiness (*sukha*) as steps five and six in the scheme of the *Ānāpānasati Sutta* does not necessarily require the experience of absorption,

---

68 According to Vism 277, and 287–90, the second and third tetrads are practicable for *jhāna*-attainers only. (Cf. also Ehara 1995: p.161; and Ledi 1999c: pp.27 and 29.) Vism suggests two alternatives, either actual development of *jhāna*, or insightful contemplation after emerging from *jhāna*. Nevertheless, both of these would only be practicable for someone able to enter absorption. The net result is that, for someone unable to attain *jhāna*, a considerable part of the Buddha's exposition on mindfulness of breathing moves beyond reach. Quite possibly because of this, additional methods came into being for the less proficient in concentration, such as counting the breaths (cf. Vism 278–83 for detailed instructions). Instructions of this type are not found anywhere in the discourses of the Buddha. Though counting the breaths may be helpful for the newcomer to mindfulness of breathing, it does to some extent constitute a change in the mood of this contemplation, since sustained counting can dull the mind (which is the reason underlying the traditional advice to use counting exercises to conquer insomnia) and also tends to stimulate the conceptual activity of the mind instead of quietening it.

69 Kheminda 1992: p.5: "the four foundations of mindfulness begin with a serenity (*samatha*) subject of meditation, namely, mindfulness of in-breathing and out-breathing". Soma 1995: p.360: "the placing of the first tetrad of the *Ānāpānasati Sutta* at the very beginning of the two main *Satipaṭṭhāna Sutta*s is clear indication of the necessity of at least the first *jhāna* … the development of insight is impossible to one who has not brought into being … at least the first *jhāna*." Ps I 249, however, only suggests that based on the breath *jhāna* may be attained, not that mindfulness of breathing in the *Satipaṭṭhāna Sutta* is only a *samatha* object of meditation. This impression is further supported by the fact that the *Satipaṭṭhāna* subcommentary Ps-pṭ I 349 makes a point of stating that an external development of mindfulness of breathing cannot yield absorption attainment. This shows that in the eyes of the commentaries mindfulness of breathing in the *satipaṭṭhāna* context can be undertaken independently of absorption attainment.

since both can occur apart from such attainment.[70] According to a verse in the *Dhammapada*, for example, joy (*pīti*) can arise as a result of insight meditation.[71] Thus awareness of the breath whilst experiencing joy or happiness is not necessarily confined to retrospective analysis after emerging from an absorption attainment, nor to the stages of calmness meditation immediately preceding such attainment.

Although the breath can undoubtedly be used for the development of concentration, the instructions throughout the sixteen steps are invariably based on distinct awareness of each in- and out-breath. The central purpose of this distinction is to cultivate awareness of the impermanent nature of the breath. Any bodily or mental phenomena coming within the focus of awareness during the sixteen steps are experienced against the background of the ever-changing rhythm of in- and out-breaths, which provides a constant reminder of impermanence (cf. Fig. 6.2 opposite).[72]

Thus a closer inspection of the sixteen steps reveals an underlying progressive pattern which proceeds through increasingly subtle aspects of subjective experience against a constant background of impermanence.[73] In contrast, on approaching absorption attainment experience becomes more and more unified, so that one is no longer clearly aware of the distinction between in- and out-breaths, or related phenomena.

The basic difference between mindfulness of breathing as a *samatha* or as a *vipassanā* practice depends on what angle is taken when observing the breath, since emphasis on just mentally knowing the presence of the breath is capable of leading to deep levels of

---

70 In fact the definition of joy (*pīti*) in this context at Paṭis I 187 uses a set of expressions that are not restricted to absorption attainment. Similarly at M II 203 the joy of the first two absorptions is contrasted with the joy arising through sensuality, documenting a type of joy (*pīti*) distinctly different from that experienced during absorption attainment. Cf. also Buddhadāsa 1989: p.51.

71 Dhp 374.

72 Such use of the breath as a means to develop insight into impermanence has a parallel at A III 306 and A IV 319, where a recollection of the inevitability and unpredictability of death is related to the unpredictability of the next breath. Cf. also S V 319, where the practice of the sixteen steps of mindfulness of breathing leads to realization of the impermanent nature of feelings.

73 Cf. e.g. Th 548, which recommends practice of mindfulness of breathing in "right order", demonstrating a clear awareness of this inherent progressive character. A detailed exposition of the sixteen steps as a single integrated practice can be found in Buddhadāsa 1989: pp.53–89. Cf. also Gethin 1992: p.59; Levine 1989: pp.32–6; Ṭhānissaro 1993: p.67; and Vimalo 1987: p.158.

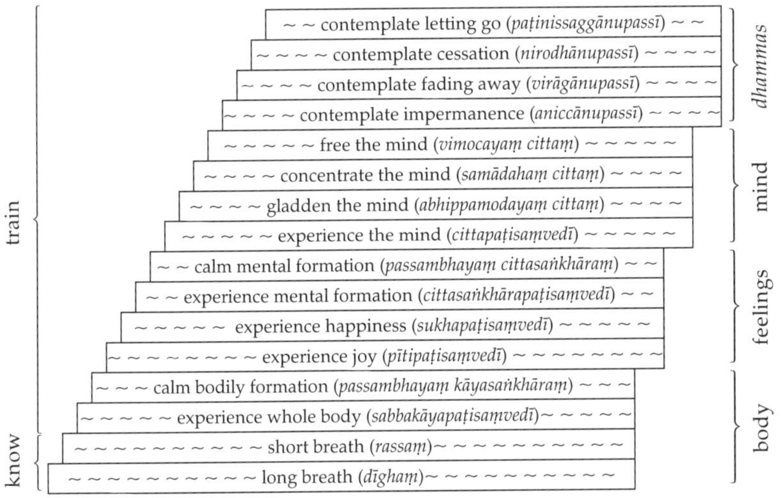

The use of ~ indicates that awareness of breathing in and out forms the background to each step

Fig. 6.2 Survey of *ānāpānasati* in sixteen steps

concentration, while emphasis on various phenomena related to the process of breathing does not lead to a unitary type of experience but stays in the realm of variety and of sensory experience, and thus is more geared towards the development of insight. These considerations suggest that the sixteen steps are not solely a concentration practice, but also introduce an insight perspective on the development of mindfulness of breathing.

An examination of the context in which the sixteen steps are taught in the *Ānāpānasati Sutta* supports this suggestion. According to the introductory section of the discourse the Buddha's rationale for giving this discourse was to demonstrate to a group of monks, who were already using the breath as a meditation object (possibly as a concentration exercise), how to develop it as a *satipaṭṭhāna*.[74] That is, the Buddha took up the breath as a meditation object in order to demonstrate how *sati* can naturally lead from mindfulness of breathing to a comprehensive awareness of feelings, mind, and *dhammas*, and hence to a development of all *satipaṭṭhānas* and to the arising of the seven awakening factors.[75] Thus the main purpose of the Buddha's exposition was to broaden the scope of mindfulness of

74 M III 78. Cf. also S V 315, where the Buddha introduced a monk, who was already practising some form of mindfulness of breathing, to the sixteen steps in order to further his practice. Cf. also Debes 1994: p.197.

breathing from awareness of the bodily phenomenon breath to awareness of feelings, mind, and *dhammas*, and in this way employ it as a means to gain insight.[76] In view of this it seems reasonable to conclude that the purpose of the sixteen steps of mindfulness of breathing described in the *Ānāpānasati Sutta*, and by implication the purpose of the four steps of mindfulness of breathing in the *Satipaṭṭhāna Sutta*, is not restricted to the development of concentration, but covers both calm and insight.

VI.5 POSTURES AND ACTIVITIES

Returning to the *satipaṭṭhāna* contemplations, the next two exercises described in the discourse, awareness of the four postures and clear knowledge in regard to activities, are both concerned with directing mindfulness to the body in activity. The instructions for contemplating the four postures are:

> **When walking, he knows "I am walking"; when standing, he knows "I am standing"; when sitting, he knows "I am sitting"; when lying down, he knows "I am lying down"; or he knows accordingly however his body is disposed.**[77]

The enumeration of the four postures in the above instruction proceeds from the more active walking to comparatively more refined and passive postures.[78] The instruction here is to "know" each of these postures, probably implying some form of proprioceptive awareness.[79] In other discourses, these four postures often convey the sense of doing something "at any time".[80] Applied to the context

75 At M III 83 the Buddha related each tetrad from the sixteen-step scheme to a particular *satipaṭṭhāna*, while at M III 87 he provided the relation to the awakening factors. The same correlations occur at S V 323–36. S V 312 moreover relates mindfulness of breathing to each awakening factor singly.

76 The insight potential of any of the sixteen steps is described at Paṭis I 95, which points out that each step can lead to realization. Paṭis I 178–82 illustrates this potential by relating the first step of mindfulness of breathing (long breath) to experiencing the rise and fall of feelings, cognitions, and thoughts, to the awakening factors, and to the experience of *Nibbāna*. Cf. also Ñāṇamoli 1982b: p.163.

77 M I 56.

78 Cf. M I 120, where a progression from fast walking to slow walking, to standing, to sitting, and finally to lying down, is each time accompanied by the comment that in this way a gross posture is substituted by a subtler one. Cf. also Fessel 1999: p.111.

79 Proprioception is the ability to sense the position, location, and movement of the body and its parts.

80 e.g. at A IV 301.

of *satipaṭṭhāna*, this usage suggests continuity of body awareness during all activities. In fact, according to the above instruction this contemplation is not limited to the four postures, but includes any way one's body might be positioned. Thus what this particular contemplation means, practically speaking, is to be aware of the body in a general manner, to be "with" the body during its natural activities, instead of being carried away by various thoughts and ideas, and therefore to be mentally anchored in the body.

This particular exercise constitutes the *satipaṭṭhāna* contemplation that most prominently fulfils the role of providing a firm grounding of awareness in the body. Because of this foundational role, it seems reasonable to follow the *Madhyama Āgama* version of *satipaṭṭhāna* and place it at the beginning of the body contemplations. For the beginner in *satipaṭṭhāna*, this simple exercise of being aware of the body, in whatever position, helps to build up continuity of *sati*. By performing even the least important movement of the body in a conscious and deliberate manner, the most mundane activities can be turned into occasions for mental development. Awareness trained in this way constitutes an important foundation for more formal meditation, since diligent practice of this contemplation will bring the mind's tendency to distraction considerably under control.

Awareness of the four postures is not only a way to build up mindfulness; the four bodily postures can also be used as objects of insightful investigation. A verse from the *Theragāthā*, for example, relates the ability to assume any of the four postures to the inter- action of the bones and tendons in the body responsible for that posture.[81] By describing the mechanics behind bodily activities in this way, this verse points to a perspective on contemplating the body which has received much attention from modern meditation teachers.[82] The mechanics involved in assuming a bodily posture or performing a movement usually escape notice owing to one's preoccupation with the outcome of one's action. In particular, a practical example for investigating the activity of walking can be found in the commentaries, which suggest breaking down the process of walking into the successive stages of a single step, which can then be correlated with the four elements.[83]

---

81 Th 570.
82 Detailed practical instructions can be found in Mahasi 1991: pp.9–16. Cf. also Debes 1994: p.113; and Lily de Silva (n.d.): p.13.
83 Vism 622: predominance of earth + water = placing; predominance of fire + air = lifting. Cf. also Sīlananda 1995: p.7.

As mentioned above, the four postures are often used in the discourses as a way to indicate that something should be done "at any time". In this way, they are at times related to various predominantly mental events such as fear, unwholesome thoughts, or overcoming the five hindrances.[84] These passages relate each of the four postures to awareness of the concurrent state of mind. This indicates that removing unwholesome states of mind, for example, is not confined to formal sitting meditation, but can and should be undertaken in any situation or posture. The fact that meditation does not have to be exclusively associated with the sitting posture is also recognized in the *Vimuttimagga* and the *Visuddhimagga*, which indicate that, depending on the character of individual meditators, other postures may be adopted for carrying out the practice of meditation.[85]

Another possibility suggested by the fact that the discourses relate the four postures to various states of mind is to observe the interrelation between states of mind and the way one performs activities like walking, sitting, etc. Through such observation one can become aware of how a particular state of mind expresses itself through one's bodily posture, or how the condition, position, and motion of the body affects the mind.[86] Bodily posture and state of mind are intrinsically interrelated, so that clear awareness of the one naturally enhances awareness of the other. In this way, contemplation of the four postures can lead to an investigation of the body's conditional interrelation with the mind.

---

84 M I 21 relates the four postures to overcoming fear; M III 112 to avoiding desires and discontent; A II 13 and It 116 to not tolerating unwholesome thoughts; and A II 14 and It 118 to overcoming the five hindrances.

85 According to Ehara 1995: p.61, the standing and walking postures are particularly suitable for lustful natured (*rāgacarita*) personalities, while sitting and reclining are more appropriate for anger natured (*dosacarita*) personalities. Vism 128 adds that whichever posture is effective for developing concentration is the one to be adopted. According to the *satipaṭṭhāna* commentary, Ps I 264, clearly knowing in regard to stretching and bending, an aspect of the next body contemplation, implies knowing the right time for performing such action, since the feelings arising from maintaining an uncomfortable posture for too long might obstruct the development of the meditation. Chah 1993: p.40, points out that "some people think that the longer you can sit, the wiser you must be ... wisdom comes from being mindful in all postures." Similarly Vimalaramsi 1997: p.47, suggests "it is far more important to observe what is happening in the mind than to sit with uncomfortable or painful sensations ... there is no magic in sitting on the floor. The magic comes from a clear, calm mind."

This particular contemplation can also lead one to question the sense of identity underlying any of the four postures.[87] The commentaries give a practical shape to this suggestion, since according to them the decisive difference between simple walking and walking meditation as a *satipaṭṭhāna* is that a meditator keeps in mind the question: "Who goes? Whose is this going?"[88]

Another perspective on the development of insight can be gained by turning awareness to minor postural adjustments. The main reason for these adjustments is to avoid the physical pain that develops when the same posture is maintained for a long time. Through closer observation it will become evident that most of the semi-conscious adjustments made in any posture are a constant effort to alleviate the pain inherent in having a body.[89]

Of these four postures, the discourses individually relate walking and reclining to the development of awareness. Walking meditation often comes up circumstantially in the discourses when a visitor, on approaching a settlement of monks, finds them practising walking meditation in the open.[90] Several passages report the Buddha and some of his senior disciples engaged in walking meditation.[91] This

86 Dhammiko 1961: p.188. Fryba 1989: p.125, even suggests deliberately assuming the posture of an insecure and anxious person, then changing to express self-confidence in one's posture, and in this way to experiment with various postures and their relationship to different emotions. Van Zeyst 1989: p.31, instructs: "one observes and is aware of how these movements are the expressions of one's mental attitude: aggressive in walking, or maybe escaping; defeated in lying down ... standing in perplexity or expectation; sitting in satisfaction or in fear ... neatness of movement in the desire to please ... roughness of movement in anger and defeat ... lack of movement in doubt and fear."

87 Cf. e.g. S III 151, which describes how the worldling's mistaken notion of a self is intricately bound up with his or her adopting any of the four postures. According to Ñāṇaponika 1992: p.64, "mindfulness on postures will bring an initial awareness of the impersonal nature of the body".

88 Ps I 251, because in this way the notion of an acting self can be overcome. Ps I 252 adds that this is to be applied to any posture.

89 Vism 640 explains that the characteristic of *dukkha* is concealed by the four postures. Naeb 1993: p.143, explains: "it is pain forcing ... to change position at all times ... we change in order to cure the pain ... it is like nursing a continuous sickness ... there is pain in all positions". Similar suggestions can be found in the *Mahāprajñāpāramitāśāstra* (in Lamotte 1970: p.1157); and in Ñāṇārāma 1997: p.29.

90 e.g. at D I 89; M I 229; M I 332; M II 119; M II 158; A V 65; and Ud 7.

91 The Buddha is reported practising walking meditation at D I 105; D III 39; D III 80; S I 107; S I 179; S I 212; Th 480 and Th 1044. His walking meditation took place during the night (at S I 107), and also during the day (at S I 179 and S I 212). S II 155 reports all the senior disciples engaged in walking meditation, each with a group of other monks.

shows that even accomplished practitioners considered walking meditation a worthwhile practice. According to the discourses, walking meditation benefits bodily health and digestion, and leads to the development of sustained concentration.[92] The commentaries document the insight potential of walking meditation with instances of its use that led to full realization.[93]

Unlike the way in which walking meditation is usually practised nowadays, the standard instructions for walking meditation found in the discourses take mental events as their main object of observation. The instructions in this context do not mention awareness of one's bodily posture or of the dynamics of walking, but speak of purifying the mind from obstructive states.[94] Since the same expression is also used for sitting meditation, it simply implies a continuation of the same meditation that has earlier been practised while seated, albeit in a different posture.

A discourse in the *Aṅguttara Nikāya* recommends walking meditation as an antidote for drowsiness. In this case, however, the instructions are different from the standard descriptions: the meditator is to focus on the walking path, to keep the senses withdrawn, and to prevent the mind from getting distracted outwardly.[95]

To cultivate awareness in regard to the reclining posture, meditators should lie down mindfully on their right side to rest during the middle part of the night, keeping in mind the time to wake up.[96] The instructions for falling asleep mindfully appear to be mainly concerned with waking up at a predetermined time.[97] According to other passages, falling asleep with awareness improves

---

92 A III 29. Improvement in health and digestion as benefits of walking meditation are also documented at Vin II 119. On the practice of walking meditation cf. also Khantipālo 1981: p.95; Kundalābhivaṃsa 1993: pp.75–8; and Ṭhitavaṇṇo 1988: pp.120–2.

93 Ps I 257 relates the story of a monk who realized arahantship after twenty years of sustained walking meditation. Ps I 258 records the same realization for another monk after sixteen years of walking meditation.

94 M I 273: "while walking and sitting, we will purify our minds of obstructive states." The expression "obstructive state" is a synonym for the five hindrances (cf. e.g. S V 94).

95 A IV 87.

96 e.g. at M I 273. The recommendation to sleep on one's right side (in the "lion's posture") could arise from the fact that in this way the smooth working of the heart during sleep is less obstructed by the weight of the body than when sleeping on one's left side (which can cause unpleasant dreams).

97 Ñāṇavīra 1987: p.158.

the quality of one's sleep and prevents bad dreams and nocturnal emissions.[98]

By way of conclusion it should be underlined that, in spite of these various perspectives on developing insight related to the four postures, what the instructions in the *Satipaṭṭhāna Sutta* itself suggest is simply awareness of the whole body in general, and of its disposition in space.

Once mindfulness of the four postures has led to a grounding of awareness in the body, one can turn to the next contemplation introduced in the *Satipaṭṭhāna Sutta*: clear knowing (*sampajāna*) in regard to a range of bodily activities.[99] The instructions for such clear knowing are:

> **When going forward and returning he acts clearly knowing; when looking ahead and looking away he acts clearly knowing; when flexing and extending his limbs he acts clearly knowing; when wearing his robes and carrying his outer robe and bowl he acts clearly knowing; when eating, drinking, consuming food, and tasting he acts clearly knowing; when defecating and urinating he acts clearly knowing; when walking, standing, sitting, falling asleep, waking up, talking, and keeping silent he acts clearly knowing.**[100]

Apart from being one of the body contemplations in the *Satipaṭṭhāna Sutta*, this exercise also forms a distinct step in the gradual path of training, referred to as "mindfulness and clear knowledge" (*sati-sampajañña*).[101] In the sequence of this gradual path of training, mindfulness and clear knowledge in regard to bodily activities occupy a transitional place between a preparatory development and actual

---

98 Vin I 295 and A III 251.

99 Cf. A III 325, according to which awareness of the four postures forms the basis for mindfulness and clear knowledge.

100 M I 57. It is notable that most of the Pāli verb forms in this instruction are past participles, giving a nuance of passivity to the activities under observation. According to Kalupahana 1999: p.283, the Buddha used passive forms as a pedagogical device to highlight the characteristic of not-self. Another point worth considering is that the postures mentioned in the previous exercise recur in the present context. The commentary, Ps I 269, explains that the difference between contemplating walking, standing, and sitting under contemplation of the postures and in the present exercise is that here they are of comparatively shorter duration. The point the commentary is trying to make could be that clear knowledge is particularly relevant to the moment when one assumes a particular posture (in terms of purpose and suitability etc.), whereas postural awareness is more profitably applied to being in a posture.

101 e.g. at D I 70.

sitting meditation.[102] To be more precise, mindfulness and clear knowledge complete the preliminary stages concerned with ethical conduct, restraint, and contentment, and form the starting point for the formal practice of meditation, when one resorts to a secluded place in order to overcome the hindrances, to progress through the levels of absorption, and to gain realization.[103] Thus the development of mindfulness and clear knowledge is a foundation for more formal meditations such as, in the present context, the remaining contemplations described in the *Satipaṭṭhāna Sutta*.[104]

The combined expression "mindfulness and clear knowledge" indicates that, in addition to being mindful of the activities mentioned, the presence of "clear knowledge" plays an important role. Since "clearly knowing" on its own, and also in combination with *sati*, occurs in the discourses in a variety of contexts and can assume a broad range of meanings,[105] the question arises of the implications of "clear knowledge" in regard to the various activities mentioned.

---

102 On the basis of the common characteristics of the gradual path of training, as it is described in various discourses (e.g. at D I 63–84; M I 179–84; M I 271–80; and M I 354–7), this pattern can be subsumed under five main stages: I. initial conviction and going forth; II. foundational training in ethical conduct and contentment; III. sense-restraint and mindfulness and clear knowledge in regard to bodily activities; IV. abandonment of the hindrances and development of absorption; V. realization. These five steps represent, to some extent, the five faculties/powers: I. confidence, II. energy, III. mindfulness, IV. concentration, and V. wisdom; cf. Crangle 1994: p.163. However, it should be added that the five faculties and powers are not to be developed only sequentially, but should be brought into being together. Barnes 1981: p.237, suggests an alternative scheme of six steps by distinguishing between sense-restraint, on the one hand, and mindfulness and clear knowledge, on the other, as two separate stages.

103 Several discourses (e.g. M I 181; M I 269; and M I 346) explicitly mention clearly knowing in regard to activities as a precondition for subsequent formal sitting meditation. This foundational role is echoed at Ps I 290 and Ps-pṭ I 380, which recommend clearly knowing in regard to activities as a basis for developing *sati* as an awakening factor. Cf. also Bronkhorst 1985: p.311; and Bucknell 1984: p.29.

104 The difference in character between clear knowledge of activities and the later body contemplations has led Schmithausen 1976: pp.253–5, to the conclusion that the contemplations of the anatomical parts, of the elements, and of a corpse could be later additions, because their character is somewhat different from the type of awareness practised during contemplation of bodily postures and clearly knowing in regard to bodily activities. However, several discourses (e.g. D II 94; A V 116; and A V 119) mention clear knowledge in regard to bodily activities separately from the four *satipaṭṭhānas*, indicating that both existed independently. This suggests that, if there was any later addition, it was clear knowledge in regard to bodily activities that was added to the *satipaṭṭhāna* scheme.

105 Cf. page 41.

Neither the *Satipaṭṭhāna Sutta* nor the expositions of the gradual path offer further information. The commentaries make up for this by presenting a detailed analysis of clear knowledge into four aspects (cf. Fig. 6.3 below). According to them, clear knowledge should be directed to the purpose of an activity and also to its suitability. Moreover one should clearly understand how to relate this activity to one's meditation practice (one's "pasture") and one should also develop "non-delusion" by clearly understanding the true nature of reality.[106] A closer inspection of the discourses brings to light several passages that support or further clarify this commentarial presentation.

purpose (*sātthakasampajañña*)
suitability (*sappāyasampajañña*)
"pasture" (*gocarasampajañña*)
non-delusion (*asammohasampajañña*)

Fig. 6.3 Four aspects of "clear knowledge" in the commentaries

According to the *Mahāsuññata Sutta*, talking can be carried out clearly knowing by refraining from topics unsuitable for one who has gone forth.[107] Here, "clearly knowing" implies that one discusses topics related to contentment, seclusion, concentration, wisdom, etc., since in this way speech becomes "purposeful" in regard to one's progress on the path. This instance parallels the first aspect of clear knowledge mentioned in the commentaries, which is concerned with the purpose of an activity.

Several of the activities listed in this part of the *Satipaṭṭhāna Sutta*, such as "going forward and returning", "looking ahead and looking away", "flexing and extending one's limbs", and "wearing one's robes and carrying one's outer robe and bowl", occur as a set

106 At Ps I 253–61.

107 M III 113. This parallels an explanation found in the *Satipaṭṭhāna* subcommentary, Ps-pṭ I 364, which relates the development of clear knowledge in regard to speech to refraining from topics unsuitable for conversation.

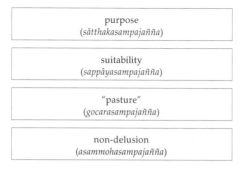

elsewhere in the discourses.[108] These instances do not explicitly mention clear knowledge, but are instructions given to monks regarding proper behaviour. What the discourses emphasize in regard to these activities, is that they should be performed in a graceful and pleasing way (*pāsādika*).[109] Similarly, the Chinese *Madhyama Āgama* speaks of a monk's "dignified and quiet behaviour" when practising clear knowledge in regard to bodily activities.[110] Judging from these passages, this particular set of activities stands for a careful and dignified way of behaving, appropriate to one who is living as a monk or nun.

The need to maintain such standards of good conduct has found its expression in the numerous training rules for the monastic community. These regulate, in great detail, various aspects of daily conduct.[111] The importance accorded to the externals of conduct in ancient India is also evident in the *Brahmāyu Sutta*, where a close examination of the Buddha's daily conduct formed part of an attempt to assess his spiritual accomplishment.[112] This need for a monk or nun to behave in a careful and dignified manner parallels the second aspect of clear knowledge mentioned in the commentaries, which relates it to the suitability of an action.

A passage from the *Aṅguttara Nikāya* associates clearly knowing with the activity of looking. This passage reports the monk Nanda, who was a particularly lustful character, marshalling all his effort in order to avoid the arising of desires and discontent (*abhijjhādomanassa*) when looking in any direction.[113] The terminology used in this instance shows that this form of clearly knowing is related to sense-restraint. A similar nuance can be found in the

---

108 At M I 460 and A II 123 as part of an instruction to a monk how to perform these bodily activities properly. At A IV 169 the whole set occurs again as a reference to proper behaviour, where a bad monk is trying to hide behind proper outer behaviour.

109 e.g. at A II 104 and at A V 201; cf. also Th 927 and Pp 44. Th 591 has the same qualification for the four postures. Law 1922: p.81, translates *sampajañña* in this context as "deliberately."

110 Minh Chau 1991: p.83.

111 These are in particular the seventy-five *sekhiya* rules, Vin IV 184–206. The importance of such outward behaviour is noted by Collins 1997: p.198. Holt 1999: p.102, points out that "the *sekhiya* rules ... are much more than mere social etiquette: they are outward reflections of the inner state of a bhikkhu's mental condition". A convenient exposition of the *sekhiya* rules can be found in Ṭhānissaro 1994: pp.489–510.

112 M II 137, giving a detailed account of the Buddha's way of performing various activities such as walking, looking, sitting down, etc.

113 A IV 167.

Mahāsuññata Sutta, which relates clearly knowing in regard to the four postures to sense-restraint.[114] Both passages correspond to the third aspect of clear knowledge mentioned in the commentaries, which speaks of "pasture". The same expression came up earlier in relation to *sati* imagery, depicting *satipaṭṭhāna* as the proper pasture of a monk, while improper pasture represented sensual distraction.[115] This suggests that clear knowledge in regard to "pasture" refers in particular to sense-restraint.

The fourth aspect mentioned in the commentaries, which associates clear knowledge with the absence of delusion (*asammoha*), goes beyond the context of body contemplation. To have a clear understanding of the true nature of reality is a task of clearly knowing (*sampajāna*) in general, a quality that, according to the "definition", needs to be developed with all the *satipaṭṭhāna* contemplations.

The commentarial presentation of the four aspects inherent in clear knowledge can be seen to follow a progressive sequence, with clearly knowing in regard to purpose (one's progress to awakening) establishing the background for corresponding "suitable" conduct, which in turn facilitates sense-restraint and one's meditative development, which then enables insight into the true nature of reality to arise. In this way, the *satipaṭṭhāna* practice of developing clear knowledge in regard to activities combines purposeful and dignified conduct with sense-restraint in order to build up a foundation for the arising of insight. In fact, both proper conduct and sense-restraint overlap to some degree, since several aspects of a monk's or a nun's code of conduct are intended to facilitate sense-restraint, while on the other hand one's bodily activities will become more graceful and dignified if a certain degree of mental equilibrium through the absence of sensual distractions has been established.

Compared to contemplation of the four postures, clear knowledge in regard to activities introduces an additional element, since the former consists only in bare awareness of whatever posture or movement occurred naturally, while the latter includes purposely adopting a restrained and dignified behaviour.

---

114 M III 113.
115 A V 352 and S V 149; cf. also page 56.

VI.6 ANATOMICAL PARTS AND ELEMENTS

The next two exercises listed in the *Satipaṭṭhāna Sutta*, contemplating the anatomical constitution of the body and contemplating the body in terms of the four elements, both direct mindfulness to an analysis of the body's constitution. The first of these two analytical meditations surveys the constitution of one's body by listing various anatomical parts, organs, and fluids.[116] The passage reads:

> **He reviews this same body up from the soles of the feet and down from the top of the hair, enclosed by skin, as full of many kinds of impurity thus: "in this body there are head-hairs, body-hairs, nails, teeth, skin, flesh, sinews, bones, bone-marrow, kidneys, heart, liver, diaphragm, spleen, lungs, bowel, mesentery, contents of the stomach, faeces, bile, phlegm, pus, blood, sweat, fat, tears, grease, spittle, snot, oil of the joints, and urine".**[117]

In other discourses, this list of anatomical parts is followed by the expression: "and whatever other parts there may be".[118] This indicates that the *satipaṭṭhāna* list is not exhaustive and the items mentioned are examples of the kinds of bodily parts that can be contemplated. In fact, other passages mention several bodily parts or fluids missing from this list, such as the brain, the male organ, or ear-wax, which demonstrates that the *satipaṭṭhāna* list does not exhaust the ancient Indian knowledge of human anatomy.[119]

The set of anatomical parts given in the *Satipaṭṭhāna Sutta* follows a natural sequence from the solid and outer parts, through the internal

---

116 Detailed descriptions of each part can be found in Ehara 1995: pp.171–7, and Vism 248–65. The *Madhyama Āgama* list of anatomical parts corresponds quite closely to the Pāli version (in Minh Chau 1991: p.90; and Nhat Hanh 1990: p.157), while the *Ekottara Āgama* has only twenty-four parts (Nhat Hanh 1990: p.170). According to Hayashima 1967: p.272, the Sanskrit versions of this *satipaṭṭhāna* contemplation mention altogether thirty-six parts. (Indeed, a passage from the *Ratnamegha*, quoted in Bendall 1990: p.202, lists thirty-six anatomical parts for body contemplation.) The fact that in the *Satipaṭṭhāna Sutta* the anatomical parts listed are thirty-one could have some additional significance, since in Buddhist cosmology the realms of existence are of the same number. Thus the descriptions of material existence on the microcosmic and the macrocosmic level were moulded on a similar pattern. Some of the anatomical parts listed in the *Satipaṭṭhāna Sutta* can also be found at *Maitrī Upaniṣad* 1.3. Although this passage quite probably postdates the Pāli discourses, it nevertheless shows that this type of body contemplation was the domain not only of Buddhist practitioners.

117 M I 57.

118 M I 421 and M III 240.

organs, to the organic liquids. This sequence represents a progressive penetration of awareness. The parts most easily accessible to awareness are mentioned first, while the aspects of the body listed further on in the sequence require a deeper degree of awareness and sensitivity. Alternatively, the sequence can also be taken to correspond to an exercise in imaginative visualization, during which one strips one's body of each part in turn.[120]

The *Visuddhimagga* indicates that the practice of this exercise progresses from giving attention to each individual anatomical part to becoming aware of all of them together.[121] This suggests that with the more advanced stages of this contemplation the individual parts recede in importance and awareness turns to the composite and unattractive nature of the body in its entirety. According to the *Sampasādanīya Sutta*, contemplation can also proceed from the anatomical parts to awareness of the skeleton only.[122]

A progressive pattern similar to the *satipaṭṭhāna* instructions can be found in the *Vijaya Sutta* of the *Sutta Nipāta*, where a thorough investigation of the body leads from its outer anatomical parts to its inner organs and liquids.[123] In the *Vijaya Sutta*, this investigation of the body concludes with the rhetorical question: "How else, except through lack of insight, could one exalt oneself or disparage another because of such a body?"[124] This conclusion shows that the aim of the contemplation described is to reduce one's attachment to the body, a suggestion that holds true also for the *Satipaṭṭhāna Sutta*.

The Chinese *Ekottara Āgama* lists a related contemplation as part of

---

119 Sn 199 mentions the brain. The brain is in fact added to the *satipaṭṭhāna* list by Paṭis I 7, and is also mentioned in the corresponding Chinese version in the *Madhyama Āgama* (in Minh Chau 1991: p.90). Vism 240 explains that the brain was not listed in the *Satipaṭṭhāna Sutta* because it was already covered by "bone-marrow". The male organ is mentioned at D I 106 and Sn 1022. The omission of the male organ from the *satipaṭṭhāna* list is not surprising, since the instructions have to be practicable for both male and female meditators; van Zeyst 1982: p.80, however, thinks that "with Victorian prudence the thought of sex has been eliminated or by-passed". Ear-wax occurs at Sn 197.

120 Debes 1994: p.124.

121 Vism 265.

122 These are the first two of four "attainments of vision" presented at D III 104. Cf. also S V 129, which points out that contemplation of the bones has many benefits.

123 Sn 193–201. The progression in this discourse also parallels the progression of the body contemplations listed in the *Satipaṭṭhāna Sutta*, since it commences by directing awareness to the four postures and to stretching and bending, and concludes with a description of a dead body eaten by animals.

124 Sn 206.

its version of body contemplation. This exercise is concerned with the bodily orifices, directing awareness to the repulsive nature of the excretions from each of them.[125] The same exercise occurs in other discourses in the Pāli *Nikāyas*.[126] The main purpose of this exercise, and of contemplating the anatomical parts, is to drive home the realization that one's own body and the bodies of others are not inherently attractive.[127] A related nuance can be found in another discourse which refers to contemplating the anatomical constitution of the body with the heading: "as below, so above, as above, so below".[128] This suggests that a detached observation of the various parts of the body leads to the understanding that they are all of equal nature. Once one clearly apprehends their true nature, it becomes evident that there is nothing inherently beautiful in any particular aspect of the body (such as, for example, eyes, hair, and lips). In the *Therīgāthā*, a nun vividly illustrates this insight by pointing out that if one were to turn the body inside out, even one's mother would be disgusted and unable to bear the smell of it.[129]

Following the instructions in the *Satipaṭṭhāna Sutta*, to contemplate the unattractive nature of the body refers in the first instance to one's own body.[130] Realizing the absence of beauty in one's own body thereby serves in particular as a countermeasure to conceit.[131] Subsequently, as indicated in the *satipaṭṭhāna* refrain, the same contemplation is then to be applied "externally", to the bodies of others. Such an external application can become a powerful antidote to sensual desire.[132] The potential of this contemplation as a countermeasure to sensuality has led to its inclusion in Buddhist ordination ceremonies, part of which consists in instructing a novice monk or nun to contemplate the first five anatomical parts listed in the

125 In Nhat Hanh 1990: p.170.

126 Sn 197 and A IV 386.

127 According to A V 109, contemplation of the anatomical parts is concerned with "unattractiveness" (*asubha*), which It 80 explains to have the purpose of countering lust.

128 S V 278. A consideration of this passage needs to take into account the traditional Indian respect for higher parts of the body over its lower parts.

129 Thī 471.

130 Cf. also Vibh 193, which clearly indicates that contemplation of the anatomical parts has to be developed on oneself first, before it can be applied to others.

131 This is documented at M I 336, where the former Buddha Kakusandha recommended contemplation of unattractiveness (of the anatomical parts) to his monks in order to counterbalance possible conceit at the excessive honour and veneration they were receiving from householders.

satipaṭṭhāna instruction.

Despite these benefits, the exercise has possible dangers. Excessive contemplation of "impurity" can lead to loathing and repugnance. Loathing one's own body or that of others, however, is only an expression of frustrated desire and does not correspond to the calming of desire intended by the exercise. The discourses describe a rather drastic case of excessive and unwise use of this particular meditation practice. After the Buddha had instructed a group of monks in this practice and retired into solitude, the monks engaged with such fervour in contemplating the anatomical constitution of their own bodies that they felt thoroughly ashamed and disgusted by it. In the end, a substantial number of them committed suicide.[133]

The need for a balanced attitude is exemplified by the simile in this part of the *Satipaṭṭhāna Sutta*, which compares the contemplation of the anatomical parts to examining a bag full of grains and beans.[134] Just as examining these grains and beans will quite probably not stimulate any affective reaction, so contemplating the anatomical constitution of the body should be carried out with a balanced and detached attitude, so that the effect is to cool desire, not to stimulate aversion.

If sufficient precautions are taken to establish the appropriate attitude, a wise and balanced contemplation of the unattractiveness of the body has the potential to lead to realization. This is documented in the *Therīgāthā*, which reports two nuns gaining full awakening by contemplating the anatomical constitution of their own bodies.[135]

Several discourses categorize the whole set of thirty-one anatomical parts listed in the *Satipaṭṭhāna Sutta* under the elements earth

---

132 A III 323 relates contemplation of the anatomical parts to removal of lust; A IV 47 to developing disgust in regard to sexuality. Bodhi 1984: p.92, explains that "the meditation aims at weakening sexual desire by depriving the sexual urge of its cognitive underpinning, the perception of the body as sensually alluring". Cf. also Khantipālo 1981: p.98; and Mendis 1985: p.44. An additional external application is described at Vism 306, where the list of bodily parts is used for counteracting anger by reflecting whether one is angry with the other person's hair, or skin, or bones, etc.

133 Vin III 68 and S V 320. On this passage cf. Mills 1992: p.74.

134 This "double-mouthed" bag (*ubhatomukhā mutoḷī*) is, according to Schlingloff 1964: p.33 n.10, a piece of cloth used for sowing, with an upper opening for placing the grains inside, while the lower opening is used to sow the grains. This simile might have suggested itself because of the somewhat similar "double-mouthed" nature of the body, with an "upper opening" for placing food in, and a "lower opening" as the outlet for faeces.

135 Thī 33 and Thī 82–6.

and water in the context of a general exposition of the four elements.[136] This indicates that the next exercise in the *Satipaṭṭhāna Sutta*, where the body is analysed into its four elementary qualities, constitutes a related type of contemplation. The instructions for this contemplation are:

> **He reviews this same body, however it is placed, however disposed, as consisting of elements thus: "in this body there are the earth element, the water element, the fire element, and the air element".**[137]

The ancient Indian scheme of four elements, mentioned here, represents four basic qualities of matter: solidity, liquidity (or cohesion), temperature, and motion.[138] Since contemplation of the thirty-one anatomical parts has covered mainly the first two of these qualities, solidity and liquidity, the four-element analysis entails a more comprehensive approach, extending awareness to aspects of the body that manifest the qualities of temperature and motion. Thus the present exercise further develops the analysis of the body on a more comprehensive and refined level.[139]

Contemplation of the body's earthy and watery qualities can be undertaken by observing the physical sensations of the solid and liquid parts of the body. Awareness of its fiery quality can be developed through noting variations in bodily temperature, and to some extent also by turning awareness to the processes of digestion and ageing. Air, representing the quality of motion, can be covered by directing awareness to the different movements that take place within the organism, such as the circulation of the blood or the cycle of the breaths.[140] The same elementary qualities can be combined in a single contemplation, by being aware of these four qualities as characteristics of each part or particle of the body.

The corresponding simile illustrates the effect of this particular method of contemplation with a butcher who has slaughtered and cut up a cow to sell. According to the commentaries, the butcher

---

136 M I 185; M I 421; and M III 240. According to Vism 348, the detailed expositions on the elements in these discourses are intended for the more slow-witted practitioners, while the comparatively brief instructions in the *Satipaṭṭhāna Sutta* are for those of quick understanding.

137 M I 57.

138 Cf. e.g. A III 340, according to which a tree trunk can be seen as a manifestation of each of the four elements, since each of them is but a quality of the same tree.

139 According to Vism 351, the four element analysis is a refinement of the previous contemplation.

simile indicates a change of cognition (*saññā*), since after the slaughter the butcher thinks no longer in terms of "cow", but only in terms of "meat".[141] A similar shift of cognition takes place when a meditator dissects the body into its elementary qualities: the body is no longer experienced as "I" or "mine", but simply as a combination of these four qualities.

To experience oneself as a combination of material qualities reveals the qualitative identity of one's own body with the external environment.[142] In this way, a healthy degree of detachment develops, counteracting the grasping at what is, in the end, merely a combination of material qualities. With sustained contemplation a meditator may come to realize that this apparently so solid and compact material body, and with it the whole material world, is entirely without essence.[143] There are simply different degrees of hardness or softness, of wetness or dryness, of hotness or coldness and some degree of motion (at least on the subatomic level). Contemplation of the four elements has thus the potential to lead to a penetrative realization of the insubstantial and selfless nature of material reality.[144]

The discourses relate the scheme of the four elements not only to the human body, but also to material existence in general. The

---

140 M I 188; M I 422; and M III 241 explain the bodily manifestations of the elements fire and air. Practical instructions can be found in Fryba 1989: p.123; or in Pa Auk 1996: p.17; cf. also Ehara 1995: pp.197–205; and Vism 351. In some contexts the scheme of the four elements is extended to cover five or even six elements, e.g. at M III 240, by including space and consciousness. These six elements form part of the *satipaṭṭhāna* instructions in the *Madhyama Āgama* version, while the version from the *Ekottara Āgama* has the same four that occur in the *Satipaṭṭhāna Sutta* (cf. Nhat Hanh 1990: pp.140, 158, 170). The element "space", according to M III 242, refers to the empty and hollow aspects of the body.

141 Ps I 272 and Vism 348. A butcher occurs also at M I 364, where it is precisely his skill in cutting out a bone so that no flesh is left on it for a dog to satisfy its hunger which forms the central aspect of the simile.

142 e.g. M I 186 gives an extensive application of the four element meditation to both oneself and to the external environment; cf. also Debes 1994: p.139; and King 1992: p.39. Ñāṇananda 1993: p.10, aptly brings out the effect of this type of contemplation by speaking of conceit as "a misappropriation of public property (i.e. earth, water, fire, air)".

143 Sn 937 points out that the world is entirely without essence. Cf. also M III 31, according to which realization of the selfless nature of the four elements is a determining characteristic of full awakening.

144 M I 185 and M I 421 relate contemplation of the four elements to insight into not-self. The same discourses follow this by applying the understanding of not-self to a situation when one is being abused or harassed by others. A II 164 similarly relates contemplation of the four elements to insight into not-self, which in this way can lead to full awakening. Cf. also Vism 640.

Mahāhatthipadopama Sutta takes up the similarity between one's own "internal" four elements and their "external" counterparts in order to bring home the truth of impermanence. The argument is that, since (according to ancient Indian cosmology) at some point in time the whole planet will meet with destruction, what permanence could there be in this insignificant accumulation of the same elements, called "body"?[145] Appreciating the impermanent nature of all material phenomena in this way serves to counteract the search for material pleasure. Relinquishing desire through disenchantment with material phenomena will then lead to freedom from the bondage caused by the four elements.[146]

An additional perspective on the four elements can be found in the *Mahārāhulovāda Sutta*, which uses the four elements as an inspiration for developing the mental qualities of loving kindness (*mettā*) and compassion (*karuṇā*). Just as the earth is free from resentment, even when various types of refuse are thrown on it, so too a meditator should develop a mind free from resentment.[147] Keeping the mind free from resentment in this way, one will be able to react with loving kindness and compassion even in adverse circumstances.[148]

These passages show that contemplation of the four elements can be employed in a variety of ways, linking the nature of one's body to the constitution of the whole material environment, or employing these material characteristics in order to develop wholesome mental attitudes.

VI.7 CORPSE IN DECAY AND MEDITATION ON DEATH

The last meditation practice among the body contemplations involves some degree of visualization, or at least reflection, since meditators have to compare their own body with what they would

---

145 M I 185. Cf. also Ledi 1986b: p.72, who suggests beginning insight meditation with this particular exercise as a basis, as it will help to rapidly develop an understanding of impermanence.

146 S II 170 points out that against the pleasure and enjoyment arising in dependence on the four elements stands their impermanent and therefore unsatisfactory nature; thus the only way out of this predicament is to develop detachment in regard to them.

147 M I 423.

148 This is exemplified at A IV 374 by Sāriputta who, wrongly accused of an offence, reacted by stating that his mind was free from resentment, just as the earth does not resent refuse being thrown on it.

see in a charnel ground.[149] The instructions for such comparison are:

> **As though he were to see a corpse thrown aside in a charnel ground – one, two, or three days dead, bloated, livid, and oozing matter ... being devoured by crows, hawks, vultures, dogs, jackals, or various kinds of worms ... a skeleton with flesh and blood, held together with sinews ... a fleshless skeleton smeared with blood, held together with sinews ... a skeleton without flesh and blood, held together with sinews ... disconnected bones scattered in all directions ... bones bleached white, the colour of shells ... bones heaped up, more than a year old ... bones rotten and crumbling to dust – he compares this same body with it thus: "this body too is of the same nature, it will be like that, it is not exempt from that fate".[150]**

In ancient India, corpses were apparently left out in the open in such charnel grounds, where they either decayed or were devoured by wild animals.[151] The above passage from the *Satipaṭṭhāna Sutta* vividly depicts the ensuing decomposition in nine stages.[152] According to Tibetan sources, the Buddha himself contemplated decaying corpses in a charnel ground, when he was still a *bodhisatta*.[153]

This exercise highlights two things: the repulsive nature of the body as revealed during the stages of its decay, and the fact that death is the inescapable destiny of all living beings. The former links this exercise to the contemplation of the body's anatomical constitution, serving as an additional tool for counteracting sensual desires.[154] This suggestion finds support in the *Mahādukkhakkhandha*

---

149 Ñāṇamoli 1995: p.1191 n.150: "*seyyathāpi* suggests that this meditation ... need not be based upon an actual encounter with a corpse ... but can be performed as an imaginative exercise". Vism 180 describes in detail how a meditator can gain the first vision of a decaying corpse in a charnel ground and subsequently develop this vision while meditating in his lodging. According to Ledi (n.d): p.58, this contemplation might similarly be developed based on sick or wounded persons (including oneself), or with dead animals as the object. Cf. also Thate 1997: p.11.

150 M I 58.

151 T.W. Rhys Davids 1997: p.80.

152 M III 91 and A III 323 subsume the same description under four main stages: the bloated body, the body eaten by animals, the skeleton, and the bones. The *Madhyama Āgama* version describes a contemplation of the same process in five stages, while the *Ekottara Āgama* version gives altogether eight stages (in Nhat Hanh 1990: pp.158 and 170).

153 Rockhill 1907: p.23.

154 e.g. Dhp-a III 108 reports that the Buddha conducted his disciples to see the rotting corpse of the beautiful courtesan Sirimā as a countermeasure to sensual desires. As 197 recommends the contemplation of a rotting corpse for those whose character

Sutta, which employs the same set of terms as a way of contemplating the inherent "disadvantage" (*ādīnava*) in material bodies.[155] Although one might be drawn to dwell on the "advantage" (*assāda*) of the beautiful bodily aspects of a young member of the opposite sex, the "disadvantage" becomes only too apparent once that same body has succumbed to old age, sickness, and finally to death, at which point this same body, which formerly appeared so attractive, proceeds through the stages of decomposition described above. This passage confirms that a central purpose of contemplating a corpse in decay is to counteract sensual desire.

Following the instructions given in the *Satipaṭṭhāna Sutta*, the vision or memory of the decomposing body is applied to one's own body, reflecting that in future one's own body will undergo the same process of decay. This kind of contemplation then also constitutes a means for counteracting conceit.[156] Subsequently, as indicated in the "refrain", the same understanding is then to be applied to the living bodies of others. Here, too, the precaution mentioned above in regard to the contemplation of the anatomical constitution applies, namely that the exercise should not lead to aversion or depression.[157]

The *Theragāthā* reports the actual practice of this *satipaṭṭhāna* exercise in a charnel ground. Two monks each contemplated a female corpse, but with different results. While one monk was able to gain insight, the other was unable to develop the contemplation, since the sight of the body provoked sensual desire in him.[158] This danger is also reflected in the commentaries, which caution against the use of a corpse belonging to the opposite sex.[159] Yet even though to contemplate a corpse of the opposite sex might not be advisable to a novice meditator, nevertheless, if carried out successfully, one would expect such a contemplation to constitute a particularly powerful antidote to sensuality.[160] In fact the *Theragāthā* also describes

---

disposition is predominantly lustful natured.

155 M I 88.

156 According to A III 323, contemplation of a corpse counters conceit.

157 Ṭhānissaro 1993: p.55.

158 Th 393–5 and Th 315–16. Another instance of a monk meditating in a cemetery can be found at Th 151–2.

159 Ps I 254.

160 In fact Ledi (n.d): p.59, recommends corpses of the opposite sex for *vipassanā* purposes, while corpses of the same sex are according to him suitable for the development of *samatha*. On contemplating a corpse as a *samatha* practice cf. Vism 178–96.

the case of a monk contemplating a female body while still alive, this being a beautiful girl singing and dancing.[161] He was able to put this vision to good use, since by wisely attending to this visual impact he became an *arahant*.

An alternative insight to be gained through this meditation practice is the inevitability of death. The stages of decay of a dead body vividly depict the truth that whatever one clings to as an embodiment of "I" or "mine" will endure only a limited time. Although this seems an obvious implication of this contemplation, the discourses usually describe recollection of death without bringing in the stages of decay. The approaches to recollecting death particularly recommended by the Buddha relate to eating and breathing: bringing to mind the fact that even the next mouthful to be eaten and the next breath to be inhaled are not certain to take place.[162] Indeed, the presence or absence of breath spells life or death, so mindfulness of breathing also has the potential to be used for recollecting death. Whatever approach one may decide to use, recollection of death helps to stir up effort in order to avoid and eradicate unwholesomeness, and can ultimately culminate in realizing the "deathless".[163]

Recollection of death also serves as a useful preparation for the time when one actually has to face death. As the concluding exercise among the body contemplations, a regular recollection of death can lead to the realization that death is fearful only to the extent to which one identifies with the body.[164] With the aid of the body contemplations one can come to realize the true nature of the body and thereby overcome one's attachment to it. Being free from attachment to the body, one will be freed from any fear of physical death.[165]

---

161 Th 267–70.

162 A III 306 and A IV 319.

163 A III 308 and A IV 320 relate recollection of death to stirring up effort to counter evil; A III 304 and A IV 317 relate the same exercise to realization of the deathless.

164 Debes 1994: p.151; and Kor 1993: p.18. A certain degree of de-identification with the body during actual contemplation is in fact directly implied in the instructions for the last three contemplations (anatomical parts, elements, corpse), where one's own body is referred to as "this same body" (M I 57–8), an expression that seems deliberately to be voiced in an impersonal manner.

165 Cf. e.g. Th 20, where an *arahant* remarks that he is not afraid of death, ready to let go of the body mindfully. Cf. also A IV 48, which relates absence of attachment to life to having repeatedly recollected death.

VII

FEELINGS

VII.1 CONTEMPLATION OF FEELINGS

The Pāli term for "feeling" is *vedanā*, derived from the verb *vedeti*, which means both "to feel" and "to know".[1] In its usage in the discourses, *vedanā* comprises both bodily and mental feelings.[2] *Vedanā* does not include "emotion" in its range of meaning.[3] Although emotions arise depending on the initial input provided by feeling, they are more complex mental phenomena than bare feeling itself and are therefore rather the domain of the next *satipaṭṭhāna*, contemplation of states of mind.

The *satipaṭṭhāna* instructions for contemplation of feelings are:

When feeling a pleasant feeling, he knows "I feel a pleasant feeling"; when feeling an unpleasant feeling, he knows "I feel an unpleasant feeling"; when feeling a neutral feeling, he knows "I feel a neutral feeling." When feeling a worldly pleasant feeling, he knows "I feel a worldly pleasant feeling"; when feeling an unworldly pleasant feeling, he knows "I feel an unworldly pleasant feeling"; when feeling a worldly unpleasant feeling, he knows "I feel a worldly unpleasant feeling"; when feeling an unworldly unpleasant feeling, he knows "I feel an unworldly unpleasant feeling"; when feeling a worldly neutral feeling, he knows "I feel a worldly neutral feeling"; when feeling

1 Hamilton 1996: p.45; and C.A.F. Rhys Davids 1978: p.299.

2 Cf. e.g. M I 302 or S IV 231; cf. also C.A.F. Rhys Davids 1978: p.300.

3 Bodhi 1993: p.80; Padmasiri de Silva 1992b: p.33; Dhīravaṃsa 1989: p.109; and Ñāṇaponika 1983: p.7.

> **an unworldly neutral feeling, he knows "I feel an unworldly neutral feeling".**[4]

The first part of the above instructions distinguishes between three basic kinds of feelings: pleasant, unpleasant, and neutral. According to the discourses, developing understanding and detachment in regard to these three feelings has the potential to lead to freedom from *dukkha*.[5] Since such understanding can be gained through the practice of *satipaṭṭhāna*,[6] contemplation of feelings is a meditation practice of considerable potential. This potential is based on the simple but ingenious method of directing awareness to the very first stages of the arising of likes and dislikes, by clearly noting whether the present moment's experience is felt as "pleasant", or "unpleasant", or neither.

Thus to contemplate feelings means quite literally to know how one feels, and this with such immediacy that the light of awareness is present before the onset of reactions, projections, or justifications in regard to how one feels. Undertaken in this way, contemplation of feelings will reveal the surprising degree to which one's attitudes and reactions are based on this initial affective input provided by feelings.

The systematic development of such immediate knowing will also strengthen one's more intuitive modes of apperception, in the sense of the ability to get a feel for a situation or another person. This ability offers a helpful additional source of information in everyday life, complementing the information gained through more rational modes of observation and consideration.

In the *satipaṭṭhāna* instructions, mindfulness of these three feelings is followed by directing awareness to an additional subdivision of feelings into "worldly" (*sāmisa*) and "unworldly" (*nirāmisa*).[7] According to a passage in the *Aṅguttara Nikāya*, this sixfold classification represents the range of diversity of feelings.[8] Thus with this sixfold scheme, contemplation of feeling comprehensively surveys the whole scale of diversity of the phenomenon "feeling" (cf. Fig. 7.1 overleaf).

---

4 M I 59.

5 A V 51. Cf. also S II 99.

6 According to S V 189, for a penetrative understanding of the three types of feelings the four *satipaṭṭhānas* are to be developed. It is remarkable that according to this passage all four *satipaṭṭhānas* are required for fully understanding feelings.

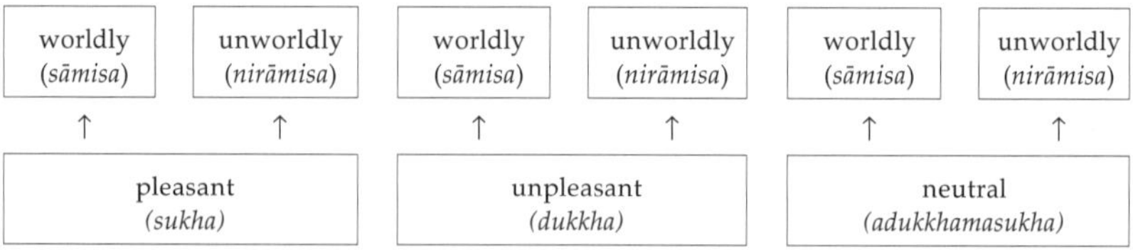

Fig. 7.1 Three and six types of feeling

The distinction between worldly (*sāmisa*) and unworldly (*nirāmisa*) feelings is concerned with the difference between feelings related to the "flesh" (*āmisa*) and feelings related to renunciation.[9] This additional dimension revolves around an evaluation of feeling that is based not on its affective nature, but on the ethical context of its arising. The basic point introduced here is awareness of whether a particular feeling is related to progress or regress on the path.

Unlike his ascetic contemporaries, the Buddha did not categorically reject all pleasant feelings, nor did he categorically recommend unpleasant experiences for their supposedly purifying effect. Instead, he placed emphasis on the mental and ethical consequences

---

7 The Chinese version of this contemplation in the *Madhyama Āgama* additionally lists feelings connected with desire (and those which are not), and feelings related to food, while the *Ekottara Āgama* version directs awareness to the fact that the presence of one type of feeling excludes the presence of the other two (in Minh Chau 1991: p.93; and Nhat Hanh 1990: pp.161 and 173). The latter suggestion has its Pāli parallel at D II 66. Additional categories can also be found at Paṭis II 233, which includes feelings differentiated according to the six senses under contemplation of feelings. In fact, according to M I 398 the sixfold classification in the above *satipaṭṭhāna* instructions can be further expanded not only by bringing in the six senses, but also by distinguishing occurrences in past, future, and present times, thereby totalling one-hundred-and-eight types of feeling altogether. An alternative threefold scheme for contemplation of feelings has been developed by Mogok Sayadaw (in Than Daing 1970: p.90) by distinguishing between five sense door feelings as "external visitors", mental feelings as "internal visitors", and feelings related to in- and out-breathing as "host visitors".

8 A III 412.

9 Ps I 279 explains that worldly pleasant feelings are those related to the five sense-pleasures, whereas their unworldly counterparts are those related to renunciation. Cf. also S IV 235, which distinguishes between joy or happiness that is worldly (sensuality), unworldly (absorption), and completely unworldly (realization). The qualification *āmisa* is often used in the discourses in the sense of "materialistic" as opposed to "*dhamma*", e.g. monks honouring "material" things more than the *Dhamma* at M I 12 and A I 73 (cf. also A I 91–4); or a "material" gift at It 98. According to Goenka 1999: p.53, and Soni 1980: p.6, the same two terms are used in present-day India to distinguish between vegetarian and non-vegetarian food. Nhat Hanh 1990: p.71, understands the two terms to represent the distinction between physiological and psychological causes of feelings (e.g. a bad feeling resulting from having gone to bed late the night before would be "worldly"). Maurice Walshe 1987: p.591 n.658 and n.659 suggests "carnal" and "spiritual" as renderings.

of all types of feeling. With the help of the above sixfold classification, this ethical dimension becomes apparent, uncovering in particular the relation of feelings to the activation of a latent mental tendency (*anusaya*) towards lust, irritation, or ignorance.[10] As the *Cūḷavedalla Sutta* points out, the arising of these underlying tendencies is mainly related to the three worldly types of feelings, whereas unworldly pleasant or neutral feelings arising during deep concentration, or unworldly unpleasant feelings arising owing to dissatisfaction with one's spiritual imperfection, do not stimulate these underlying tendencies.[11]

The conditional relation between feelings and such mental tendencies is of central importance, since by activating these latent tendencies, feelings can lead to the arising of unwholesome mental reactions. The same principle underlies the corresponding section of the twelve links of dependent co-arising (*paṭicca samuppāda*), where feelings form the condition that can lead to the arising of craving (*taṇhā*).[12]

This crucially important conditional dependence of craving and mental reactions on feeling probably constitutes the central reason why feelings have become one of the four *satipaṭṭhānas*. In addition, the arising of pleasant or unpleasant feelings is fairly easy to notice, which makes feelings convenient objects of meditation.[13]

A prominent characteristic of feelings is their ephemeral nature. Sustained contemplation of this ephemeral and impermanent nature of feelings can then become a powerful tool for developing disenchantment with them.[14] A detached attitude towards feelings, owing to awareness of their impermanent nature, is characteristic of the experiences of an *arahant*.[15]

---

10 Cf. M I 303; M III 285; and S IV 205. The relation of the three types of feeling to their respective latent tendencies has inspired a variation of contemplation of feelings in the *Ratnacūḍa Sūtra* (quoted in Bendall 1990: p.219), where the instructions are that if one experiences a pleasant feeling, one should develop compassion towards beings indulging in passion, while in the case of unpleasant feeling compassion is to be directed towards beings indulging in hatred, and with neutral feeling towards beings subject to delusion.

11 M I 303.

12 Described in detail at D II 58.

13 According to Ps I 277, feelings are a clearer object for *satipaṭṭhāna* than consciousness or contact, because the arising of pleasant or unpleasant feelings is easily noticed.

14 This is exemplified at A IV 88, where the Buddha elaborated the injunction "nothing is worth clinging to" by teaching contemplation of the impermanent nature of feelings, a contemplation he then showed to be capable of leading to realization.

Another aspect inviting contemplation is the fact that the affective tone of any feeling depends on the type of contact that has caused its arising.[16] Once this conditioned nature of feelings is fully apprehended, detachment arises naturally and one's identification with feelings starts to dissolve.

A poetic passage in the *Vedanā Saṃyutta* compares the nature of feelings to winds in the sky coming from different directions.[17] Winds may be sometimes warm and sometimes cold, sometimes wet and sometimes dusty. Similarly, in this body different types of feelings arise. Sometimes they are pleasant, sometimes neutral, and sometimes unpleasant. Just as it would be foolish to contend with the vicissitudes of the weather, one need not contend with the vicissitudes of feelings. Contemplating in this way, one becomes able to establish a growing degree of inner detachment with regard to feelings. A mindful observer of feelings, by the very fact of observation, no longer fully identifies with them and thereby begins to move beyond the conditioning and controlling power of the pleasure–pain dichotomy.[18] The task of undermining identification with feelings is also reflected in the commentaries, which point out that to inquire "who feels?" is what leads from merely experiencing feeling to contemplating them as a *satipaṭṭhāna*.[19]

For the sake of providing some additional information about the importance and relevance of contemplation of feelings, I will now briefly consider the relation of feelings to the forming of views (*diṭṭhi*) and opinions, and examine in more detail the three types of feelings presented in the *satipaṭṭhāna* instructions.

---

15 M III 244 describes the *arahant*'s detached attitude to feelings owing to his or her understanding of their impermanent nature.

16 M III 242.

17 S IV 218.

18 Debes 1994: p.227.

19 Ps I 275. The commentary explains that the purpose of this form of inquiry is to overcome the notion of a self that feels. Cf. also D II 68, which points out two prominent identification patterns for feelings: "feeling is my self" and "my self feels". These come, together with the view "my self is without feeling", as three ways of construing a sense of self in regard to feeling. Their removal then leads to realization. On this passage cf. Bodhi 1995: pp.34–6. The importance of dissociating feeling from any notion of "I" or "mine" is also stressed by Ñāṇapoṇika 1983: p.4.

VII.2 FEELINGS AND VIEWS (*DIṬṬHI*)

The cultivation of a detached attitude towards feelings is the introductory theme of the *Brahmajāla Sutta*. At the outset of this discourse, the Buddha instructed his monks to be neither elated by praise nor displeased by blame, since either reaction would only upset their mental composure. Next, he comprehensively surveyed the epistemological grounds underlying the different views prevalent among ancient Indian philosophers and ascetics. By way of conclusion to this survey he pointed out that, having fully understood feelings, he had gone beyond all these views.[20]

The intriguing feature of the Buddha's approach is that his analysis focused mainly on the psychological underpinnings of views, rather than on their content.[21] Because of this approach, he was able to trace the arising of views to craving (*taṇhā*), which in turn arises dependent on feeling.[22] Conversely, by fully understanding the role of feeling as a link between contact and craving, the view-forming process itself can be transcended.[23] The *Pāsādika Sutta* explicitly presents such transcendence of views as an aim of *satipaṭṭhāna* contemplation.[24] Thus the second *satipaṭṭhāna*, contemplation of feelings, has an intriguing potential to generate insight into the genesis of views and opinions.

---

20 D I 16.

21 In fact, the *Brahmajāla Sutta* discusses sixty-two "grounds" for formulating views (D I 39: *dvāsaṭṭhiyā vatthūhi*), not sixty-two "views". The actual number of views is much less, as e.g. the first four "grounds" make up the one "view" of eternalism, formulated in each instance in exactly the same terms. This shows that the Buddha's analysis was mainly concerned with the epistemological grounds for formulating views, much less with the individual content of any of these views. When S IV 287 speaks of sixty-two "views" (*dvāsaṭṭhi diṭṭhigatāni Brahmajāle bhaṇitāni*) or Sn 538 of "heresies" (*osaraṇāni*), this does not really correspond to the terminology employed in the *Brahmajāla Sutta* itself.

22 At D I 39 the Buddha pointed out that all these different views arose for lack of knowledge and vision on the part of those who propounded them, who were simply under the influence of feelings and craving. The commentary Sv-pṭ I 180 explains the genesis of such views to be the outcome of not understanding the arising of feelings and therefore reacting to feelings with craving. Katz 1989: p.150, fittingly speaks of a "psychoanalysis of metaphysical claims".

23 At D I 45 the Buddha explained that one who has understood the arising and disappearance of contact (contact being the necessary condition for the arising of feelings and therewith of craving), has thereby realized what goes beyond all these views.

24 D III 141.

Sustained contemplation will reveal the fact that feelings decisively influence and colour subsequent thoughts and reactions.[25] In view of this conditioning role of feeling, the supposed supremacy of rational thought over feelings and emotions turns out to be an illusion.[26] Logic and thought often serve merely to rationalize already existing likes and dislikes, which in turn are conditioned by the arising of either pleasant or unpleasant feelings.[27] The initial stages of the perceptual process, when the first traces of liking and disliking appear, are usually not fully conscious, and their decisive influence on subsequent evaluations often passes undetected.[28]

Considered from a psychological perspective, feeling provides quick feedback during information processing, as a basis for motivation and action.[29] In the early history of human evolution, such rapid feedback evolved as a mechanism for surviving dangerous situations, when a split-second decision between flight or fight had to be made. Such decisions are based on the evaluative influence of the first few moments of perceptual appraisal, during which feeling plays a prominent role. Outside such dangerous situations, however, in the comparatively safe average living situation in the modern world, this survival function of feelings can sometimes produce inadequate and inappropriate reactions.

Contemplation of feelings offers an opportunity to bring these evaluative and conditioning functions back into conscious awareness. Clear awareness of the conditioning impact of feeling can lead to a restructuring of habitual reaction patterns that have become meaningless or even detrimental. In this way, emotions can be deconditioned at their point of origin.[30] Without such deconditioning, any affective bias, being the outcome of the initial evaluation triggered by feeling, can find its expression in apparently well-reasoned "objective" opinions and views. In contrast, a realistic appraisal of the conditional dependence of views and opinions on the initial evaluative input provided by feeling uncovers the affective attachment underlying personal views and opinions. This

---

25 Cf. e.g. M I 111, which describes how one's thoughts and reactions depend on the decisive first input provided by feeling and cognition.

26 Khantipālo 1981: p.35.

27 Premasiri 1972: p.20.

28 Burns 1994: p.33.

29 Brown 1986a: p.271.

30 Padmasiri de Silva 1981: p.22; and Dwivedi 1977: p.255.

dependency of views and opinions on the first evaluative impact of feeling is a prominent cause of subsequent dogmatic adherence and clinging.[31]

In ancient India, the Buddha's analytical approach to views formed a striking contrast to the prevalent philosophical speculations. He dealt with views by examining their affective underpinnings. For the Buddha, the crucial issue was to uncover the psychological attitude underlying the holding of any view,[32] since he clearly saw that holding a particular view is often a manifestation of desire and attachment.

An important aspect of the early Buddhist conception of right view is therefore to have the "right" attitude towards one's beliefs and views. The crucial question here is whether one has developed attachment and clinging to one's own views,[33] which often manifests in heated arguments and disputation.[34] The more right view can be kept free from attachment and clinging, the better it can unfold its full potential as a pragmatic tool for progress on the path.[35] That is, right view as such is never to be given up; in fact, it constitutes the culmination of the path. What is to be given up is any attachment or clinging in regard to it.

In the context of actual meditation practice, the presence of right view finds its expression in a growing degree of detachment and disenchantment with conditioned phenomena, owing to a deepening realization of the truth of *dukkha*, its cause, its cessation, and the

---

31 This is a recurrent theme throughout the *Aṭṭhakavagga*; see especially Sn 781; Sn 785; Sn 824; Sn 878; Sn 892; and Sn 910 on the dogmatic grasp engendered through views, and Sn 832; Sn 883; Sn 888–9; Sn 894; and Sn 904 on how this dogmatic grasp leads to deprecating others and to endless quarrelling. Cf. also Premasiri 1989: p.655, who aptly relates "view" to the concept of dogmatism.

32 Cf. also Bodhi 1992a: p.9; Burford 1994: p.47; Collins 1982: p.119; Gethin 1997b: p.222; and Gomez 1976: p.141.

33 The standard formulation of right view in the discourses is in fact directly concerned with attachment and clinging, formulated by way of the four noble truths (cf. e.g. D II 312). This scheme of the four noble truths is then applied to views themselves at A IV 68.

34 At M I 108 the Buddha, on being challenged to proclaim his view, answered that his view was such that it led to the absence of quarrelling with anyone. Cf. also M I 500, which relates understanding the impermanent nature of the three types of feeling to freedom from disputation. At S III 138 the Buddha summed up his non-contentious attitude with: "I do not dispute with the world, it is the world that disputes with me."

35 A pragmatic attitude towards one's own view is recommended at M I 323 and at A III 290, both instances specifying that the purpose of one's view should be to bring about inner tranquillity and lead to freedom from *dukkha*.

way leading to its cessation. Such detachment is also reflected in the absence of "desires and discontent", stipulated in the *satipaṭṭhāna* "definition", and in the instruction to avoid "clinging to anything in the world", mentioned in the *satipaṭṭhāna* "refrain".

VII.3 PLEASANT FEELING AND THE IMPORTANCE OF JOY

The conditioning role of pleasant feelings in leading to likes and eventually to dogmatic attachment has some far-reaching implications. But this does not mean that all pleasant feelings have simply to be avoided. In fact, the realization that pleasant feelings are not simply to be shunned was a direct outcome of the Buddha's own quest for liberation.

On the eve of his awakening, the Buddha had exhausted the traditional approaches to realization, without gaining awakening.[36] While recollecting his past experiences and considering what approach might constitute an alternative, he remembered a time in his early youth when he experienced deep concentration and pleasure, having attained the first absorption (*jhāna*).[37] Reflecting further on this experience, he came to the conclusion that the type of pleasure experienced then was not unwholesome, and therefore not an obstacle to progress.[38] The realization that the pleasure of absorption constitutes a wholesome and advisable type of pleasant feeling marked a decisive turning point in his quest. Based on this crucial

---

36 Neither highly refined degrees of concentration, nor the pursuit of various ascetic practices, had been able to lead him to full awakening, so (at M I 246) he questioned himself: "Could there be another way to realization?" His unremitting effort to continue his quest even after exhausting all known approaches to realization might underlie M I 219 and also A I 50, both instances presenting his awakening as the outcome of undaunted striving. His departure from all hitherto known ways of approaching realization is indicated by the expression "things unheard of before" (e.g. at M II 211 and S V 422).

37 M I 246. On this passage cf. also Horsch 1964: p.107. The discourse does not give his exact age, though judging from the context it must have been at some point during his childhood. Mil 289 makes the rather improbable suggestion that he was only one month old and attained not just the first but all four *jhānas*. The Tibetan sources (Rockhill 1907: p.23) place this episode on the eve of his going forth, which also seems improbable.

38 M I 246 reports him as reflecting: "Why am I afraid of a happiness that has nothing to do with sensuality and unwholesome states? I am not afraid of such a happiness!" Based on this insight he realized awakening. Such understanding of the importance of an ethical evaluation of mental events is also reflected at M I 114 with his pre-awakening division of thoughts into wholesome and unwholesome ones.

understanding, the Buddha was soon able to break through to awakening, which earlier, in spite of considerable concentrative attainments and a variety of ascetic practices, he had been unable to achieve.

After his awakening, the Buddha declared himself to be one who lived in happiness.[39] This statement clearly shows that, unlike some of his ascetic contemporaries, the Buddha was no longer afraid of pleasant feelings. As he pointed out, it was precisely the successful eradication of all mental unwholesomeness that caused his happiness and delight.[40] In a similar vein, the verses composed by awakened monks and nuns often extol the happiness of freedom gained through the successful practice of the path.[41] The presence of delight and non-sensual joy among the awakened disciples of the Buddha often found its expression in poetic descriptions of natural beauty.[42] Indeed, the early Buddhist monks delighted in their way of life, as testified by a visiting king who described them as "smiling and cheerful, sincerely joyful and plainly delighting, living at ease and unruffled".[43] This description forms part of a comparison made by the king between the followers of the Buddha and other ascetics, whose demeanour was comparatively gloomy. To him, the degree of joy exhibited by the Buddha's disciples corroborated the appropriateness of the Buddha's teaching. These passages document the significant role of non-sensual joy in the life of the early Buddhist monastic community.

The skilful development of non-sensual joy and happiness was an outcome of the Buddha's first-hand realization, which had shown

---

39 A I 136; cf. also Dhp 200.

40 D I 196; cf. also D II 215. According to Ps I 297 with full awakening, joy (as an awakening factor) also reaches perfection.

41 Th 35; Th 526; Th 545; Th 888; and Thī 24.

42 e.g. at M I 212, where the beauty of the moon-lit Gosiṅga forest became the occasion for several senior disciples to extol various qualities of a monk; or the descriptions of natural beauty in the verses of awakened monks at Th 13; Th 22; Th 113; Th 307–10; Th 523; Th 527–8; Th 601; Th 1062; Th 1064; Th 1065; Th 1068–70; and Th 1136. At D II 267, the Buddha even expressed his appreciation for a slightly sensuous piece of music performed by the *gandhabba* Pañcasikha, whose song drew comparisons between the beauty of his beloved and the beauty of the life of *arahants*; on this passage cf. Gnanarama 1998: pp.119–21. On the appreciation of natural beauty by the Buddha and his monks cf. also Gokhale 1976: p.106; Kariyawasam 1984: p.359; and Nhat Hanh 1990: p.62.

43 M II 121; cf. also Rahula 1997: p.52. In fact, according to A V 122, one who delights in the Buddha's teaching will experience happiness, whether walking, standing, sitting, or lying down.

him the need to differentiate between wholesome and unwholesome types of pleasure.[44] The *satipaṭṭhāna* instructions for contemplating feelings reflect this wisdom by distinguishing between worldly and unworldly types of pleasant feelings.

The ingenuity of the Buddha's approach was not only his ability to discriminate between forms of happiness and pleasure which are to be pursued and those which are to be avoided, but also his skilful harnessing of non-sensual pleasure for the progress along the path to realization. Numerous discourses describe the conditional dependence of wisdom and realization on the presence of non-sensual joy and happiness. According to these descriptions, based on the presence of delight (*pāmojja*), joy (*pīti*) and happiness (*sukha*) arise and lead in a causal sequence to concentration and realization. One discourse compares the dynamics of this causal sequence to the natural course of rain falling on a hilltop, gradually filling the streams and rivers, and finally flowing down to the sea.[45] Once non-sensual joy and happiness have arisen, their presence will lead naturally to concentration and realization.[46] Conversely, without gladdening the mind when it needs to be gladdened, realization will not be possible.[47]

The importance of developing non-sensual joy is also reflected in the *Araṇavibhaṅga Sutta*, where the Buddha encouraged his disciples to find out what really constitutes true happiness and, based on this understanding, to pursue it.[48] This passage refers in particular to the experience of absorption, which yields a form of happiness that far surpasses its worldly counterparts.[49] Alternatively, non-sensual pleasure can also arise in the context of insight meditation.[50]

---

44 M I 476 and M I 454. The same understanding is also reflected at Th 742, which recommends those type of pleasure that are related to the *Dhamma*; and in the expression "auspicious joy" (*kalyāṇapīti*) at Sn 969. Cf. also Premasiri 1981: p.69.

45 S II 30. Same sequence at Vin I 294, D I 73; D I 182; D I 207; D I 214; D I 232; D I 250; D III 241; D III 279; D III 288; M I 37; M I 283; S IV 78; S IV 351–8; S V 156; S V 398; A I 243; A III 21; A III 285; A V 1–6; A V 312; A V 315; A V 317; A V 329; and A V 333 (cf. also Paṭis I 85; and Vism 144). The supportive role of delight for realization is documented at Dhp 376; Dhp 381; and Th 11. According to Ayya Khema 1991: p.105, "inner joy is an absolute necessity for successful meditation". Buddhadāsa 1956: p.109, speaks of the need to develop "perpetual spiritual joy". The importance of pīti is also noted by Cousins 1973: p.120; Debes 1997: p.497; Gruber 1999: p.231; Ñāṇapoṇika 1988: p.20 n.9; and Sekhera 1995: p.104.

46 A V 2.

47 A III 435; the commentary Mp III 413 explains this as referring particularly to the need to avoid mental dullness. The importance of developing joy in the context of *satipaṭṭhāna* practice is also mentioned at S V 156.

48 M III 230.

A close examination of the *Kandaraka Sutta* brings to light a progressive refinement of non-sensual happiness taking place during the successive stages of the gradual training. The first levels of this ascending series are the forms of happiness that arise owing to blamelessness and contentment. These in turn lead to the different levels of happiness gained through deep concentration. The culmination of the series comes with the supreme happiness of complete freedom through realization.[51]

The important role of non-sensual joy is also reflected in the *Abhidhammic* survey of states of mind. Out of the entire scheme of one-hundred-and-twenty-one states of mind, the majority are accompanied by mental joy, while only three are associated with mental displeasure.[52] This suggests that the *Abhidhamma* places great emphasis on the role and importance of joy.[53] The *Abhidhammic* scheme of states of mind has moreover kept a special place for the smile of an *arahant*.[54] Somewhat surprisingly, it occurs among a set of so-called "rootless" (*ahetu*) and "inoperative" (*akiriya*) states of mind.

---

49 M III 233; cf. also M I 398.

50 M III 217 relates the experience of mental joy to gaining insight into the impermanent nature of all sense experience; according to Th 398 and Th 1071 the pleasure of insight surpasses that of fivefold music; Th 519 points out that meditating free from craving yields the highest possible form of pleasure; Dhp 373 speaks of the divine pleasure of insight; and according to Dhp 374 insight into the arising and passing away of the aggregates leads to joy and delight.

51 M I 346 speaks of the happiness gained through maintaining pure ethical conduct (*anavajjasukhaṃ*), followed by the happiness derived from restraint of the senses (*abyāsekasukhaṃ*), which in turn leads to the progressive degrees of happiness experienced during the first absorption (*vivekajaṃ pītisukhaṃ*), the second absorption (*samādhijaṃ pītisukhaṃ*), and the third absorption (*sukhavihārī*), and culminates in the happiness of realization (*nibbuto sītibhūto sukhapaṭisaṃvedī*). Cf. also Th 63 and Th 220, who speak of gaining happiness through happiness. Govinda 1991: p.61 explains: "cessation of suffering is supreme happiness and ... every step towards that aim is accompanied by ever-increasing joy". Warder 1956: p.57, even goes so far as to compare the Buddha's emphasis on the importance of joy with Epicureanism.

52 Abhidh-s 1–7 presents a scheme consisting of sixty-three states of mind accompanied by mental joy (*somanassa*), three accompanied by mental displeasure (*domanassa*), and fifty-five accompanied by equanimity (*upekkhā*); cf. also Govinda 1991: p.63.

53 A similar emphasis can be found at Kv 209, which lists a total of twenty-eight types of happiness. Cf. also Vism 143, which reports that non-sensual joy can occur at five different levels, and details eleven factors conducive to its development (at Vism 132). Various types of happiness are also listed in the *Vimuttimagga* (cf. Ehara 1995: p.5).

54 The "smile-producing state of mind, accompanied by mental joy" mentioned at Abhidh-s 2 among the rootless states of mind; cf. also Bodhi 1993: p.45. The *arahant*'s smile is documented in several discourses for the Buddha and for Moggallāna, e.g. at Vin III 105–8; M II 45; M II 74; S I 24; S II 254–8; and A III 214.

These states of mind are neither "rooted" in wholesome or unwholesome qualities, nor related to the "operation" of karma. Out of this particular group of states of mind, only one is accompanied by joy (*somanassahagatā*): the smile of the *arahant*. The unique quality of this smile was apparently sufficient ground for the *Abhidhamma* to allot it a special place within its scheme.

Extrapolating from the above, the entire scheme of the gradual training can be envisaged as a progressive refinement of joy. To balance out this picture, it should be added that progress along the path invariably involves unpleasant experiences as well. However, just as the Buddha did not recommend the avoidance of all pleasant feelings, but emphasized their wise understanding and intelligent use, so his position regarding unpleasant feelings and experiences was clearly oriented towards the development of wisdom.

VII.4 UNPLEASANT FEELING

In the historical context of ancient India, the wise analysis of feeling proposed by the Buddha constituted a middle path between the worldly pursuit of sensual pleasures and ascetic practices of penance and self-mortification. A prominent rationale behind the self-mortifications prevalent among ascetics at that time was an absolutist conception of karma. Self-inflicted pain, it was believed, brings an immediate experience of the accumulated negative karmic retribution from the past, and thereby accelerates its eradication.[55]

The Buddha disagreed with such mechanistic theories of karma. In fact, any attempt to work through the retribution of the entire sum of one's past unwholesome deeds is bound to fail, because the series of past lives of any individual is without a discernible beginning,[56] so the amount of karmic retribution to be exhausted is

---

55 e.g. M II 214, cf. also Jayawardhana 1988: p.409. Additional reasons for these practices might have been the prevalence of the idea that self-inflicted pain builds up spiritual power (*iddhi*), which can then be used to attain supernormal powers or attain liberation; or the idea that the body is the source of craving and thus, in order to eliminate craving, the body is to be mortified.

56 S II 178; S III 149; and A V 113. Goldstein 1994: p.131, rightly points out: "the idea that enlightenment comes when we clear up our karma ... is a mistaken view, because we are all trailing an infinite amount of past karma ... enlightenment does not happen because we have gotten rid of a certain amount of karmic activity. It happens when our mind cuts through delusion."

unfathomable. Besides, painful feelings can arise from a variety of other causes.[57]

Although karmic retribution cannot be avoided and will quite probably manifest in one form or another during one's practice of the path,[58] awakening is not simply the outcome of mechanically eradicating the accumulated effects of past deeds. What awakening requires is the eradication of ignorance (*avijjā*) through the development of wisdom.[59] With the complete penetration of ignorance through insight, *arahants* go beyond the range of most of their accumulated karmic deeds, apart from those still due to ripen in this present lifetime.[60]

The Buddha himself, prior to his own awakening, had also taken for granted that painful experiences have purifying effects.[61] After abandoning ascetic practices and gaining realization, he knew better. The *Cūḷadukkhakkhandha Sutta* reports the Buddha's attempt to convince some of his ascetic contemporaries of the fruitlessness of self-inflicted suffering. The discussion ended with the Buddha making the ironic point that, in contrast to the painful results of self-mortification, he was able to experience degrees of pleasure vastly

---

57 At S IV 230 the Buddha mentioned feelings originating from disorders of bile, phlegm, wind, imbalance of the bodily humours, change of climate, careless behaviour, or violence as alternatives to feelings resulting from karmical retribution. These alternatives are also enumerated at A II 87; A III 131; and A V 110; cf. also Ledi 1999d: p.66. In fact, according to A I 173 and A I 249 karma conceived as sole and absolute cause would imply a form of determinism and thereby logically exclude the possibility of living a life devoted to purification.

58 A V 292; A V 297; and A V 299 emphasize the impossibility of completely avoiding karmic retribution. Dhp 127 points out that there is no spot in the whole world where one could escape the retribution of one's evil deeds. Cf. also Ud 21, which reports a monk, seated in meditation, experiencing pain because of former deeds. However, as A I 249 points out, the intensity of karmic retribution depends to a great extent on the present moral and mental condition of the person in question, in the sense that a particularly unwholesome deed might lead an immoral person to hell, but will not have the same consequences in the case of an otherwise moral person.

59 A IV 382 clearly denies that the holy life under the Buddha is lived for the purpose of altering or eradicating karmic results that have not yet ripened, clarifying that the purpose is rather to develop knowledge and wisdom. To attempt to eradicate the results of past karma was a Jain position, which the Buddha criticized at M II 216 and M II 222.

60 The simple logic behind this it that the karmic results bound to ripen in future lives will no longer have an opportunity to produce results (cf. e.g. Th 81). In the case of the *arahant* Aṅgulimāla, for example, retribution for his former crimes could only take place within the limited scope of that same lifetime (cf. M II 104).

61 M II 93.

superior even to those available to the king of the country.[62] Clearly, for the Buddha, realization did not depend on merely enduring painful feelings.[63] In fact, considered from the psychological viewpoint, intentional subjection to self-inflicted pain can be an expression of deflected aggression.[64]

The experience of unpleasant feelings can activate the latent tendency to irritation and lead to attempts to repress or avoid such unpleasant feelings. Moreover, aversion to pain can, according to the Buddha's penetrating analysis, fuel the tendency to seek sensual gratification, since from the unawakened point of view the enjoyment of sensual pleasures appears to be the only escape from pain.[65] This creates a vicious circle in which, with each experience of feeling, pleasant or unpleasant, the bondage to feeling increases.

The way out of this viscious circle lies in mindful and sober observation of unpleasant feelings. Such non-reactive awareness of pain is a simple but effective method for skilfully handling a painful experience. Simply observing physical pain for what it is prevents it from producing mental repercussions. Any mental reaction of fear or resistance to pain would only increase the degree of unpleasantness of the painful experience. An accomplished meditator might be able to experience solely the physical aspect of an unpleasant feeling without allowing mental reactions to arise. Thus meditative skill and insight have an intriguing potential for preventing physical sickness from affecting the mind.[66]

The discourses relate this ability of preventing physical pain from affecting mental composure to the practice of *satipaṭṭhāna* in particular.[67] In this way, a wise observation of pain through *satipaṭṭhāna* can transform experiences of pain into occasions for deep insight.

---

62 M I 95.

63 M I 241.

64 Cf. Padmasiri de Silva 1991: p.71.

65 S IV 208. The Buddha then illustrated the unawakened worldling's predicament in the case of pain with being shot by two darts, since over and above the "dart" of physical pain, the mental reaction leads to more *dukkha*, viz. another dart. Cf. also Lily de Silva 1987: p.19; Kor 1991: p.6, and 1995: p.18.

66 S III 1 instructs: "you should train like this: my body may be sick, yet my mind will not be afflicted." The discourse explains that the point is to avoid identification with any of the five aggregates (and thereby with the pain). This suggests a sense of dissociation from the experience of pain, as if the affected part of the body did not belong to one. Although one continues to be aware of the pain as an objective phenomenon, this act of dissociation or de-identification diminishes or even removes the affective impact of the pain on the mind.

VII.5 NEUTRAL FEELING

While pleasant and unpleasant feelings can activate the respective latent tendencies to lust and irritation, neutral feelings can stimulate the latent tendency to ignorance.[68] Ignorance in regard to neutral feelings is to be unaware of the arising and disappearance of neutral feelings, or not to understand the advantage, disadvantage, and escape in relation to neutral feelings.[69] As the commentaries point out, awareness of neutral feelings is not an easy task and should best be approached by way of inference, by noting the absence of both pleasant and unpleasant feelings.[70]

Of further interest in a discussion of neutral feeling is the *Abhidhammic* analysis of feeling tones arising at the five physical sense doors. The *Abhidhamma* holds that only the sense of touch is accompanied by pain or pleasure, while feelings arising at the other four sense doors are invariably neutral.[71] This *Abhidhammic* presentation offers an intriguing perspective on contemplation of feeling, since it invites an inquiry into the degree to which an experience of delight or displeasure in regard to sight, sound, smell, or taste is simply the outcome of one's own mental evaluation.

In addition to this inquiry, a central feature to be contemplated in regard to neutral feelings is their impermanent nature.[72] This is of particular importance because, in actual experience, neutral feeling appears easily to be the most stable of the three types of feeling. Thus to counteract the tendency to regard it as permanent, its impermanent nature need to be observed. Contemplated in this way, neutral feeling will lead to the arising of wisdom, thereby counteracting the latent tendency to ignorance.

---

67 According to S V 302, painful bodily feelings cannot overpower a mind well established in *satipaṭṭhāna*. The Buddha himself, by remaining mindful and clearly knowing, was able to endure unperturbed the intense pain of a serious injury to his foot (at S I 27 and S I 110).

68 M I 303.

69 M III 285.

70 Ps I 277. The commentary illustrates this using the example of a hunter seeing tracks before and after a rock, thereby inferring the path an animal had taken.

71 Dhs 139–45; more explicitly at Abhidh-s 2; cf. also C.A.F. Rhys Davids 1922: p.171 n.2. The discourses offer a somewhat different perspective, since they speak of pleasant and unpleasant sights, sounds, smells, and tastes, these in turn providing the conditions for the arising of corresponding feelings of pleasure or displeasure; cf. e.g. S IV 115; S IV 119; S IV 125; and S IV 126.

72 It 47.

The *Saḷāyatanavibhaṅga Sutta* points out that the difference between neutral feelings associated with ignorance and those associated with wisdom is related to whether such feelings transcend their object.[73] In the deluded case, neutral feeling is predominantly the result of the bland features of the object, where the lack of effect on the observer results in the absence of pleasant or unpleasant feelings. Conversely, neutral feeling related to the presence of wisdom transcends the object, since it results from detachment and equanimity, and not from the pleasant or unpleasant features of the object.

According to the same discourse, the establishment of such equanimity is the result of a progressive refinement of feelings, during which at first the three types of feelings related to a life of renunciation are used to go beyond their more worldly and sensual counterparts.[74] In the next stage, mental joy related to renunciation is used to confront and go beyond difficulties related to renunciation. This process of refinement then leads up to equanimous feelings, transcending even non-sensual feelings of mental joy. Equanimity and detachment as a culmination of practice also occur in the *satipaṭṭhāna* refrain for contemplation of feelings, which instructs the meditator to contemplate all kinds of feeling "free from dependencies" and "without clinging".[75]

73 M III 219.
74 M III 220.
75 M I 59: "he abides independent, not clinging to anything in the world. That is how in regard to feelings he abides contemplating feelings."

VIII

MIND

VIII.1 CONTEMPLATION OF THE MIND

During the later part of the previous *satipaṭṭhāna*, contemplation of feeling, awareness was concerned with the ethical distinction between worldly and unworldly feelings. The same distinction occurs at the start of the next *satipaṭṭhāna*, which directs awareness to the ethical quality of the mind, namely to the presence or absence of lust (*rāga*), anger (*dosa*), and delusion (*moha*).[1] The instructions are:

> **He knows a lustful mind to be "lustful", and a mind without lust to be "without lust"; he knows an angry mind to be "angry", and a mind without anger to be "without anger"; he knows a deluded mind to be "deluded", and a mind without delusion to be "without delusion"; he knows a contracted mind to be "contracted", and a distracted mind to be "distracted"; he knows a great mind to be "great", and a narrow mind to be "narrow"; he knows a surpassable mind to be "surpassable", and an unsurpassable mind to be "unsurpassable"; he knows a concentrated mind to be "concentrated", and an unconcentrated mind to be "unconcentrated"; he knows a liberated mind to be "liberated", and an unliberated mind to be "unliberated".**[2]

Contemplation of the mind makes use of altogether eight categories

---

1 Cf. also Khantipālo 1981: p.37.
2 M I 59.

(cf. Fig. 8.1 below).[3] In each case, the task of *sati* is to know a particular mental quality or its opposite, so that contemplation of the mind actually covers sixteen states of mind. The same set of sixteen states appears elsewhere in the discourses in relation to telepathic abilities.[4] Thus from the perspective of the discourses this set forms a representative list of states of mind that is relevant both to personal introspection and to assessing another's mind.

These sixteen states of mind (or eight categories) can be subdivided into two sets. The first set contrasts unwholesome and wholesome states of mind, while the second set is concerned with the presence or absence of higher states of mind. I will examine these different states of mind individually, following an introductory assessment of contemplation of the mind in general.

"ordinary" states of mind	"higher" states of mind
lustful (*sarāga*)	great (*mahaggata*)
angry (*sadosa*)	unsurpassable (*anuttara*)
deluded (*samoha*)	concentrated (*samāhita*)
distracted (*vikkhitta*)	liberated (*vimutta*)

Fig. 8.1 Eight categories for contemplation of the mind

Underlying this *satipaṭṭhāna* is an implicit shift in emphasis from the ordinary way of experiencing mind as an individual entity to considering mental events as mere objects, analysed in terms of their qualitative characteristics.[5] Contemplation of the mind also includes, in accordance with the *satipaṭṭhāna* "refrain", awareness of the arising and passing away of the states of mind being contemplated, thereby revealing the momentary character of all mental events. In addition, sustained contemplation of the mind will also expose the degree to which what one takes to be one's own mind is in fact influenced by external conditions. In this way, realizing the

3 In addition to these eight categories, the Chinese version of this contemplation in the *Madhyama Āgama* lists the mind "with blemishes", and "without blemishes", while the *Ekottara Āgama* has "craving" and "mastery of the mind" as additional categories (in Minh Chau 1991: p.93; and Nhat Than 1990: pp.162 and 174). Paṭis II 234 includes the six types of consciousness (differentiated according to the six sense doors) in its list for contemplation of the mind.

4 e.g. at M I 495.

5 Bodhi 1984: p.98; and Piatigorski 1984: p.41. C.A.F. Rhys Davids 1978: p.8, draws attention to the novelty of this approach in the history of Indian thought.

impermanent and conditioned nature of the mind accords with the general thrust of *satipaṭṭhāna* towards detachment and non-identification.

VIII.2 NON-REACTIVE AWARENESS OF ONE'S STATE OF MIND

It is noteworthy that contemplation of the mind does not involve active measures to oppose unwholesome states of mind (such as lust or anger). Rather, the task of mindfulness is to remain receptively aware by clearly recognizing the state of mind that underlies a particular train of thoughts or reactions. Such uninvolved receptivity is required because of one's instinctive tendency to ignore whatever contradicts or threatens one's sense of importance and personal integrity. The habit of employing self-deception to maintain one's self esteem has often become so ingrained that the first step to developing accurate self-awareness is honest acknowledgment of the existence of hidden emotions, motives, and tendencies in the mind, without immediately suppressing them.[6] Maintaining non-reactive awareness in this way counters the impulse towards either reaction or suppression contained in unwholesome states of mind, and thereby deactivates their emotional and attentional pull.[7]

The *Vitakkasaṇṭhāna Sutta* offers a description of such deactivation: in order to come to grips with the repeated occurrence of unwholesome thoughts, attention turns to the nature of these thoughts and to the volitional disposition or driving force that produced them.[8] The discourse explains this simple but ingenious method of turning the full light of attention on the mental condition underlying one's thoughts with the help of a simile. One is walking quite fast for no particular reason. Becoming fully aware of what one is doing, one might walk slower, or even stand still, or instead of

---

6 Bullen 1982: p.29.

7 Newman 1996: pp.35 and 46. Cf. also A V 39, which explains that while unwholesome conduct by way of body or speech is to be overcome by adopting more appropriate ways of conduct, the proper approach for overcoming mental defilements is repeated wise observation. A clinical case supporting the ingenuity of this approach is documented by Deatherage 1975: p.140, where a twenty-three-year-old male, hospitalized for extreme periodic aggressiveness and alcohol abuse, was cured within eight weeks simply by being taught to recognize and mentally name the emotions he experienced, without even knowing that what he was doing was related to "meditation". Another chronic anger case-study involving awareness of mind as cure can be found in Woolfolk 1984: p.551.

8 M I 120.

standing one might sit or lie down. This progressive increase in physical comfort and tranquillity vividly illustrates how the mental agitation and tension of unwholesome thought processes can be gradually reduced and overcome through direct observation. Watching an unwholesome state of mind without involvement in this way will deprive it of its fuel so that it will gradually lose its power.

Such mindful observation without involvement is illustrated in a simile in the discourses in which the Buddha compared awareness of one's states of mind to the use of a mirror to see one's reflection.[9] Just as a mirror simply reflects whatever is presented to it, meditators should try to maintain bare awareness of the present condition of their mind without allowing reactions to arise.

However, the same *Vitakkasaṇṭhāna Sutta* speaks also of "beating down and crushing mind with mind" as an alternative approach in order to deal with unwholesome thoughts.[10] This appears to disagree with the aforementioned. But once this instruction is considered in its context, it becomes clear that it comes only as a last resort, after all other alternative approaches, including the above discussed deactivation, have proved ineffective.[11] Thus to "beat down and crush mind with mind" is an emergency measure when all else has failed. When the situation is about to get out of hand, the use of force will at least prevent the obsessive negative thoughts from spilling over into unwholesome activity. "To beat down and crush mind with mind" is in fact on another occasion counted by the Buddha among those fruitless exercises which he himself had tried and discarded prior to his awakening.[12] This goes to show that the use of mere force is not intended for mental development in general, but in cases of emergency only.

---

9 A V 92; the same simile occurs also at D I 80 and M I 100. Cf. also Samararatne 1997: p.141, who recommends maintaining a "mirror-like mind", especially in regard to unpleasant emotions.

10 M I 120.

11 The other approaches, in addition to the above-mentioned directing of attention to the nature of these thoughts and to the volitional disposition underlying them, are to direct attention to something wholesome instead, or to reflect on the danger of succumbing to these unwholesome thoughts, or to try to forget these thoughts. A similar case can be found at A IV 87, where after an extensive list of different methods for staying awake and countering drowsiness, the final recommendation is to go to sleep mindfully. Clearly, in this case too, the last method is not really helpful for staying awake, but is also the last resort when all other measures had failed.

12 At M I 242.

VIII.3 FOUR "ORDINARY" STATES OF MIND

Citta, the Pāli term used in this *satipaṭṭhāna*, usually refers in the discourses to "mind" in the conative and emotional sense, in the sense of one's mood or state of mind.[13]

The first three among the states of mind listed in the *satipaṭṭhāna* instruction are lust (*rāga*), anger (*dosa*), and delusion (*moha*), the three main roots of all unwholesome mental events.[14] The basic principle underlying the contemplation of these unwholesome roots, which also underlies the distinction between worldly and unworldly feelings in the previous *satipaṭṭhāna*, is the clear distinction between what is wholesome and what is unwholesome. Systematic development of this ability nurtures an intuitive ethical sensitivity which constitutes an important asset in one's progress on the path and a reliable guide to proper conduct in daily life.

The *Satipaṭṭhāna Sutta* presents each of these "roots" together with its opposite: the absence of lust, anger, or delusion. This way of presentation is common in canonical usage, allowing the negative term to cover not only the opposite notion, but also to imply a wider range of meaning.[15] Thus to be "without anger", for example, could refer simply to a state of mind free from irritation, but also to a mind overflowing with loving kindness.

During meditation, each of these three unwholesome roots can manifest in a distinctive manner: the fever of lust may be compared to being on fire within, the physical tension of anger to being overpowered and controlled by a forceful opponent, and the confusion of delusion to being hopelessly entangled in a net.[16]

Taken in an absolute sense, a mind without lust, anger, and delusion is the mind of an *arahant*.[17] This way of understanding is in fact

---

13 T.W. Rhys Davids 1993: p.266; on the term *citta* cf. also page 205, footnote 21.

14 Taking *rāga* as a synonym for *lobha*. A detailed exposition of the three roots can be found in Ñāṇaponika 1978.

15 Khantipālo 1981: p.38.

16 Dhp 251 poetically points out that there is no fire like lust, no grip like anger, and no net like delusion. Buddhadāsa 1989: p.67, suggests distinguishing between mental tendencies such as "pulling in", "pushing away", and "running around in circles", in order to recognize the three unwholesome roots.

17 Cf. e.g. M I 5, where *arahants* are said to be free from these three through their eradication; M I 65, which refers to realized ascetics as free from lust, anger, and delusion; M I 236 and S I 220, where the Buddha referred to himself as free from lust, anger, and delusion; and A III 43; A III 336; and A III 347, which associate such freedom to absence of the influxes.

the most frequent usage of the qualification "without lust", "without anger", and "without delusion" in the discourses. Thus contemplation of the mind appears to be not only concerned with momentary states of mind, but also with the overall condition of the mind. Understood in this way, to contemplate mind unaffected by lust, anger, or delusion would also include awareness of the degree to which these three unwholesome roots are no longer "rooted" in one's mental continuum.[18]

The two states of mind listed next for contemplation, contracted (*saṅkhitta*) and distracted (*vikkhitta*), both appear to have negative implications.[19] The same two terms occur elsewhere in the discourses, with inward "contraction" being the result of sloth-and-torpor, and external "distraction" the outcome of pursuing sensual pleasures.[20] The commentaries on the *Satipaṭṭhāna Sutta* indeed relate the "contracted" state of mind to sloth-and-torpor, while according to them the "distracted" state of mind represents restlessness.[21]

The ability to balance the mind, by avoiding both contraction and distraction, is an important skill required for the development of deeper levels of concentration or insight. The placing of these two states of mind at this point in the instructions for contemplation of the mind indicates the need to cultivate such balance, once one has at least temporarily moved beyond the reach of the grosser types of mental unwholesomeness and is aiming towards the development

---

18 Cf. e.g. A IV 404, where awareness of their absence is part of the reviewing knowledge of an *arahant*.

19 Alternatively, in order to conform with the pattern in this *satipaṭṭhāna* of presenting a positive state of mind together with its negative counterpart, the contracted (*saṅkhitta*) state of mind could be taken in a positive sense, as a "concentrated" or "attentive" state of mind (cf. T.W. Rhys Davids 1993: p.665). The corresponding verb *saṅkhipati* does indeed occur in this positive sense at Ja I 82, when the Buddha radiated loving kindness to his five earlier followers on their first meeting after his awakening. Cf. also Goenka 1999: p.57, who translates *saṅkhitta* as "collected" and "concentrated."

20 S V 279. The relation of these two to "internal" and "external" occurs again at A IV 32.

21 Ps I 280. However, in the above mentioned discourse at S V 279 the hindrance restlessness occurs separately, apparently not forming part of "distracted", whereas according to the commentarial explanation the two should be identical. The relation of "distracted" to the search for sense gratification (as at S V 279) occurs also at M III 225. The consequences of a distracted state of mind are, according to A V 147, that one becomes unable to direct one's attention skilfully, avoid unwholesome behaviour, or overcome mental inertia.

of "higher" states of mind, such as are described in the remainder of this *satipaṭṭhāna*.

VIII.4 FOUR "HIGHER" STATES OF MIND

The next qualification, "great" (*mahaggata*), occurs in other discourses often in the context of calmness meditation, for instance when describing the meditative practice of radiating the four divine abodes (*brahmavihāra*) in all directions.[22] Similarly, in the *Anuruddha Sutta* "great" represents the ability to pervade a broad area with one's meditation object, in this case apparently as the result of *kasiṇa* meditation.[23] These instances support the commentarial explanation of this part of the *satipaṭṭhāna* instructions, according to which a "great" state of mind (*mahaggata*) is related to the development of absorption.[24]

The same commentaries relate the next category mentioned for contemplation, the "surpassable" (*sa-uttara*) state of mind, to the development of concentration.[25] "Surpassable", then, indicates the need to clearly recognize the constituents of a particular level of absorption to be left behind in order to proceed to a higher level of absorption.[26] This finds support in the *Sekha Sutta*, which refers to the fourth absorption as a state of "unsurpassable" equanimity and mindfulness.[27] On the other hand, in the discourses the qualification "unsurpassable" frequently occurs in relation to full awakening.[28] Understood in this way, the present category also includes the reviewing knowledge after realization, when one investigates the degree to which the mind has been freed from fetters and mental defilements.

---

22 e.g. at M II 207.

23 M III 146. The commentary Ps IV 200 explains this pervasion to be related to *kasiṇa* meditation. A *kasiṇa* is a meditation device, for example a coloured disk, used to help develop concentration.

24 Ps I 280.

25 Ps I 280 explains "unsurpassable" to refer to absorption attainment. Sīlananda 1990: p.94, takes "unsurpassable" as a specific reference to the immaterial attainments.

26 The need to abandon lower absorption attainments is described e.g. at M I 455. Nhat Hanh 1990: p.13, renders *sa-uttara* with the expression: "my mind is capable of reaching a higher state".

27 e.g. at M I 357. The fourth *jhāna* as a level of concentration is indeed "unsurpassable", since the immaterial attainments take place with the same level of concentration, but directed towards progressively more refined objects.

28 e.g. at D II 83; M I 163; M I 303; M II 237; S I 105; S I 124; A I 168; A III 435; and Th 415.

The next term in the series, the "concentrated" (*samāhita*) state of mind, is self-explanatory. According to the commentaries, this expression includes access concentration and full absorption.[29] Since in the discourses *samādhi* refers to concentration in the context of the development of both calm and insight, the expression "concentrated mind" has a fairly broad range of reference.

The qualification "liberated" (*vimutta*) frequently occurs in the discourses in relation to full awakening.[30] Understood in this way, the "liberated" mind parallels the more frequent usage of the expression "unsurpassable mind" and also the mind that is forever "without lust", "without anger", and "without delusion", all these referring to the mind of an *arahant*.[31] The commentaries, moreover, relate the qualification "liberated" to temporary freedom from defilements during insight meditation.[32] Elsewhere in the discourses the qualification of being "liberated" occurs also in relation to the development of concentration, as "freedom of the mind" (*cetovimutti*).[33] Thus the expression "liberated mind" can be taken to refer to experiences of mental freedom in relation to both calm and insight.

The theme underlying the contemplation of these four higher states of mind is the ability to monitor the more advanced stages of one's meditative development. In this way, within the scope of contemplation of the mind, *sati* can range from recognition of the presence of lust or anger to awareness of the most lofty and sublime types of mental experience, each time with the same basic task of calmly noticing what is taking place.

The emphasis given in this *satipaṭṭhāna* to mindful contemplation of deep levels of concentration is noteworthy. Among the Buddha's contemporaries, experiences of absorption often gave rise to

---

29 Ps I 280.

30 e.g. at M I 141; S III 45; S III 51; Ud 24; and It 33.

31 The standard descriptions of full awakening use the expression "liberated" to describe the *arahant*'s knowledge of his or her realization (e.g. at D I 84). At times the expression "liberated" is combined with "unsurpassable" as references to full awakening, cf. e.g. M I 235; S I 105; or A IV 106. D III 270 and A V 31 relate the "well liberated mind" to freedom from the three unwholesome roots.

32 Ps I 280. This suggestion by the commentary can claim some support from S V 157, which speaks of a calm and undistracted state of mind, fit for *satipaṭṭhāna*, as "liberated".

33 Various types of "freedom of the mind" are listed at M I 296. Similarly, A III 16 refers to the absence of the five hindrances as a mind "liberated" from them.

speculative views.[34] The Buddha's distinctive departure from these speculations was his thoroughly analytical treatment of the meditative absorptions, aimed at understanding their composite and conditioned nature.[35] This analytical treatment is exemplified in the *Aṭṭhakanāgara Sutta*, which states that one should regard the experience of absorption as merely a product of the mind, a conditioned and volitionally produced experience.[36] Such understanding then leads to the conclusion that whatever is a product of conditions is also impermanent and subject to cessation. Insight into the impermanent nature of deep levels of concentration also forms part of *satipaṭṭhāna* practice, when the instruction in the "refrain" to contemplate the nature of arising and passing away is applied to the higher states of mind listed for contemplation.[37] Undertaken in this way, *satipaṭṭhāna* in regard to higher states of mind becomes a practical expression of the Buddha's analytical attitude towards the entire range of mental experience.

---

34 Of the sixty-two grounds for views presented in the *Brahmajāla Sutta* (D I 12–39), forty-nine appear to be related to concentrative attainments of various types: recollection of past lives [nos 1–3, 5–7, 17]; the divine eye [31–4, 51–7]; kasiṇa meditation [9–11, 19, 23–5, 29–30, 35, 39–41, 43, 47–9]; and *jhāna* in general [20–2, 27, 36–8, 44–6, 59–62]; (correlations given with the help of the commentary). This ratio (nearly 80%) constitutes an overwhelming testimony to the view-generating propensity of deep concentration experiences. The fact that *jhānic* experiences can easily lead to the formation of wrong views is also noted by Wijebandara 1993: p.21.

35 Piatigorski 1984: p.44: "in early historical Buddhism some non-Buddhist yogic experiences were realized, analysed and reworked so that they could be used without their previous or actual religious contents". Premasiri 1987b: p.178: "the distinctive feature of Buddhism is that it described these *jhāna* states purely in psychological terms, without bringing in mystical or supernatural explanations for them."

36 M I 350. Cf. also M I 436, which analyses *jhānic* experience with the help of the aggregate scheme, followed by the consideration that all these phenomena are impermanent, unsatisfactory, and not-self.

37 M I 60: "he abides contemplating the nature of arising ... of passing away ... of both arising and passing away in regard to the mind."

IX

DHAMMAS: THE HINDRANCES

IX.1 CONTEMPLATION OF *DHAMMAS*

The next contemplation in the *Satipaṭṭhāna Sutta* is concerned with a specific set of mental qualities, the five hindrances. These come as the first among the contemplations of "*dhammas*". Before embarking on a closer inspection of this exercise, I will examine the implications of the term "*dhammas*", in order to provide some background to the exercises listed under this fourth and last *satipaṭṭhāna*.

The Pāli term *dhamma* can assume a variety of meanings, depending on the context in which it occurs. Most translators take the term *dhammas* in the *Satipaṭṭhāna Sutta* to mean "mental objects", in the sense of whatever can become an object of the mind, in contradistinction to the objects of the other five senses. In regard to *satipaṭṭhāna*, however, this rendering appears strange. If the term *dhammas* were to refer to "objects of the mind", then the other three *satipaṭṭhānas* should also be included here, since they too can become objects of the mind. Moreover, one of the exercises listed under the fourth *satipaṭṭhāna* is contemplation of the six senses together with their respective objects, so this contemplation of *dhammas* is not confined to the objects of the mind as the sixth sense only. In fact, the *dhammas* listed in the fourth *satipaṭṭhāna*, such as the hindrances and the aggregates, etc., do not naturally evoke the classification "mental objects".[1]

---

1 Ṭhānissaro 1996: p.73. Paṭis II 234 simply suggests that whatever is not included in the previous three *satipaṭṭhānas* is to be understood as *dhammas* in this context. Sīlananda

What this *satipaṭṭhāna* is actually concerned with are specific mental qualities (such as the five hindrances and the seven awakening factors), and analyses of experience into specific categories (such as the five aggregates, the six sense-spheres, and the four noble truths). These mental factors and categories constitute central aspects of the Buddha's way of teaching, the *Dhamma*.[2] These classificatory schemes are not in themselves the objects of meditation, but constitute frameworks or points of reference to be applied during contemplation. During actual practice one is to look at whatever is experienced in terms of these *dhammas*.[3] Thus the *dhammas* mentioned in this *satipaṭṭhāna* are not "mental objects", but are applied to whatever becomes an object of the mind or of any other sense door during contemplation.

The expression "contemplation of *dhammas*" occurs also in the *Ānāpānasati Sutta* in relation to the last four of the sixteen steps for developing mindfulness of breathing, which are concerned with contemplating "impermanence", "fading away", "cessation", and "letting go".[4] At first sight, the four steps described here appear to be

---

1990: p.95, rejects a translation as "mental objects" and suggests leaving *dhammas* untranslated, a suggestion which I have followed. Alternative translations could be: "facts in general" (in Kalupahana 1992: p.74); "phenomena" (in Bodhi 2000: p.44, and in Jayasuriya 1988: p.161); "patterns of events" (in Harvey 1997: p.354); "conditions" (in Vajirañāṇa 1975: p.59); or "principles" (in Watanabe 1983: p.16).

2 Ñāṇamoli 1995: p.1193 n.157 explains: "in this context *dhammā* can be understood as comprising all phenomena classified by way of the categories of the Dhamma, the Buddha's teaching". Gyori 1996: p.24, in regard to contemplation of *dhammas* suggests that "the exercises ... in this section are specifically intended to invest the mind with a soteriological orientation".

3 In this context it is noticeable that the instruction for contemplation of *dhammas* employs the locative case twice, once for *dhammas* and again for the five hindrances, the five aggregates, etc. Thus one is to "contemplate *dhammas* in regard to *dhammas* in regard to the five hindrances, (etc.)", that is, one contemplates phenomena "in terms of" the categories listed as *dhammas*. This way of introducing each contemplation differs from the earlier three *satipaṭṭhānas*. Cf. also S V 184, according to which the *dhammas* contemplated in this *satipaṭṭhāna* are conditionally related to attention, while body is related to nutriment, feelings to contact, and mind to name-and-form. This suggests that contemplation of *dhammas* requires the deliberate act of directing attention to its objects, in terms of the *dhammas* listed, to a stronger degree than the other *satipaṭṭhānas*. Carrithers 1983: p.229, explains that "the propositions of doctrine are transmuted into immediate perception, here and now". Similarly Gombrich 1996: p.36, speaks of learning "to see the world through Buddhist spectacles"; while Gyatso 1992: p.8, suggests: "previously learned categories and skills inform present experience without being recollected as such". Cf. also Collins 1994: p.78.

4 M III 83.

quite different from the mental factors and categories listed under contemplation of *dhammas* in the *Satipaṭṭhāna Sutta*. The Buddha's reason for classifying these final four steps of mindfulness of breathing as contemplation of *dhammas* was that at this more advanced point of practice a meditator will have overcome desires and discontent, thereby becoming established in equanimity.[5] The commentaries indicate that this is a reference to the removal of the hindrances.[6]

Although taking desires and discontent to represent the whole set of the five hindrances is questionable,[7] this explanation provides a link between the final four steps of mindfulness of breathing and the sequence of *dhammas* in the *Satipaṭṭhāna Sutta*, since these begin with the hindrances. According to the commentaries, the hindrances lead the contemplations of *dhammas* because their removal serves as a basis for developing the comparatively sophisticated contemplations in this last *satipaṭṭhāna*.[8] A further parallel between the two discourses is that the sixteen-step scheme for mindfulness of breathing leads to the development of the awakening factors,[9] since the awakening factors also form part of the contemplation of *dhammas* in the *Satipaṭṭhāna Sutta*.

These parallels suggest that a temporal progression towards realization could form the key aspect of contemplation of *dhammas* in both cases. In the *satipaṭṭhāna* context, this progression underlies the sequential order of the mental factors and categories detailed for contemplation of *dhammas* (cf. Fig. 9.1 below): Based on a sufficient degree of mental stability through overcoming the hindrances, contemplation of *dhammas* proceeds to an analysis of subjective personality, in terms of the five aggregates, and to an analysis of the relation between subjective personality and the outer world, in terms of the six sense-spheres.[10] These two analyses form a convenient basis for developing the awakening factors, whose successful establishment constitutes a necessary condition for awakening. To

---

5 M III 84.
6 Ps IV 142.
7 Cf. page 69.
8 Ps-pṭ I 373.
9 At M III 87. Cf. also Paṭis I 191, which relates contemplation of impermanence to experiencing the rise and fall of the aggregates and sense-spheres, thereby providing an additional relation to the *satipaṭṭhāna* context.
10 Although these two contemplations would not necessarily have to be practised in this order, it seems meaningful to follow an inquiry into subjective personality with an investigation of its relationship to the external world by way of the senses.

awaken is to fully understand the four noble truths "as they really are", this being the final exercise among the contemplations of *dhammas* and the successful culmination of *satipaṭṭhāna* practice.[11]

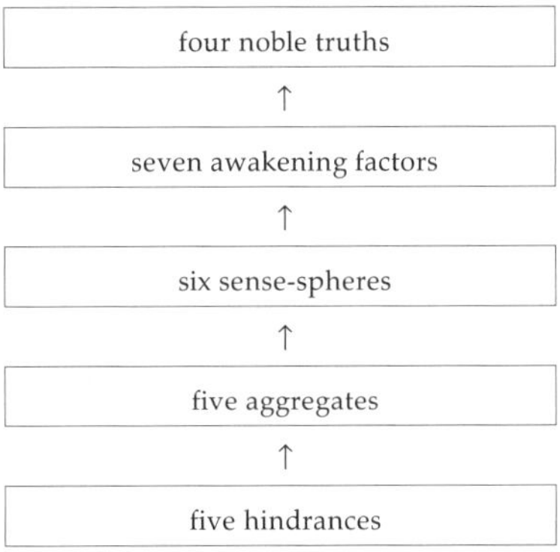

Fig. 9.1 Survey of contemplation of *dhammas*

With the final four steps of mindfulness of breathing, however, the emphasis is mainly directed towards the insights gained through contemplation of *dhammas*. These proceed from the direct experience of the impermanent nature of phenomena (*aniccānupassī*), to giving attention to their "fading away" (*virāgānupassī*) and "cessation" (*nirodhānupassī*). These in turn lead to detachment, or "letting go" (*paṭinissaggānupassī*): a state of mind fit for awakening.[12]

Contemplation of *dhammas* in both the *Satipaṭṭhāna Sutta* and the *Ānāpānasati Sutta*, then, indicates a temporal progression towards detachment and realization. Although the breakthrough to realization can take place while practising any of the sixteen steps of mindfulness of breathing, the final four steps appear to be specifically designed to this end. Similarly, although realization can take place while one is engaged in any of the *satipaṭṭhāna* contemplations, the

11 With this presentation I do not intend to suggest that these contemplations of *dhammas* necessarily have to be practised in this order and in conjunction, only that they are presented in a progressive order in the *Satipaṭṭhāna Sutta*.

12 Cf. M I 251, where the same four-step sequence, in the context of contemplating feelings, leads directly to realization. Paṭis I 194 explains contemplation of letting go to be of two types: "giving up" (the aggregates) and "leaping forward" (to realization). On "letting go" cf. also Ñāṇārāma 1997: pp.85–7; and van Zeyst 1961a: p.3. The Chinese *Saṃyukta Āgama* has preserved a different sequence for the last four steps of mindfulness of breathing, which proceeds from impermanence to "abandoning", followed by "fading away" and then culminates with "cessation" (in Choong 2000: p.227).

final section of the *Satipaṭṭhāna Sutta*, concerned with the contemplation of *dhammas*, stands out for its particular emphasis on achieving this goal.

In contrast to the previous *satipaṭṭhānas*, contemplation of *dhammas* is particularly concerned with recognizing the conditioned nature of the phenomena under observation. In fact, the main instruction for most of the contemplations of *dhammas* directly mentions conditionality, while in the previous *satipaṭṭhānas* this happens only in the "refrain". The prominence of conditionality in this *satipaṭṭhāna* brings to mind the well-known statement that one who sees dependent co-arising sees the *Dhamma*.[13] Such "seeing" (*passati*) of the *Dhamma* may well come about through "contemplating" (*anu-passati*) *dhammas*, a suggestion which also squares well with the acquisition of the "method" (*ñāya*) mentioned in the "direct path" passage of the *Satipaṭṭhāna Sutta* as a goal of practice.[14]

Thus contemplation of *dhammas* skilfully applies *dhammas* (classificatory categories) as taught in the *Dhamma* (the teaching of the Buddha) during contemplation in order to bring about an understanding of the *dhamma* (principle) of conditionality and lead to the realization of the highest of all *dhammas* (phenomena): *Nibbāna*.[15]

IX.2 CONTEMPLATION OF THE FIVE HINDRANCES

The first of the contemplations of *dhammas* is, in a way, a more specific version of contemplation of states of mind, since it turns awareness to five manifestations of the three unwholesome roots: the five hindrances. In contrast to the preceding contemplation of the mind, however, contemplation of the hindrances covers not only the presence or absence of a hindrance, but also the conditions underlying the presence or absence of each hindrance. In my exploration I will follow the two-stage pattern of this instruction, by focusing initially on the five hindrances and the importance of recognizing them, and considering subsequently the conditions for their presence or absence.

The *satipaṭṭhāna* instructions for contemplating the hindrances are:

---

13 M I 190.

14 Cf. page 111.

15 D III 102 speaks of *Nibbāna* as the highest of all wholesome *dhammas*; cf. also A II 34 and Sn 225.

If sensual desire is present in him, he knows "there is sensual desire in me"; if sensual desire is not present in him, he knows "there is no sensual desire in me"; and he knows how unarisen sensual desire can arise, how arisen sensual desire can be removed, and how a future arising of the removed sensual desire can be prevented. If aversion is present in him, he knows.... If sloth-and- torpor is present in him, he knows.... If restlessness-and-worry is present in him, he knows.... If doubt is present in him, he knows "there is doubt in me"; if doubt is not present in him, he knows "there is no doubt in me"; and he knows how unarisen doubt can arise, how arisen doubt can be removed, and how a future arising of the removed doubt can be prevented.[16]

The use of the term "hindrance" (*nīvaraṇa*) clearly indicates why these mental qualities have been singled out for special attention: they "hinder" the proper functioning of the mind.[17] Under the influence of the hindrances one is unable to understand one's own good or that of others, or to gain concentration or insight.[18] Learning to withstand the impact of a hindrance with awareness is therefore an important skill for one's progress on the path. According to the discourses, difficulties in counterbalancing a hindrance are a good reason for approaching an experienced meditator to ask for practical guidance.[19]

These five hindrances actually cover seven distinct mental qualities.[20] That these seven are subsumed under a fivefold presentation is probably due to the similarities in effect and character between sloth (*thīna*) and torpor (*middha*), and between restlessness (*uddhacca*) and worry (*kukkucca*).[21] According to the commentaries, this fivefold presentation makes it possible to correlate each hindrance with

---

16 M I 60.
17 Cf. e.g. D I 246; S V 96; and S V 97.
18 M II 203; S V 92; S V 127; and A III 63.
19 A III 317 and A III 321.
20 At S V 110 a tenfold presentation is given, by distinguishing between internal sensual desire, aversion, and doubt, and their external counterparts, while the remaining two compounds are separated into sloth, torpor, restlessness, and worry. This presentation supports the notion of seven actual mental qualities. Cf. also Gunaratana 1996: p.32. A variation of the usual fivefold presentation can be found at It 8, which has a single hindrance, the hindrance of ignorance. Another variation occurs at Paṭis I 31, Paṭis I 103, and Paṭis I 163, where enumerations of the hindrances omit worry and give ignorance and dissatisfaction instead.

one of the five mental factors needed to attain absorption (*jhāna-aṅga*).[22]

The hindrances not only obstruct absorption attainment, they also impede the establishment of the awakening factors (*bojjhaṅga*).[23] This antagonistic relationship between the hindrances and the awakening factors is of considerable importance, since the removal of the former and the development of the latter are necessary conditions for realization.[24]

Two sets of similes in the discourses depict the specific character and effect of the five hindrances. The first set of similes illustrates

---

21 The similarity between sloth and torpor is noted by Vibh 254, according to which both refer to "inability" or "unreadiness", with the difference that sloth is of a mental type, while torpor represents the bodily variation. Vibh-a 369 understands this explanation in the case of torpor to refer to mental factors, not to the physical body. But if one considers the antidotes listed for torpor at A IV 85 it becomes probable that to speak of "torpor" does refer to physical torpor. The similarity of the other two hindrances is mentioned at Ps-pṭ I 375.

22 Vism 141 explains that concentration is incompatible with sensual desire, joy with aversion, initial mental application with sloth-and-torpor, happiness with restlessness-and-worry, and sustained mental application with doubt. (On this correlation cf. also Buddhadāsa 1976: p.112; and Upali Karunaratne 1996: p.51.) The point that Vism is trying to make here could be, in the case of the first four correlations, that unification of the mind through concentration is opposed to the mental diversification caused by sensual desire, that the mental bliss and physical ease caused by the arising of joy is incompatible with the mental rigidity and physical tension of aversion, that the clear grasp of the object through initial mental application counteracts the unclarity and mental fogginess of sloth-and-torpor, and that the mental contentment and physical tranquillity engendered by happiness does not leave scope for restlessness or worry to arise (cf. Vism-mhṭ I 165). As for the fifth hindrance, if doubt (*vicikicchā*) is understood more broadly, implying not only doubt but a generally distracted state of mind (cf. T.W. Rhys Davids 1993: p.615, where the corresponding verb *vicikicchati* is related to being distracted in thought), this would then find its counterbalance in the mental stability and undistractedness produced by sustained mental application. On the other hand, it should be pointed out that in the discourses a listing of the hindrances and the individual *jhāna* factors together occurs only at M I 294. This passage does not directly relate each hindrance to an individual *jhāna* factor, but merely enumerates both, and that in a sequence not corresponding to the commentarial correlation. This passage is moreover absent from the Chinese version of this discourse (cf. Minh Chau 1991: p.100, and Stuart-Fox 1989: p.90), which otherwise corresponds to the Pāli version. For a critical discussion of the *jhāna* factor analysis cf. also Rahula 1962: p.192.

23 This is especially the case for sloth-and-torpor versus energy; restlessness-and-worry versus tranquillity; and doubt versus investigation-of-*dhammas* (e.g. at S V 104). In numerous instances throughout the *Bojjhaṅga Saṃyutta* (S V 63–140) the awakening factors and the hindrances are presented as diametrically opposed mental qualities. Cf. also page 239.

24 A V 195. D II 83; D III 101; and S V 161 stipulate the same conditions for becoming a Buddha.

the effect of each hindrance through the image of a bowl filled with water and used as a mirror in order to look at the reflection of one's face. According to these similes, the effect of sensual desire is similar to water mixed with dye; aversion resembles water heated to the boil; sloth-and-torpor is compared to water overgrown with algae; restlessness-and-worry affect the mind like water stirred by wind; and doubt is like dark and muddy water.[25] In all five cases, one is unable to see one's reflection properly in the water. These similes vividly illustrate the individual character of each hindrance: sensual desire colours one's perception; because of aversion one gets heated; sloth-and-torpor result in stagnation; through restlessness-and-worry one is tossed about; and doubt obscures.[26]

The other set of similes illustrates the absence of the hindrances. According to this set, to be free from sensual desire is like being relieved from a debt; to be free from aversion is like recovering from physical illness; to be unobstructed by sloth-and-torpor is akin to being released from prison; to be free from the agitation of restlessness-and-worry is like being liberated from slavery; and to overcome doubt resembles crossing a dangerous desert safely.[27] This second set of similes provides additional illustrations of the hindrances: sensual desire agitating the mind is comparable to being heavily in debt; the tension created through aversion is quite literally a dis-ease; sloth-and-torpor dulls and imprisons the mind; restlessness-and-worry can control the mind to such an extent that one is completely at its mercy; and doubt leaves one in a state of insecurity, not knowing which way to turn.

Since the first set of similes illustrates the presence of the hindrances (in terms of their debilitating effect), while the second describes the relief of being free of them, these two sets correspond to the two alternatives for contemplating the hindrances: awareness of their presence or of their absence.

25 S V 121 and A III 230.
26 Cf. also Fryba 1989: p.202, who suggests the following correlations: sensual desire distorts perception and fragments awareness, aversion creates divisions and cramps the mind, sloth-and-torpor befogs awareness, restlessness-and-worry consumes the mind with no sense of direction, doubt creates irresolute vacillation.
27 D I 71 and M I 275.

IX.3 THE IMPORTANCE OF RECOGNIZING THE HINDRANCES

According to the discourses, if a hindrance is present and one does not recognize it, one is "mis-meditating", a form of practice the Buddha did not approve of.[28] But if one does recognize the presence of a hindrance and contemplates it as a *satipaṭṭhāna* meditation, one's practice will lead to purification of the mind.[29]

A passage in the *Aṅguttara Nikāya* demonstrates the importance of clearly recognizing mental defilements for what they are. This discourse reports the monk Anuruddha complaining to his friend Sāriputta that despite concentrative attainments, unshaken energy, and well-established mindfulness, he was unable to break through to full realization.[30] In reply, Sāriputta pointed out that Anuruddha's boasting of concentration attainments was nothing but a manifestation of conceit, his unshaken energy was simply restlessness, and his concern about not yet having awakened was just worry. Helped by his friend to recognize these as hindrances, Anuruddha was soon able to overcome them and achieve realization.

This technique of simple recognition constitutes an ingenious way of turning obstacles to meditation into meditation objects.[31] Practised in this way, bare awareness of a hindrance becomes a middle path between suppression and indulgence.[32] Several discourses beautifully illustrate the powerful effect of this simple act of recognition by describing how the tempter Māra, who often acts as a personification of the five hindrances, loses his powers as soon as he is recognized.[33]

The ingenuity of this approach of bare recognition can be illustrated by considering the case of anger from a medical perspective. The arising of anger leads to an increase in the release of adrenaline, and such an increase in adrenaline will in turn further stimulate the anger.[34] The presence of non-reactive *sati* puts a brake on this vicious

---

28 M III 14.

29 A I 272.

30 A I 282.

31 Gunaratana 1996: p.44; and Ñāṇapoṇika 1986b: p.21.

32 This function of *satipaṭṭhāna* as a middle path between sense indulgence and self-mortification is mentioned at A I 295.

33 Several of these episodes can be found in the *Māra* and *Bhikkhuṇī Saṃyuttas*, S I 103–35; cf. also the injunction at Sn 967 to recognize mental defilements as manifestations of Māra, the "dark one". Goldstein 1994: p.85, illustratively speaks of "wagging the finger at Māra". Cf. also Marasinghe 1974: p.197.

34 Lily de Silva (n.d.): p.25.

cycle.[35] By simply remaining receptively aware of a state of anger, neither the physical reaction nor the mental proliferation is given scope. If, on the other hand, one abandons the balanced state of awareness and resents or condemns the arisen anger, the act of condemnation becomes just another manifestation of aversion.[36] The vicious cycle of anger continues, albeit with a different object.

Once the hindrances are at least temporarily removed,[37] the alternative aspect of contemplating the hindrances becomes relevant: awareness of their absence. In several expositions of the gradual path, such absence of the hindrances forms the starting point for a causal sequence that leads via delight, joy, tranquillity, and happiness (*pāmojja, pīti, passaddhi,* and *sukha*) to concentration and the attainment of absorption. The instruction in this context is "to contemplate the disappearance of the five hindrances within oneself".[38] This suggests a positive act of recognizing and even rejoicing in the absence of the hindrances, which then paves the way for deep concentration. Such a conscious act of recognizing and rejoicing in the absence of the hindrances is vividly illustrated in the second set of similes mentioned above, which compare this state of mental freedom to freedom from debt, disease, imprisonment, slavery, and danger.

Several discourses refer to such a tranquil state of mind, temporarily unaffected by any hindrance or mental defilement, as "luminous".[39] According to a passage in the *Aṅguttara Nikāya*, to come to know this luminous nature of the mind is in fact an important requirement for the development of the mind (*cittabhāvanā*).[40]

---

35 A study with the help of Rorschach testing corroborates this, where Brown 1986b: p.189, comes to the conclusion that advanced meditators are not without the experience of conflict, but are remarkably non-defensive in experiencing such conflicts. This observation points to their ability to maintain non-reactive and equanimous awareness.

36 Goldstein 1985: p.57: "often there is a tendency to condemn the hindrances when they arise. The condemning mind is itself the factor of aversion."

37 Complete eradication of all five hindrances takes place only with full awakening (cf. S V 327). In fact, when commenting on this part of the *Satipaṭṭhāna Sutta*, Ps I 282 correlates the "future non-arising" of each hindrance with corresponding levels of realization, these being in most cases non-returning or arahantship.

38 e.g. at D I 73. The use of the Pāli verb *sam-anupassati* in this instruction indicates that a form of contemplation (*anupassanā*) is intended here.

39 S V 92; A I 10; A I 257; and A III 16. These passages relate the luminosity of the mind to the development of a concentrated state of mind that is free from defilements and

IX.4 CONDITIONS FOR PRESENCE OR ABSENCE OF A HINDRANCE

After the first stage of recognizing the presence or absence of a hindrance, the second stage of the same contemplation follows: awareness of the conditions that have led to the arising of a hindrance, that assist in removing an arisen hindrance, and that prevent future arising of a hindrance (see Fig. 9.2 below). The task of *sati* during this second stage follows a progressive pattern, proceeding from diagnosis, via cure, to prevention.

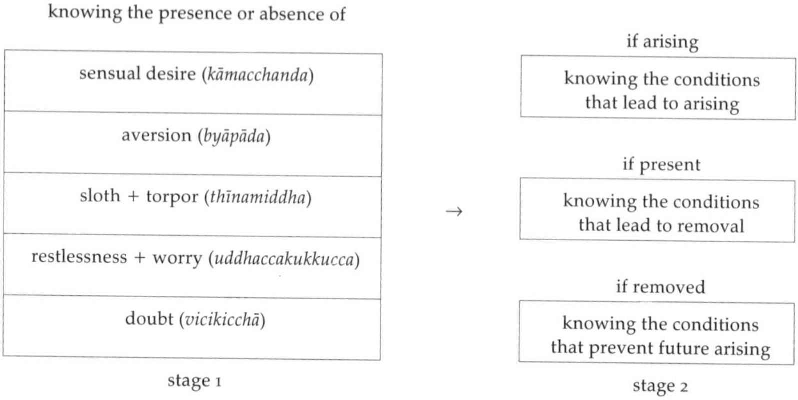

Fig. 9.2 Two stages in the contemplation of the five hindrances

---

ready for realization. Cf. also D III 223, where a form of concentration leads to a mind full of "radiance" (*sappabhāsa*); M III 243, where "luminous" is related to a high level of equanimity; and S V 283, where even the Buddha's body is said to be "luminous" as a result of concentration. Upali Karunaratne 1999c: p.219, explains: "what is meant by lustrous and pure mind (*pabhassara*) is not a state of mind which is absolutely pure, nor the pure mind which is synonymous with emancipation ... pure only in the sense, and to the extent, that it is not disturbed or influenced by external stimuli".

40 A I 10. The commentaries Mp I 60 and As 140 identify the luminous mind with the *bhavaṅga* (subconscious life-continuum). Here it could, however, be objected that the term *bhavaṅga* in the context of the commentarial description of mental processes refers to a subconscious moment that occurs between each conscious part of the mental process. (In fact, sleep is referred to as *bhavaṅgaṃ otāreti* at Ps-pṭ I 364.) In contrast, the luminous state of mind at A I 10 clearly refers to a conscious experience, since it is to be "known" (*pajānāti*). On *bhavaṅga* cf. the excellent exposition in Gethin 1994; also Harvey 1989: pp.94–8; and Sarachchandra 1994: p.90. The attempt by Wijesekera 1976: p.348, to establish a historically early existence of the term with the help of a passage from the *Aṅguttara Nikāya* and several occurrences in the *Paṭṭhāna* is not convincing, as A II 79 in the PTS, the Burmese, and the Sinhalese editions invariably reads *bhavagga* (best of existences, which also fits the context much better) instead of *bhavaṅga*, and occurrences in the *Paṭṭhāna* could also be taken as betraying the comparatively late age of this part of the *Abhidhamma*; cf. also Ñāṇatiloka 1988: p.246.

By turning a hindrance into an object of meditation, the mere presence of awareness can often lead to dispelling the hindrance in question. Should bare awareness not suffice, more specific antidotes are required. In this case, *sati* has the task of supervising the measures undertaken for removing the hindrance, by providing a clear picture of the actual situation, without however getting involved itself and thereby losing its detached observational vantage point.

Clearly recognizing the conditions for the arising of a particular hindrance not only forms the basis for its removal, but also leads to an appreciation of the general pattern of its arising. Such appreciation lays bare the levels of conditioning and misperceptions that cause the arising of a hindrance, and thereby contributes to preventing its recurrence.

Sustained observation will reveal the fact that frequently thinking or dwelling on a particular issue produces a corresponding mental inclination, and thus a tendency to get caught up in ever more thoughts and associations along the same lines.[41] In the case of sensual desire (*kāmacchanda*), for example, it will become evident that its arising is due not only to outer objects, but also to an inclination towards sensuality embedded within one's own mind.[42] This sensual tendency influences the way one perceives outer objects and thence leads to the full-blown arising of desire, and various attempts to satisfy this desire.[43]

The particular dynamic of sensual desire is such that, every time a sensual desire is gratified, the act of gratification fuels ever stronger subsequent manifestations of the same desire.[44] With detached observation it will become apparent that gratification of sensual desires is based on a misconception, on searching for pleasure in the wrong place.[45] As the Buddha pointed out, the way to inner peace and composure necessarily depends on gaining independence from this vortex of desire and gratification.[46]

A passage in the *Aṅguttara Nikāya* offers an intriguing psychological analysis of the underlying causes of sensual desire. According to this discourse, the search for satisfaction through a partner of the

---

41 M I 115.
42 S I 22.
43 S II 151.
44 M I 508.
45 M I 507.
46 M I 508.

other gender is related to one's identification with the characteristics and behaviour of one's own gender.[47] That is, to search for union externally implies that one is still caught up in the limitations of one's own gender identity. This shows that the affective investment inherent in identifying with one's gender role and behaviour forms an important link in the arising of sensual desire. In contrast *arahants*, who have eradicated even the subtlest traces of identification, are unable to engage in sexual intercourse.[48]

Just as the arising of sensual desire can be analysed in terms of its psychological underpinnings, so too the absence of sensual desire depends on an intelligent management of the same psychological mechanisms. Once one has at least temporarily escaped from the vicious circle of continuous demands for satisfaction, it becomes possible to develop some form of counterbalance in one's perceptual appraisal.[49] If excessively dwelling on aspects of external beauty has led to frequent states of lust, contemplation directed towards the less appealing aspects of the body can lead to a progressive decrease in such states of mind.

Examples for such counterbalancing can be found among the *satipaṭṭhāna* meditation practices, in particular the contemplations of the anatomical constitution of the body and of a decaying corpse. In addition to these, restraint of the senses, moderation with food, wakefulness, and awareness of the impermanent nature of all mental events are helpful measures in order to prevent the arising of sensual desire.[50]

Similar approaches are appropriate for the other hindrances, in each case entailing the establishment of some form of counterbalance to the conditions that tend to stimulate the arising of the hindrance. In the case of aversion (*byāpāda*), often the irritating or repulsive feature of phenomena has received undue attention. A

---

47 A IV 57; on this passage cf. Lily de Silva 1978: p.126.

48 e.g. at D III 133. The eradication of sensual desire has already taken place at the level of non-returning.

49 Th 1224–5 explains that a distorted cognition of sensuality can be counterbalanced by avoiding sensually alluring objects, by directing attention to the unattractive aspects of the body, by mindfulness of the body (in general), and by developing disenchantment.

50 A IV 166. At S IV 110 monks are encouraged to look on women as if they are their own mother, sister, or daughter. The same discourse (at S IV 112) documents the particular importance of sense-restraint, since out of the various methods mentioned for countering sensual desire, sense-restraint turned out to be the only acceptable explanation for the ability of even young monks to live in celibacy.

direct antidote to such one-sided perception is to ignore the negative qualities of whoever is causing one's irritation, and to pay attention instead to whatever positive qualities can be found in him or her.[51] By no longer paying attention to the matter, or by reflecting on the inevitability of karmic retribution, it becomes possible to develop equanimity.[52]

An important remedy for a tendency to anger and aversion is the development of loving kindness (*mettā*).[53] According to the discourses, developing loving kindness helps to establish harmonious relations not only towards other human beings, but also towards non-human beings.[54] In the present context, the concept of "non-human beings" can also be understood in a psychological way, as representing subjective psychological disorders.[55] The development of loving kindness indeed counteracts pathological feelings of alienation and low self-esteem, and thereby provides an important foundation for successful insight meditation.

Loving kindness not only provides the proper preparatory ground for the practice of insight meditation, but it can also directly contribute to realization.[56] According to the Buddha, the distinctive

---

51 A III 186.

52 These come at A III 185 as part of altogether five antidotes: developing loving kindness, compassion, equanimity, inattention, and reflecting on karma.

53 M I 424. According to Fenner 1987: p.226, the divine abodes (*brahmavihāras*) are based on accurate cognitions and thus counter errant cognitions leading to unwholesome mental qualities. An inspiring description of loving kindness can be found in Ñāṇapoṇika 1993: pp.9–12.

54 S II 264.

55 In fact, at S II 265, non-human beings are apparently set on creating psychological disorders, which can be prevented by developing loving kindness. Katz 1989: p.161, suggests: "one possible interpretation of 'non-human beings' could be those psychological functions which endanger spiritual growth".

56 M I 352 describes in detail how to combine loving kindness with insight: on emergence from an absorption developed through loving kindness, one develops insight into the impermanent and conditioned nature of this attainment. M I 38 and A I 196 describe the transition from loving kindness to insight with the reflection: "there is this, there is what is inferior, there is what is superior, and there is a complete escape from this entire field of cognition". (Ps I 176 and Mp II 306 explain the last to be a reference to *Nibbāna*.) Cf. also A IV 150 and It 21, who point out that the development of loving kindness helps to weaken the fetters. According to Aronson 1986: p.51: "the meditation on love is the soil within which concentration and ... insight are cultivated". Meier 1978: p.213, suggests that both *vipassanā* and loving kindness meditation have a similar aim, namely, to weaken the sense of "I", so that their different approaches (*vipassanā* by way of analytical dissection, loving kindness by way of expansion) can be considered complementary (though it should be kept in mind that loving kindness on its own will not be able completely to remove all attachment to a sense of "I").

character of loving kindness meditation as taught by him lies in combining it with the awakening factors, in this way directly harnessing loving kindness to the progress towards realization.[57] Several discourses relate the practice of loving kindness in particular to progress from the stage of stream-entry to that of non-returning.[58] Clearly, the advantages of developing loving kindness are not confined to its function as an antidote to anger and irritation.

---

57 At S V 119 the Buddha pointed out that this combination formed the distinguishing feature between the Buddhist approach and the way loving kindness was practised by contemporary ascetics. When considering the Buddha's way of teaching loving kindness meditation it might also be of relevance to point out that what he originally taught was an unspecified pervasion of all directions with an attitude of loving kindness (cf. e.g. M I 38). D I 251, M II 207, and S IV 322 make the spatially pervasive character of radiating loving kindness all the more evident by comparing it to a vigorous trumpeter making himself heard in all four directions. Although such pervasion often indicates absorption, this is not invariably the case, since according to M I 129 this pervasion is to be undertaken when being verbally insulted or even physically maltreated, a situation hardly conducive to entering absorption. Or else at M II 195 a Brahmin on his deathbed, suffering from agonizing headaches, severe stomach cramps, and high fever, soon after being instructed to practise this pervasion, passed away and was reborn in the Brahmā world. This circumstance suggests that he must have been able to put the instructions to good use, even though his physical condition would have made it impossible for him to develop absorption. It is only with the commentaries, possibly because they associated the pervasion exclusively with absorption (cf. Vism 308), that meditation on loving kindness becomes an exercise in conceptual imagination, directed towards oneself, a friend, a neutral person, and an enemy in turn (cf. Vism 296). This method of practice is not found anywhere in the discourses.

58 S V 131 and A V 300. (This is in both instances repeated for the other three *brahmavihāras.*) Similarly, Sn 143 describes the practice of loving kindness based on "having experienced that state of peace", with the result that the practitioner will not be born again in a womb (Sn 152). This suggests that the practice of loving kindness can lead one who has experienced the "state of peace", i.e. one who is a stream-enterer, to transcending rebirth in a womb, i.e. to non-returning. This way of understanding is supported by the commentary, Pj II 193, which explains "state of peace" to refer to *Nibbāna*. This explanation is also confirmed by Dhp 368, where loving kindness is again related to "state of peace", the connotation of which is further clarified by the expression "calming of formations". However, Jayawickrama 1948: vol.2, p.98, argues against taking "state of peace" to refer to a realization of *Nibbāna*. The Sanskrit fragments from the Turfan discoveries also mention the realization of non-returning as one of the advantages of developing loving kindness (in Schlingloff 1964: p.133). The reason loving kindness is linked to progress from stream-entry to non-returning could be related to the two fetters that are to be removed at this stage: sensual desire and aversion. Loving kindness, especially if developed up to absorption level, can act as an antidote to both, since the intense mental happiness experienced during deep concentration counteracts the search for pleasure through the external senses, while loving kindness, by its very nature, counters aversion.

Returning to the remaining hindrances, an antidote to sloth (*thīna*) and torpor (*middha*) is to develop "clarity of cognition" (*ālokasaññā*).[59] In the discourses and the *Vibhaṅga*, "clarity of cognition" seems to refer to the development of mental clarity.[60] The commentaries take the expression more literally and suggest the use of real light, either from an external source, or else light as an internal mental image.[61]

Such "clarity of cognition" takes place with the aid of mindfulness and clearly knowing (*sampajāna*), which brings into play two essential qualities of *satipaṭṭhāna* as a remedy against sloth-and-torpor. This points back to the fact that *satipaṭṭhāna* itself can at times suffice for countering a hindrance. The same is also the case in regard to sensual desire, where contemplation of the anatomical parts or a corpse can act as an antidote. Nevertheless, it needs to be kept in mind that the emphasis in the *Satipaṭṭhāna Sutta* is not on actively opposing a hindrance, but on clearly recognizing a hindrance together with the conditions related to its presence or absence. More active measures are the domain of right effort, another factor of the noble eightfold path.

The arising of sloth-and-torpor can be caused by discontent, boredom, laziness, drowsiness caused by overeating, and by a depressed state of mind.[62] An effective antidote for these can then be found in a sustained application of energy.[63] The *Aṅguttara Nikāya* dedicates an entire discourse to discussing the hindrance torpor, offering a variety of remedies. Initially, presumably while still maintaining the formal meditation posture, one can attempt to counter torpor by changing one's meditation subject, or else by reflecting on or reciting passages from the Buddha's teachings. Should this not work, one can pull one's ears, massage the body, get up, sprinkle one's eyes with water and look up at the sky. If torpor still persists, walking meditation should be practised.[64]

In the opposite case, when restlessness (*uddhacca*) and worry (*kukkucca*) have arisen, factors leading to an increase of mental calmness and stability should be developed. Here, mindfulness of

---

59 e.g. at D I 71.
60 A IV 86 relates "clarity of cognition" to developing a radiant mind. Vibh 254 explains that "clarity of cognition" refers to bright, clear, and pure cognitions, which Vibh-a 369 explains as cognitions free from the hindrances.
61 Ps I 284 and Ps-pṭ I 375.
62 S V 64; S V 103; and A I 3.
63 S V 105.
64 A IV 85.

breathing stands out as a particularly effective method for calming the thinking activity of the mind.[65] In addition, any of the other subjects of calmness meditation are appropriate in this situation, together with improving the general degree of mental calmness and composure during one's activities.[66]

According to the discourses, restlessness-and-worry can sometimes arise because of excessive energetic striving.[67] Here a less pushy attitude towards one's practice can help to remedy the situation. In relation to restlessness in particular, it is moreover advisable to avoid any provocative talk, since such talk easily leads to prolonged discussions and thereby causes the arising of restlessness.[68] The arising of worry is often related to guilt, such as when one has done an unwholesome deed and feels regret about it.[69] Thus maintaining an impeccable level of ethical conduct goes a long way in preventing the arising of this hindrance. The discourses also relate a monk's experience of "worry" to lack of clarity concerning the *Dhamma*, and describe how this was then countered by an instruction or explanation given by the Buddha.[70]

In the case of the last of the five hindrances, a clear distinction between what is wholesome or skilful and what is unwholesome or unskilful serves to counter the obstruction caused by doubt (*vicikicchā*).[71] This obstruction is of considerable importance, since without clearly knowing what is wholesome and what is unwholesome one will be unable to overcome lust, anger, and delusion.[72] The hindrance of doubt plays a role not only in relation to the development

---

65 A III 449; A IV 353; A IV 358; Ud 37; and It 80.

66 D I 71; S V 105; and A III 449.

67 A I 256 and A III 375.

68 A IV 87.

69 Cf. e.g. Vin III 19, where the monk Sudinna experienced worry due to having engaged in sexual intercourse.

70 e.g. at S IV 46 the Buddha, visiting a sick monk, enquired whether that monk had any worries. His question was in the first instance related to "guilt", but once the sick monk in question reported that he had nothing to reproach himself for, the question was repeated and led to some clarification or specific instruction concerning the *Dhamma*. Another nuance of "worry" can be found at A I 282, where it indicates excessive worry about realization. Cf. furthermore A II 157, which also relates "restlessness" to the *Dhamma*.

71 D III 49. Such doubt can occur "internally", in relation to oneself, or "externally", in relation to others (cf. S V 110).

72 A V 147. Cf. also D II 283, where a detailed exposition of wholesomeness and unwholesomeness from different perspectives enabled Sakka to fully overcome doubt and realize stream-entry.

of insight, but also in the context of calmness meditation. This can be inferred from the *Upakkilesa Sutta*, a discourse concerned mainly with the development of concentration, where doubt heads a list of mental obstructions to the attainment of absorption.[73]

The ability to distinguish between wholesomeness and unwholesomeness needed for overcoming doubt can be developed with the help of the awakening factor investigation-of-*dhammas* (*dhamma-vicaya*).[74] This indicates that from a Buddhist perspective the task of overcoming doubt is not a question of belief or faith. Rather, overcoming doubt takes place through a process of investigation, which leads to clarity and understanding.

Overcoming these five hindrances is a matter of crucial importance for all types of meditative practices. For this purpose, the commentaries list a set of factors helpful for overcoming or inhibiting each hindrance, a survey of which can be found in Fig. 9.3 overleaf. With increasing meditative proficiency it will become possible to dispel any hindrance as soon as it is recognized, as quickly as a drop of water evaporates when it falls on a hot frying pan.[75] The centrally important factor for removing a hindrance, whether slowly or quickly, is *sati*, since without awareness of the presence or arising of a hindrance, little can be done in terms of prevention or removal. This task of mindful recognition is the central theme of contemplation of the hindrances.

---

73 M III 128, where doubt is mentioned as the first of a particular set of mental obstructions not encountered as such elsewhere in the discourses, and which are specifically related to the development of concentration. It is particularly noticeable that the hindrances of sensual desire and aversion are not mentioned, suggesting that these have been overcome before the stage of practice in question. The mental obstructions listed are doubt, inattention, sloth-and-torpor, consternation, elation, unease, excessive energy, deficient energy, longing, cognition of diversity, and excessive meditation on forms. Their successful removal then leads to the attainment of absorption.

74 This is suggested by the fact that the nutriment for investigation-of-*dhammas* is presented in exactly the same terms as the "anti"-nutriment of doubt, cf. S V 104 and S V 106.

75 This simile occurs at M I 453 in relation to dispelling attachment; at M III 300 in relation to dispelling likes and dislikes that have arisen in the mind; and at S IV 190 in relation to dispelling unwholesome thoughts and memories.

sensual desire	general acquaintance with and formal meditation on the body's unattractiveness guarding the senses moderation in food good friends and suitable conversation
aversion	general acquaintance with and formal meditation on loving kindness reflecting on the karmic consequences of one's deeds repeated wise consideration good friends and suitable conversation
sloth + torpor	lessening food intake changing meditation postures mental clarity/ cognition of light staying outdoors good friends and suitable conversation
restlessness + worry	good knowledge of the discourses clarification of the discourses through questioning being well versed in ethical conduct visiting experienced elders good friends and suitable conversation
doubt	good knowledge of the discourses clarification of the discourses through questioning being well versed in ethical conduct strong commitment good friends and suitable conversation

Fig. 9.3 Commentarial survey of factors for overcoming or inhibiting the hindrances[76]

76 Ps I 281–6.

X

DHAMMAS: THE AGGREGATES

X.1 THE FIVE AGGREGATES

The present *satipaṭṭhāna* exercise examines the five aggregates which constitute the basic components that make up "oneself". The instructions are:

> **He knows "such is material form, such its arising, such its passing away; such is feeling, such its arising, such its passing away; such is cognition, such its arising, such its passing away; such are volitions, such their arising, such their passing away; such is consciousness, such its arising, such its passing away."[1]**

Underlying the above instructions are two stages of contemplation: clear recognition of the nature of each aggregate, followed in each case by awareness of its arising and passing away (cf. Fig. 10.1 below). I will first attempt to clarify the range of each aggregate. Then I will examine the Buddha's teaching of *anattā* within its historical context, in order to investigate the way in which the scheme of the five aggregates can be used as an analysis of subjective experience. After that I will consider the second stage of practice, which is concerned with the impermanent and conditioned nature of the aggregates.

---

1 M I 61.

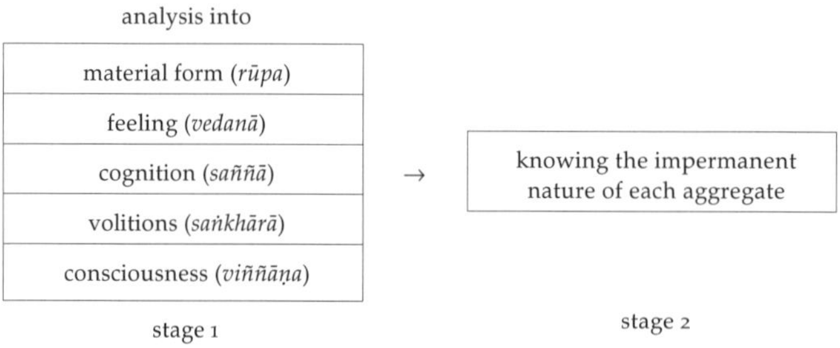

Fig. 10.1 Two stages in the contemplation of the five aggregates

Clearly recognizing and understanding the five aggregates is of considerable importance, since without fully understanding them and developing detachment from them, it will not be possible to gain complete freedom from *dukkha*.[2] Indeed, detachment and dispassion regarding these five aspects of subjective personality leads directly to realization.[3] The discourses, and the verses composed by awakened monks and nuns, record numerous cases where a penetrative understanding of the true nature of the five aggregates culminated in full awakening.[4] These instances highlight the outstanding potential of this particular *satipaṭṭhāna* contemplation.

These five aggregates are often referred to in the discourses as the "five aggregates of clinging" (*pañcupādānakkhandha*).[5] In this context

2 S III 27.

3 A V 52. Cf. also S III 19–25, where several discourses relate an understanding of the aggregates to full realization.

4 At M III 20, a detailed exposition on the aggregates led sixty monks to full realization. At S III 68, the Buddha's first five disciples became *arahants* after an exposition of *anattā*, again by way of the five aggregates. Cf. also Th 87; Th 90; Th 120; Th 161; Th 369; and Th 440; each relating full awakening to insight into the five aggregates.

5 e.g. at D II 305. The expression "five aggregates" seems to have been easily intelligible in ancient India, since it occurs in the Buddha's first discourse, at S V 421, apparently without any need for elaboration or explanation. Similarly, at M I 228, the five aggregates form part of a description of the Buddha's teaching to the disputer Saccaka (who was presumably unfamiliar with Buddhism, but appears to have readily understood what was being said). This suggests that the five- aggregate scheme might have already been in existence at the time of Gotama Buddha. Since the discourses also include contemplation of the five aggregates in their description of the awakening of the ancient Buddha Vipassī (at D II 35), it seems that from their perspective, too, the scheme of the five aggregates was known before the advent of Gotama Buddha. Stcherbatsky 1994: p.71, mentions parallels to the aggregates in the *Brāhmaṇas* and *Upaniṣads*; and according to Warder 1956: p.49 n.2, the aggregates were a known concept among the Jains and possibly also among the Ājīvikas.

"aggregate" (*khandha*) is an umbrella term for all possible instances of each category, whether past, present, or future, internal or external, gross or subtle, inferior or superior, near or far.[6] The qualification "clinging" (*upādāna*) refers to desire and attachment in regard to these aggregates.[7] Such desire and attachment in relation to the aggregates is the root cause for the arising of *dukkha*.[8]

The sequence of these five aggregates leads from the gross physical body to increasingly subtle mental aspects.[9] The first of the aggregates, material form (*rūpa*), is usually defined in the discourses in terms of the four elementary qualities of matter.[10] A discourse in the *Khandha Saṃyutta* explains that material form (*rūpa*) refers to whatever is affected (*ruppati*) by external conditions such as cold and heat, hunger and thirst, mosquitoes and snakes, emphasizing

---

6 e.g. at M III 16. On the term "aggregate" cf. also Boisvert 1997: p.16; Upali Karunaratne 1999b: p.194; and Ñāṇamoli 1978: p.329. C.A.F. Rhys Davids 1937: p.410, suggests that the reason it should be five aggregates in particular could be related to the fact that the number five represents a comprehensive unit in ancient Indian thought, something which in turn is derived from the number of fingers on the human hand. The range of applicability of the five-aggregate scheme is documented at M I 435, which applies the five-aggregate structure to the experience of *jhāna*. Cf. also M I 190, which analyses the sense-spheres with the help of the five-aggregate scheme. Khanti 1984: p.49, applies the five aggregates to mindfulness of breathing, by distinguishing between breath, sensation of breathing, noting in/out-breath, effort to breathe, and knowing the breath.

7 M I 300; M III 16; S III 47; and S III 167. Cf. also Ayya Khema 1984: p.8; and Bodhi 1976: p.92.

8 As an abridged statement of the first noble truth, e.g. at D II 305: "in short, the five aggregates of clinging are *dukkha*". Similarly, S III 7 points out that lust and desire in regard to the five aggregates leads to *dukkha*; and S III 31 explains that to delight in the five aggregates is to delight in *dukkha*. Cf. also Gethin 1986: p.41.

9 Stcherbatsky 1994: p.23.

10 e.g. at M III 17. Such definitions in the discourses also speak frequently of the material form "derived" (*upādāya*) from the four elements (e.g. at M I 53). Judging from M I 421, this expression might simply refer to those bodily parts or processes that are predominantly "derived" (*upādiṇṇa*) from the respective element, such as the harder bodily parts like hair and bones in the case of the element earth, the liquid bodily parts like blood and urine in the case of the element water, the process of digestion in the case of the element fire, and the breath in the case of the element air. According to the *Abhidhamma* and the commentaries, however, "derived" material form refers to twenty-three or twenty-four types of secondary matter, in addition to the four elements (twenty-three types at Dhs 134; twenty-four at Vism 444 by adding the heart-base). A detailed survey of these can be found in Bodhi 1993: pp.235–42; and Karunadasa 1989: pp.31–116. According to Kor 1993: p.6, from the viewpoint of practical meditation an understanding of the four elements as exemplifying basic characteristics of matter suffices for the development of insight. Cf. also Ñāṇavīra 1987: p.102, who warns against analysis carried out for its own sake.

the subjective experience of *rūpa* as a central aspect of this aggregate.[11]

Next in the sequence of the aggregates come feeling (*vedanā*) and cognition (*saññā*), which represent the affective and the cognitive aspects of experience.[12] In the context of the process of perception, cognition (*saññā*) is closely related to the arising of feeling, both depending on stimulation through the six senses by way of contact (*phassa*).[13] The standard presentations in the discourses relate feeling to the sense organ, but cognition to the respective sense object.[14] This indicates that feelings are predominantly related to the subjective repercussions of an experience, while cognitions are more concerned with the features of the respective external object. That is, feelings provide the "how" and cognitions the "what" of experience.

To speak of a "cognition" of an object refers to the act of identifying raw sensory data with the help of concepts or labels, such as when one sees a coloured object and "re-cognizes" it as yellow, red, or white, etc.[15] Cognition to some extent involves the faculty of memory, which furnishes the conceptual labels used for recognition.[16]

The fourth aggregate comprises volitions (*saṅkhārā*), representing the conative aspect of the mind.[17] These volitions or intentions corre-

---

11 S III 86. Strictly speaking, *ruppati* and *rūpa* are not etymologically related. Nevertheless, this passage offers an illustrative explanation of the term. Kalupahana 1992: p.17, comments: "*rūpa* … the definition of it provided by the Buddha makes it a function rather than an entity". Sarachchandra 1994: p.103, explains: "*rūpa* is not interpreted as mere matter, but as organic sensations" (i.e. as a subjective factor).

12 Padmasiri de Silva 1991: p.17; and W.S. Karunaratne 1988a: p.96.

13 M I 111: "with contact as condition there is feeling, what one feels, that one cognizes". M I 293 clarifies that feeling and cognition occur as a conjoined pair. M III 17 points out that contact is the condition for the manifestation of the aggregates of feeling and cognition.

14 The standard descriptions (e.g. at D II 309) speak of "eye-contact feeling" and of "cognition of visible form" (the same applies to the other senses); cf. Hamilton 1996: p.15.

15 S III 87. Cf. also Boisvert 1997: p.89; Hamilton 1996: pp.54, 57–9; Harvey 1995: p.141 (whose suggested translation of *saññā* as "cognition" I have followed); Premasiri 1987a: pp.53–5; and C.A.F. Rhys Davids 1922: p.6 n.4. Cf. also Gruber 1999: p.192, who suggests that the prefix *saṁ-* of *saññā* could be taken to refer to the gathering "together" of sense experiences under a conceptual label through the activity of cognition.

16 Cf. D I 93, where "to cognize" (*sañjānāti*) is used in the sense of "giving a name"; or M III 234 where "cognition" occurs for the various terms used to refer to a bowl. On the relation of cognition to memory cf. Ñāṇapoṇika 1985: p.71.

17 e.g. M I 389 distinguished between afflictive and non-afflictive volitions by way of body, speech, and mind. S III 60 and S III 63 explain "volitions" to comprise intentions related to visible form, sound, smell, taste, touch, and mental objects. Cf. also Padmasiri de Silva 1992a: p.16; and Schumann 1957: p.90.

spond to the reactive or purposive aspect of the mind, that which reacts to things or their potentiality.[18] The aggregate of volitions and intentions interacts with each of the aggregates and has a conditioning effect upon them.[19] In the subsequent developments of Buddhist philosophy, the meaning of this term expanded until it came to include a wide range of mental factors.[20]

The fifth aggregate is consciousness (*viññāṇa*). Although at times the discourses use "consciousness" to represent mind in general,[21] in the context of the aggregate classification it refers to being conscious of something.[22] This act of being conscious is most prominently responsible for providing a sense of subjective cohesiveness, for the notion of a substantial "I" behind experience.[23] Consciousness

---

18 Ñāṇavīra 1987: p.70, aptly brings out the nature of "volition" by providing the following example for the five aggregates: a solid (material form) pleasant (feeling) shady tree (cognition) "for lying under" (volition) visible to me (consciousness).

19 S III 87; (cf. also Vibh 7). Bodhi 2000: p.1071 n.112, comments: "this passage shows the active role of ... volition in constructing experienced reality. Not only does volition influence the objective content of the experience, but it also shapes the psychophysical organism within which it has arisen and, via its role as kamma, shapes the future configurations of the five aggregates to be produced by kamma."

20 Cf. the long list of mental factors given under *saṅkhārā* in Dhs (e.g. 17–18) each time a state of mind is presented; also at Vism 462–72. Cf. also Bodhi 2000: p.45; W.S. Karunaratne 1988a: p.118; McGovern 1979: p.87; C.A.F. Rhys Davids 1978: p.324; and Stcherbatsky 1994: p.20.

21 A typical instance is the expression "this body with consciousness" (*saviññāṇake kāye*), e.g. at S III 80, where "consciousness" stands for all four mental aggregates. Cf. also D I 21 and S II 94, which use "consciousness" (*viññāṇa*) on a par with the two Pāli terms *citta* and *mano*, all three referring to "mind" in this context. Bodhi 2000: p.769 n.154, aptly clarifies the implications of these three Pāli terms in the discourses: "*viññāṇa* signifies the particularizing awareness through a sense faculty ... as well as the underlying stream of consciousness, which sustains personal continuity through a single life and threads together successive lives.... *Mano* serves as the third door of action (along with body and speech) and as the sixth internal sense base.... *Citta* signifies mind as the centre of personal experience, as the subject of thought, volition, and emotion." A detailed survey of differences in the usage of these three terms in the discourses can be found in Johansson 1965: p.208.

22 M I 292 explains that "feeling" just feels, whereas "consciousness" is conscious "of" such a feeling. S III 87 alternatively illustrates the activity of consciousness by it being conscious of various tastes. Cf. also Hamilton 1996: pp.54 and 92; Harvey 1995: p.154; Premasiri 1987a: p.57; Wayman 1976: p.331; and Wijesekera 1994: pp.87, 104, and 111. Concerning the difference between cognition and consciousness, Ñāṇamoli 1978: p.338 explains: "a hint of what is referred to may perhaps be got from the prefixes ... the prefix *vi-* might be taken dissociatively as the division and distribution of bare *(vi-)ññāṇa* over the six bases, while the prefix *saṃ-* might be taken associatively as the perception of synthesis of the objective fields into 'things' and 'percepts' in each of the six pairs of bases."

23 Cf. the wrong view at M I 258 that the same consciousness feels, experiences karmic retribution, and fares on in the round of rebirths.

depends on the various features of experience supplied by name-and-form (*nāmarūpa*), just as name-and-form in turn depend on consciousness as their point of reference.[24] This conditional interrelationship creates the world of experience, with consciousness being aware of phenomena that are being modified and presented to it by way of name-and-form.[25]

To provide a practical illustration of the five aggregates: during the present act of reading, for example, consciousness is aware of each word through the physical sense door of the eye. Cognition understands the meaning of each word, while feelings are responsible for the affective mood: whether one feels positive, negative, or neutral about this particular piece of information. Because of volition one either reads on, or stops to consider a passage in more depth, or even refers to a footnote.

The discourses describe the characteristic features of these five aggregates with a set of similes. These compare material form to the insubstantial nature of a lump of foam carried away by a river; feelings to the impermanent bubbles that form on the surface of water during rain; cognition to the illusory nature of a mirage; volitions to the essenceless nature of a plantain tree (because it has no heartwood); and consciousness to the deceptive performance of a magician.[26]

This set of similes points to central characteristics that need to be understood with regard to each aggregate. In the case of material form, contemplating its unattractive and insubstantial nature corrects mistaken notions of substantiality and beauty. Concerning feelings, awareness of their impermanent nature counteracts the tendency to search for pleasure through feelings. With regard to cognition, awareness of its deluding activity uncovers the tendency to project one's own value judgements onto external phenomena as if these were qualities of the outside objects. With volitions, insight

---

24 The importance of this conditional interrelation is highlighted at D II 34 and S II 105, where Buddha Vipassī and Buddha Gotama respectively (both still at the *bodhisatta* stage at this point), on investigating dependent co-arising up to this reciprocal relationship between consciousness and name-and-form, concluded: "I have found the path of insight leading to awakening."

25 D II 56: "Consciousness conditions name-and-form … name-and-form conditions consciousness." ("Name", according to M I 53, comprises feeling, cognition, volition, contact, and attention.)

26 S III 142; with further explanations in Vism 479. On these similes cf. also Mahasi 1996: pp.68–79.

into their selfless nature corrects the mistaken notion that willpower is the expression of a substantial self. Regarding consciousness, understanding its deceptive performance counterbalances the sense of cohesiveness and substantiality it tends to give to what in reality is a patchwork of impermanent and conditioned phenomena.

Owing to the influence of ignorance, these five aggregates are experienced as embodiments of the notion "I am". From the unawakened point of view, the material body is "Where I am", feelings are "How I am", cognitions are "What I am" (perceiving), volitions are "Why I am" (acting), and consciousness is "Whereby I am" (experiencing). In this way, each aggregate offers its own contribution to enacting the reassuring illusion that "I am".

By laying bare these five facets of the notion "I am", this analysis of subjective personality into aggregates singles out the component parts of the misleading assumption that an independent and unchanging agent inheres in human existence, thereby making possible the arising of insight into the ultimately selfless (*anattā*) nature of all aspects of experience.[27]

In order to assess the implications of the aggregate scheme, a brief examination of the teaching of *anattā* against the background of the philosophical positions in existence in ancient India will be helpful at this point.

X.2 THE HISTORICAL CONTEXT OF THE TEACHING ON *ANATTĀ*

At the time of the Buddha, a variety of differing views about the nature of the self existed. The Ājīvika teachings, for example, proposed a soul having a particular colour and considerable size as the true self.[28] The Jains posited a finite soul, similarly possessed of size and weight.[29] According to them, the soul survived physical death, and in its pure state it possessed infinite knowledge.[30] The *Upaniṣads* proposed an eternal self (*ātman*), unaffected by the vicissitudes of

---

27 On the relevance of the five aggregates as a philosophical refutation of notions of self cf. Kalupahana 1975: p.116; Thiṭṭila 1969: p.xxii; and Wijesekera 1994: p.262.

28 According to Basham 1951: p.270, the Ājīvika soul had the colour of a blue fruit and its size reached the height of five hundred *yojanas*. (A *yojana* is the ancient Indian measure for distances and represents the distance that can be covered with one yoke of oxen in a day, approximately seven miles.) Could this description of the soul refer to the sky?

29 Malalasekera 1965: p.569.

30 Pande 1957: p.356.

change. *Upaniṣadic* conceptions about such an eternal self ranged from a physical self the size of a thumb abiding in the heart area and leaving the body during sleep, to an unobservable and unknowable self, immaterial, free from death and sorrow, beyond any worldly distinction between subject and object.[31] In the *Upaniṣadic* analysis of subjective experience, this eternal self, autonomous, permanent, and blissful, was taken to be the agent behind all the senses and activities.[32]

The materialist schools, on the other hand, rejected all immaterial conceptions of a self or soul. In order to account for causality, they proposed a theory based on the inherent nature (*svabhāva*) of material phenomena.[33] According to them, a human individual was just an automaton functioning according to the dictates of matter. From their perspective, human effort was of no avail and there was no such thing as ethical responsibility.[34]

In this context, the Buddha's position cuts a middle path between the belief in an eternal soul and the denial of anything beyond mere matter. By affirming karmic consequences and ethical responsibility, the Buddha clearly opposed the teachings of the materialists.[35] At the same time, he was able to explain the operation of karmic retribution over several lifetimes with the help of dependent co-arising (*paṭicca samuppāda*) and thereby without bringing in a substantial unchanging essence.[36] He pointed out that the five aggregates, which together account for subjective experience, on closer investigation turn out to be impermanent and not amenable to complete personal control. Therefore a permanent and self-sufficient self cannot be found within or apart from the five aggregates.[37] In this way,

---

31 Malalasekera 1965: p.567.

32 Collins 1982: p.80, and Jayatilleke 1980: p.297.

33 Kalupahana 1994: p.13.

34 A typical example is the position taken by Ajita Kesakambalī (at D I 55) that there are no such things as good and evil deeds, since a human being is nothing more than a combination of the four elements. Along similar lines Pakudha Kaccāyana (at D I 56) proposed human beings to be made up of seven immutable principles, which led him to the conclusion that even cutting off someone's head with a sword should not be considered killing, but should be reckoned only as inserting the blade in the space intervening between these seven principles. Cf. also Jayatilleke 1980: p.444; and Kalupahana 1975: pp.25–32.

35 The importance of considering the *anattā* teaching in the light of the karma theory is highlighted by Sasaki 1992: pp.32–5.

36 W.S. Karunaratne 1988b: p.72: "the teaching of *anattā* is an ... adaptation of the central truth of causality".

the Buddha's teaching of *anattā* denied a permanent and inherently independent self, and at the same time affirmed empirical continuity and ethical responsibility.

X.3 EMPIRICAL SELF AND CONTEMPLATION OF THE AGGREGATES

Not only does the Buddha's penetrating analysis of self provide a philosophical refutation of theories proposing a substantial and unchanging self, it also has an intriguing psychological relevance. "Self", as an independent and permanent entity, is related to notions of mastery and control.[38] Such notions of mastery, permanence, and inherent satisfactoriness to some degree parallel the concepts of "narcissism" and the "ideal ego" in modern psychology.[39]

These concepts do not refer to articulate philosophical beliefs or ideas, but to unconscious assumptions implicit in one's way of perceiving and reacting to experience.[40] Such assumptions are based on an inflated sense of self-importance, on a sense of self that continuously demands to be gratified and protected against external threats to its omnipotence. Contemplating *anattā* helps to expose these assumptions as mere projections.

The *anattā* perspective can show up a broad range of manifestations of such a sense of self. According to the standard instructions for contemplating *anattā*, each of the five aggregates should be considered devoid of "mine", "I am", and "my self".[41] This analytical approach covers not only the last-mentioned view of a self, but also the mode of craving and attachment underlying the attribution of "mine" to phenomena and the sense of "I am" as a manifestation of conceit and grasping.[42] A clear understanding of the range of each aggregate forms the necessary basis for this investigation.[43] Such a

37 That it is the very absence of permanence that disqualifies phenomena from being considered "self" becomes evident at M III 282. The lack of control over the five aggregates, in addition to their impermanent nature, is, according to S III 66, what disqualifies them from being "I" or "mine". Cf. also M I 231.

38 Vism 640 explains that to speak of "not-self" implies not being susceptible to the free exercise of control. Ñāṇavīra 1987: p.70, points out that "*attā*, 'self', is fundamentally a notion of mastery over things".

39 Cf. Epstein 1988: p.65, 1989: p.66; and Hanly 1984: p.254. On Buddhist and Western notions of "self" cf. also West 1991: pp.200–4.

40 In fact, as Ps I 251 indicates, even animals are under the influence of self notions, which would certainly not be a philosophical belief.

41 e.g. at S III 68, a consideration to be applied to all possible instances of the five aggregates.

clear understanding can be gained through *satipaṭṭhāna* contemplation. In this way, contemplation of the five aggregates commends itself for uncovering various patterns of identification and attachment to a sense of self.

A practical approach to this is to keep inquiring into the notion "I am" or "mine", that lurks behind experience and activity.[44] Once this notion of an agent or owner behind experience has been clearly recognized, the above non-identification strategy can be implemented by considering each aggregate as "not mine, not I, not my self".

In this way, contemplation of the five aggregates as a practical application of the *anattā* strategy can uncover the representational aspects of one's sense of self, those aspects responsible for the formation of a self image.[45] Practically applied in this way, contemplation of *anattā* can expose the various types of self-image responsible for identifying with and clinging to one's social position, professional occupation, or personal possessions. Moreover, *anattā* can be employed to reveal erroneous superimpositions on experience, particularly the sense of an autonomous and independent subject reaching out to acquire or reject discrete substantial objects.[46]

According to the Buddha's penetrative analysis, patterns of identification and attachment to a sense of self can take altogether twenty different forms, by taking any of the five aggregates to be self, self to be in possession of the aggregate, the aggregate to be inside self, or self to be inside the aggregate.[47] The teaching on *anattā* aims to completely remove all these identifications with, and the corresponding attachments to, a sense of self. Such removal proceeds in stages: with the realization of stream-entry any notion of a permanent self

---

42 Spk II 98 explains that the notion "this is mine" is related to craving, the notion "I am this" to conceit, and the notion "this is my self" to views. S III 105 points out that the self-image "I am" comes about because of the existence of some form of grasping.

43 S IV 197 enjoins thorough investigation of the range of each aggregate, this investigation forming the basis for the insight that no I or mine can be found.

44 A simple device to start this type of practice could be to question oneself: "who?" or "whose?" in regard to any activity or experience. This is in fact suggested by the *satipaṭṭhāna* commentary at Ps I 251 and Ps I 274; cf. also Khantipālo 1981: p.71.

45 Engler 1983: p.33; and Epstein 1990: p.30. An interesting point in this context is suggested by Wayman 1984: p.622, according to whom *ātman* might refer to "embodiment" in certain Vedic contexts, which further supports relating it to the "representational self".

46 Hamilton 1997: p.281.

47 e.g. at M III 17.

(*sakkāyadiṭṭhi*) is eradicated, whilst the subtlest traces of attachment to oneself are removed only with full awakening.

The teaching of *anattā*, however, is not directed against what are merely the functional aspects of personal existence, but aims only at the sense of "I am" that commonly arises in relation to it.[48] Otherwise an *arahant* would simply be unable to function in any way. This, of course, is not the case, as the Buddha and his *arahant* disciples were still able to function coherently.[49] In fact, they were able to do so with more competence than before their awakening, since they had completely overcome and eradicated all mental defilements and thereby all obstructions to proper mental functioning.

A well-known simile of relevance in this context is that of a chariot which does not exist as a substantial thing apart from, or in addition to, its various parts.[50] Just as the term "chariot" is simply a convention, so the superimposition of "I"-dentifications on experience are nothing but conventions.[51] On the other hand, to reject the existence of an independent, substantial chariot does not mean that it is impossible to ride in the conditioned and impermanent functional assemblage of parts to which the concept "chariot" refers. Similarly, to deny the existence of a self does not imply a denial of the conditioned and impermanent interaction of the five aggregates.

Another instance showing the need to distinguish between emptiness and mere nothingness, in the sense of annihilation, occurs in a discourse from the *Abyākata Saṃyutta*. Here, the Buddha, on being directly questioned concerning the existence of a self (*attā*), refused to give either an affirmative or a negative answer.[52] According to his own explanation later on, if he had simply denied the existence of a self, it might have been misunderstood as a form of annihilationism, a position he was always careful to avoid. Such a misunderstanding can in fact have dire consequences, since to mistakenly believe that *anattā* implies there to be nothing at all can lead to wrongly assuming that consequently there is no karmic responsibility.[53]

In fact, although the scheme of the five aggregates opposes the

---

48 Harvey 1995: p.17, illustrates this difference by distinguishing between "Self" (permanent, substantial, etc.) and "self" (empirical and changing). Ñāṇananda 1993: p.10, aptly sums up: "accept yourself – and reject your self."

49 Lily de Silva 1996: p.4.

50 S I 135. This same simile forms part of the introductory dialogue at Mil 25. A modern version can be found in Claxton 1991: p.27. Cf. also Ñāṇavīra 1987: p.46.

51 "I" and "mine" are then used simply as conventions by an *arahant* (cf. S I 14).

52 S IV 400.

notion of a self and therefore appears essentially negative in character, it also has the positive function of defining the components of subjective empirical existence.[54] As a description of empirical personality, the five aggregates thus point to those central aspects of personal experience that need to be understood in order to progress towards realization.[55]

A breakdown into all five aggregates might not be a matter of absolute necessity, since some passages document less detailed analytical approaches to insight. According to the *Mahāsakuludāyi Sutta*, for example, the simple distinction between body and consciousness constituted a sufficient degree of analysis for several disciples of the Buddha to gain realization.[56] Even so, most discourses operate with the more usual analysis of the mental side of experience into four aggregates. This more detailed analysis might be due to the fact that it is considerably more difficult to realize the impersonal nature of the mind than of the body.[57]

Compared with the previous *satipaṭṭhāna* contemplations of similar phenomena (such as body, feelings, and mind), contemplation of the aggregates stands out for its additional emphasis on exposing identification-patterns. Once these patterns of identification are seen for what they really are, the natural result will be disenchantment and detachment in regard to these five aspects of subjective experience.[58] A key aspect for understanding the true nature of the aggregates, and thereby of oneself, is awareness of their impermanent and conditioned nature.

---

53 Cf. e.g. the mistaken reasoning at M III 19 that if actions are performed by a not-self, what self could be affected by the result of these actions?

54 M I 299: "the five aggregates of clinging are called personality"; cf. also Hamilton 1995a: p.54; and Kalupahana 1994: pp.70–2.

55 Hamilton 1996: p.xxiv.

56 M II 17. In this passage "consciousness" acts as a representative of mind in its entirety. Cf. also M I 260, which comprehensively refers to the entire set of the five aggregates as something that has "come to be" in conditional dependence on nutriment, a way of developing deep insight leading to freedom from doubt and purified view which does not seem to require analysing them separately. Ps II 307 explains that "come to be" refers to the entire set of the five aggregates in this context.

57 S II 94.

58 This disenchantment is described at M I 511 with the insight that for a long time one has been tricked and cheated by one's own mind, since when clinging one has been clinging just to these five aggregates.

X.4 ARISING AND PASSING AWAY OF THE AGGREGATES

According to the *Satipaṭṭhāna Sutta*, to contemplate the five aggregates requires a clear recognition of each, followed by directing awareness to their arising (*samudaya*) and their passing away (*atthagama*). This second stage of practice reveals the impermanent character of the aggregates, and to some extent thereby also points to their conditioned nature.[59]

In the discourses, contemplation of the impermanent nature of the aggregates, and thereby of oneself, stands out as a particularly prominent cause for gaining realization.[60] Probably because of its powerful potential for awakening, the Buddha spoke of this particular contemplation as his "lion's roar".[61] The reason underlying the eminent position of contemplating the impermanent nature of the aggregates is that it directly counters all conceit and "I"- or "mine"-making.[62] The direct experience of the fact that every aspect of oneself is subject to change undermines the basis on which conceit and "I"- or "mine"-making take their stand. Conversely, to the extent to which one is no longer under the influence of "I" or "mine" notions in regard to the five aggregates, any change or alteration of the aggregates will not lead to sorrow, lamentation, pain, grief, and despair.[63] As the Buddha emphatically advised: "give up the aggregates, since none of them is truly your own!"[64]

In practical terms, contemplating the arising and passing away of each aggregate can be undertaken by observing change taking place in every aspect of one's personal experience, be these, for example, the cycle of breaths or circulation of the blood, the change of feelings from pleasant to unpleasant, the variety of cognitions and volitional reactions arising in the mind, or the changing nature of conscious-

---

59 Cf. e.g. S II 28, where contemplating the arising and passing away of the five aggregates is immediately followed by an exposition of dependent co-arising (*paṭicca samuppāda*).

60 At D II 35 the former Buddha Vipassī realized full awakening by contemplating the impermanence of the five aggregates. The same contemplation and result by a nun is documented at Thī 96. The potential of this contemplation to lead to full awakening is documented also at D III 223; S II 29; S II 253; A II 45; and A IV 153. Gethin 1992: p.56, concludes: "the practice of watching rise and fall with regard to the five aggregates of grasping seems to be particularly associated with the gaining of the insight that leads ... directly to awakening".

61 S III 84.

62 Cf. M I 486; M III 115; and S III 157.

63 S III 4.

64 M I 140 and S III 33.

ness, arising at this or that sense door. Such practice can then build up to contemplating the arising and passing away of all five aggregates together, when one comprehensively surveys the five aggregate-components of any experience and at the same time witnesses the impermanent nature of this experience.

Contemplating the arising and passing away of the five aggregates also highlights their conditioned nature. The interrelatedness of impermanence and conditionality with regard to the five aggregates is practically depicted in a discourse from the *Khandha Saṃyutta*, in which realization of the impermanent nature of the five aggregates takes place based on understanding of their conditioned nature.[65] Since the conditions for the arising of each aggregate are impermanent, this passages points out, how could the conditionally arisen aggregate be permanent?

Another discourse in the *Khandha Saṃyutta* relates the arising and passing away of the material aggregate to nutriment, while feelings, cognitions, and volitions depend on contact, and consciousness on name-and-form.[66] Dependent on nutriment, contact, and name-and-form, these five aggregates in turn constitute the condition for the arising of pleasant and unpleasant experiences. The same discourse points out that against the all too apparent "advantage" (*assāda*) of experiencing pleasure through any of the aggregates stands the "disadvantage" (*ādīnava*) of their impermanent and therefore unsatisfactory nature. Thus the only way out (*nissaraṇa*) is to abandon desire and attachment towards these five aggregates.

A related viewpoint on "arising" (*samudaya*) is provided in yet another discourse from the same *Khandha Saṃyutta*, which points out that delight provides the condition for the future arising of the aggregates, while the absence of delight leads to their cessation.[67] This passage links the conditioned and conditioning nature of the aggregates to a comprehension of dependent co-arising. In the *Mahāhatthipadopama Sutta*, such comprehension of dependent co-arising leads to an understanding of the four noble truths.[68]

From a practical perspective, contemplation of the conditioned and conditioning nature of the five aggregates can be undertaken by

---

65 S III 23.

66 S III 62 and S III 59.

67 S III 14.

68 M I 191. Cf. also S IV 188, which relates contemplation of the arising and passing away of the aggregates to understanding the arising and passing away of *dukkha*.

becoming aware how any bodily or mental experience depends on, and is affected by, a set of conditions. Since these conditions are not amenable to full personal control, one evidently does not have power over the very foundation of one's own subjective experience.[69] "I" and "mine" turn out to be utterly dependent on what is "other", a predicament which reveals the truth of *anattā*.

The one centrally important condition, however, which can be brought under personal control through systematic training of the mind, is identification with the five aggregates. This crucial conditioning factor of identification is the central focus of this *satipaṭṭhāna* contemplation, and its complete removal constitutes the successful completion of the practice.

According to the discourses, detachment from these constituent parts of one's personality through contemplating the conditioned and impermanent nature of the aggregates is of such significance that direct knowledge of the arising and passing away of the five aggregates is a sufficient qualification for becoming a stream-enterer.[70] Not only that, but contemplation of the five aggregates is capable of leading to all stages of awakening, and is still practised even by *arahants*.[71] This vividly demonstrates the central importance of this contemplation, which progressively exposes and undermines self identifications and attachments and thereby becomes a powerful manifestation of the direct path to realization.

---

69 S III 66 points out that each aggregate is not-self, since it is not possible to have them conform to one's wishes (such as, for example, always having a healthy body, experiencing only pleasant feelings, etc.).

70 S III 160 and S III 193.

71 S III 167.

XI

DHAMMAS: THE SENSE-SPHERES

XI.1 THE SENSE-SPHERES AND THE FETTERS

The previous *satipaṭṭhāna* exercise was concerned with analysing subjective personality with the help of the aggregate scheme. An alternative or complementary approach is to turn to the relationship between oneself and the outer world.[1] This is the topic covered by contemplation of the sense-spheres, which directs awareness to the six "internal" and "external" sense-spheres (*ajjhattikabāhira āyatana*), and to the fetter arising in dependence on them. Here are the instructions for this exercise:

He knows the eye, he knows forms, and he knows the fetter that arises dependent on both, and he also knows how an unarisen fetter can arise, how an arisen fetter can be removed, and how a future arising of the removed fetter can be prevented.

He knows the ear, he knows sounds, and he knows the fetter that arises dependent on both, and.... He knows the nose, he knows odours, and he knows the fetter that arises dependent on both, and.... He knows the tongue, he knows flavours, and he knows the fetter that arises dependent on both, and.... He knows the body, he knows tangibles, and he knows the fetter that arises dependent on both, and....

---

1 Cf. e.g. M III 279 and S IV 106, which directly relate contemplation of the sense-spheres to the aggregate scheme; cf. also S IV 68. On the contemplations of the aggregates and the senses as complementary approaches cf. Bodhi 2000: p.1122; and Gethin 1986: p.50.

> **He knows the mind, he knows mind-objects, and he knows the fetter that arises dependent on both, and he also knows how an unarisen fetter can arise, how an arisen fetter can be removed, and how a future arising of the removed fetter can be prevented.**[2]

According to the discourses, to develop understanding and detachment in regard to these six internal and external sense-spheres is of central importance for the progress towards awakening.[3] An important aspect of such understanding is to undermine the misleading sense of a substantial "I" as the independent experiencer of sense objects. Awareness directed to each of these sense-spheres will reveal that subjective experience is not a compact unit, but rather a compound made up of six distinct "spheres", each of which is dependently arisen.

Each of these sense-spheres includes both the sense organ and the sense object. Besides the five physical senses (eye, ear, nose, tongue, and body) and their respective objects (sight, sound, smell, flavour, and touch), the mind (*mano*) is included as the sixth sense, together with its mental objects (*dhamma*). In the present context, "mind" (*mano*) represents mainly the activity of thought (*maññati*).[4] While the five physical senses do not share each other's respective field of activity, all of them relate to the mind as the sixth sense.[5] That is, all perceptual processes rely to some extent on the interpretative role of the mind, since it is the mind which "makes sense" out of the other senses. This shows that the early Buddhist scheme of six sense-spheres does not set pure sense perception against the conceptual activity of the mind, but considers both as interrelated processes, which together bring forth the subjective experience of the world.

It is particularly intriguing that early Buddhism treats the mind just like the other sense organs. Thought, reasoning, memory, and reflection are dealt with in the same manner as the sense data of any other sense door. Thus the thinking activity of the mind shares the impersonal status of external phenomena perceived through the five senses.

---

2 M I 61.
3 S IV 89 and A V 52 present insight and detachment regarding the six sense-spheres as enabling one to make an end of *dukkha*.
4 Cf. Johansson 1965: pp.183–7; and T.W. Rhys Davids 1993: p.520.
5 M I 295 and S V 218.

Insight into this impersonal character of "one's own" thoughts can be gained even with the first few attempts at meditation, when one discovers how difficult it is to avoid getting lost in all kinds of reflections, daydreams, memories, and fantasies, despite being determined to focus on a particular object of meditation. Just as it is impossible only to see, hear, smell, taste, and touch what is wished for, so too, with an untrained mind, it is not possible to have thoughts only when and how one would like to have them. For precisely this reason a central purpose of meditative training is to remedy this situation by gradually taming the thinking activity of the mind and bringing it more under conscious control.[6]

The above passage from the *Satipaṭṭhāna Sutta* lists both the sense organs and sense objects for contemplation. On the face of it, the instruction to "know" (*pajānāti*) eye and forms, ear and sounds, etc. seems rather flat, but on further consideration this instruction may reveal some deeper implications.

Often these six senses and their objects occur in descriptions of the conditioned arising of consciousness (*viññāṇa*).[7] An intriguing aspect of this conditional situation is the role that subjective influence plays in the perceptual process. Experience, represented by the six types of consciousness, is the outcome of two determinant influences: the "objective" aspect on the one hand, that is, the in-coming sensory impressions; and the "subjective" aspect on the other hand, namely, the way in which these sense impressions are received and cognized.[8] Supposedly objective perceptual appraisal is in reality conditioned by the subject as much as by the object.[9] One's experi-

---

6 This has found its expression in various passages such as at M I 122, where to develop mastery of the mind means to be able to think only what one wishes to think; or at M I 214, which speaks of gaining control over the mind and thereby being no longer controlled by it; or Dhp 326, which poetically compares controlling one's wandering mind to a mahout controlling a rutting elephant.

7 e.g. at M I 111.

8 Ñāṇamoli 1980: p.159, aptly expresses this: "*ajjhattikāyatana* = the organization of experience ... *bahiddhāyatana* = the experience as organized"; van Zeyst 1967b: p.470, explains: "the inner sphere ... constitutes the subjective element which is the capacity of reaction, and the outer sphere constitutes the objective element which produces the impact". In fact, several of the terms used in this *satipaṭṭhāna* refer exclusively to the senses as faculties of perception (*cakkhu, sota, ghāna*), while the discourses use a different set of Pāli terms for the corresponding physical organs (*akkhi, kaṇṇa, nāsā*), a finding which points to an emphasis on the subjective, in the sense of one's ability to see, hear, etc., underlying the *satipaṭṭhāna* instructions.

9 Cf. e.g. Bodhi 1995: p.16; Padmasiri de Silva 1991: p.21; Guenther 1991: p.16; and Naranjo 1971: p.189.

ence of the world is the product of an interaction between the "subjective" influence exercised by how one perceives the world, and the "objective" influence exercised by the various phenomena of the external world.

Understood in this way, the fact that the *satipaṭṭhāna* instruction directs awareness to each sense organ could have deeper implications, in the sense of pointing to the need to recognize the subjective bias inherent in each process of perception. The influence of this subjective bias has a decisive effect on the first stages of perception and can lead to the arising of a fetter (*saṃyojana*). Such subsequent reactions are often based on qualities and attributes assumed to belong to the perceived object. In actual fact, these qualities and attributes are often projected on the object by the perceiver.

Satipaṭṭhāna contemplation of the six sense-spheres can lead to recognizing this influence of personal biases and tendencies on the process of perception. Contemplating in this way will uncover the root cause for the arising of unwholesome mental reactions. This reactive aspect forms in fact part of the above instructions, where the task of *sati* is to observe the fetter that can arise in dependence on sense and object.

Although a fetter arises in dependence on sense and object, the binding force of such a fetter should not be attributed to the senses or objects per se. The discourses illustrate this with the example of two bulls, bound together by a yoke. Just as their bondage is not caused by either of the bulls, but by the yoke, so too the fetter should not be imputed to either its inner or its outer conditions (for example eye and forms), but to the binding force of desire.[10]

In the discourses there is considerable variation in the usage of the term "fetter",[11] which suggests that to speak of "fetters" does not always necessarily refer to a fixed set, but may sometimes include whatever falls under the same principle, in the sense of fettering and causing bondage. The most common presentation of "fetters" in the discourses lists altogether ten types: belief in a substantial and permanent self, doubt, dogmatic clinging to particular rules and

10 S IV 163; S IV 164; and S IV 283. Cf. also S IV 89 and S IV 108.

11 M I 361 has eight "fetters" in relation to killing, stealing, false speech, malicious speech, rapacious greed, spiteful scolding, angry despair, and arrogance. D III 254; A IV 7; and A IV 8 list seven: complaisance, irritation, views, doubt, conceit, lust for existence, and ignorance. Single fetters occur at M I 483, which has the fetter of householdership, and at It 8, which speaks of the fetter of craving.

observances, sensual desire, aversion, craving for fine-material existence, craving for immaterial existence, conceit, restlessness, and ignorance.[12]

The eradication of these ten fetters takes place with the different stages of realization.[13] Since all these ten fetters might not necessarily manifest in the context of actual *satipaṭṭhāna* practice, and since the term "fetter" has a certain breadth of meaning in the discourses, during contemplation of the sense-spheres awareness can be directed in particular to the fettering force of desire and aversion in regard to whatever is experienced.

The pattern of a fetter's arising proceeds from what has been perceived, via various thoughts and considerations, to the manifestation

---

12 Cf. e.g. S V 61. Ps I 287 lists sensual lust, irritation, conceit, view, doubt, clinging to particular rules and observances, lust for existence, envy, avarice, and ignorance as fetters for the *satipaṭṭhāna* context. Concerning clinging to particular rules and observances, Bodhi 2000: p.727 n.5, explains that the expression "rules and observances" (*sīlabbata*) can refer to such ascetic practices as, for example, behaving like a dog (cf. M I 387, which speaks of the "dog-rule" and the "dog-observance"). Some ascetics adopted such practices in the hope of gaining purification or rebirth in heaven (cf. M I 102). Cf. also Ud 71, where "rules and observances" replaces the more usual "self-mortification" as one of the two extremes to be avoided. However, at Dhp 271 the Buddha spoke to his own monks about the need to go beyond "rules and observances" in order to reach realization; so this verse indicates that "rules and observances" can also become a problem for Buddhist monks. In fact, the equivalent term *sīlavata* occurs in several instances as a positive quality of a Buddhist monk (e.g. at A III 47; Sn 212; It 79; and Th 12). This suggests, as in fact expressly stated at A I 225, that "rules and observances" can be either wholesome or unwholesome, so the fettering aspect is to be found in dogmatic clinging (*parāmāsa*). The absence of such dogmatic clinging is indeed explicitly mentioned in the standard descriptions of the qualities of a stream-enterer (cf. e.g. D II 94; S II 70; or A II 57), which indicate that a stream-enterer is endowed with pure moral conduct, but does not dogmatically cling to it. (The Pāli term used is *aparāmaṭṭha*, which according to Vism 222 refers in this context to clinging by way of craving and views.)

13 Cf. e.g. D I 156. The dynamics of this progressive eradication of the ten fetters is that with the first direct experience of *Nibbāna* at stream-entry, belief in a permanent self becomes impossible. Since this experience comes as the successful outcome of following the right path, doubt about what is wholesome and skilful for progress on this path, and also doubt in the more existential sense regarding the whence and whither of oneself, together with dogmatic clinging to particular rules and observances, are left behind. With continued practice, the next two fetters of sensual desire and aversion are diminished at once-returning and then fully overcome with the realization of non-returning. With full awakening, the last remnants of attachment in the form of craving for deep states of concentration (and corresponding forms of existence) are extinguished, together with any traces of the notion "I am" as a manifestation of conceit and its possible repercussions in the form of restlessness, and therewith all ignorance is overcome as well.

of desire and thereby to bondage.[14] A mindful observation of the conditions that lead to the arising of a fetter constitutes the second stage of contemplation of the sense-spheres (cf. Fig. 11.1 below). The task of awareness in this case, paralleling contemplation of the hindrances, is non-reactive observation. Such non-reactive observation is directed towards individual instances in which perception causes desire and bondage, and also towards discovering the general patterns of one's mental inclinations, in order to be able to prevent the future arising of a fetter.

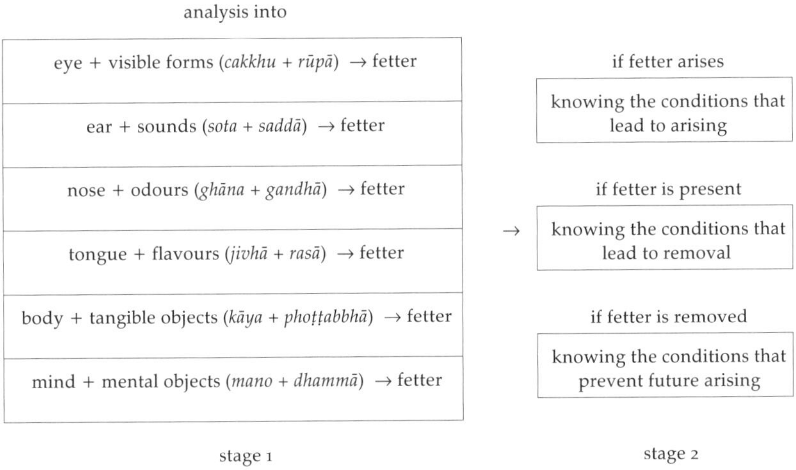

Fig. 11.1 Two stages in the contemplation of the six sense-spheres

As with the contemplation of the hindrances, the second stage of contemplation of the sense-spheres (concerned with the arising and removal of a fetter) follows a progressive pattern from diagnosis, via cure, to prevention. In contrast to the contemplation of the hindrances, however, contemplation of the sense-spheres places a stronger emphasis on the perceptual process. This constitutes an additional degree of refinement, since attention is here directed to the first stages of the perceptual process, which, if left unattended, can lead to the arising of unwholesome mental reactions.

To fill in some background to this aspect of *satipaṭṭhāna*, I will briefly survey the Buddha's analysis of the perceptual process, with particular attention to the implications of the "latent tendencies"

---

14 A I 264 relates the state of being fettered to desire, this in turn being due to thinking and pondering over desirable things of the past, present, or future.

(*anusaya*) and "influxes" (*āsava*), and also to restraint at the sense doors. This will provide the necessary basis for evaluating the early Buddhist approach to "cognitive training", and for examining the Buddha's pithy instruction to the ascetic Bāhiya that led to his immediate full awakening.

XI.2 THE PERCEPTUAL PROCESS

The conditioned character of the perceptual process is a central aspect of the Buddha's analysis of experience. According to the *Madhupiṇḍika Sutta*, the conditional sequence of the average perceptual process leads from contact (*phassa*) via feeling (*vedanā*) and cognition (*saññā*) to thought (*vitakka*), which can in turn stimulate conceptual proliferation (*papañca*).[15] Such conceptual proliferations tend to give rise to further concoctions of proliferations and cognitions (*papañcasaññāsaṅkhā*), which lead from the originally perceived sense data to all kinds of associations concerning past, present, and future.

The Pāli verb forms employed in this passage from the *Madhupiṇḍika Sutta* indicate that the last stage of this perceptual process is an event of which one is the passive experiencer.[16] Once the conditioned sequence of the perceptual process has reached the stage of conceptual proliferation one becomes, as it were, a victim of one's own associations and thoughts. The thought process proliferates, weaving a net built from thoughts, projections, and associations, of which the "thinker" has become almost a helpless prey.

The crucial stage in this sequence, where the subjective bias can set in and distort the perceptual process, occurs with the initial appraisal of feeling (*vedanā*) and cognition (*saññā*). Initial distortions of the sense data arising at this stage will receive further reinforcement by thinking and by conceptual proliferation.[17] Once the stage of conceptual proliferation is reached, the course is set. The proliferations are projected back onto the sense data and the mind continues proliferating by interpreting experience in line with the original biased cognition. The stages of cognition and initial conceptual reaction are therefore decisive aspects of this conditioned sequence.

---

15 M I 111.
16 Cf. Ñāṇananda 1986: p.5.
17 Sn 874 emphasizes the dependence of conceptual proliferation on cognition in particular.

The perceptual sequence described in the *Madhupiṇḍika Sutta* occurs in an elucidation of a short statement made by the Buddha, in which he related his teaching to the dispelling of various latent (*anuseti*) types of cognitions (*saññā*), and to overcoming the "latent tendencies" (*anusaya*) that can come into operation during the process of perception.[18]

The discourses mention various types of latent tendencies. A commonly occurring set of seven includes sensual desire, irritation, views, doubt, conceit, craving for existence, and ignorance.[19] The central characteristic of a latent tendency is unconscious activation. As the verb *anuseti*, "to lie along with", suggests, a latent tendency lies dormant in the mind, but can become activated during the process of perception. In their dormant stage, the underlying tendencies are already present in newborn babies.[20]

A term of similar importance in relation to the process of perception is influx (*āsava*).[21] These influxes can "flow" (*āsavati*) into and thereby "influence" the perceptual process.[22] As with the underlying tendencies, this influence operates without conscious intention. The influxes arise owing to unwise attention (*ayoniso manasikāra*) and to ignorance (*avijjā*).[23] To counteract and prevent the arising of the influxes is the central aim of the monastic training rules laid

18 M I 108. Cf. also M III 285, which relates a part of the same conditioned perceptual sequence to the activation of the latent tendencies.

19 e.g. at A IV 9. Apart from this standard set one finds the latent tendency to mental standpoints and adherences at S II 17 and S III 135, the latent tendency to lust at S IV 205, and the latent tendency to craving at Dhp 338. To contemplate the effects these underlying tendencies can create in the mind may be undertaken by directing awareness to the untrained mind's "tendency" to react to sensory experience with either lust or irritation; to its "tendency" to respond to more theoretical information by either forming views and opinions or else by feeling confused and doubtful; and by contemplating how the sense of "I" underlying subjective experience "tends" to manifest as conceit and moreover "tends" to clamour for eternal continuation (viz. craving for existence). Contemplating in this way will reveal the surprising degree to which the unawakened mind in some way or other "tends" towards ignorance. Ñāṇapoṇika 1977: p.238, points out that "latent tendency" includes both the actually arisen mental defilement and the corresponding mental disposition, this being the result of long-time habits.

20 M I 432; cf. also M II 24.

21 *Āsava* also means "outflow", as when a sore festers (cf. A I 124), or "fermentation", as when liquor is brewed from flowers etc. (cf. Sv III 944).

22 e.g. M I 9 recommends guarding the senses in order to avoid the activation of the influxes.

23 M I 7 relates the arising of the influxes to unwise attention; A III 414 to ignorance.

down by the Buddha,[24] and their successful eradication (*āsavakkhaya*) is a synonym for full awakening.[25]

The discourses often mention three types of influx: the influx of sensual desire, desire for existence, and ignorance.[26] Sensual desire and desire for existence come up also in the second noble truth as main factors in the arising of *dukkha*,[27] while ignorance forms the starting point of the "twelve links" depicting the "dependent co-arising" (*paṭicca samuppāda*) of *dukkha*. These occurrences indicate that the scheme of the influxes is intrinsically related to the causes for the arising of *dukkha*.[28] That is, desire for sensual enjoyment, desire for becoming this or that, and the deluding force of ignorance, are those "influences" responsible for the genesis of *dukkha*.

The whole purpose of practising the path taught by the Buddha is to eradicate the influxes (*āsava*), uproot the latent tendencies (*anusaya*), and abandon the fetters (*saṃyojana*).[29] These three terms refer to the same basic problem from slightly different perspectives, namely to the arising of craving (*taṇhā*) and related forms of unwholesomeness in relation to any of the six sense-spheres.[30] In this context, the influxes represent root causes for the arising of *dukkha* that might "flow into" perceptual appraisal, the underlying tendencies are those unwholesome inclinations in the unawakened mind

---

24 The rationale given by the Buddha for proclaiming a rule (cf. e.g. Vin III 21) was that it should restrain presently arisen influxes and avoid their arising in future (cf. also M I 445). In addition to adherence to the rules, other important methods for countering the influxes are not getting entangled in wrong views; restraining the senses; using requisites properly; enduring heat, cold, hunger, pain, etc.; avoiding dangerous animals and unsuitable intimacy with the opposite sex; removing unwholesome intentions and thoughts; and developing the factors of awakening (at M I 7–11).

25 e.g. at M I 171.

26 e.g. at M I 55. In addition to these three influxes, the influx of views is mentioned in a few instances (e.g. at D II 81); however, according to Ñāṇatiloka 1988: p.27, and T.W. Rhys Davids 1993: p.115, the set of three influxes is probably the more original version. On the influxes cf. also Johansson 1985: p.178; and Premasiri 1990a: p.58.

27 e.g. at S V 421.

28 This also underlies the fact that descriptions of the actual event of full awakening often apply the scheme of the four noble truths to *dukkha* and again to the influxes, cf. e.g. D I 84.

29 S V 28.

30 The all-pervasive range of craving is illustrated in the detailed exposition of the second noble truth in the *Mahāsatipaṭṭhāna Sutta*, D II 308, where the various stages of the perceptual process, from the six senses, their respective objects and types of consciousness, via contact, to feeling, cognition, volition, and initial and sustained mental application are all listed as possible instances for the arising of craving. This analysis of sense experience occurs again at S II 109, and also at Vibh 101 (in the *Suttanta* exposition of the four noble truths).

that "tend" to get triggered off during the perceptual process, and the fetters arising at any sense door are responsible for "binding" beings to continued transmigration in *saṃsāra*.

A way to avoid the operation of the influxes, underlying tendencies, and fetters, and thereby the arising of unwholesome states of mind and reactions at any sense door, is the practice of sense-restraint (*indriya saṃvara*). The method of sense-restraint is mainly based on *sati*, whose presence exerts a restraining influence on the reactions and proliferations that otherwise tend to occur during the perceptual process.[31] As the discourses point out, sense-restraint causes the arising of joy and happiness, which in turn form the basis for concentration and insight.[32] Indeed, living with full awareness in the present moment, free from sensual distraction, can give rise to an exquisite sense of delight.

Such cultivation of mindfulness at the sense doors does not imply that one is simply to avoid sense impressions. As the Buddha pointed out in the *Indriyabhāvanā Sutta*, if simply avoiding seeing and hearing were in itself conducive to realization, blind and deaf people would be accomplished practitioners.[33] Instead, the instruction for sense-restraint enjoins the practitioner not to dwell on the sign (*nimitta*) or secondary characteristics (*anuvyañjana*) of sense objects, in order to avoid the "flowing in" of detrimental influences.[34] In the present context, "sign" (*nimitta*) refers to the distinguishing feature by which one recognizes or remembers something.[35] In regard to the process of perception, this "sign" (*nimitta*) is related to the first evaluation of the raw sense data, because of

---

31 Bodhi 2000: p.1127, explains: "to restrain the senses ... involves stopping at the bare sensum, without plastering it over with layers of meaning whose origins are purely subjective". Upali Karunaratne 1993: p.568, relates restraint of the senses in particular to the stage of the perceptual process when feelings arise.

32 e.g. at S IV 78. Cf. also M I 346, which speaks of the pure happiness (*abyāseka sukha*) gained through sense-restraint.

33 At M III 298, in answer to a Brahmin who had proposed not seeing with the eyes and not hearing with the ears as a form of meditative development of the faculties. Cf. also Tilakaratne 1993: p.72.

34 e.g. at M I 273. The verb "to flow into", *anvāssavati*, is derived from *anu* + *ā* + *savati* (T.W. Rhys Davids 1993: p.50) and is thus reminiscent of the influxes, the *āsavas*.

35 e.g. at M I 360 "sign" refers to the outer aspect of being a householder; or at Vin III 15 and M II 62 a slave woman recognized the former son of the house, now a monk and returning after a long absence, by way of the "sign". In other passages "sign" has a more causal function (cf. e.g. S V 213; A I 82; A II 9; A IV 83; and Th 1100). On "sign" cf. also Harvey 1986: pp.31–3; and page 237, footnote 21.

which the object appears to be, for example, "beautiful" (*subhanimitta*) or "irritating" (*paṭighanimitta*), which then usually leads to subsequent evaluations and mental reactions.[36]

The instruction to bring restraint to bear on the secondary characteristics (*anuvyañjana*) could correspond to further associations in the perceptual process, which elaborate in detail the initial biased cognition (*saññā*).[37] The tendency to biased and affective reactions is rooted in the stage of sign making, when the first barely conscious evaluations that might underlie cognition (*saññā*) can arise. In the context of the *Satipaṭṭhāna Sutta*'s injunction to contemplate the causes related to the arising of a fetter, this stage of sign making is especially relevant. It is this stage, therefore, and the possibilities of influencing it, to which I will now turn in more detail.

XI.3 COGNITIVE TRAINING

According to the discourses, a penetrative understanding of the nature of cognition (*saññā*) is a prominent cause for realization.[38] Cognitions under the influence of sensuality or aversion lead to cognitive distortions and thereby cause the arising of unwholesome thoughts and intentions.[39] Distorted or biased cognitions include significant misapprehensions of reality that affect the fundamental structure of ordinary experience, such as when one wrongly perceives permanence, satisfaction, substantiality, and beauty in what

36 A I 3 relates sensual desire to unwise attention to the "sign of beauty", and aversion to unwise attention to the "sign of irritation". M I 298 explains that lust, anger, and delusion are "makers of signs". Cf. also M III 225, which describes how consciousness, because of following after the sign, becomes tied and shackled by the gratification derived from the sign, and thereby becomes fettered to the sign.

37 As 400, however, takes the term to refer to the details of the perceived object. On the other hand, in similar passages in the discourses "sign" may be followed by various types of thoughts, which could correspond to "association" (cf. e.g. M I 119). T.W. Rhys Davids 1993: p.43, translates *anuvyañjana* as "accompanying attribute", "supplementary or additional sign or mark". The corresponding Chinese version (Minh Chau 1991: p.82) speaks of not grasping the general appearance and not "taking delight in it". On *anuvyañjana* as "association" cf. Vimalo 1974: p.54.

38 A II 167. Cf. also Sn 779, pointing out that by penetrative insight into cognition one will be able to cross the flood; and Sn 847, according to which one gone beyond cognition has thereby gone beyond bondage.

39 M I 507 speaks of the cognitive distortion (*viparītasaññā*) to perceive sensual pleasures as happiness. M II 27 identifies cognitions under the influence of sensuality, aversion, and cruelty as the source of all unwholesome thoughts and intentions.

in fact is the opposite.[40] The presence of such unrealistic elements within cognition is due to the habitual projection of one's own mistaken notions onto cognized sense data, a process of which one is usually unaware. These habitual projections underlying the perceptual process are responsible for unrealistic expectations and thereby for frustration and conflict.[41]

As a countermeasure to these unrealistic cognitive appraisals, the discourses recommend cultivating beneficial cognitions.[42] Such beneficial cognitions direct awareness to the impermanence or unsatisfactoriness of all aspects of experience. Others are concerned with more specific issues, such as the unattractive features of the body or food. Regarding the nature of these cognitions, an important point to bear in mind is that to cognize something as beautiful or as impermanent does not refer to a process of reflection or consideration, but only to being aware of a particular feature of an object, in other words, to experience it from a particular point of view. In the case of ordinary cognitive appraisal, this point of view or act of selection is usually not at all conscious. Cognizing someone or something as beautiful often takes place as the combined outcome of past conditioning and one's present mental inclinations. These tend to determine which aspect of an object becomes prominent during cognition. Reflective thought only subsequently enters into the scene, influenced by the kind of cognition that has led to its arising.[43]

The crucial point, from a meditative perspective, is that cognitions are amenable to a process of training.[44] The ability to train cognitions

40 These are the four *vipallāsas*, cf. A II 52; Paṭis II 80; Bodhi 1992b: p.4; and page 25, footnote 27.

41 Fromm 1960: p.127: "man in the state of repressedness … does not see what exists, but he puts his thought image into things, and sees them in the light of his thought images and fantasies, rather than in their reality. It is the thought image … that creates his passions, his anxieties." Johansson 1985: p.96: "things are seen through the lenses of our desires, prejudices and resentments and are transformed accordingly".

42 e.g. at D III 251; D III 253; D III 289; A III 79; A III 83–5; A IV 24; A IV 46; A IV 387; A V 105–7; and A V 109.

43 M II 27. In fact, according to D I 185 cognition temporally precedes knowledge (*ñāṇa*), a temporal precedence which can lead to a considerable degree of influence exercised by cognition on what is being "known"; cf. also Ñāṇavīra 1987: p.110.

44 D I 180 explains that through training some type of cognitions will arise, others will disappear (this statement occurs in the context of *jhāna* attainment); cf. also Premasiri 1972: p.12. Claxton 1991: p.25, points out that "the Buddhist position, because it asserts that perception is changeable by psychological practices such as meditation, assumes a 'constructivist' view".

is related to the fact that cognitions are the outcome of mental habits. By way of cognitive training, one can establish new and different habits and thereby gradually alter one's cognitions. The basic procedure for such cognitive training is related to the same habit-forming mechanism, namely to becoming accustomed to, and familiar with, a certain way of viewing experience.[45] By directing awareness again and again to the true characteristics of conditioned existence, these will become more and more familiar, imprint themselves onto one's way of viewing experience, and thereby lead to the arising of similar ways of cognizing on future occasions.

The method through which cognition is trained can be conveniently exemplified with a set of terms occurring in the *Girimānanda Sutta*, where reflection (*paṭisañcikkhati*) and contemplation (*anupassanā*) are mentioned alongside cognition (*saññā*).[46] Although this is not spelled out in the discourse, this passage lists those two activities that are related to training cognition: a preliminary degree of wise reflection as a basis for the sustained practice of contemplation (*anupassanā*). Skilfully combined, these two can gradually transform the way the world is cognized.

To give a practical example: if, on the basis of an intellectual appreciation of impermanence, one regularly contemplates the arising and passing away of phenomena, the result will be the arising of *aniccasaññā*, of cognitions apprehending phenomena from the viewpoint of impermanence. With continued practice, awareness of impermanence will become increasingly spontaneous and have an increasing influence on one's daily experiences, outside of actual contemplation. In this way, sustained contemplation can lead to a gradual change in the operational mechanics of cognition, and in one's outlook on the world.

According to the discourses, such cognitive training can lead to a stage at which one is able at will to cognize phenomena as agreeable (*appaṭikkūla*) or as disagreeable (*paṭikkūla*).[47] The culmination of training one's cognitions in this way is reached when one completely transcends such evaluations and becomes firmly established in perceptual equanimity. The discourses go so far as to consider

45 A long list of such cognitive trainings is given at A V 107, each time introduced by the expression "accustomed to" or " familiar with" (*paricita*). Cf. also Paṭis I 32.

46 A V 109.

47 M III 301. A III 169 explains that the purpose of this cognitive training is to counter the arising of lust and anger.

such mastery over one's cognitions to be superior even to supernatural powers like walking on water or flying through the air.[48]

The basis for developing such intriguing kinds of mastery is *satipaṭṭhāna* contemplation.[49] The presence of *sati* directly counteracts automatic and unconscious ways of reacting that are so typical of habits. By directing *sati* to the early stages of the perceptual process, one can train cognition and thereby reshape habitual patterns. Of central importance in this context is the receptive quality of mindfulness, which gives full attention to the cognized data. Of equal significance is *sati*'s detached quality, which avoids immediate reactions.

In this way, receptive and detached *sati* applied to the early stages of the perceptual process can make habitual reactions conscious and enable an assessment of the extent to which one is reacting automatically and without conscious deliberation. This also reveals the selective and filtering mechanisms of perception, highlighting the extent to which subjective experience mirrors one's hitherto unconscious assumptions. In this manner, through *satipaṭṭhāna* contemplation, it becomes possible to access and redress a central cause of the arising of unwholesome cognitions, and thereby for the activation of influxes (*āsava*), underlying tendencies (*anusaya*), and fetters (*saṃyojana*), by de-automatizing or deconditioning habits and subconscious evaluations.

A practical application of this skill is the subject of the final section of my exploration of the contemplation of the sense-spheres.

XI.4 THE INSTRUCTION TO BĀHIYA

"Bāhiya of the Bark-Garment" was a non-Buddhist ascetic who once approached the Buddha for instructions while the latter was collecting almsfood. Still out on the roads of the city, the Buddha gave him a short instruction concerned with cognitive training, with the

---

48 D III 113.

49 Cf. S V 295, where an exposition of *satipaṭṭhāna* is followed by a description of the ability to influence cognition (*paṭikkūle appaṭikkūlasaññī*). Scientific corroboration of perceptual changes owing to meditation can be found in Brown 1984: p.727. Cf. also Brown 1977: p.248; Deikman 1969: p.204; and Santucci 1979: p.72.

result that Bāhiya immediately gained full awakening.[50] The Buddha's cryptic instruction was:

> **When in the seen will be only what is seen, in the heard only what is heard, in the sensed only what is sensed, in the known only what is known, you will not be by that; when you are not by that, you will not be therein; when you are not therein, you will be neither here, nor there, nor in between. This is the end of *dukkha*.**[51]

This instruction directs bare awareness to whatever is seen, heard, sensed, or cognized. Maintaining bare awareness in this way prevents the mind evaluating and proliferating the raw data of sense perception. This corresponds to an interception of the first stages in the sequence of the perceptual process, through mindful attention. Here, bare awareness simply registers whatever arises at a sense door without giving rise to biased forms of cognition and to unwholesome thoughts and associations.[52] In terms of sense-restraint, the stage of making a "sign" (*nimitta*) is thereby brought into conscious awareness.[53] Establishing bare awareness at this stage of the perceptual process prevents the latent tendencies (*anusaya*), influxes (*āsava*), and fetters (*saṃyojana*) from arising.

---

50 Ud 8; for this he was noted among the Buddha's disciples as pre-eminent in quick understanding (at A I 24). S IV 63 and S V 165 report the realization of a monk by the same name, Bāhiya, but based in one case on contemplating the six senses as impermanent, unsatisfactory, and not-self, and in the other case on *satipaṭṭhāna*. According to Malalasekera 1995: vol.II, pp.281–3, these last two are different from the Bāhiya of the *Udāna* episode. Another Bāhiya who caused dissension among the monks is mentioned at A II 239. At S IV 73 the monk Māluṅkyaputta received the "Bāhiya" instruction, where it again led to full awakening, although in this case after a period of practice in seclusion. The Bāhiya case also comes up in the *Satipaṭṭhāna* subcommentary Ps-pṭ I 357, in the context of clear knowledge in regard to bodily activities.

51 Ud 8.

52 This seems to be the implication of several passages in the *Sutta Nipāta* which employ the same terms (seen, heard, sensed), cf. Sn 793; Sn 798; Sn 802; Sn 812; and Sn 914. Mahasi 1992: p.42, explains: "when one concentrates only on the act of seeing without thinking over what one has seen, visual perception will last only for an instant ... in that case defilements will have no time to assert themselves". Namto 1984: p.15: instructs one to "focus on the split-second between hearing a sound and recognizing it in the conventional manner". Practical experiences that reflect the above injunctions are described in Shattock 1970: p.68; and Walsh 1984: p.267.

53 Compare the detailed treatment given by Māluṅkyaputta after receiving the "Bāhiya" instructions at S IV 73, where he pointed out how lack of mindfulness leads to giving attention to the sign of affection and thereby to an infatuated state of mind. (Same again in part at Th 98–9 and in full at Th 794–817.)

The activities of seeing, hearing, sensing, and knowing mentioned in the Bāhiya instruction occur also in the *Mūlapariyāya Sutta*.[54] This discourse contrasts the *arahant*'s direct comprehension of phenomena with the ordinary way of perception through misconceiving the cognized data in various ways. The *Chabbisodhana Sutta* relates the elaborations absent from what is seen, heard, sensed, and known by an *arahant* to freedom from attraction and rejection.[55] Other passages discuss the same set of activities with an additional emphasis on avoiding any form of identification.[56] This injunction is particularly pertinent, since according to the *Alagaddūpama Sutta* the activities of seeing, hearing, sensing, and knowing can lead to wrongly developing a sense of self.[57] Passages in the *Upaniṣads* indeed take these activities as evidence for the perceiving activity of a self.[58]

According to the Bāhiya instruction, by maintaining bare *sati* at all sense doors one will not be "by that", which suggests not being carried away by the conditioned sequence of the perceptual process, thereby not modifying experience through subjective biases and distorted cognitions.[59] Not being carried away, one is not "therein" by way of subjective participation and identification.[60] Such absence of being "therein" draws attention to a key aspect of the instruction to Bāhiya, to the realization of *anattā* as the absence of a perceiving self.

---

54 M I 1. Cf. also A II 23, which documents the Buddha's ability to see through and fully understand whatever is seen, heard, sensed, or cognized.

55 M III 30.

56 M I 136 and M III 261.

57 M I 135. Cf. also Bhattacharya 1980: p.10.

58 *Bṛhadāraṇyaka Upaniṣad* 2.4.5 states that the self should be seen, heard of, thought about, and meditated upon, since by the seeing, hearing, sensing, and cognizing of the self everything is known; *Bṛhadāraṇyaka Upaniṣad* 4.5.6 then declares that once the self is seen, heard, sensed, and cognized, everything is known.

59 "By that" (*tena*) in the sense of "thereby", cf. e.g. Dhp 258, which criticizes much talking by pointing out that "thereby" or "by that" (*tena*) one does not become a sage. According to Ireland 1977: p.160 n.3, *tena* and *tattha* "are the key words in this text".

60 "Therein", *tattha*, is a locative adverb, which can also be translated as "there", "in that place", or "to this place" (T.W. Rhys Davids 1993: p.295). Vimalo 1959: p.27, renders this passage (*tena* + *tattha*): "then you will not be influenced by that, if you are not influenced by it, you are not bound to it". For "subjective participation" in the sense of affective involvement cf. Sn 1086. Bodhi 1992b: p.13, commenting on the Bāhiya instruction, explains: "what is to be eliminated from cognition is precisely the false imputations of subjectivity that distort the incoming data and issue in erroneous judgements and beliefs".

Neither being "by that" nor "therein" also constitutes a comparatively advanced stage of *satipaṭṭhāna* practice, when the meditator has become able to continuously maintain bare awareness at all sense doors, thereby not being "by that" by remaining free from "clinging to anything in the world", nor being "therein" by continuing to "abide independently", as stipulated in the *satipaṭṭhāna* "refrain".

According to the final part of the Bāhiya instruction, by maintaining awareness in the above manner one will not be established "here" or "there" or "in between". A way of understanding "here" and "there" is to take them as representing the subject (senses) and the respective objects, with "in between" standing for the conditioned arising of consciousness.[61] According to a discourse from the *Aṅguttara Nikāya*, it is the "seamstress" craving (*taṇhā*) which "stitches" consciousness ("the middle") to the senses and their objects (the two opposite ends).[62] Applying this imagery to the Bāhiya instruction, in the absence of craving these three conditions for perceptual contact do not get sufficiently "tied" together, so to speak, for further proliferations to occur. Such absence of unnecessary proliferation is characteristic of the cognitions of *arahants*, who are no longer influenced by subjective biases and who cognize phenomena without self-reference. Free from craving and proliferations, they are not identified with either "here" (senses), or "there" (objects), or "in between" (consciousness), resulting in freedom from any type of becoming, whether it be "here", or "there", or "in between".

---

61 Following Ñāṇavīra 1987: p.435. The commentary Ud-a 92, however, relates these expressions to spheres of rebirth, but points out that in this interpretation "in between" should not be taken to refer to an intermediate existence. In fact, the Pāli commentarial tradition holds that rebirth immediately follows the moment of passing away. A close examination of the discourses, on the other hand, reveals several instances which suggest that from their perspective such a state in between existences did exist, where the being to be reborn (the *gandhabba* at M I 265 and M II 157), propelled by craving (S IV 399), seeks a new existence (*sambhavesi* at M I 48 and Sn 147), or can attain full awakening in that intermediate state if the stage of non-returning had earlier been realized (the *antarāparinibbāyi* e.g. at D III 237; S V 70; S V 201; S V 204; S V 237; S V 285; S V 314; S V 378; A I 233; A II 134; A IV 14; A IV 71; A IV 146; A IV 380; and A V 120). Cf. also Bodhi 2000: p.1902 n.65.

62 A III 400, commenting on Sn 1042. Cf. also Dhp 385, which speaks in praise of going beyond this shore and the other, a passage which according to Daw Mya Tin 1990: p.132, can be interpreted in a similar way. The seamstress (craving) occurs again at Th 663. Cf. also Ñāṇananda 1999: p.19.

XII

DHAMMAS: THE AWAKENING FACTORS

XII.1 CONTEMPLATION OF THE AWAKENING FACTORS

The mental qualities that form the topic of the next contemplation of *dhammas* provide the conditions conducive to awakening, which is why they are termed "awakening factors".[1] Just as a river inclines and flows towards the ocean, so the awakening factors incline towards *Nibbāna*.[2]

The instructions for contemplating the awakening factors are:

> **If the mindfulness awakening factor is present in him, he knows "there is the mindfulness awakening factor in me"; if the mindfulness awakening factor is not present in him, he knows "there is no mindfulness awakening factor in me"; he knows how the unarisen mindfulness awakening factor can arise, and how the arisen mindfulness awakening factor can be perfected by development.**
>
> **If the investigation-of-*dhammas* awakening factor is present in him, he knows.... If the energy awakening factor is present in him, he knows.... If the joy awakening factor is present in him, he knows.... If the tranquillity awakening factor is present in him, he knows.... If the concentration awakening factor is present in him, he knows....**
>
> **If the equanimity awakening factor is present in him, he knows "there is the equanimity awakening factor in me"; if the equanimity**

---

1 S V 72; S V 83; and Paṭis II 115. Cf. also D III 97; Dhp 89; and Thī 21. According to Norman 1997: p.29, *bodhi* is better rendered by "awakening" than by "enlightenment", a suggestion which I have followed.

2 S V 134.

awakening factor is not present in him, he knows "there is no equanimity awakening factor in me"; he knows how the unarisen equanimity awakening factor can arise, and how the arisen equanimity awakening factor can be perfected by development.[3]

Contemplation of the awakening factors proceeds similarly to the contemplation of the hindrances: first awareness turns to the presence or absence of the mental quality in question, and then to the conditions for its presence or absence (cf. Fig. 12.1 below). However, while in the case of contemplating the hindrances awareness is concerned with the conditions for their future non-arising, with the awakening factors the task is to know how to develop and firmly establish these beneficial mental qualities.

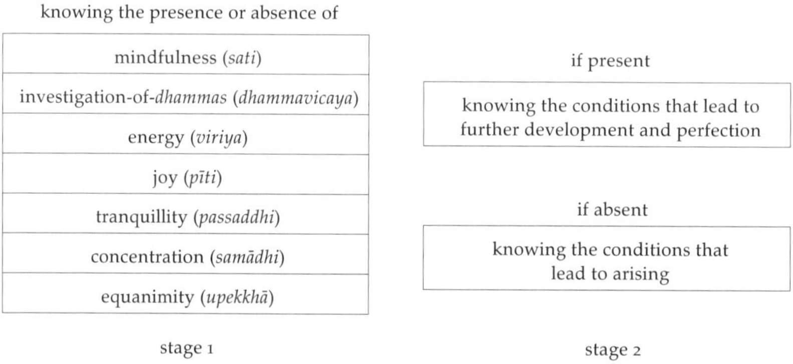

Fig. 12.1 Two stages in the contemplation of the seven awakening factors

Like the contemplation of the hindrances, the instructions for contemplating the awakening factors do not mention any active endeavour to set up or maintain a particular awakening factor, apart from the task of setting up awareness. However, just as the mere presence of *sati* can counter a hindrance, so the presence of *sati* can promote the arising of the other awakening factors. In fact, according to the *Ānāpānasati Sutta* the seven awakening factors form a conditionally related sequence, with *sati* as its initial cause and foundation.[4] This suggests that the development of the awakening factors is a natural outcome of practising *satipaṭṭhāna*.[5]

---

3 M I 61.

4 M III 85 and S V 68.

5 According to S V 73 and A V 116, the development of the four *satipaṭṭhānas* fulfils the seven awakening factors.

Besides providing the foundation for the other factors, *sati* is moreover the one awakening factor whose development is beneficial at any time and on all occasions.[6] The remaining six factors can be split into two groups of three: investigation-of-*dhammas* (*dhammavicaya*), energy (*viriya*), and joy (*pīti*) are particularly appropriate when the mind is sluggish and deficient in energy, while tranquillity (*passaddhi*), concentration (*samādhi*), and equanimity (*upekkhā*) are suitable for those occasions when the mind is excited and over-energetic.[7]

XII.2 THE CONDITIONAL SEQUENCE OF THE AWAKENING FACTORS

In the conditional sequence of the awakening factors, "investigation-of-*dhammas*" (*dhammavicaya*) develops out of well-established mindfulness. Such investigation-of-*dhammas* seems to combine two aspects: on the one hand an inquiry into the nature of experience (by taking "*dhammas*" to stand for "phenomena"), and on the other a correlation of this experience with the teachings of the Buddha (the "*Dhamma*").[8] This twofold character also underlies the word "investigation" (*vicaya*), derived from the verb *vicinati*, whose range of meaning includes both "investigating" and "discriminating".[9] Thus "investigation-of-*dhammas*" can be understood as an investigation of subjective experience based on the discrimination gained through familiarity with the *Dhamma*. Such discrimination refers in particular to the ability to distinguish between what is wholesome or skilful for progress on the path, and what is unwholesome or unskilful.[10] This directly contrasts investigation-of-*dhammas* with the

---

6 At S V 115 the Buddha emphatically stated that *sati* is always useful. This usefulness of *sati* is illustratively compared by the commentary to the need for salt when preparing food (at Ps I 292). The central importance of *sati* is also brought out at Ps I 243 and Ps-pṭ I 363, according to which *sati* forms the essential condition for "contemplation" and "knowledge".

7 S V 112.

8 At S V 68 "investigation-of-*dhammas*" refers to further reflection on earlier heard explanations by elder monks. In contrast at S V 111 "investigation-of-*dhammas*" stands for investigating internal and external phenomena.

9 T.W. Rhys Davids 1993: p.616.

10 S V 66. On investigation-of-*dhammas* cf. also Jootla 1983: pp.43–8; and Ledi 1983: p.105, who assembles the five higher stages of purification, the three contemplations, and the ten insight knowledges under this particular awakening factor. According to Mil 83, investigation-of-*dhammas* is a mental quality of crucial importance for realization.

hindrance doubt (*vicikicchā*), which arises owing to lack of clarity about what is wholesome and what is unwholesome.[11]

The development of investigation-of-*dhammas* in turn arouses the awakening factor of energy (*viriya*).[12] The arising of such "energy" is related to putting forth effort.[13] The discourses further qualify such energy with the attribute "unshaken".[14] This qualification draws attention to the need for effort or energy to be applied with continuity, a specification which parallels the quality of being diligent (*ātāpī*) mentioned in the "definition" part of the *Satipaṭṭhāna Sutta*. According to the discourses, energy can manifest either mentally or physically.[15] As an awakening factor, energy stands in direct opposition to the hindrance sloth-and-torpor (*thīnamiddha*).[16]

In the sequence of the awakening factors, energy in turn leads to the arising of joy (*pīti*). Joy as an awakening factor is clearly a non-sensual type of joy, such as the joy that can be experienced during absorption attainment.[17] The progression of the awakening factors then leads from joy (*pīti*), via tranquillity (*passaddhi*), to concentration (*samādhi*). This echoes a causal sequence often described elsewhere in the discourses, which similarly proceeds from joy, tranquillity, and happiness to concentration, and culminates with the arising of wisdom and realization.[18]

---

11 Cf. S V 104, which describes the "nutriment" for investigation-of-*dhammas* in exactly the same terms used by S V 106 to describe the "anti-nutriment" for doubt, namely wise attention in regard to what is wholesome and what is unwholesome. Such clarity is in both cases concerned with "internal" as well as "external" *dhammas* (cf. S V 110).

12 According to Debes 1994: p.292, the effect of investigation-of-*dhammas*, by finding out the validity and relevance of the Buddha's teachings to experienced reality, is to awaken energy ("Tatkraft").

13 S V 66 recommends endeavour and exertion as nutriments for the awakening factor of energy. The Chinese *Āgama* version of this discourse mentions the four right efforts as nutriment for the awakening factor of energy (cf. Choong 2000: p.213). This presentation fits well with the distinction between wholesomeness and unwholesomeness gained through cultivating the previous awakening factor, investigation-of-*dhammas*, since the same distinction underlies the four right efforts.

14 S V 68.

15 S V 111. Spk III 169 mentions the practice of walking meditation as an example for physical "energy".

16 S V 104 describes the nutriment for the awakening factor of energy in the same terms used at S V 105 for the anti-nutriment for sloth-and-torpor.

17 S V 68 speaks of "unworldly joy"; which S V 111 relates to the presence or absence of initial and sustained mental application, i.e. to the experience of absorption. "Joy" in this context is, however, not confined to *jhānic* joy only, since non-sensual joy can also be the result of insight meditation, cf. e.g. Dhp 374.

18 e.g. at S II 32; cf. also page 166, footnote 45.

As an awakening factor, tranquillity (*passaddhi*) is related to physical and mental calmness and is therefore a direct antidote to the hindrance restlessness-and-worry (*uddhaccakukkucca*).[19] As part of the causal sequence leading to concentration, the awakening factor tranquillity leads to a happy state of mind, which in turn facilitates concentration.[20] Concentration, then, arises because of the development of calmness and lack of distraction.[21] According to the discourses, concentration with and without initial mental application (*vitakka*) can serve as an awakening factor.[22]

The culmination of the development of the awakening factors comes with the establishment of equanimity (*upekkhā*), a balanced state of mind resulting from concentration.[23] Such refined mental balance and equipoise corresponds to a level of well-developed

---

19 S V 104 identifies physical and mental tranquillity as nutriment for the awakening factor of tranquillity, while S V 106 speaks of calmness of the mind (*cetaso vūpasamo*) as anti-nutriment for restlessness-and-worry. Another noteworthy point is that the discourses analyse both the awakening factor tranquillity and the hindrance sloth-and-torpor into a bodily and a mental aspect, documenting a physical and a psychological component of both.

20 S V 69.

21 S V 105 recommends the "sign of calmness" (*samathanimitta*) as nutriment for the awakening factor of concentration. This "sign of calmness" is mentioned again at D III 213 and S V 66. The "sign" (*nimitta*) occurs also in various other passages, often in apparent relation to the development of concentration. Frequently a "sign of concentration" (*samādhinimitta*) can be found (at D III 226; D III 242; D III 279; M I 249; M I 301; M III 112; A I 115; A I 256; A II 17; A III 23; and A III 321). Though at M I 301 this sign of concentration is related to the four *satipaṭṭhānas*, at M III 112 it refers to the practice of *samatha* meditation, since this passage speaks of internally unifying, quietening, and concentrating the mind on this sign of concentration, which it then explains to refer to attainment of the four *jhānas*. In some instances one also finds the "sign of the mind" (*cittanimitta*, e.g. at S V 151; A III 423; and Th 85), which Th 85 relates to non-sensual happiness, an instance reminiscent of the experience of non-sensual happiness during absorption. Similarly, A IV 419 recommends making much of the "sign", which in this passage too represents *jhānic* attainment. Another relevant passage is M III 157, where the Buddha spoke of the need to "penetrate" or "acquire" the sign (*nimittaṃ paṭivijjhitabbaṃ*) in order to overcome various mental obstructions. The set of mental obstructions to be overcome in this discourse form a unique set which does not occur as such elsewhere and is clearly related to *samatha* meditation (cf. page 199, footnote 73). Ps IV 207 however, possibly having in mind A IV 302, takes this passage to refer to the divine eye. This reading by the commentary does not make much sense, since the above passage clearly deals with a level of practice prior even to the first *jhāna*, while to develop the divine eye would necessitate attainment of the fourth *jhāna*. Shwe 1979: p.387, explains: "anything entering into a causal relation, by which its effect is signified, marked or characterized, is a *nimitta*. An object, image or concept which, on being meditated upon, induces *samādhi* (*jhāna*) is a *nimitta*." On the "sign" in a different context cf. also page 225, footnote 35.

satipaṭṭhāna, when the meditator is capable of dwelling "independently, without clinging to anything in the world", as stipulated in the "refrain".

Practically applied, the whole set of the seven awakening factors can be understood to describe the progress of *satipaṭṭhāna* practice to this level of deep equanimity. On the basis of well-established mindfulness, one investigates the nature of subjective reality (viz. investigation-of-*dhammas*). Once sustained investigation gains momentum (viz. energy), with growing insight the object of contemplation becomes clearer and the meditator feels inspired (viz. joy) to continue with the practice. If at this point the danger of getting carried away by elation and agitation can be avoided, continued contemplation leads to a state of calmness, when the mind stays effortlessly with its meditation object without succumbing to distraction (viz. concentration). With maturing insight, this process culminates in a state of firm equanimity and detachment.

It is at this point, when the inspired momentum of mindful investigation takes place against a background of tranquil composure, that the mental equipoise needed for the breakthrough to awakening comes about. At this level of practice, a deep sense of completely letting go prevails. In the discourses, such "letting go" as a central purpose of developing the *bojjhaṅgas* forms the culmination of a set of attributes frequently associated with the awakening factors. These attributes stipulate that, in order to actualize the awakening potential of the *bojjhaṅgas*, they need to be based on "seclusion" (*viveka*), on "fading away" (*virāga*), and on "cessation" (*nirodha*), since in this way they will lead to "letting go" (*vossagga*).[24]

---

22 S V 111. As Vism 126 explains, the *jhāna* factors already begin to arise during access concentration, although they become fully stable only with the attainment of the first *jhāna*. Thus the expression "concentration with initial mental application" can also be taken to include levels of concentration bordering on absorption, during which the presence of initial and sustained mental application is responsible for further deepening concentration and thereby leads to attainment of the first *jhāna*. Understood in this way, levels of concentration close to absorption, corresponding to the commentarial notion of "access concentration", could also be put into service as awakening factors.

23 S V 69. Aronson 1979: p.2, explains that *upekkhā* is formed from *upa* meaning "toward" and a derivative of the verb *ikkh* meaning "to see", and thus conveys a "notion of over-looking a situation from a distance". Gethin 1992: p.160, points out that "*upekkhā* ... is both the balance of the skilful mind and the force which maintains that balance".

Equanimity and mental balance as the consummation of the other six awakening factors also constitutes the climax in the commentarial scheme of the insight knowledges, in which "equanimity in regard to all conditioned phenomena" (*saṅkhārupekkhāñāṇa*) marks the culmination of the series and the suitable mental condition for the event of realization.

XII.3 BENEFITS OF DEVELOPING THE AWAKENING FACTORS

The profitable effect of the awakening factors stands in direct opposition to the detrimental repercussions of the hindrances, a contrast frequently mentioned in the discourses.[25] Both these sets form aspects of *satipaṭṭhāna* contemplation and are of central importance in cultivating the mental conditions conducive to realization.[26] According to the Buddha, these two aspects from among the contemplations of *dhammas* (removal of the hindrances and an establishment of the awakening factors) are the necessary conditions not only for realization, but also for developing mundane types of knowledge.[27]

The central importance of developing awareness in regard to these two sets of mental qualities is also reflected in the fact that all Chinese and Sanskrit versions of contemplation of *dhammas* include the hindrances and the awakening factors. In contrast, none of these versions mentions the contemplation of the five aggregates, and several versions omit the contemplation of the sense-spheres and the contemplation of the four noble truths.[28] Thus what remains as the unanimously accepted core of contemplation of *dhammas* in all different versions are the five hindrances and the seven awakening

---

24 e.g. at M III 88. The same awakening dynamics can be related to the noble eightfold path (S I 88; S IV 367; and S V 1–62); and to the five faculties (S IV 365; S V 239; and S V 241); or the five powers (S IV 366; S V 249; and S V 251); cf. also Gethin 1992: pp.162–8.

25 The discourses express this contrast by calling the awakening factors "anti-hindrances" (*anīvaraṇā*, e.g. at S V 93). Cf. also page 188, footnote 23. In the Chinese *Madhyama Āgama* version, contemplation of the awakening factors immediately follows contemplation of the hindrances in the sequence of the *dhamma*-contemplations, which illustrates how the removal of the latter naturally leads to a development of the former; cf. Minh Chau 1991: p.94; and Nhat Hanh 1990: p.163.

26 S V 128 points out that the awakening factors lead to knowledge and vision, while the hindrances lead to the absence of knowledge and vision.

27 According to S V 121 they constitute the reason why at times what has been well learned can be forgotten, while at other times matters not studied intensively can still be well remembered.

factors, a finding which underlines their importance.[29] This finding has a parallel in the *Vibhaṅga*, which also lists only these two meditation practices in its account of contemplation of *dhammas*.[30] To overcome the hindrances, to practise *satipaṭṭhāna*, and to establish the awakening factors are, indeed, according to several Pāli discourses, the key aspects and the distinctive features common to the awakenings of all Buddhas, past, present, and future.[31]

Developing the awakening factors can be combined with a broad range of meditation exercises, including, for example, contemplation of a decaying corpse, the divine abodes, mindfulness of breathing, or contemplation of the three characteristics.[32] This indicates that to contemplate the awakening factors does not mean that one has to relinquish one's primary object of meditation. Rather, one is aware of these seven mental qualities as facets of one's progress towards insight during actual practice, and one consciously develops and balances them so that the contemplation of one's primary object can give rise to awakening.

There is a sense of mental mastery in this ability to oversee the development of insight during *satipaṭṭhāna* practice and to supervise the harmonious interaction of the awakening factors. The discourses illustratively compare this sense of mental mastery to being able to choose any garment from a full wardrobe.[33] A survey of the supportive factors listed in the commentaries for such mental mastery can be found in Fig. 12.2.

As indicated by the discourses, a revelation of the awakening factors takes place only when a Buddha and his teaching have arisen.[34]

---

28 The four noble truths occur in neither of the two *Āgama* versions and in only one of the three other versions of *satipaṭṭhāna*, this being the *Śāriputrābhidharma* (cf. Schmithausen 1976: p.248). The six sense-spheres occur in the Chinese *Madhyama Āgama* version, while the Chinese version found in the *Ekottara Āgama* has only the awakening factors and, based on removal of the hindrances (mentioned at the outset of the discourse), the development of the four *jhānas* (cf. Nhat Than 1990: p.176).

29 Warder 1991: p.86.

30 Vibh 199. Ñāṇatiloka 1983: p.39, seems to take this "omission" on the side of the *Vibhaṅga* as a matter of intentional selection. Cf. also Ṭhānissaro 1996: p.74.

31 D II 83; D III 101; and S V 161.

32 Cf. S V 129–33.

33 S V 71. It is interesting to note that the monk possessing this ability was Sāriputta, who is characterized elsewhere in the discourses for his wisdom (e.g. S I 191, and A I 23) and his ability in mental analysis (M III 25). At M I 215 he used the same simile to illustrate mental mastery.

34 S V 77; cf. also S V 99.

Hence, in the eyes of the early Buddhists, the development of the awakening factors was a specifically Buddhist teaching. That other contemporary ascetics were also instructing their disciples to develop the awakening factors was, according to the commentaries, simply a case of imitation.[35]

The relation of the seven awakening factors to the Buddha, together with their qualification as treasures on another occasion, is reminiscent of the universal monarch (*cakkavatti rāja*), who is similarly in the possession of seven precious treasures.[36] Just as the realization of universal sovereignty depends on those seven precious possessions and is heralded by the arising of the wheel-treasure (*cakkaratana*), so too the realization of awakening depends on seven mental treasures, the awakening factors, and is heralded by the arising of *sati*.

The beneficial effect of the awakening factors is not confined to mental conditions, since several discourses report that their recollection sufficed for curing some *arahants*, including the Buddha himself, of physical illness.[37] Associations of cure and illness also underlie the formulation of the final meditation practice in the *Satipaṭṭhāna Sutta*, contemplation of the four noble truths, to which I will turn in the next chapter.

---

35 Cf. S V 108 and S V 112; and the commentary at Spk III 168; cf. also Gethin 1992: pp.177–80; and Woodward 1979: vol.V p.91 n.1.

36 S V 99 presents both the seven treasures of a Tathāgata, which are the seven awakening factors, and the seven treasures of a universal monarch, which are a wheel, an elephant, a horse, a jewel, a woman, a steward, and a counsellor, each endowed with magical qualities. Spk III 154 then correlates them individually.

37 At S V 79–81, where Kassapa, Moggallāna, and the Buddha were each cured of illness by a recitation of the awakening factors. The effect of thus recalling and probably at the same time also re-establishing the constellation of mental factors that had led each of them to full awakening was apparently powerful enough to effect an abating of their respective diseases. On the curative effect of the awakening factors cf. Dhammananda 1987: p.134; and Piyadassi 1998: pp.2–4. The Chinese *Āgamas* have only preserved the instance involving the Buddha, not the other two, cf. Akanuma 1990: p.242.

mindfulness (*sati*)	mindfulness and clear knowledge avoiding unmindful people and associating with mindful people inclining the mind accordingly (towards the development of *sati*)
investigation (*dhammavicaya*)	theoretical inquiry bodily cleanliness balance of the five faculties avoiding unwise people and associating with wise people reflecting on the deeper aspects of the *Dhamma* inclining the mind accordingly
energy (*viriya*)	reflecting on the fearfulness of the planes of misery seeing the benefits of effort reflecting on the path to be practised honouring the offerings one has received reflecting on the inspiring qualities of the tradition one is following, of one's teacher, of one's status as a follower of the Buddha, and of companions in the holy life avoiding lazy people and associating with energetic people inclining the mind accordingly
joy (*pīti*)	recollecting the Buddha, the *Dhamma*, the *Saṅgha*, one's virtue, one's acts of generosity, heavenly beings, and the peace of realization avoiding rough people and associating with refined people reflecting on inspiring discourses inclining the mind accordingly
tranquillity (*passaddhi*)	good food, agreeable weather, comfortable posture balanced behaviour avoiding restless people and associating with calm people inclining the mind accordingly
concentration (*samādhi*)	bodily cleanliness balancing the five faculties skill in taking up the sign of concentration skill in inciting, restraining, gladdening, and not interfering with the mind at the right time avoiding distracted people and associating with attentive people reflecting on the attainment of absorption inclining the mind accordingly
equanimity (*upekkhā*)	detachment towards people and things avoiding prejudiced people and associating with impartial people inclining the mind accordingly

Fig. 12.2 Commentarial survey of supportive conditions for developing the awakening factors[38]

38 Ps I 290–9.

XIII

DHAMMAS: THE FOUR NOBLE TRUTHS

The instructions for the final exercise among the *satipaṭṭhāna* contemplations are:

> **He knows as it really is, "this is *dukkha*", he knows as it really is, "this is the arising of *dukkha*", he knows as it really is, "this is the cessation of *dukkha*", he knows as it really is, "this is the way leading to the cessation of *dukkha*".**[1]

XIII.1 THE IMPLICATIONS OF *DUKKHA*

According to more detailed expositions found in other discourses, the first of the four noble truths relates *dukkha* to physical events such as disease and death, and to the mental displeasure that arises from being unable to satisfy desires and wishes.[2] As the first noble truth points out, all these forms of *dukkha* can in the final analysis be traced to the basic fivefold clinging to existence by way of the aggregates.

Although the Buddha placed much emphasis on *dukkha*, this does not mean that his analysis of reality was concerned only with the negative aspects of existence. In fact, an understanding of *dukkha*

---

1 M I 62.

2 e.g. at S V 421. Gethin 1992: p.18, comments: "understanding the first noble truth involves not so much the revelation that *dukkha* exists, as the realization of what *dukkha* is". Hamilton 1996: p.206, points out that "the first noble truth ... can most accurately be understood if it is borne in mind that this is a truth statement, not a value judgement".

and its arising leads to the third and the fourth noble truths, which are concerned with the positive values of freedom from *dukkha* and the practical path leading to that freedom. As the Buddha himself expressly stated, a realization of the four noble truths will be accompanied by happiness, and the noble eightfold path is a path productive of joy.[3] This shows that understanding *dukkha* is not necessarily a matter of frustration and despair.

Dukkha is often translated as "suffering". Suffering, however, represents only one aspect of *dukkha*, a term whose range of implications is difficult to capture with a single English word.[4] *Dukkha* can be derived from the Sanskrit *kha*, one meaning of which is "the axle-hole of a wheel", and the antithetic prefix *duḥ* (= *dus*), which stands for "difficulty" or "badness".[5] The complete term then evokes the image of an axle not fitting properly into its hole. According to this image, *dukkha* suggests "disharmony" or "friction". Alternatively *dukkha* can be related to the Sanskrit *stha*, "standing" or "abiding", combined with the same antithetic prefix *duḥ*.[6] *Dukkha* in the sense of "standing badly" then conveys nuances of "uneasiness" or of being "uncomfortable".[7] In order to catch the various nuances of "*dukkha*", the most convenient translation is "unsatisfactoriness", though it might be best to leave the term untranslated.

The need for careful translation of the term can be demonstrated with the help of a passage from the *Nidāna Saṃyutta*, where the Buddha stated that whatever is felt is included within *dukkha*.[8] To understand *dukkha* here as an affective quality and to take it as implying that all feelings are "suffering" conflicts with the Buddha's analysis of feelings into three mutually exclusive types, which are,

---

3 S V 441 and M I 118.

4 Cf. T.W. Rhys Davids 1993: p.324; and Wijesekera 1994: p.75.

5 Monier-Williams 1995: pp.334 (*kha*) and 483 (*duḥkha*); cf. also Smith 1959: p.109. The corresponding Pāli terms are the prefix *du* (difficulty, badness), and *akkha* (axle of a wheel), cf. T.W. Rhys Davids 1993: pp.2 and 324. Vism 494 gives another rather imaginative explanation of the term, by relating *kha* to space (*ākāsa*), which is then supposed to represent the absence of permanence, beauty, happiness, and self.

6 Monier-Williams 1995: p.1262.

7 Cf. also Ñāṇamoli 1991: p.823 n.8, who suggests "uneasiness" as a preferable rendering for *dukkha* when this is used as a characteristic of the whole of experience.

8 S II 53.

in addition to unpleasant feeling, pleasant and neutral feelings.[9] On another occasion the Buddha explained his earlier statement that "whatever is felt is included within *dukkha*" to refer to the impermanent nature of all conditioned phenomena.[10] The changing nature of feelings, however, need not necessarily be experienced as "suffering", since in the case of a painful experience, for example, change may be experienced as pleasant.[11] Thus all feelings are not "suffering", nor is their impermanence "suffering", but all feelings are "unsatisfactory", since none of them can provide lasting satisfaction. That is, *dukkha* as a qualification of all conditioned phenomena is not necessarily experienced as "suffering", since suffering requires someone sufficiently attached in order to suffer.

XIII.2 THE FOUR NOBLE TRUTHS

That to suffer is due to some form of attachment is in fact the implication of the second noble truth, according to which in order for the unsatisfactory nature of phenomena in the world to lead to actual suffering, it is necessary for craving (*taṇhā*) to be present.[12] As the third noble truth indicates, once all traces of attachment and craving have been eradicated by the *arahant*, such suffering is also eradicated. Thus "suffering", unlike "unsatisfactoriness", is not inherent in the phenomena of the world, only in the way in which the unawakened mind experiences them. This is indeed the underlying theme of the four noble truths as a whole: the suffering caused by attachment and craving can be overcome by awakening. For an *arahant* the unsatisfactory nature of all conditioned phenomena is no longer capable of causing suffering.

---

9 At D II 66 the Buddha pointed out that when experiencing a pleasant feeling, for example, one will not experience the other two types of feeling. Other passages indicate that according to the Buddha certain kinds of experiences and corresponding realms of existence are pure pleasure or happiness, e.g. M I 76 speaks of the experience of entirely pleasant feelings (by beings reborn in heaven), and M II 37 affirms that there is an entirely pleasant world (this being the Brahmā world corresponding to the attainment of the third *jhāna*). Cf. also Nanayakkara 1993a: p.538.

10 S IV 216. M III 208 discusses the same statement. Cf. also Ñāṇamoli 1995: p.1340 n.1227; and Ñāṇavīra 1987: p.477.

11 M I 303 points out that whereas the change of pleasurable experiences might be experienced as suffering, in the case of pain, change is experienced as pleasurable.

12 e.g. at S V 421. Cf. also Gruber 1999: pp.94 and 194; and Nanayakkara 1989: p.699.

The fourth noble truth then treats the conditions for such overcoming in detail, by depicting the practical way (*magga, paṭipadā*) to be followed. This noble eightfold path covers the central activities and qualities to be cultivated in order to bring about the transformation from ignorant worldling (*puthujjana*) to *arahant*.[13] Since in this context right mindfulness (*sammā sati*) is juxtaposed with other factors such as view, speech, and action, the noble eightfold path sets the necessary framework for a development of *satipaṭṭhāna*.[14] In other words, *satipaṭṭhāna* becomes "*sammā sati*" only when and if it is undertaken interdependently with the other seven path factors.[15]

The four noble truths express the essence of the Buddha's awakening and form the central theme of what is recorded as his first formal discourse.[16] Since these four truths accord with reality, they are further qualified as "noble", as the four "noble" truths.[17] The underlying fourfold structure parallels a fourfold method of diagnosis and prescription used in ancient Indian medicine (cf. Fig. 13.1 below).[18] Similar nuances occur in several discourses which compare the

13 In addition to the eightfold enumeration of path factors, a fivefold presentation can occasionally be found that is applicable to the context of meditation and presupposes the previous fulfilment of right speech, right action, and right livelihood, cf. M III 289; Vibh 238–240; the discussion at Kv 600; and Ñāṇatiloka 1983: p.32. A tenfold enumeration also occurs (e.g. at D II 217 and M III 76), which adds qualities of the *arahant*: right knowledge and right liberation.

14 *Satipaṭṭhāna* as the path factor of right mindfulness is in particular closely related to right view, since on the one hand right mindfulness is required to establish right view (cf. M III 72), while on the other hand, right view serves as a basis for all other path factors (cf. D II 217 and M I 71). Cf. also Vibh 242, which speaks of right view as the "root" of the other seven path factors. The need for right view as a foundation for progress on the path is also emphasized by Bodhi 1991: p.3; and Story 1965: p.167.

15 The same also underlies the nuances of *sammā* as "togetherness" or as being "connected in one", cf. page 74.

16 S V 422.

17 At S V 435. Another discourse at S V 435 offers the alternative explanation that they are so called because their author is the "Noble One". This discourse, unlike the preceding one, is missing from the Chinese *Āgamas*, cf. Akanuma 1990: p.263. According to Norman 1984: p.389, the attribute "noble" might not have been part of the historically earliest formulations of the four (noble) truths.

18 De la Vallée Poussin 1903: p.580; Padmasiri de Silva 1992a: p.166; and Pande 1957: p.398. According to Wezler 1984: pp.312–24, there is no evidence for this scheme having predated the Buddha's formulation of the four noble truths, therefore it is also possible that it was adopted from his teaching by the medical sciences. Parallels to the four noble truths occur also in the *Yoga Sūtra* by Patañjali, II 15–26, a detailed discussion of which can be found in Wezler 1984: pp.301–7.

Buddha to a doctor and his teaching to medicine.[19] This presentation underlines the pragmatic orientation of the four noble truths as a practical investigation of reality.[20]

disease:	*dukkha*
virus:	craving
health:	*Nibbāna*
cure:	path

Fig. 13.1 The fourfold structure of ancient Indian medicine and the four noble truths

Just as the footprints of all animals can fit within the footprint of an elephant, so too, whatever wholesome states there are, all of them are embraced by the four noble truths.[21] On the other hand, to believe that one can realize awakening without having understood the four noble truths is like trying to construct the upper floors of a house without having first constructed its lower floors and foundations.[22] Taken together, these statements underscore the central importance of the four noble truths.

XIII.3 CONTEMPLATION OF THE FOUR NOBLE TRUTHS

Each of the four noble truths makes its own demand on the practitioner: *dukkha* has to be "understood", its origination has to be "abandoned", its cessation has to be "realized", and the practical path to this realization has to be "developed".[23] In particular, the five aggregates are to be understood, ignorance and craving for existence are to be abandoned, knowledge and freedom are to be realized, and calm (*samatha*) and insight (*vipassanā*) are to be developed.[24]

19 e.g. at M II 260; A IV 340; It 101; Sn 560; Sn 562; and Th 1111. A III 238 explains that just as a skilled doctor can quickly dispel one's disease, so too the Buddha's teaching will dispel all one's sorrow and grief. Cf. also Ehara 1995: p.275; and Vism 512.
20 Buswell 1994: p.3, speaks of early Buddhism's "spiritual pragmatism according to which the truth of a religious proposition consists in its practical utility".
21 M I 184.
22 S V 452.
23 S V 436.
24 S V 52 and A II 247. S III 159 and S III 191 explain that to "understand" the five aggregates implies the eradication of lust, anger, and delusion.

For the purpose of contemplation (*anupassanā*), the *Dvayatānupassanā Sutta* suggests that one may focus either on *dukkha* and its arising, or on its cessation and the path leading to its cessation.[25] This corresponds to the two stage sequence found throughout the contemplation of *dhammas*: in each case recognizing the presence or absence of a particular phenomenon includes directing mindfulness to the causes of its presence or absence (see Fig. 13.2 below).

knowing *dukkha*	→	knowing the condition that leads to the arising of *dukkha*: craving
knowing the cessation of *dukkha*	→	knowing the condition that leads to the overcoming of *dukkha*: the noble eightfold path
stage 1		stage 2

Fig. 13.2 Two stages in the contemplation of the four noble truths

Applied at a mundane level, contemplation of the four noble truths can be directed to patterns of clinging (*upādāna*) to existence occurring in everyday life, as, for example, when one's expectations are frustrated, when one's position is threatened, or when things do not go as one would want.[26] The task here is to acknowledge the underlying pattern of craving (*taṇhā*) that has led to the build-up of clinging and expectations, and also its resultant manifestation in some form of *dukkha*. This understanding in turn forms the necessary basis for letting go of craving (*taṇhāya paṭinissagga*). With such letting go, clinging and *dukkha* can, at least momentarily, be overcome. Practised in this way, one will become increasingly able to "fare evenly amidst the uneven".[27]

Not only do the four noble truths, listed as the final meditation practice in this *satipaṭṭhāna*, constitute the conclusion of this series of contemplations, they can also be related to each of the other contemplations of *dhammas*.[28] The commentaries go further by relating each of the meditation practices described throughout the *Satipaṭṭhāna*

25 Sn (prose preceding verse 724).

26 The standard formulations of the first noble truth identify "not getting what one wants" as one of the aspects of *dukkha*, e.g. at S V 421.

27 S I 4 and S I 7 use this expression to illustrate the inner balance and flexibility of *arahants*.

28 S IV 86 applies the scheme of the four noble truths to an understanding of the six sense-spheres (cf. also S V 426); while M I 191 and S V 425 do the same in regard to the

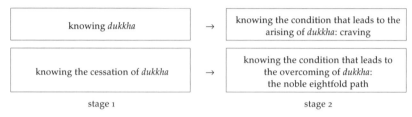

Sutta to the scheme of the four noble truths.[29] In fact, the successful completion of any *satipaṭṭhāna* contemplation is the realization of *Nibbāna*, which corresponds to knowing the third noble truth "as it really is".[30] Yet a full understanding of the third noble truth implies a penetration of all four, since each one is but a different facet of the same central realization.[31] Thus the four noble truths indeed form the culmination of any successful implementation of *satipaṭṭhāna* as the direct path to the realization of *Nibbāna*.

---

aggregates. In the *Satipaṭṭhāna Sutta* itself, the contemplations of the hindrances and of the awakening factors are structured according to an underlying pattern that parallels the diagnostic scheme of the four noble truths, since each observation turns to the presence of the respective mental quality, its absence, and the causes of its presence or absence.

29 The scheme of the four noble truths is applied at Ps I 250 to mindfulness of breathing, at Ps I 252 to the four postures, at Ps I 270 to activities, at Ps I 271 to anatomical parts, at Ps I 272 to the four elements, at Ps I 279 to feelings, at Ps I 280 to the mind, at Ps I 286 to the hindrances, at Ps I 287 to the aggregates, at Ps I 289 to the sense-spheres, and at Ps I 300 to the awakening factors.

30 Vibh 116 points out that the third noble truth is unconditioned. Cf. also S V 442, according to which a distinctive quality of a stream-enterer is full understanding of the four noble truths.

31 S V 437. Cf. also Kv 218; Vism 690–2; Bodhi 1984: p.126; and Cousins 1983: p.103. In fact, according to Sn 884 there is only one truth, which suggests that the scheme of four truths does not imply four separate truths. According to a discourse in the Chinese *Saṃyukta Āgama*, however, realization of the four noble truths has to take place sequentially, by first coming to fully know the truth of suffering, followed in turn by understanding each of the other noble truths (in Choong 2000: p.239).

XIV

REALIZATION

The concluding passage of the *Satipaṭṭhāna Sutta* gives a "prediction" of realization within a variable time period. The passage reads:

> **If anyone should develop these four *satipaṭṭhānas* in such a way for seven years ... six years ... five years ... four years ... three years ... two years ... one year ... seven months ... six months ... five months ... four months ... three months ... two months ... one month ... half a month ... seven days, one of two fruits could be expected for him: either final knowledge here and now, or, if there is a trace of clinging left, non-returning. So it was with reference to this that it was said:**
>
> **Monks, this is the direct path for the purification of beings, for the surmounting of sorrow and lamentation, for the disappearance of *dukkha* and discontent, for acquiring the true method, for the realization of *Nibbāna*, namely, the four *satipaṭṭhānas*.**[1]

I will first examine this prediction and discuss whether the progress towards realization is "gradual" or "sudden". In the remainder of this chapter I will try to explore some ideas, perspectives, and suggestions on the goal of *satipaṭṭhāna* mentioned in the above passage, the "realization of *Nibbāna*".

---

1 M I 62. The prediction concerning the higher two stages of awakening occurs again for *satipaṭṭhāna* at S V 181, and for mindfulness of breathing at S V 314, but also in a variety of other contexts, e.g. at S V 129–33; S V 236; A III 82; A III 143; A V 108; Sn 724–65; and It 39–41.

XIV.1 GRADUAL AND SUDDEN

According to the above prediction, *satipaṭṭhāna* practice has the potential to lead to the higher two of the four stages of awakening, non-returning and arahantship. The fact that this passage speaks immediately of the two higher stages of realization underlines the thoroughness of *satipaṭṭhāna* as the "direct path" to *Nibbāna*, drawing attention to its capability of leading "at least" to the eradication of the five lower fetters (*saṃyojana*), and therewith to complete freedom from sensual desire and aversion.[2]

The other notable feature of this prediction is the variation in the length of time for *satipaṭṭhāna* practice to bear fruit.[3] Apparently, even someone of inferior ability can gain freedom from desire and aversion within a maximum of seven years, while someone of superior ability can do so within only seven days.[4] However, in evaluating this prediction it needs to be kept in mind that the number seven might have a more symbolic character in this context, indicating simply a complete period or cycle of time.[5]

The prediction to realization in the Chinese *Madhyama Āgama* allows for even quicker awakening than the Pāli discourses, suggesting that realization can occur in the evening even if practice has begun only that same morning.[6] The possibility of such instant

---

2 The freedom from sensual desire and aversion envisaged in the prediction echoes to some extent the "definition" part of the *Satipaṭṭhāna Sutta* (M I 56), which relates the practice of *satipaṭṭhāna* to freedom from desires and discontent. Horner 1934: p.792, however, understands the expression "if there is a trace of clinging left" literally, as representing the *arahant*'s awakening as opposed to his or her passing away; cf. also Masefield 1979: p.221.

3 The same occurs in a different context at D III 55, where the Buddha stated that within such a variable time period he could guide a disciple to realization. This could be a reference to *satipaṭṭhāna*, since the Buddha did not further specify in what he would instruct the disciple.

4 On this passage cf. Knight 1985: p.3; and Solé-Leris 1992: p.103.

5 According to T.W. Rhys Davids 1993: p.673, the number seven is invested with a "peculiar magic nimbus" in Pāli, which mitlitates against taking this prediction too literally. An example of such symbolic use of the number seven can be found at A IV 89, where the Buddha related a past life of his in which, as a fruit of seven years of loving kindness practice, he was not reborn in this world for seven aeons, for seven times he became a Mahā Brahmā, for many times seven he became a universal monarch, possessed of the seven treasures. Furthermore, in the above prediction at the end of the *Satipaṭṭhāna Sutta* it is noticeable that, when counting down, "one year" is not followed by "eleven months", as should be expected, but by "seven months", indicating that the sequence does not follow mathematical logic. According to Dumont 1962: p.73: "the number seven ... indicates a totality" (in ancient India).

6 Minh Chau 1991: p.94; and Nhat Than 1990: p.166.

realization through *satipaṭṭhāna*, within just one day or night, is also recognized by the Pāli commentaries,[7] while the discourses state this only in relation to the five "factors of striving" (*pañca padhāniyaṅga*).[8]

The variations in the time periods for *satipaṭṭhāna* to bear fruit suggest that the decisive breakthrough to realization can happen at any time during correct practice. That is, once *sati* is well established (*supatiṭṭhita*), every moment is pregnant with potential awakening.

This raises the question of the extent to which progress to realization follows a "gradual" pattern, as against an unexpected "sudden" breakthrough to awakening.[9]

According to the discourses, it is impossible to measure exactly the quantity of defilements eradicated during a day of practice, just as a carpenter cannot measure the extent to which the handle of his adze has worn out during a day of use.[10] Nevertheless, just as after repeated use a carpenter will realize that the handle has worn out, so will a meditator, after repeated practice, realize that the defilements are growing weaker and are being eradicated. This simile indicates a gradual, though not precisely measurable, progress towards realization.

The gradual nature of the progress towards realization is in fact a recurring theme in the discourses.[11] They explain that progress in the practice of the *Dhamma* deepens gradually, in a way comparable to the gradual deepening of the ocean.[12] A passage in the *Aṅguttara Nikāya* illustrates the gradual character of the process of purification with the example of gradually refining gold, where at first gross and middling impurities are removed, followed by finer impurities.[13]

---

7 Ps I 302.

8 M II 96, however, with the specification that the Buddha himself was to train the practitioner, a specification not stipulated in the *Satipaṭṭhāna Sutta*. This suggests that for realization within a single day the personal presence of the Buddha as the teacher is required. The five factors of striving mentioned in this discourse are confidence, physical health, honesty, energy, and wisdom regarding the arising and disappearance of phenomena. (The last of these could represent the outcome of *satipaṭṭhāna* practice, especially of contemplating the nature of arising and passing away stipulated in the "refrain".)

9 On "sudden" and "gradual" cf. also Gethin 1992: pp.132 and 246; and Nanayakkara 1993b: p.581. Pensa 1977: p.335, relates this distinction to the difference between peak- and plateau-experiences.

10 S III 154 and A IV 127.

11 e.g. at M I 479; M III 2; or A I 162. Cf. also Strenski 1980: pp.4 and 8.

12 Vin II 238; A IV 200; A IV 207; and Ud 54.

13 A I 254. Cf. also Dhp 239.

Similarly, in the realm of mental culture one at first removes the gross types of impurities, and is only then able to proceed to subtler levels.

Another simile compares the practice of the threefold training in ethical conduct (*sīla*), concentration (*samādhi*), and wisdom (*paññā*) to a farmer, who has to plant and water his crop in due time.[14] Neither the farmer nor a practitioner of the threefold training has the magical power to say: "let my effort ripen now and bear fruit", yet their constant effort will bring about the desired results. This simile indicates that progress to awakening follows a natural dynamic, comparable to the growth of plants in nature.

Another canonical illustration of the progress towards realization is that of a hen sitting on her eggs. In due course the hen's unrelenting sitting on her eggs will lead to the hatching of the chicks, just as, in due course, a practitioner's unrelenting practice will lead to realization.[15] The chicks' sudden emergence from their shells depends on a gradual process of inner development through the hen incubating the eggs. Similarly, the sudden breakthrough to *Nibbāna* depends on a gradual process of inner development and mental cultivation. Just as the hen cannot directly cause the chicks to break their shells, the breakthrough to *Nibbāna* cannot be directly made to happen. Both will occur in their own time, if the necessary conditions are in place.

These passages clearly indicate that progress to awakening follows a gradual course. On the other hand, however, several realizations of stream-entry described in the discourses take place in a rather "sudden" manner, usually while listening to a discourse given by the Buddha. On considering these instances it seems almost as if to hear a discourse were sufficient for awakening, without much need to develop concentration gradually and engage in

---

14 A I 240.

15 M I 104; M I 357; S III 154; and A IV 125. This simile has a slightly humorous undertone, since in a way it relates a meditator engaged in intensive practice to a hen on her eggs, both of whom spend much of their time sitting.

insight meditation.[16] Here, however, it needs to be taken into consideration that if someone had realized stream-entry while meditating alone and in seclusion, this did not occasion a discourse and therefore was not recorded later.[17] But when someone realized stream-entry while listening to the Buddha, the circumstances of the event caused it to become part of the later reported discourse. Thus it is to be expected that mainly the latter type of stream-entry realizations are recorded in the discourses. The same discourses do in fact document the potential for insight meditation to lead to the realization of stream-entry, which would be a meaningless statement if stream-entry were to depend solely on listening to a discourse.[18] Besides, if simply listening to and understanding a discourse were sufficient for realization, the Buddha would not have given so many exhortations to meditate.[19]

A fairly condensed version of the gradual path can be found in one instance when a layman, despite being slightly drunk, was nevertheless able to gain stream-entry. On meeting the Buddha for the first time, this man sobered up and, after receiving a gradual dis-

---

16 In fact Dhammavuddho 1999: p.10, suggests translating *sotāpanna* as "ear-entry", being realized upon hearing a discourse. Similarly Masefield 1987: p.134, proposes that *sota* in the term *sotāpanna* refers to "hearing" rather than "stream". However, on considering the discourses one finds that although listening to the *Dhamma* is mentioned at S V 347 as one of the factors of stream-entry, the same discourse clearly defines "stream" to refer to the noble eightfold path and a "stream-enterer" to be one who is in full possession of this noble eightfold path. In addition it could be pointed out that the Pāli term for receiving the *Dhamma* by hearing is *sotānugata*, not *sotāpanna* (cf. A II 185). The "stream" image comes up also at S V 38, where the noble eightfold path is compared to the Gaṅgā river, since it leads towards *Nibbāna* just as the Gaṅgā leads towards the sea.

17 Only the realization of arahantship was deemed of sufficient significance to merit being reported to the Buddha (*aññā vyākaraṇa*).

18 e.g. S III 167 relates realization of stream-entry to contemplation of the impermanent, unsatisfactory, and selfless nature of the five aggregates; A I 44 presents well-developed mindfulness of the body as capable of leading to stream-entry; and A III 442–3 propose the same potential for contemplating all formations as impermanent, unsatisfactory, and not-self. Cf. also D III 241 and A III 21, where listening to the *Dhamma* constitutes one out of five occasions for awakening, the others being teaching the *Dhamma*, reciting the *Dhamma*, reflecting on the *Dhamma*, and, last but not least, meditation.

19 Cf. e.g. the Buddha's admonition: "meditate, don't be negligent!" (e.g. at M I 46; M I 118; M II 266; M III 302; S IV 133; S IV 359; S IV 361; S IV 368; S IV 373; S V 157; A III 87; A III 88; A IV 139; and A IV 392); or the frequent description of a meditator going off into seclusion for intensive practice and retreat (e.g. at D I 71; D I 207; D II 242; D III 49; M I 181; M I 269; M I 274; M I 346; M I 440; M II 162; M II 226; M III 3; M III 35; M III 115; M III 135; A II 210; A III 92; A III 100; A IV 436; and A V 207).

course, he then and there realized stream-entry.[20] In this particular case, the impact of personally meeting the Buddha was apparently so powerful that the breakthrough to stream-entry could take place, in spite of the fact that just a few moments earlier he had been inebriated. This layman is not the only such case, for the discourses also report the attainment of stream-entry at the time of death by another layman, who during his lifetime had been unable to abstain from alcohol.[21] A closer consideration of this discourse suggests that this layman was probably someone who had earlier progressed so far on the path that stream-entry had to take place (at the latest) at death, despite the fact that in the meantime his ethical foundation had deteriorated.[22]

"Sudden" experiences of awakening can even lead all the way to arahantship. A case in point is the ascetic Bāhiya, whose full awakening came within minutes of his first meeting with the Buddha, immediately after receiving a short but penetrative instruction.[23] Bāhiya is certainly a prototype for "sudden" awakening. From consideration of the background to his awakening it becomes apparent that Bāhiya's gradual development took place outside the Buddhist scheme of training. At the time of his encounter with the Buddha, Bāhiya already possessed a high degree of spiritual maturity, so that the brief instructions he received were sufficient to trigger a complete breakthrough.[24]

---

20 A IV 213.

21 S V 375.

22 According to S V 380, Sarakāni completed (*paripūrakārī*) the training at the time of his death, which indicates that Sarakāni attained stream-entry at that time. Since S V 379 has the same set of terms used in the definitions of the "*Dhamma*-follower" (*dhammānusārī*) and the "faith-follower" (*saddhānusārī*) at M I 479, it seems highly probable that he had been such a "follower" and was thus bound to realize stream-entry latest at death (cf. S III 225, which states that it is impossible for a *Dhamma*-follower or a faith-follower to pass away without having realized the fruit of stream-entry).

23 Ud 8; cf. page 229.

24 Bāhiya must have developed a high degree of mental purification by whatever type of practice he was following, since, according to the *Udāna* account, he (mistakenly) deemed himself already fully awakened. The sincerity of his aspiration becomes evident from the fact that, once a doubt about his presumed realization had arisen, he immediately undertook the journey across half the Indian subcontinent to meet the Buddha. His sense of urgency was so strong that he even went to search for the Buddha on his almsround, unable to await his return to the monastery. (The commentary Ud-a 79 gives a rather incredible account of Bāhiya as a shipwrecked hypocrite, wearing bark in order to make an easy living, while his long journey across half of India was, according to Ud-a 86, a feat of supernormal power.)

Most of the instances mentioned so far reveal the powerful influence of the Buddha's personal presence, which provided a potent catalyst for realization. On further perusing the discourses, additional examples of at times remarkably "sudden" realizations can be found. In an all-out attempt to reach realization, Ānanda finally gained full awakening at precisely the moment when he had given up striving and was about to lie down to rest.[25] Elsewhere, a nun, and on another occasion a monk, both on the verge of committing suicide, were "saved", as it were, by awakening.[26] The commentaries even recount the story of an acrobat who gained realization while balancing on the top of his pole.[27] All these instances demonstrate the sudden and unpredictable nature of the event of awakening. They show that, although a gradual progress towards realization is the rule, the time required for such gradual preparation to bear fruit varies greatly according to the individual. This is also a central implication of the different time periods listed in the prediction of realization at the close of the *Satipaṭṭhāna Sutta*.

Thus early Buddhism proposes a gradual development as the necessary preparation for an eventual sudden breakthrough to realization. Viewing the path in this way, as a combination of these two aspects, reconciles the apparent contradiction between the frequently recurring emphasis in the discourses on the need for a particular type of conduct and for the development of knowledge, while other passages show that the realization of *Nibbāna* is not simply the result of conduct or knowledge.[28]

Not only is it impossible to predict the precise moment when realization will take place, but, from the viewpoint of actual practice, even the gradual progress towards realization does not necessarily unfold uniformly. Instead, most practitioners experience a cyclic succession of progression and regression, oscillating within a fairly broad spectrum.[29] If these recurring cycles are considered within a

25 Vin II 285.
26 Thī 80–1 and Th 408–9.
27 Dhp-a IV 63.
28 At A II 163 Sāriputta was asked whether realization was a matter of knowledge or of conduct, to both of which he replied in the negative, explaining that both were necessary, yet not sufficient conditions for realization to take place. (On this passage cf. Jayatilleke 1967: p.456.) Similarly, according to Sn 839 purity is not simply the result of view, learning, knowledge, or conduct, nor can purity be gained in the absence of these.
29 Debes 1994: pp.204 and 208; and Kornfield 1979: p.53.

longer time frame, however, they reveal a slow but consistent gradual development, with an ever-increasing potential to culminate in a sudden realization of *Nibbāna*. To the implications of such a realization I will now turn in more detail.

XIV.2 *NIBBĀNA* AND ITS ETHICAL IMPLICATIONS

Taken in its literal sense, "*Nibbāna*" refers to the going out of a lamp or a fire. The image of an extinguished lamp occurs in fact several times in the discourses as a description of the experience of *Nibbāna*.[30] The corresponding verb *nibbāyati* means "to be extinguished" or "to become cool". Such extinction is probably best understood in a passive sense, when the fires of lust, aversion, and delusion become cool through lack of fuel.[31] The metaphor of an extinguished fire in its ancient Indian context has nuances of calmness, independence, and release.[32]

Judging by the evidence in the discourses, contemporary ascetics and philosophers used the term *Nibbāna* with predominantly positive connotations. The *Brahmajāla Sutta*, for example, lists five positions advocating *Nibbāna* "here and now", which were five different conceptions of happiness: the pleasures of worldly sensuality and of the four levels of absorption.[33] Another discourse reports a wanderer taking "*Nibbāna*" to refer to health and mental well-being.[34] Similar positive connotations underlie the standard definition in the Pāli discourses, according to which *Nibbāna* stands for freedom from the unwholesome mental roots of lust, anger, and delusion.[35]

30 D II 157; S I 159; A I 236; A IV 3; A IV 4; and Th 906. Thī 116 has a slightly different formulation, when Paṭācārā's experience of *Nibbāna* actually coincided with the "*nibbāna*" of her lamp.

31 Cf. M III 245 and S V 319. Collins 1998: p.191, and T.W. Rhys Davids 1993: p.362, point out that *Nibbāna* refers to the extinction of a fire for lack of fuel, not through active blowing out.

32 Ṭhānissaro 1993: p.41. For parallels in the *Upaniṣads* employing the imagery of extinguished fire cf. Schrader 1905: p.167.

33 D I 36. The Buddha's definition of *Nibbāna* "here and now" can be found at A V 64.

34 M I 509. In the eyes of the Buddha this was clearly a mistaken view of *Nibbāna*.

35 e.g. at S IV 251; S IV 261; and S IV 371. S V 8 has the same definition for the "deathless"; while S I 39 and Sn 1109 define *Nibbāna* as the eradication of craving. This parallels a rather imaginative way of deriving the term *Nibbāna* found in the commentaries that takes *Nibbāna* to be composed of *ni* (absence) and *vāna* (as a metaphorical expression of craving), the entire compound then representing "absence of craving" (e.g. at Vism 293; also in Vajirañāṇa 1984: p.20).

This definition highlights in particular the ethical implications of realizing *Nibbāna*. These ethical implications require further examination, since at times realization of *Nibbāna* has been taken to imply the transcendence of ethical values.[36] Such transcendence seems, at first sight, to be advocated in the *Samaṇamaṇḍikā Sutta*, since this discourse associates awakening with the complete cessation of wholesome ethical conduct.[37] On similar lines, other passages in the Pāli canon speak in praise of going beyond both "good" and "evil".[38]

Taking the passage from the *Samaṇamaṇḍikā Sutta* first, a close examination of the discourse reveals that this particular statement does not refer to the abandoning of ethical conduct, but only to the fact that *arahants* no longer identify with their virtuous behaviour.[39] Regarding the other passages, which speak of "going beyond good and evil", one needs to distinguish clearly between the Pāli terms translated as "good", which can be either *kusala* or *puñña*. Although the two terms cannot be completely separated from each other in canonical usage, they often carry quite distinct meanings.[40] While *puñña* mostly denotes deeds of positive merit, *kusala* includes any type of wholesomeness, including the realization of *Nibbāna*.[41]

What *arahants* have "gone beyond" is the accumulation of karma. They have transcended the generation of "good" (*puñña*) and of its opposite "evil" (*pāpa*). But the same cannot be said of wholesomeness (*kusala*). In fact, by eradicating all unwholesome (*akusala*) states of mind, *arahants* become the highest embodiment of wholesomeness (*kusala*). So much is this the case that, as indicated in the *Samaṇamaṇḍikā Sutta*, they are spontaneously virtuous and do not even identify with their virtue.

---

36 This is maintained e.g. by van Zeyst 1961c: p.143.

37 M II 27.

38 e.g. Dhp 39; Dhp 267; Dhp 412; Sn 547; Sn 790; and Sn 900.

39 Ñāṇamoli 1995: p.1283 n.775, comments: "this passage shows the arahant, who maintains virtuous conduct but no longer identifies with his virtue". Wijesekera 1994: p.35, explains that the practitioner should "master morality, but not allow morality to get the better of him". Cf. also M I 319, where the Buddha pointed out that although he was possessed of a high level of virtue he did not identify with it.

40 According to Carter 1984: p.48, some degree of overlap exists between *kusala* and *puñña* in the context of the threefold volition, but a clear distinction between both terms can be drawn in regard to a person's qualities.

41 In fact, according to D III 102, the realization of *Nibbāna* is the highest among wholesome phenomena; cf. Premasiri 1976: p.68. Cf. also Collins 1998: p.154; and Nanayakkara 1999: p.258.

Nibbāna, at least as understood by the Buddha, has quite definite ethical implications. *Arahants* are simply unable to commit an immoral act, since with their full realization of *Nibbāna*, all unwholesome states of mind have been extinguished.[42] The presence of any unwholesome thought, speech, or deed would therefore directly contradict the claim to being an *arahant*.

In the *Vīmaṃsaka Sutta*, the Buddha applied this principle even to himself, openly inviting prospective disciples to examine his claim to full awakening by thoroughly investigating and observing his behaviour and deeds.[43] Only if no trace of unwholesomeness was found, he explained, would it be reasonable for them to place their confidence in him as a teacher. Even a Buddha should exemplify his teachings by his deeds, as indeed he did. That which the Buddha taught was in complete conformity with his behaviour.[44] This was so much the case that even after his full awakening the Buddha still engaged in those activities of restraint and careful consideration that had brought about purification in the first place.[45] If the Buddha made himself measurable by common standards of ethical purity, there is little scope for finding moral double-standards in his teaching.

Even if awakening takes place only at the level of stream-entry, the experience of *Nibbāna* still has definite ethical consequences. A major consequence of realizing stream-entry is that stream-enterers become unable to commit a breach of ethical conduct serious

---

42 According to (e.g.) D III 133; D III 235; M I 523; and A IV 370 the ethical perfection of *arahants* is such that they are incapable of deliberately depriving a living being of life, of stealing, of engaging in any form of sexual intercourse, of lying, and of enjoying sensual pleasures by storing things up as householders do. Cf. also Lily de Silva 1996: p.7.

43 M I 318. Cf. also Premasiri 1990b: p.100.

44 D II 224; D III 135; A II 24; and It 122 point out that the Buddha acted as he spoke and spoke as he acted. This comes up in a different way at A IV 82, where the Buddha clarified that for him there was no need to conceal any of his actions in order to avoid others coming to know of them. The Buddha's moral perfection is also mentioned at D III 217 and M II 115.

45 M I 464. (On correlating the activities mentioned in this passage with M I 11 or A III 390, the fact that "removing" is also mentioned appears strange and could be due to a textual corruption, as for the Buddha there would be no need to remove unwholesome thoughts, since they will not arise in the first place.)

enough to lead to a lower rebirth.[46] Although they have not yet reached the level of ethical perfection of the Buddha or an *arahant*, the first realization of *Nibbāna* has already caused an irreversible ethical change.

In order to provide additional perspectives on *Nibbāna*, I will now briefly consider some canonical descriptions of it.

XIV.3 THE EARLY BUDDHIST CONCEPTION OF *NIBBĀNA*

The early Buddhist conception of *Nibbāna* was not easily understood by contemporary ascetics and philosophers. The Buddha's consistent refusal to go along with any of the four standard propositions about the survival or the annihilation of an *arahant* after death was rather bewildering to his contemporaries.[47] According to the Buddha, to entertain these different propositions was as futile as to speculate about the direction in which a fire had departed once it had gone out.[48]

The Buddha found the existing ways of describing a state of realization or awakening inadequate to his realization.[49] His understanding of *Nibbāna* constituted a radical departure from the conceptions of the time. He was well aware of this himself, and after his awakening he immediately reflected on the difficulty of conveying what he had realized to others.[50]

Despite these difficulties, the Buddha did try to explain the nature of *Nibbāna* on several occasions. In the *Udāna*, for instance, he spoke of *Nibbāna* as something beyond this world or another world, beyond coming, going, or staying, beyond the four elements representing material reality, and also beyond all immaterial realms. This

46 M III 64 lists the following as impossibilities for a stream-enterer: killing one's mother, killing one's father, killing an *arahant*, wounding a Buddha, and causing a schism in the monastic community. The inability to commit such serious breaches of ethical conduct comes as one of the four limbs of stream-entry, a topic that occurs frequently in the discourses (e.g. at S V 343). In addition, according to M I 324 and Sn 232, stream-enterers are also unable to hide their wrongdoings.

47 e.g. at M I 486.

48 M I 487.

49 At M I 329 the *Nibbānic* realization (the "non-manifestative consciousness") forms part of what almost amounts to a contest in which the Buddha proved that his realization was entirely beyond the ken of Brahmā, demonstrating metaphorically that it went beyond the hitherto known and valued types of realization. (On this passage cf. Jayatilleke 1970: p.115.)

50 M I 167 and S I 136. On the difficulty of describing *Nibbāna* with ordinary language cf. also Burns 1983: p.20; and Story 1984: p.42.

"sphere" (*āyatana*), he pointed out, objectless and without any support, constitutes "the end of suffering".[51] This description shows that *Nibbāna* refers to a dimension completely different from ordinary experiences of the world, and also different from experiences of meditative absorption.

Other discourses refer to such a totally different experience as a "non-manifestative" consciousness.[52] A related nuance comes up in a somewhat poetic passage that compares the "unstationed" consciousness of an *arahant* to a ray of sunlight passing through the window of a room without an opposing wall: the ray does not land anywhere.[53]

Another discourse in the *Udāna* describes *Nibbāna* with the help of a set of past participles as "not-born" (*a-jāta*), "not-become" (*a-bhūta*), "not-made" (*a-kata*), and "not-conditioned" (*a-saṅkhata*).[54] This passage again emphasizes that *Nibbāna* is completely "other", in that it is not born or made, not produced or conditioned. It is owing to this "otherness" that *Nibbāna* constitutes freedom from birth (*jāti*), becoming (*bhava*), karma (*kamma*), and formations (*saṅkhārā*).[55] Birth (*jāti*) in a way symbolizes existence in time, while *Nibbāna*, not being subject to birth or death, is timeless or beyond time.[56]

These passages show that *Nibbāna* is markedly different from any other experience, sphere, state, or realm. They clearly indicate that as long as there is even a subtle sense of a somewhere, a something, or a someone, it is not yet an experience of *Nibbāna*.

---

51 Ud 80. In this context "sphere" (*āyatana*) could be taken to refer to a "sphere" of experience, since on other occasions the same set of terms forms part of a description of a meditative experience, cf. A V 7; A V 319; A V 353; A V 355; A V 356; and A V 358. Mp V 2 relates these passages to the fruition-attainment of an *arahant*.

52 The *anidassana viññāṇa* at D I 223. On this passage cf. also Harvey 1989: p.88; Ñāṇananda 1986: p.66; and Ñāṇamoli 1980: p.178.

53 S II 103, where due to the complete absence of craving for any of the four nutriments, consciousness is "unstationed" (*appatiṭṭhita*), this in turn resulting in freedom from future becoming.

54 Ud 80 and It 37. On this passage cf. Kalupahana 1994: p.92; and Norman 1991–3: p.220.

55 D III 275 and It 61. On this passage cf. Premasiri 1991: p.49.

56 Cf. e.g. M I 162, where one's wife, children, and material possessions are defined as phenomena subject to birth, followed by classifying *Nibbāna* as not subject to birth. On possible implications of the term "birth" cf. also Buddhadāsa 1984: p.26; Govinda 1991: p.50; Harvey 1989: p.90; and Karunadasa 1994: p.11.

XIV.4 *NIBBĀNA*: NEITHER ALL-EMBRACING UNITY NOR ANNIHILATION

In order further to clarify the distinctive character of the Buddha's conception of *Nibbāna*, in the remainder of this chapter I will set it off against the realization of all-embracing unity (as envisaged by the "non-dual" religious traditions), and also against annihilationism. While early Buddhism does not deny the distinction between subject and object, it does not treat this distinction as particularly important. Both are insubstantial, the subject being nothing other than a complex of interactions with the world (object), while to speak of a "world" is to speak of what is being perceived by the subject.[57]

Unity, in terms of subjective experience, entails a merging of the subject with the object. Experiences of this kind are often the outcome of deep levels of concentration. *Nibbāna*, on the other hand, entails a complete giving up of both subject and object, not a merger of the two.[58] Such an experience constitutes an "escape" from the entire field of cognition.[59] Although *Nibbāna* partakes of non-duality in so far as it has no counterpart,[60] its implications nevertheless go far beyond experiences of oneness or unity.[61]

---

57 Tilakaratne 1993: p.74.

58 e.g. S IV 100 speaks of a cessation of all six sense-spheres, an expression which the commentary explains to refer to *Nibbāna* (Spk II 391). Another relevant reference could be the standard description of stream-entry (e.g. at S V 423), which speaks of the insight into the fact that whatever arises will also cease, an expression that may well hint at the subjective experience of *Nibbāna*, whence all conditionally arisen phenomena cease. Similarly the declarations of realization at M III 265 and S IV 58 point to a cessation experience. Realization as a cessation experience is also reflected in the writings of modern meditation teachers and scholars, cf. e.g. Brown 1986b: p.205; Goenka 1994a: p.113, and 1999: p.34; Goleman 1977b: p.31; Griffith 1981: p.610; Kornfield 1993: p.291; Mahasi 1981: p.286; and Ñāṇārāma 1997: p.80. Cf. also footnote 30, page 257 above.

59 M I 38; this "escape" from the whole field of cognition is identified by the commentary with *Nibbāna* (Ps I 176). Similarly Thī 6 refers to *Nibbāna* as the stilling of all cognitions.

60 The question "what is the counterpart of *Nibbāna*?" (at M I 304) was a question which, according to the *arahant* nun Dhammadinnā, cannot be answered. The commentary Ps II 369 explains that *Nibbāna* has no counterpart.

61 This much can be deduced from a statement made by the Buddha (M II 229–33) that with the direct experience of *Nibbāna* all views and standpoints related to an experience of unity are left behind and transcended. Cf. also S II 77, where the Buddha rejected the view "all is one" as one of the extremes to be avoided. Furthermore, according to A IV 40 and A IV 401, in different celestial realms either unitary or diversified experiences prevail, so that a categorical statement like "all is one" would not accord with the early Buddhist description of cosmic reality. Cf. also Ling 1967: p.167.

Experiences of oneness were actually not unknown to the early Buddhist community, but even their most refined forms, experienced with the immaterial attainments, were not considered to be the final goal.[62] Just as the Buddha himself did not feel satisfied with what he had experienced based on the indications received from his first teachers,[63] so he admonished his disciples to go beyond and transcend such "transcendental" experiences.[64] Some of his disciples had achieved various non-dual experiences, while others had realized full awakening without experiencing any of the immaterial attainments.[65] The latter were the living proof that such attainments, far from being identifiable with *Nibbāna*, are not even necessary for its realization.

In order properly to assess the early Buddhist concept of *Nibbāna*, it needs not only to be distinguished from views based on experiences of unity, but also has to be differentiated from the theories of annihilation held among the deterministic and materialistic schools of ancient India. On several occasions the Buddha was in fact wrongly accused of being an annihilationist.[66] His humorous reply to such allegations was that he could rightly be called so if this meant the annihilation of unwholesome states of mind.

A consideration of the discourses shows that *Nibbāna* is described in both positive and negative terms. Negative expressions occur

---

62 The immaterial attainments are explicitly identified with "unity" at M III 220. In fact the whole series begins with the injunction not to pay attention to diversified cognitions as a basis for developing the sphere of infinite space (e.g. at A IV 306), which clearly indicates the unitary character of these experiences. At M III 106 the four immaterial attainments are again qualified as "unity" (*ekatta*), each of them forming part of a gradual "descent" into emptiness. The culmination of this gradual descent is reached with the destruction of the influxes (M III 108), at which point the qualification "unity" is no longer used. This passage clearly demonstrates that full awakening goes beyond even the most refined experiences of oneness. This discourse also indicates that there may be various types of "emptiness" experience, but that it is the complete destruction of the influxes that determines whether (or not) an experience of emptiness does indeed constitute full awakening.

63 Cf. M I 165, where the Buddha remarked about Āḷāra Kālāma and Uddaka Rāmaputta that their teaching was not conducive to complete disenchantment and therefore not sufficient to realize *Nibbāna*.

64 e.g. at M I 455–6, where the Buddha commented on each of the meditative absorptions in turn: "this is not enough, abandon it, I say, surmount it!"

65 These were the *arahants* "freed by wisdom", who according to their canonical definition (e.g. at M I 477) had destroyed the influxes without having experienced the immaterial attainments.

66 Vin III 2; A IV 174; and A IV 183. Cf. also Vin I 234; Vin III 3; M I 140; and A V 190; where the Buddha is called a "nihilist".

frequently in a practical context, indicating the work still to be done.[67] Other passages, however, refer to *Nibbāna* with a variety of positive epithets, calling it a state of peace, of purity, and of freedom, sublime and auspicious, wonderful and marvellous, an island, a shelter, and a refuge.[68] The happiness of freedom contingent upon having realized *Nibbāna* constitutes the highest possible form of happiness.[69] Described as the source of supreme happiness, as a state of freedom, sublime and auspicious, *Nibbāna* seems to have little in common with mere annihilation.

In fact, according to the Buddha's penetrating analysis the attempt to annihilate self still revolves around a sense of selfhood, though being motivated by disgust with this self. In this way annihilationism is still in bondage to a sense of self, comparable to a dog moving in circles around a post to which it is bound.[70] Such craving for non-existence (*vibhavataṇhā*) forms indeed an obstacle to the realization of *Nibbāna*.[71] As the *Dhātuvibhaṅga Sutta* explains, to think in terms of: "I shall not be" is a form of conceiving as much as the thought: "I shall be".[72] Both are to be left behind in order to proceed to awakening.

To maintain that an *arahant* will be annihilated at death is a misunderstanding, since such a proposition argues the annihilation of

---

67 Bodhi 1996: p.171; Ñāṇapoṇika 1986a: p.25; and Sobti 1985: p.134.

68 S IV 368–73 gives a long list of such epithets. A similar but shorter list occurs at A IV 453.

69 *Nibbāna* as the highest happiness occurs e.g. at M I 508; Dhp 203; Dhp 204; and Thī 476. These expressions refer to the *arahant*'s experience of the happiness of liberation, cf. e.g. M II 104; S I 196; Ud 1; Ud 10; and Ud 32. The superiority of this happiness over all other types of happiness is stated at Ud 11. However, it should be pointed out that *Nibbāna* itself is not a felt type of happiness, since with *Nibbāna* all feelings cease. This is documented at A IV 414, where Sāriputta stated that *Nibbāna* is happiness. When questioned how there could possibly be happiness in the absence of any feeling, he explained that for him it was precisely the absence of feeling that constituted happiness. Similarly at M I 400 the Buddha explained that he considered even the cessation of feelings and cognitions to constitute happiness, since he did not limit the concept of "happiness" to happy feelings only. Johansson 1969: p.25, explains that *Nibbāna* is "'a source of happiness' and not 'a state of happiness'".

70 M II 232.

71 Since it is one of the forms of craving included in the second noble truth (cf. e.g. S V 421).

72 M III 246.

something that cannot be found in a substantial sense even while one is still alive.[73] Therefore any statement concerning the existence or annihilation of an *arahant* after death turns out to be meaningless.[74] What *Nibbāna* does imply is that the ignorant belief in a substantial self is annihilated, an "annihilation" which has already taken place with stream-entry. With full awakening, then, even the subtlest traces of grasping at a sense of self are forever "annihilated", which is but a negative way of expressing the freedom gained through realization. Fully awakened to the reality of selflessness, the *arahant* is free indeed, like a bird in the sky, leaving no tracks.[75]

73 At S IV 383, the destiny of an *arahant* after death posed a dilemma for the monk Anurādha, which he attempted to resolve by stating that it could be described in a way other than the four standard propositions used in ancient India in such discussions. After dismissing this (according to Indian logic impossible) fifth alternative, the Buddha led Anurādha to the conclusion that even while still alive an *arahant* cannot be identified with any of the five aggregates, or with anything outside of them. The same reasoning can be found at S III 112, where Sāriputta rebuked the monk Yamaka for presuming that *arahants* are annihilated at death.

74 Sn 1074 compares the *arahant* to a flame which, once gone out, can no longer be reckoned in terms of "flame". Sn 1076 explains that there is no measuring of one who has thus gone out, since with all phenomena removed, all pathways of language are also removed. The only acceptable declaration to be made about *arahants* at death (cf. D II 109 and D III 135) is that they "enter the *Nibbāna* element without remainder". This declaration is further explained at It 38 to imply that in the case of an *arahant* passing away, all that is felt and experienced, because it is no longer delighted in, will simply become cool.

75 Dhp 93 and Th 92.

XV

CONCLUSION

The Buddha once said he would be able to answer questions about *satipaṭṭhāna* without repeating himself or exhausting his answers, even if the inquiry were to continue for a whole century.[1] If the topic of *satipaṭṭhāna* could not be exhausted by the Buddha, then clearly the present work can at best attempt only to offer a starting point for further discussion and exploration. Nevertheless, the time has now come to sum up the present discussion by attempting to highlight some key aspects of *satipaṭṭhāna*. In addition, I will place *satipaṭṭhāna* within a wider context by considering its place and importance in the context of the Buddha's teaching.

XV.1 KEY ASPECTS OF *SATIPAṬṬHĀNA*

The "direct path" to *Nibbāna* described in the *Satipaṭṭhāna Sutta* presents a comprehensive set of contemplations that progressively reveal ever subtler aspects of subjective experience. The mental qualities required for this direct path of *satipaṭṭhāna* are, according to the "definition" part of the discourse, a balanced and sustained application of effort (*ātāpī*), the presence of clearly knowing (*sampajāna*), and a balanced state of mind, free from desires (*abhijjhā*) and discontent (*domanassa*). These three qualities revolve like the three spokes of a wheel around the central mental quality of *sati*.

---

1 M I 82. The commentary on this passage, Ps II 52, has each of the four questioners specialize in one of the four *satipaṭṭhānas*.

As a mental quality, *sati* represents the deliberate cultivation and a qualitative improvement of the receptive awareness that characterizes the initial stages of the perceptual process. Important aspects of *sati* are bare and equanimous receptivity, combined with an alert, broad, and open state of mind. One of the central tasks of *sati* is the de-automatization of habitual reactions and perceptual evaluations. *Sati* thereby leads to a progressive restructuring of perceptual appraisal, and culminates in an undistorted vision of reality "as it is". The element of non-reactive watchful receptivity in *sati* forms the foundation for *satipaṭṭhāna* as an ingenious middle path which neither suppresses the contents of experience nor compulsively reacts to them.

This mental quality of *sati* has a broad variety of possible applications. Within the context of *satipaṭṭhāna*, *sati* can range from the coarsest activities, such as defecation and urination, all the way up to the most sublime and exalted state, when *sati* is present as a mental factor during the breakthrough to *Nibbāna*. A similar breadth of applications can be found in the context of calmness meditation, where the tasks of *sati* range from recognizing the presence of a hindrance, to emerging with awareness from the highest meditative absorption.

On the basis of the central characteristics and qualities of *satipaṭṭhāna* described in the "definition" and in the "refrain", the main thrust of *satipaṭṭhāna* can be summed up as:

Keep Calmly Knowing Change

With the injunction "keep" I intend to cover both continuity and comprehensivity in *satipaṭṭhāna* contemplation. Continuity of awareness underlies the quality "diligent" (*ātāpī*) mentioned in the "definition". The element of comprehensiveness comes up in the "refrain", which enjoins to contemplate both internally (*ajjhatta*) and externally (*bahiddhā*), that is, to comprehensively contemplate both oneself and others.

The qualification "calmly" stands for the need, mentioned in the "definition" and the "refrain", to undertake *satipaṭṭhāna* free from desires and discontent (*vineyya loke abhijjhādomanassaṃ*), and also free from any clinging or dependence (*anissito ca viharati, na ca kiñci loke upādiyati*).

The verb "knowing" echoes the frequent use of the verb *pajānāti* in the discourse. Such "knowing" represents the quality of bare mindfulness (*sati*) combined with clearly knowing (*sampajāna*), both mentioned in the "definition". Both occur also in the "refrain", which speaks of contemplating merely for the sake of "bare knowledge and continuous mindfulness" (*ñāṇamattāya paṭissatimattāya*).

The "refrain" also explains the particular aspect of body, feelings, mind, and *dhammas* to which this quality of knowing is to be directed, namely their arising and passing away (*samudaya-vaya-dhammānupassī*). Such contemplation of impermanence can either lead to an understanding of conditionality, or form the basis for understanding the other two characteristics of conditioned phenomena, *dukkha* and *anattā*. It is this growth of insight into the unsatisfactory and empty nature of conditioned existence, based on the direct realization of impermanence, to which I intend to refer with the term "change".

The essential features of *satipaṭṭhāna* contemplation can also be brought out visually. In Fig. 15.1 below I have attempted to illustrate

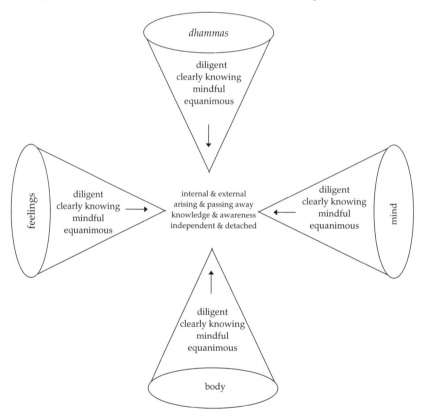

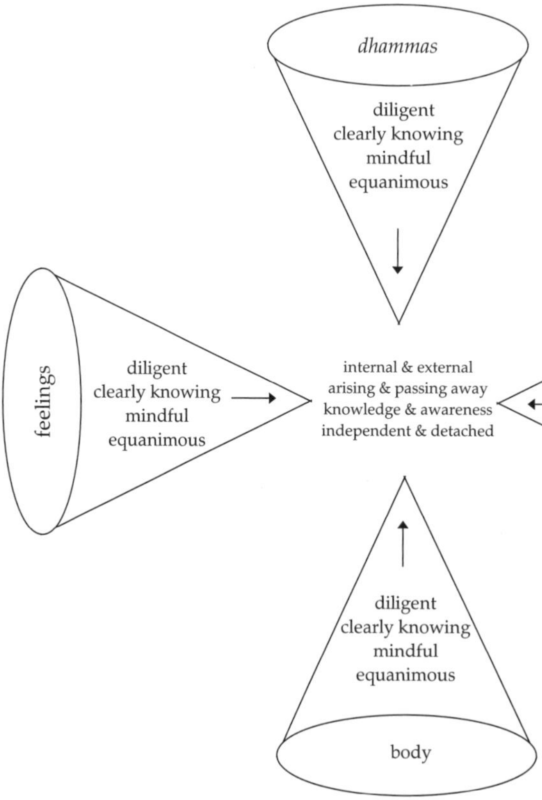

Fig. 15.1 Central characteristics and aspects of *satipaṭṭhāna*

the relationship between the "definition", the four *satipaṭṭhānas*, and the "refrain". The central aspects mentioned in the "refrain" are in the centre of the figure, while the qualities listed in the "definition" are repeated in each cone. These four cones represent the four *satipaṭṭhānas*, each of which can become the main focus of practice and lead to deep insight and realization.

As the diagram indicates, undertaking *satipaṭṭhāna* contemplation of body, feelings, mind, or *dhammas* requires the combination of all the four qualities listed in the "definition". Such contemplation leads to the development of the four aspects of *satipaṭṭhāna* found in the centre of the above figure and mentioned in the "refrain" of the *Satipaṭṭhāna Sutta*.

In this diagram I intend to show that each of the four *satipaṭṭhānas* constitutes a "door" or perhaps a "stepping-stone". The contemplations included under the four *satipaṭṭhānas* are not ends in themselves, rather, they are only tools for developing the central aspects described in the "refrain". Whichever door or stepping-stone is used to develop insight, the main task is to employ it skilfully in order to gain a comprehensive and balanced vision of the true nature of subjective experience.

In the *Saḷāyatanavibhaṅga Sutta* the Buddha spoke of three "*satipaṭṭhānas*" distinct from the practices listed in the four *satipaṭṭhāna* scheme.[2] This suggests that the contemplations described in the *Satipaṭṭhāna Sutta* do not determine the only proper and suitable ways for carrying out "*satipaṭṭhāna*" contemplation, but only recommendations for possible applications. Thus the practice of *satipaṭṭhāna* is not necessarily restricted to the range of objects explicitly listed in the *Satipaṭṭhāna Sutta*.

The contemplations in the *Satipaṭṭhāna Sutta* progress from gross to subtle aspects of experience. It should be kept in mind, however, that this discourse represents a theoretical model of *satipaṭṭhāna*, not a case study. In actual practice, the different contemplations described in the discourse can be combined in a variety of ways and it would be a misunderstanding to take the progression in the discourse as prescribing the only possible sequence for the development of *satipaṭṭhāna*.

The flexible interrelation of the *satipaṭṭhāna* contemplations in actual practice can be illustrated by taking a cross-section, as it were,

2 M III 221 (cf. also page 30).

through the direct path of *satipaṭṭhāna*. Such a sectional view would resemble a twelve-petalled flower (see Fig. 15.2 below), with the main object of contemplation (here the breath is used as an example) constituting the centre of the "flower".

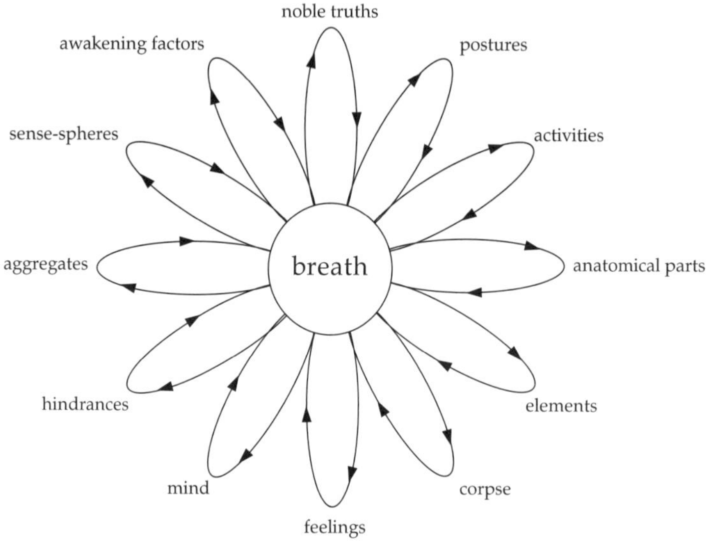

Fig. 15.2 Dynamic interrelation of the *satipaṭṭhāna* contemplations

From awareness of the main object of meditation, the dynamics of contemplation can at any given moment lead to any of the other *satipaṭṭhāna* exercises, and then revert to the main object. That is, from being aware of the process of breathing, for example, awareness might turn to any other occurrence in the realm of body, feelings, mind, or *dhammas* which has become prominent, and then revert to the breath. Otherwise, in the event that the newly-arisen object of meditation should require sustained attention and deeper investigation, it can become the new centre of the flower, with the former object turned into one of the petals.

Any meditation practice from the four *satipaṭṭhānas* can serve as the main focus of insight contemplation and lead to realization. At the same time, meditations from one *satipaṭṭhāna* can be related with those from other *satipaṭṭhānas*. This indicates the flexibility of the *satipaṭṭhāna* scheme, which allows freedom for variation and combination according to the character and level of development of the meditator. Understood in this way, practising *satipaṭṭhāna* should not be a question of practising one or another *satipaṭṭhāna*, but of contemplating one as well as the others. In fact, during the deeper stages of the practice, when one is able to abide "independent and free from clinging to anything in the world", the practice of *satipaṭṭhāna* progresses from any particular object or area to a more and more comprehensive form of contemplation that embraces all aspects of experience. Expressed in the terms of Fig. 15.2 it would be as if, when the sun was about to set, the twelve petals of the flower gradually came together to form a single bud. Practised in this way, *satipaṭṭhāna* becomes an integrated four-faceted survey of one's present experience, taking into account its material, affective, and mental aspects from the perspective of the *Dhamma*. In this way one's present experience becomes an occasion for swift progress on the direct path to realization.

XV.2 THE IMPORTANCE OF *SATIPAṬṬHĀNA*

The Buddha recommended the practice of *satipaṭṭhāna* to newcomers and beginners, and also included advanced practitioners and *arahants* among the cultivators of *satipaṭṭhāna*.[3]

For the beginner embarking on *satipaṭṭhāna* practice, the discourses stipulate a basis in ethical conduct and the presence of "straight" view as necessary foundations.[4] According to a passage in the *Aṅguttara Nikāya*, the practice of *satipaṭṭhāna* leads to overcoming weakness with regard to the five precepts.[5] This suggests that the ethical foundation required to begin *satipaṭṭhāna* might be weak at the outset, but will be strengthened as practice proceeds. Similarly, the "straight" view mentioned earlier might refer to a preliminary degree of motivation and understanding that will develop

---

3 S V 144. That different levels of disciples should practise *satipaṭṭhāna* comes up again at S V 299. (Woodward 1979: vol.V p.265, translates this passage as if the practice of *satipaṭṭhāna* "should be abandoned". This rendering is not convincing, since in the present context the Pāli term *vihātabba* is better translated as a future passive form of *viharati*, not of *vijahati*.)

4 The need for a basis in ethical conduct before embarking on *satipaṭṭhāna* is stated e.g. at S V 143; S V 165; S V 187; and S V 188. Cf. also S V 171, according to which the very purpose of ethical conduct is to lead up to the practice of *satipaṭṭhāna*. S V 143 and 165 add "straight view" (*diṭṭhi ca ujukā*) to the necessary conditions for *satipaṭṭhāna*.

5 A IV 457.

further with the progress of *satipaṭṭhāna* contemplation.[6] Additional requisites for undertaking *satipaṭṭhāna* practice are to limit one's activities, to refrain from gossiping, excessive sleep, and socializing, and to develop sense restraint and moderation with regard to food.[7]

It might already have come as a surprise that a newcomer to the path should be encouraged to cultivate *satipaṭṭhāna* right away.[8] That the Buddha and his fully-awakened disciples should still engage in the practice of *satipaṭṭhāna* might be even more surprising. Why would one who has realized the goal continue with *satipaṭṭhāna*?

The answer is that *arahants* continue with insight meditation because for them this is simply the most appropriate and pleasant way to spend their time.[9] Proficiency in *satipaṭṭhāna*, together with delight in seclusion, are indeed distinguishing qualities of an *arahant*.[10] Once true detachment has set in, the continuity of insight meditation becomes a source of delight and satisfaction. Thus *satipaṭṭhāna* is not only the direct path leading to the goal, but also the perfect expression of having realized the goal. To borrow from the poetic language of the discourses: path and *Nibbāna* merge into one, like one river merging with another.[11]

---

6 S III 51 and S IV 142 present the direct experience of the impermanent nature of the aggregates or the sense-spheres as "right view", a form of right view that is clearly an outcome of insight meditation.

7 A III 450.

8 It should be pointed out, however, that there is a clear qualitative difference between *satipaṭṭhāna* practised by a beginner and by an *arahant*. S V 144 describes this qualitative progression, which leads from the initial insight of the beginner, via the penetrative comprehension of the advanced practitioner, to the full freedom from any attachment during the contemplation undertaken by an *arahant*. Even for the beginner's initial insight, this discourse stipulates that *satipaṭṭhāna* is to be undertaken with a calm and concentrated mind for true insight to arise, a requirement not easily met by those who have just started to practise.

9 S III 168 explains that although *arahants* have nothing more to do, they continue to contemplate the five aggregates as impermanent, unsatisfactory, and not-self, because for them this is a pleasant form of abiding here and now and a source of mindfulness and clear knowledge. At S I 48 the Buddha explained again that *arahants*, although meditating, have nothing more to do since they have "gone beyond". Cf. also Ray 1994: p.87.

10 S V 175 defines an *arahant* as one who has perfected the cultivation of *satipaṭṭhāna*. According to S V 302, *arahants* often dwell established in *satipaṭṭhāna*. The *arahant*'s delight in seclusion is documented at D III 283; A IV 224; and A V 175. The *arahant*'s proficiency in *satipaṭṭhāna* comes up again at A IV 224 and at A V 175. Katz 1989: p.67, concludes: "*satipaṭṭhāna* ... *arahants* enjoy this practice, which would mean ... that it is a natural expression of their attainment".

A similar nuance underlies the final part of the "refrain", according to which contemplation continues for the sake of continued contemplation.[12] This indicates that there is no point at which a practitioner goes beyond the practice of meditation. Thus the relevance of *satipaṭṭhāna* extends from the very beginning of the path all the way through to the moment of full realization, and beyond.

The continued relevance of formal meditation practice even for *arahants* is documented in various discourses. These discourses show that the Buddha and his disciples were always given to meditation, irrespective of their level of realization.[13] The Buddha was well known in contemporary ascetic circles for being in favour of silence and retreat.[14] An illustrative episode in the *Sāmaññaphala Sutta* reports the Buddha and a large congregation of monks meditating in such deep silence that an approaching king feared being led into an ambush, because it seemed impossible to him that so many people could be assembled together without making any noise.[15] The Buddha's appreciation of silence went so far that he would readily

11 According to D II 223, *Nibbāna* and the path coalesce, just as the Gaṅgā and the Yamunā rivers coalesce. Malalasekera 1995: vol.I p.734, explains that "the junction of the Gaṅgā and the Yamunā ... is used as a simile for perfect union".

12 M I 56: "mindfulness ... is established in him to the extent necessary for ... continuous mindfulness".

13 e.g. S V 326 reports the Buddha and some *arahants* engaged in the practice of mindfulness of breathing. From among the *arahant* disciples, Anuruddha was known for his frequent practice of *satipaṭṭhāna* (cf. S V 294–306). Sn 157 stresses again that the Buddha did not neglect meditation. Cf. also M III 13, where the Buddha is characterized as one who practised meditation and followed the conduct of a meditator.

14 e.g. at D I 179; D III 37; M I 514; M II 2; M II 23; M II 30; A V 185; and A V 190; the Buddha and his followers are characterized as being "in favour of silence, practising silence, praising silence". Cf. also S III 15 and S IV 80, where the Buddha emphatically exhorted his disciples to make an effort at living in seclusion. According to A III 422, seclusion is in fact a necessary requirement for gaining real control over the mind. Cf. also It 39 and Sn 822, where the Buddha spoke again in praise of seclusion. At Vin I 92 the Buddha even exempted junior monks from the need to live in dependence on a teacher if they were meditating in seclusion. Living in community almost appears to be a second-rate alternative, since at S I 154 such community life is recommended to those monks who are unable to find delight in seclusion (cf. also Ray 1994: p.96). The importance of seclusion in the historically early stages of the Buddhist monastic community is also noted by Panabokke 1993: p.14. To live in seclusion, however, requires some degree of meditative proficiency, as the Buddha pointed out at M I 17 and A V 202. If such meditative proficiency was lacking, the Buddha would advise monks against going off into seclusion (cf. the cases of Upāli at A V 202 and Meghiya at Ud 34).

15 D I 50.

dismiss noisy monks or lay supporters from his presence.[16] If the hustle and bustle around him reached a level he found excessive, he was capable of just walking off by himself, leaving the congregation of monks, nuns, and lay followers to themselves.[17] Seclusion, he explained, was a distinctive quality of the *Dhamma*.[18]

The discourses report that even after his full awakening the Buddha still went into solitary silent retreat.[19] Even outside of intensive retreat, distinguished visitors were sometimes not allowed to approach him if he was engaged in his daily meditation.[20] According to the Buddha's own statement in the *Mahāsuññata Sutta*, if while abiding in emptiness meditation he was visited by monks, nuns, or laity, his mind inclined to seclusion to such an extent that he would talk to them in a way that was intended to dismiss them.[21]

His secluded lifestyle earned the Buddha some undeserved ridicule from other ascetics, who insinuated that he might fear being vanquished in debate with others.[22] This, however, was not the case; the Buddha was not afraid of debate or of anything else. His

---

16 At M I 457 a newly-ordained group of monks was dismissed by the Buddha for being too noisy. The same happened again at Ud 25. At A III 31 (= A III 342 and A IV 341), the Buddha was disinclined to accept food brought by a group of householders because they were creating a lot of noise. On the other hand, however, merely to observe silence for its own sake was criticized by the Buddha. At Vin I 157 he rebuked a group of monks who had spent a rainy season together in complete silence, apparently in order to avoid communal discord. This case needs to be considered in the light of M I 207, where the silent cohabitation of a group of monks is described in the same terms, but met with the Buddha's approval. Here the decisive difference was that every fifth day this group of monks would interrupt their silence and discuss the *Dhamma*, i.e. in this case silence was not observed to avoid dissension, but was employed as a means to create a suitable meditative atmosphere and at the same time wisely balanced with regular discussions about the *Dhamma*. In fact these two activities, either discussing the *Dhamma* or observing silence, were often recommended by the Buddha as the two appropriate ways of spending time with others (e.g. at M I 161).

17 Ud 41. A similar action was undertaken at A V 133 by a group of senior monks who departed without even taking their leave of the Buddha in order to avoid the noise created by some visitors, an action which the Buddha, on being told later, approved.

18 Vin II 259 and A IV 280.

19 Vin III 68; S V 12; and S V 320 report the Buddha spending two weeks in complete seclusion on a silent retreat, while Vin III 229; S V 13; and S V 325 report the same for a three-month period.

20 e.g. at D I 151. According to D II 270, even Sakka, king of gods, had once to depart without being able to meet the Buddha, because he was not allowed to disturb the Buddha's meditation.

21 M III 111.

22 D I 175 and D III 38.

secluded and meditative lifestyle was simply the appropriate expression of his realization, and at the same time a way of setting an example to others.[23]

The passages mentioned so far clearly show the importance given in the early Buddhist community to retiring into seclusion and engaging in the practice of intensive meditation. This importance is also reflected in the statement that practice of the four *satipaṭṭhānas*, together with removing the hindrances and establishing the awakening factors, constitutes a common feature of the awakening of all Buddhas, past, present, and future.[24] In fact, not only Buddhas, but all those who have realized or will realize awakening, do so by overcoming the hindrances, establishing *satipaṭṭhāna*, and developing the awakening factors.[25] In view of the fact that both the hindrances and the awakening factors are objects of contemplation of *dhammas*, it becomes evident that *satipaṭṭhāna* is an indispensable ingredient for growth in the *Dhamma*.[26] Little wonder then that the Buddha equated neglecting *satipaṭṭhāna* with neglecting the path to freedom from *dukkha*.[27]

The relevance of *satipaṭṭhāna* to all the Buddha's disciples is also indicated by the fact that, according to the discourses, many nuns were accomplished practitioners of *satipaṭṭhāna*.[28] Several instances also refer to lay-meditators proficient in *satipaṭṭhāna* contemplation.[29] These instances clearly show that the word "monks" (*bhikkhave*), used in the *Satipaṭṭhāna Sutta* by the Buddha as a form of

---

23 At D III 54 the Buddha pointed out that all Awakened Ones of past times had similarly been dedicated to seclusion and silence. M I 23 and A I 60 explain his reasons for living in seclusion to be a pleasant abiding here and now and out of compassion for future generations. Cf. also Mil 138.

24 D II 83; D III 101; and S V 161. At S I 103 the Buddha explicitly stated that his awakening took place based on *sati*.

25 A V 195. This statement appears to be of such crucial importance that in the *satipaṭṭhāna* version preserved in the Chinese *Madhyama Āgama* it has become part of the introductory part of the discourse itself, cf. Nhat Hanh 1990: p.151.

26 In fact, according to A V 153, mindfulness is essential for growth in the *Dhamma*. The usefulness of *satipaṭṭhāna* is further corroborated by the substantial list of its possible benefits at A IV 457–60.

27 S V 179.

28 S V 155.

29 e.g. according to M I 340 the lay disciple Pessa engaged from time to time in *satipaṭṭhāna*. Pessa's practice is qualified in this discourse with the expression "well established" (*supatiṭṭhita*), which clearly indicates that it must have been of a rather advanced level. S V 177 and S V 178 report the laymen Sirivaḍḍha and Mānadinna both engaged in the practice of *satipaṭṭhāna*. Both were then declared by the Buddha to have achieved non-returning.

address to his audience, was not intended to restrict the instructions to fully ordained monks.[30]

Although the practice of *satipaṭṭhāna* is clearly not limited to members of the monastic community, it nevertheless holds particular benefits for them, since it counters tendencies towards personal and communal decline.[31] As the Buddha pointed out, once a monk or a nun has practised *satipaṭṭhāna* for a sufficient length of time, nothing in the world can tempt them to disrobe and forsake their way of life, since they have become thoroughly disenchanted with worldly temptations.[32] Well established in *satipaṭṭhāna*, they have become truly self-reliant and are no longer in need of any other form of protection or refuge.[33]

The wholesome effects of *satipaṭṭhāna* are not restricted to oneself. The Buddha emphatically advised that one should encourage one's friends and relatives to also practise *satipaṭṭhāna*.[34] In this way, *satipaṭṭhāna* practice can become a tool for assisting others. The Buddha once illustrated the proper procedure for such assistance with the example of two acrobats about to perform a balancing act together.[35] In order for both to perform safely, each first of all had to pay attention to his own balance, not to the balance of his companion. Similarly, the Buddha advised, one should first of all establish balance within oneself by developing *satipaṭṭhāna*. Based on establishing such inner balance one will be able to relate to external circumstances with patience, non-violence, and compassion, and therefore be truly able to benefit others.

The simile of the two acrobats suggests that self-development by way of *satipaṭṭhāna* forms an important basis for the ability to help others. According to the Buddha, to try to assist others without first

---

30 Ps I 241 explains that in the present context "monk" includes whoever engages in the practice.

31 D II 77; D II 79; S V 172; S V 173; and S V 174.

32 S V 301. It is revealing to contrast this statement with A III 396, according to which even a fourth *jhāna* attainer is still liable to disrobing and returning to a worldly lifestyle.

33 D II 100; D III 58; D III 77; S V 154; S V 163; and S V 164 speak of those engaging in *satipaṭṭhāna* as becoming like an island and thereby a refuge to themselves. Commenting on this statement, Sv II 549 emphasizes that it is the practice of *satipaṭṭhānas* that will lead to the highest.

34 S V 189. It is a little surprising that this discourse has not made its way into the Chinese *Āgamas* (cf. Akanuma 1990: 247).

35 S V 169. On this passage cf. also Ñāṇapoṇika 1990: p.3; Ñāṇavīra 1987: p.211; Piyadassi 1972: p.475; and Ṭhānissaro 1996: p.81.

having developed oneself is like trying to save someone from a quagmire while one is oneself sinking.[36] He compared attempts to lead others to realize what one has not yet realized oneself to someone carried away by a swift river, yet attempting to help others to cross it.[37]

All these passages document the central position and importance of *satipaṭṭhāna* in the context of the Buddha's teaching. Indeed, it is the practice of *satipaṭṭhāna*, the systematic development of this unobtrusive quality of mindfulness, that constitutes the direct path to the realization of *Nibbāna*, to the perfection of wisdom, to the highest possible happiness, and to unsurpassable freedom.[38]

---

36 M I 45. Likewise Dhp 158 recommends being well established oneself before teaching others. Cf. also A II 95–9, where the Buddha distinguished between four possibilities of practice: for one's own benefit only, or for others' benefit only, or for the benefit of neither, or for the benefit of both. His perhaps surprising position was that to practise for one's own benefit only is superior to practising for the benefit of others only (cf. also Dhp 166). The underlying rationale is that unless one is established oneself in overcoming unwholesomeness (A II 96) or in ethical restraint (A II 99), one will be unable to benefit others. Cf. also Premasiri 1990c: p.160, who points out the need for a basis of internal peace before proceeding to serve others.

37 Sn 320.

38 *Nibbāna* is referred to as the "perfection of wisdom" at M III 245 and Th 1015; as the highest happiness at Dhp 204; and as unsurpassable freedom at M I 235.

BIBLIOGRAPHY

In quoting Pāli sources, my references are to the volume and page of the PTS edition. In the case of the *Dhammapada*, the *Sutta Nipāta* and the *Thera/Therīgāthā*, quotations are by verse number of the PTS edition, instead of the page number. Quotations from the subcommentary/*Ṭīkā* and the Abhidh-s are referenced according to the volume and page of the Burmese Chaṭṭha Saṅgāyana edition, published on CD-ROM by the Vipassanā Research Institute, Igatpuri, India 1997. For matters of comparison, I have also consulted the Sinhalese Buddha Jayanti edition, published by the Sri Lanka Tripitaka Project, Colombo.

Akanuma, Chizen, 1990 (1929): *The Comparative Catalogue of Chinese Āgamas & Pāli Nikāyas*, Delhi: Sri Satguru.

Alexander, F., 1931: "Buddhist Training as an Artificial Catatonia", in *Psychoanalytical Review*, vol.18, no.2, pp.129–45.

Ariyadhamma, Nauyane, 1994: *Satipaṭṭhāna Bhāvanā*, Gunatilaka (tr.), Sri Lanka, Kalutara.

Ariyadhamma, Nauyane, 1995 (1988): *Ānāpānasati, Meditation on Breathing*, Kandy: BPS.

Aronson, Harvey B., 1979: "Equanimity in Theravāda Buddhism", in *Studies in Pāli and Buddhism*, Delhi: pp.1–18.

Aronson, Harvey B., 1986 (1980): *Love and Sympathy in Theravāda Buddhism*, Delhi: Motilal Banarsidass.

Ayya Khema, 1984 (1983): *Meditating on No-Self*, Kandy: BPS.

Ayya Khema, 1991: *When the Iron Eagle Flies; Buddhism for the West*, London: Arkana, Penguin Group.

Ayya Kheminda (n.d.): *A Matter of Balance*, Colombo: Printing House.

Ba Khin, U, 1985: "The Essentials of Buddha-Dhamma in Practice", in *Dhamma Text by Sayagyi U Ba Khin*, Saya U Chit Tin (ed.), England, Heddington.
Ba Khin, U, 1994 (1991): "Revolution with a View to Nibbāna", in *Sayagyi U Ba Khin Journal*, India, Igatpuri: VRI, pp.67–74.
Barnes, Michael, 1981: "The Buddhist Way of Deliverance", in *Studia Missionalia*, vol.30, pp.233–77.
Basham, A.L., 1951: *History and Doctrines of the Ājīvikas*, London: Luzac.
Bendall, Cecil (et al, tr.), 1990 (1922): *Śikṣā Samuccaya*, Delhi: Motilal Banarsidass.
Bhattacharya, Kamaleswar, 1980: "Diṭṭham, Sutam, Mutam, Viññātam", in *Buddhist Studies in Honour of Walpola Rahula*, Balasoorya (et al, ed.) London: pp.10–15.
Bodhi, Bhikkhu, 1976: "Aggregates and Clinging Aggregates", in *Pāli Buddhist Review*, vol.1, no.1, pp.91–102.
Bodhi, Bhikkhu, 1984: *The Noble Eightfold Path*, Kandy: BPS.
Bodhi, Bhikkhu, 1989: *The Discourse on the Fruits of Recluseship*, Kandy: BPS.
Bodhi, Bhikkhu (et al), 1991: *The Discourse on Right View*, Kandy: BPS.
Bodhi, Bhikkhu, 1992a (1978): *The All Embracing Net of Views: The Brahmajāla Sutta and its Commentaries*, Kandy: BPS.
Bodhi, Bhikkhu, 1992b (1980): *The Discourse on the Root of Existence*, Kandy: BPS.
Bodhi, Bhikkhu, 1993: *A Comprehensive Manual of Abhidhamma, the Abhidhammattha Saṅgaha*, Kandy: BPS.
Bodhi, Bhikkhu, 1995 (1984): *The Great Discourse on Causation: The Mahānidāna Sutta and its Commentaries*, Kandy: BPS.
Bodhi, Bhikkhu, 1996: "Nibbāna, Transcendence and Language", in *Buddhist Studies Review*, vol.13, no.2, pp.163–76.
Bodhi, Bhikkhu, 1998: "A Critical Examination of Ñāṇavīra Thera's 'A Note on Paṭiccasamuppāda'", in *Buddhist Studies Review*, vol.15, no.1, pp.43–64; no.2, pp.157–81.
Bodhi, Bhikkhu (tr.), 2000: *The Connected Discourses of the Buddha*, 2 vols., Boston: Wisdom.
Boisvert, Mathieu, 1997 (1995): *The Five Aggregates; Understanding Theravāda Psychology and Soteriology*, Delhi: Sri Satguru.
Brahmavaṃso, Ajahn, 1999: *The Basic Method of Meditation*, Malaysia: Buddhist Gem Fellowship.
Bronkhorst, Johannes, 1985: "Dharma and Abhidharma", in *Bulletin of the School of Oriental and African Studies*, no.48, pp.305–20.
Bronkhorst, Johannes, 1993 (1986): *The Two Traditions of Meditation in Ancient India*, Delhi: Motilal Banarsidass.
Brown, Daniel P., 1977: "A Model for the Levels of Concentrative Meditation", in *International Journal of Clinical and Experimental Hypnosis*, vol.25, no.4, pp.236–73.

Brown, Daniel P. (et al), 1984: "Differences in Visual Sensitivity among Mindfulness Meditators and Non-Meditators", in *Perceptual & Motor Skills*, no.58, pp.727–33.

Brown, Daniel P. (et al), 1986a: "The Stages of Meditation in Cross-Cultural Perspective", in *Transformations of Consciousness*, Wilber (et al, ed.), London: Shambhala, pp.219–83.

Brown, Daniel P. (et al), 1986b: "The Stages of Mindfulness Meditation: A Validation Study", in *Transformations of Consciousness*, Wilber (et al, ed.), London: Shambhala, pp.161–217.

Bucknell, Roderick S., 1984: "The Buddhist Path to Liberation", in *Journal of the International Association of Buddhist Studies*, vol.7, no.2, pp.7–40.

Bucknell, Roderick S., 1993: "Reinterpreting the Jhānas" in *Journal of the International Association of Buddhist Studies*, vol.16, no.2, pp.375–409.

Bucknell, Roderick S., 1999: "Conditioned Arising Evolves: Variation and Change in Textual Accounts of the Paṭicca-samuppāda Doctrine", in *Journal of the International Association of Buddhist Studies*, vol.22, no.2, pp.311–42.

Buddhadāsa, Bhikkhu, 1956: *Handbook for Mankind*, Thailand: Suan Mok.

Buddhadāsa, Bhikkhu, 1976 (1971): *Ānāpānasati (Mindfulness of Breathing)*, Nāgasena (tr.), Bangkok: Sublime Life Mission, vol.1.

Buddhadāsa, Bhikkhu, 1984: *Heart-Wood from the Bo Tree*, Thailand: Suan Mok.

Buddhadāsa, Bhikkhu, 1989 (1987): *Mindfulness with Breathing*, Santikaro (tr.), Thailand: Dhamma Study & Practice Group.

Buddhadāsa, Bhikkhu, 1992: *Paṭiccasamuppāda, Practical Dependent Origination*, Thailand: Vuddhidhamma Fund.

Buddhadāsa, Bhikkhu, 1993 (1977): "Insight by the Nature Method", in Kornfield: *Living Buddhist Masters*, Kandy: BPS, pp.119–29.

Bullen, Leonard A., 1982: *A Technique of Living, Based on Buddhist Psychological Principles*, Kandy: BPS.

Bullen, Leonard A., 1991 (1969): *Buddhism: A Method of Mind Training*, Kandy: BPS.

Burford, Grace G., 1994 (1992): "Theravāda Buddhist Soteriology and the Paradox of Desire", in *Paths to Liberation*, Buswell (et al, ed.), Delhi: Motilal Banarsidass, pp.37–62.

Burns, Douglas M., 1983 (1968): *Nirvāna, Nihilism and Satori*, Kandy: BPS.

Burns, Douglas M., 1994 (1967): *Buddhist Meditation and Depth Psychology*, Kandy: BPS.

Buswell, Robert E. (et al), 1994 (1992): Introduction to *Paths to Liberation*, Buswell (et al, ed.), Delhi: Motilal Banarsidass, pp.1–36.

Carrithers, Michael, 1983: *The Forest Monks of Sri Lanka*, Delhi: Oxford University Press.

Carter, John Ross, 1984: "Beyond 'Beyond Good and Evil'", in *Buddhist Studies in Honour of H. Saddhātissa*, Dhammapāla (et al, ed.), Sri Lanka: University of Jayewardenepura, pp.41–55.

Chah, Ajahn, 1992: *Food for the Heart*, Thailand: Wat Pa Nanachat.

Chah, Ajahn, 1993 (1977): "Notes from a Session of Questions and Answers", in Kornfield: *Living Buddhist Masters*, Kandy: BPS pp.36–48.

Chah, Ajahn, 1996 (1991): *Meditation, Samādhi Bhāvanā*, Malaysia: Wave.

Chah, Ajahn, 1997 (1980): *Taste of Freedom*, Malaysia: Wave.

Chah, Ajahn, 1998: *The Key to Liberation*, Thailand: Wat Pa Nanachat.

Chakravarti, Uma, 1996: *The Social Dimensions of Early Buddhism*, Delhi: Munshiram Manoharlal.

Chit Tin, Saya U, 1989: *Knowing Anicca and the Way to Nibbāna*, Trowbridge, Wiltshire: Sayagyi U Ba Khin Memorial Trust.

Choong, Mun-keat, 1999 (1995): *The Notion of Emptiness in Early Buddhism*, Delhi: Motilal Banarsidass.

Choong, Mun-keat, 2000: *The Fundamental Teachings of Early Buddhism*, Wiesbaden: Harrassowitz.

Claxton, Guy, 1991 (1978): "Meditation in Buddhist Psychology", in *The Psychology of Meditation*, West (ed.), Oxford: Clarendon Press, pp.23–38.

Collins, Steven, 1982: *Selfless Persons: Imagery and Thought in Theravāda Buddhism*, Cambridge: University Press.

Collins, Steven, 1994: "What Are Buddhists Doing When They Deny the Self?", in *Religion and Practical Reason*, Tracy (et al ed.), Albany: State University New York Press, pp.59–86.

Collins, Steven, 1997: "The Body in Theravāda Buddhist Monasticism", in *Religion and the Body*, Coakley (ed.), Cambridge: University Press, pp.185–204.

Collins, Steven, 1998: *Nirvana and other Buddhist Felicities*, Cambridge: University Press.

Conze, Edward, 1956: *Buddhist Meditation*, London: Allen and Unwin.

Conze, Edward, 1960 (1951): *Buddhism, its Essence and Development*, Oxford: Cassirer.

Conze, Edward, 1962: *Buddhist Thought in India*, London: Allen and Unwin.

Cousins, Lance S., 1973: "Buddhist Jhāna: Its Nature and Attainment according to the Pāli Sources", in *Religion*, no.3, pp.115–31.

Cousins, Lance S., 1983: "Nibbāna and Abhidhamma", in *Buddhist Studies Review*, vol.1, no.2, pp.95–109.

Cousins, Lance S., 1984: "Samatha-Yāna and Vipassanā-Yāna", in *Buddhist Studies in Honour of H. Saddhātissa*, Dhammapāla (et al, ed.), Sri Lanka: University of Jayewardenepura, pp.56–68.

Cousins, Lance S., 1989: "The Stages of Christian Mysticism and Buddhist Purification", in *The Yogi and the Mystic*, Werner (ed.), London: pp.103–20.

Cousins, Lance S., 1992: "Vitakka/Vitarka and Vicāra, Stages of Samādhi in Buddhism and Yoga", in *Indo-Iranian Journal*, no.35, pp.137–57.

Cox, Collett, 1992: "Mindfulness and Memory", in *In the Mirror of Memory*, Gyatso (ed.), New York: State University Press, pp.67–108.

Cox, Collett, 1994 (1992): "Attainment through Abandonment", in *Paths to Liberation*, Buswell (et al, ed.), Delhi: Motilal Banarsidass, pp.63–105.

Crangle, Edward F., 1994: *The Origin and Development of Early Indian Contemplative Practices*, Wiesbaden: Harrassowitz.

Daw Mya Tin, 1990 (1986): *The Dhammapada*, Varanasi: Central Institute of Higher Tibetan Studies.

Deatherage, Gary, 1975: "The Clinical Use of 'Mindfulness' Meditation Techniques in Short-Term Psychotherapy", in *Journal of Transpersonal Psychology*, vol.7, no.2, pp.133–43.

Debes, Paul, 1994: "Die 4 Pfeiler der Selbstbeobachtung – Satipatthāna", in *Wissen und Wandel*, vol.40, nos.3/4, 5/6, 7/8, 9/10; pp.66–127, 130–90, 194–253, 258–304.

Debes, Paul, 1997 (1982): *Meisterung der Existenz durch die Lehre des Buddha*, 2 vols., Germany: Buddhistisches Seminar Bindlach.

Debvedi, Phra, 1990 (1988): *Sammāsati; an Exposition of Right Mindfulness*, Dhamma-Vijaya (tr.), Thailand: Buddhadhamma Foundation.

Debvedi, Phra, 1998 (1990): *Helping Yourself to Help Others*, Puriso (tr.), Bangkok: Wave.

Deikman, Arthur J., 1966: "De-automatization and the Mystic Experience", in *Psychiatry*, New York: no.29, pp.324–38.

Deikman, Arthur J., 1969: "Experimental Meditation", in *Altered States of Consciousness*, Tart (ed.), New York: Anchor Books, pp.203–223.

De la Vallée Poussin, Louis, 1903: "Vyādhisūtra on the Four Āryasatyas", in *Journal of the Royal Asiatic Society*, pp.578–80.

De la Vallée Poussin, Louis, 1936/37: "Musīla et Nārada; le Chemin du Nirvāna", in *Mélanges Chinois et Bouddhiques*, Bruxelles: Institut Belge des Hautes Études Chinoises, no.5, pp.189–222.

Delmonte, M.M., 1991 (1978): "Meditation: Contemporary Theoretical Approaches", in *The Psychology of Meditation*, West (ed.), Oxford: Clarendon Press, pp.39–53.

Demieville, Paul, 1954: "Sur la Mémoire des Existences Antérieures", in *Bulletin de l'École Française d'Extrême Orient*, Paris: vol.44, no.2, pp.283–98.

De Silva, Lily (n.d.): *Mental Culture in Buddhism (based on the Mahāsatipaṭṭhānasutta)*, Colombo: Public Trustee.

De Silva, Lily, 1978: "Cetovimutti, Paññāvimutti and Ubhatobhāgavimutti", in *Pāli Buddhist Review*, vol.3, no.3, pp.118–45.

De Silva, Lily, 1987: "Sense Experience of the Liberated Being as Reflected in Early Buddhism", in *Buddhist Philosophy and Culture*, Kalupahana (et al, ed.), Colombo, pp.13–22.

De Silva, Lily, 1996 (1987): *Nibbāna as Living Experience*, Kandy: BPS.

De Silva, Padmasiri, 1981: *Emotions and Therapy, Three Paradigmatic Zones*, Sri Lanka: University of Peradeniya.

De Silva, Padmasiri, 1991 (1977): *An Introduction to Buddhist Psychology*, London: Macmillan.

De Silva, Padmasiri, 1992a (1973): *Buddhist and Freudian Psychology*, Singapore: University Press.

De Silva, Padmasiri, 1992b (1991): *Twin Peaks: Compassion and Insight*, Singapore: Buddhist Research Society.

Devendra, Kusuma, ?1985: *Sati in Theravāda Buddhist Meditation*, Sri Lanka: Maharagama.

Dhammadharo, Ajahn, 1987: *Frames of Reference*, Ṭhānissaro (tr.), Bangkok.

Dhammadharo, Ajahn, 1993 (1977): "Questions and Answers on the Nature of Insight Practice", in Kornfield: *Living Buddhist Masters*, Kandy: BPS, pp.259–70.

Dhammadharo, Ajahn, 1996 (1979): *Keeping the Breath in Mind & Lessons in Samādhi*, Thailand/Malaysia: Wave.

Dhammadharo, Ajahn, 1997: *The Skill of Release*, Ṭhānissaro (tr.), Malaysia: Wave.

Dhammananda, K. Sri, 1987: *Meditation, the Only Way*, Malaysia, Kuala Lumpur: Buddhist Missionary Society.

Dhammasudhi, Chao Khun Sobhana, 1968 (1965): *Insight Meditation*, London: Buddhapadīpa Temple.

Dhammasudhi, Chao Khun Sobhana, 1969: *The Real Way to Awakening*, London: Buddhapadīpa Temple.

Dhammavuddho Thera, 1994: *Samatha and Vipassanā*, Malaysia, Kuala Lumpur.

Dhammavuddho Thera, 1999: *Liberation, Relevance of Sutta-Vinaya*, Malaysia, Kuala Lumpur: Wave.

Dhammiko, Bhikkhu, 1961: "Die Übung in den Pfeilern der Einsicht", in *Buddhistische Monatsblätter*, Hamburg, pp.179–91.

Dhīravaṃsa, 1988 (1974): *The Middle Path of Life; Talks on the Practice of Insight Meditation*, California: Blue Dolphin.

Dhīravaṃsa, 1989 (1982): *The Dynamic Way of Meditation*, Wellingborough: Crucible.

Dumont, Louis, 1962: "The Conception of Kingship in Ancient India", in *Contributions to Indian Sociology*, vol.VI, pp.48–77.

Dwivedi, K.N., 1977: "Vipassanā and Psychiatry", in *Maha Bodhi*, Calcutta, vol.85, no.8–10, pp.254–6.

Earle, J.B.B., 1984: "Cerebral Laterality and Meditation", in *Meditation: Classic and Contemporary Perspectives*, Shapiro (ed.), New York: Aldine, pp.396–414.

Eden, P.M., 1984: "The Jhānas", in *Middle Way*, vol.59, no.2, pp.87–90.

Edgerton, Franklin, 1998 (1953): *Buddhist Hybrid Sanskrit Grammar and Dictionary*, Delhi: Motilal Banarsidass.

Ehara, N.R.M. (et al, tr.), 1995 (1961): *The Path of Freedom (Vimuttimagga)*, Kandy: BPS.

Engler, John H., 1983: "Vicissitudes of the Self According to Psychoanalysis and Buddhism", in *Psychoanalysis and Contemporary Thought*, vol.6, no.1, pp.29–72.

Engler, John H., 1986: "Therapeutic Aims in Psychotherapy and Meditation", in *Transformations of Consciousness*, Wilber (et al, ed.), London: Shambhala, pp.17–51.

Epstein, Mark, 1984: "On the Neglect of Evenly Suspended Attention", in *Journal of Transpersonal Psychology*, vol.16, no.2, pp.193–205.
Epstein, Mark, 1986: "Meditative Transformations of Narcissism", in *Journal of Transpersonal Psychology*, vol.18, no.2, pp.143–58.
Epstein, Mark, 1988: "The Deconstruction of the Self", in *Journal of Transpersonal Psychology*, vol.20, no.1, pp.61–9.
Epstein, Mark, 1989: "Forms of Emptiness: Psychodynamic, Meditative and Clinical Perspectives", in *Journal of Transpersonal Psychology*, vol.21, no.1, pp.61–71.
Epstein, Mark, 1990: "Psychodynamics of Meditation: Pitfalls on the Spiritual Path", in *Journal of Transpersonal Psychology*, vol.22, no.1, pp.17–34.
Epstein, Mark, 1995: *Thoughts without a Thinker, Psychotherapy from a Buddhist Perspective*, New York: Basic Books.
Fenner, Peter, 1987: "Cognitive Theories of the Emotions in Buddhism and Western Psychology", in *Psychologia*, no.30, pp.217–27.
Fessel, Thorsten K. H., 1999: *Studien zur "Einübung von Gegenwärtigkeit" (Satipaṭṭhāna) nach der Sammlung der Lehrreden (Sutta-Piṭaka) der Theravādin*, M.A. thesis, University of Tübingen.
Festinger, Leon, 1957: *A Theory of Cognitive Dissonance*, New York: Row, Peterson & Co.
Fleischman, Paul R., 1986: *The Therapeutic Action of Vipassanā*, Kandy: BPS.
Fraile, Miguel, 1993: *Meditación Budista y Psicoanalisis*, Madrid: EDAF.
Frauwallner, Erich: "Abhidharma Studien", in *Wiener Zeitschrift für die Kunde Süd- und Ostasiens*; no.7 (1963) pp.20–36; no.8 (1964) pp.59–99, no.15 (1971) pp.69–121, no.16 (1972) pp.95–152, no.17 (1973) pp.97–121.
Fromm, Erich, 1960: "Psychoanalysis and Zen Buddhism", in *Zen Buddhism and Psychoanalysis*, Suzuki (ed.), London: Allen and Unwin, pp.77–141.
Fryba, Mirko, 1989 (1987): *The Art of Happiness, Teachings of Buddhist Psychology*, Boston: Shambhala.
Gethin, Rupert, 1986: "The Five Khandhas", in *Journal of Indian Philosophy*, no.14, pp.35–53.
Gethin, Rupert, 1992: *The Buddhist Path to Awakening: A Study of the Bodhi-Pakkhiyā Dhammā*, Leiden: Brill.
Gethin, Rupert, 1994: "Bhavaṅga and Rebirth According to the Abhidhamma", in *The Buddhist Forum*, London: School of Oriental and African Studies, vol.3 (1991–3), pp.11–35.
Gethin, Rupert, 1997a: "Cosmology and Meditation", in *History of Religions*, Chicago, vol.36, pp.183–217.
Gethin, Rupert, 1997b: "Wrong View and Right View in the Theravāda Abhidhamma", in *Recent Researches in Buddhist Studies*, Dhammajoti (et al, ed.), Colombo/Hong Kong, pp.211–29.
Gnanarama, Pategama, 1998: *Aspects of Early Buddhist Sociological Thought*, Singapore: Ti-Sarana Buddhist Association.
Goenka, S.N., 1994a (1991): "Buddha's Path is to Experience Reality", in *Sayagyi U Ba Khin Journal*, India, Igatpuri: VRI, pp.109–13.

Goenka, S.N., 1994b: "Sensation, the Key to Satipaṭṭhāna", in *Vipassanā Newsletter*, India, Igatpuri: VRI, vol.3, no.5.

Goenka, S.N., 1999: *Discourses on Satipaṭṭhāna Sutta*, India, Igatpuri: VRI.

Gokhale, Balkrishna Govind, 1976: "The Image World of the Thera-Therī-Gāthās", in *Malalasekera Commemoration Volume*, Wijesekera (ed.), Colombo, pp.96–110.

Goldstein, Joseph, 1985 (1976): *The Experience of Insight: A Natural Unfolding*, Kandy: BPS.

Goldstein, Joseph, 1994: *Insight Meditation*, Boston: Shambhala.

Goleman, Daniel, 1975: "Meditation and Consciousness: An Asian Approach to Mental Health", in *American Journal of Psychotherapy*, vol.30, no.1, pp.41–54.

Goleman, Daniel, 1977a: "The Role of Attention in Meditation and Hypnosis", in *International Journal of Clinical and Experimental Hypnosis*, vol.25, no.4, pp.291–308.

Goleman, Daniel, 1977b: *The Varieties of the Meditative Experience*, New York: Irvington.

Goleman, Daniel, 1980 (1973): *The Buddha on Meditation and Higher States of Consciousness*, Kandy, BPS.

Gomez, Louis O., 1976: "Proto-Mādhyamika in the Pāli Canon", in *Philosophy East and West*, Hawaii, vol.26, no.2, pp.137–65.

Gombrich, Richard F., 1996: *How Buddhism Began, the Conditioned Genesis of the Early Teachings*, London: Athlone Press.

Govinda, Lama Anagarika, 1991 (1961): *The Psychological Attitude of Early Buddhist Philosophy*, Delhi: Motilal Banarsidass.

Griffith, Paul J., 1981: "Concentration or Insight, the Problematic of Theravāda Buddhist Meditation Theory", in *Journal of the American Academy of Religion*, vol.49, no.4, pp.605–24.

Griffith, Paul J., 1983: "Buddhist Jhāna: a Form-Critical Study", in *Religion*, no.13, pp.55–68.

Griffith, Paul J., 1986: *On Being Mindless: Buddhist Meditation and the Mind-Body Problem*, Illinois, La Salle: Open Court.

Griffith, Paul J., 1992: "Memory in Classical Yogācāra", in *In the Mirror of Memory*, Gyatso (ed.), New York: State University Press, pp.109–31.

Gruber, Hans, 1999: *Kursbuch Vipassanā*, Frankfurt: Fischer.

Guenther, Herbert von, 1991 (1974): *Philosophy and Psychology in the Abhidharma*, Delhi: Motilal Banarsidass.

Gunaratana, Mahāthera Henepola, 1981: *The Satipatthāna Sutta and its Application to Modern Life*, Kandy: BPS.

Gunaratana, Mahāthera Henepola, 1992: *Mindfulness in Plain English*, Malaysia: Wave.

Gunaratana, Mahāthera Henepola, 1996 (1985): *The Path of Serenity and Insight*, Delhi: Motilal Banarsidass.

Gyatso, Janet, 1992: Introduction to *In the Mirror of Memory*, Gyatso (ed.), New York: State University Press, pp.1–19.

Gyori, T.I., 1996: *The Foundations of Mindfulness (Satipatthāna) as a Microcosm of the Theravāda Buddhist World View*, M.A. diss., Washington: American University.

Hamilton, Sue, 1995a: "Anattā: A Different Approach", in *Middle Way*, vol.70, no.1, pp.47–60.

Hamilton, Sue, 1995b: "From the Buddha to Buddhaghosa: Changing Attitudes toward the Human Body in Theravāda Buddhism", in *Religious Reflections on the Human Body*, Law (ed.), Bloomington: Indiana University Press, pp.46–63.

Hamilton, Sue, 1996: *Identity and Experience; the Constitution of the Human Being According to Early Buddhism*, London: Luzac Oriental.

Hamilton, Sue, 1997: "The Dependent Nature of the Phenomenal World", in *Recent Researches in Buddhist Studies*, Dhammajoti (et al, ed.), Colombo/Hong Kong, pp.276–91.

Hanly, Charles, 1984: "Ego Ideal and Ideal Ego", in *International Journal of Psychoanalysis*, no.65, pp.253–61.

Hare, E.M. (tr.), 1955: *The Book of the Gradual Sayings*, vol.IV, London: PTS.

Harvey, Peter, 1986: "Signless Meditations in Pāli Buddhism", in *Journal of the International Association of Buddhist Studies*, vol.9, no.1, pp.25–52.

Harvey, Peter, 1989: "Consciousness Mysticism in the Discourses of the Buddha", in *The Yogi and the Mystic*, Werner (ed.), London: Curzon Press, pp.82–102.

Harvey, Peter, 1995: *The Selfless Mind: Personality, Consciousness and Nirvāna in Early Buddhism*, England, Richmond: Curzon.

Harvey, Peter, 1997: "Psychological Aspects of Theravāda Buddhist Meditation Training", in *Recent Researches in Buddhist Studies*, Dhammajoti (et al, ed.), Colombo/Hong Kong, pp.341–66.

Hayashima, Kyosho, 1967: "Asubha", in *Encyclopaedia of Buddhism*, Sri Lanka, vol.2, pp.270–81.

Hecker, Hellmuth, 1999: "Achtsamkeit und Ihr Vierfacher Aspekt", in *Buddhistische Monatsblätter*, Hamburg, vol.45, no.1, pp.10–12.

Heiler, Friedrich, 1922: *Die Buddhistische Versenkung*, München: Reinhardt.

Holt, John C., 1999 (1981): *Discipline, the Canonical Buddhism of the Vinayapiṭaka*, Delhi: Motilal Banarsidass.

Horner, I.B., 1934: "The Four Ways and the Four Fruits in Pāli Buddhism", in *Indian Historical Quarterly*, pp.785–96.

Horner, I.B. (tr.), 1969: *Milinda's Questions*, vol.1, London: Luzac.

Horner, I.B., 1979 (1936): *The Early Buddhist Theory of Man Perfected*, Delhi: Oriental Books.

Horsch, P., 1964: "Buddhas erste Meditation", in *Asiatische Studien*, vol.17, pp.100–54.

Hurvitz, Leon, 1978: "Fa-Sheng's Observations on the Four Stations of Mindfulness", in *Mahāyāna Buddhist Meditation*, Kiyota (ed.), Honolulu, pp.207–48.

Ireland, John D., 1977: "The Buddha's Advice to Bāhiya", in *Pāli Buddhist Review*, vol.2, no.3, pp.159–61.

Janakabhivaṃsa, U, ?1985: *Vipassanā Meditation the Path to Enlightenment*, Sri Lanka: Systematic Print.

Jayasuriya, W.F., 1988 (1963): *The Psychology & Philosophy of Buddhism*, Malaysia, Kuala Lumpur: Buddhist Missionary Society.

Jayatilleke, K.N., 1948: "Some Problems of Translation and Interpretation, I", in *University of Ceylon Review*, vol.7, pp.208–24.

Jayatilleke, K.N., 1967: "Avijjā", in *Encyclopaedia of Buddhism*, Sri Lanka, vol.2, pp.454–9.

Jayatilleke, K.N., 1970: "Nirvāna", in *Middle Way*, London, vol.45, no.3, pp.112–17.

Jayatilleke, K.N., 1980 (1963): *Early Buddhist Theory of Knowledge*, Delhi: Motilal Banarsidass.

Jayawardhana, Bandula, 1988: "Determinism", in *Encyclopaedia of Buddhism*, Sri Lanka, vol.4, pp.392–412.

Jayawickrama, N.A., 1948: "A Critical Analysis of the Sutta Nipāta", Ph.D. diss., University of London, in *Pāli Buddhist Review*, 1976–8, vol.1, pp.75–90, 137–63; vol.2, pp.14–41, 86–105, 141–58; vol.3, pp.3–19, 45–64, 100–12.

Johansson, Rune E.A., 1965: "Citta, Mano, Viññāṇa – a Psychosemantic Investigation", in *University of Ceylon Review*, vol.23, nos 1 & 2, pp.165–215.

Johansson, Rune E.A., 1969: *The Psychology of Nirvana*, London: Allen and Unwin.

Johansson, Rune E.A., 1985 (1979): *The Dynamic Psychology of Early Buddhism*, London: Curzon.

Jootla, Susan Elbaum, 1983: *Investigation for Insight*, Kandy: BPS.

Jotika, U; Dhamminda, U (tr.), 1986: *Mahāsatipaṭṭhāna Sutta*, Burma: Migadavun Monastery.

Jumnien, Ajahn, 1993 (1977): "Recollections of an Interview", in Kornfield: *Living Buddhist Masters*, Kandy: BPS pp.275–85.

Kalupahana, David J., 1975: *Causality: The Central Philosophy of Buddhism*, Hawaii: University Press.

Kalupahana, David J., 1992 (1987): *The Principles of Buddhist Psychology*, Delhi: Sri Satguru.

Kalupahana, David J., 1994 (1992): *A History of Buddhist Philosophy: Continuities and Discontinuities*, Delhi: Motilal Banarsidass.

Kalupahana, David J., 1999: "Language", in *Encyclopaedia of Buddhism*, Sri Lanka, vol.6, pp.282–4.

Kamalashila, 1994 (1992): *Meditation: the Buddhist Way of Tranquillity and Insight*, Glasgow: Windhorse.

Kariyawasam, A.G.S, 1984: "Delight", in *Encyclopaedia of Buddhism*, Sri Lanka, vol.4, pp.358–9.

Karunadasa, Y., 1989 (?1967): *Buddhist Analysis of Matter*, Singapore, Buddhist Research Society.

Karunadasa, Y., 1994: "Nibbānic Experience: a Non-Transcendental Interpretation", in *Sri Lanka Journal of Buddhist Studies*, vol.4, pp.1–13.

Karunadasa, Y., 1996: *The Dhamma Theory*, Kandy, BPS.

Karunaratne, Upali, 1989: "Dhammānupassanā", in *Encyclopaedia of Buddhism*, Sri Lanka, vol.4, pp.484–6.

Karunaratne, Upali, 1993: "Indriya Saṃvara", in *Encyclopaedia of Buddhism*, Sri Lanka, vol.5, pp.567–8.

Karunaratne, Upali, 1996: "Jhāna", in *Encyclopaedia of Buddhism*, Sri Lanka, vol.6, pp.50–5.

Karunaratne, Upali, 1999a: "Kāyagatāsati", in *Encyclopaedia of Buddhism*, Sri Lanka, vol.6, pp.168–9.

Karunaratne, Upali, 1999b: "Khandha", in *Encyclopaedia of Buddhism*, Sri Lanka, vol.6, pp.192–201.

Karunaratne, Upali, 1999c: "Kilesa", in *Encyclopaedia of Buddhism*, Sri Lanka, vol.6, pp.213–22.

Karunaratne, W.S., 1979: "Change", in *Encyclopaedia of Buddhism*, Sri Lanka, vol.4, pp.115–23.

Karunaratne, W.S., 1988a: *Buddhism: Its Religion and Philosophy*, Singapore: Buddhist Research Society.

Karunaratne, W.S., 1988b: *The Theory of Causality in Early Buddhism*, Sri Lanka, Nugegoda.

Kassapa, Bhikkhu, 1966: "Meditation – Right and Wrong", in *Maha Bodhi*, Calcutta, vol.74, no.11/12, pp.242–5.

Katz, Nathan, 1979: "Does the 'Cessation of the World' Entail the Cessation of the Emotions?" in *Pāli Buddhist Review*, vol.4, no.3, pp.53–65.

Katz, Nathan, 1989 (1982): *Buddhist Images of Human Perfection*, Delhi: Motilal Banarsidass.

Keown, Damien, 1992: *The Nature of Buddhist Ethics*, London: Macmillan.

Khanti, Sayadaw, 1984: *Ānāpāna*, Ashin Parama (tr.), Myanmar, Rangoon: Department for Religious Affairs.

Khantipālo, Bhikkhu, 1981: *Calm and Insight: A Buddhist Manual for Meditators*, London: Curzon.

Khantipālo, Bhikkhu, 1986 (1968): *Practical Advice for Meditators*, Kandy: BPS.

Khemacari Mahathera, 1985: "A Discourse on Satipaṭṭhāna", in Sujīva: *Hop on Board the Ship of Mindfulness*, Singapore: Kowah Printing, pp.17–39.

Kheminda Thera, 1980: *The Way of Buddhist Meditation (Serenity and Insight according to the Pāli Canon)*, Colombo: Lake House.

Kheminda Thera, 1990 (1979): *Satipatthana Vipassanā Meditation: Criticism and Replies*, Malaysia: Selangor Buddhist Vipassanā Meditation Society.

Kheminda Thera, 1992 (1965): *Path, Fruit and Nibbāna*, Colombo: Balcombe.

King, Winston L., 1992 (1980): *Theravāda Meditation: The Buddhist Transformation of Yoga*, Delhi: Motilal Banarsidass.

Kloppenborg, Ria, 1990: "The Buddha's Redefinition of Tapas", in *Buddhist Studies Review*, vol.7, no.1/2, pp.49–73.

Knight, Charles F., 1985 (1970): *Mindfulness – an all Time Necessity*, Kandy: BPS.

Kor Khao Suan Luang, 1985: *Directing to Self-Penetration*, Kandy: BPS.

Kor Khao Suan Luang, 1991: *Looking Inward: Observations on the Art of Meditation*, Kandy: BPS.

Kor Khao Suan Luang, 1993: *Reading the Mind, Advice for Meditators*, Kandy: BPS.

Kor Khao Suan Luang, 1995: *A Good Dose of Dhamma, for Meditators when they are ill*, Kandy: BPS.

Kornfield, Jack, 1977: *The Psychology of Mindfulness Meditation*, Ph.D. diss., USA: Saybrook Institute.

Kornfield, Jack, 1979: "Intensive Insight Meditation", in *Journal of Transpersonal Psychology* , vol.11, no.1, pp.41–58.

Kornfield, Jack, 1993 (1977): *Living Buddhist Masters*, Kandy: BPS.

Kundalābhivaṃsa, Sayadaw U, 1993: *Dhamma Discourses*, Khin Mya Mya (tr.), Singapore (no publ.).

Kyaw Min, U, 1980: *Buddhist Abhidhamma: Meditation & Concentration*, Singapore: Times Books International.

Lamotte, Étienne (tr.), 1970: *Le Traité de la Grande Vertu de Sagesse de Nāgārjuna (Mahāprajñāpāramitāśāstra)*, Louvain: Institut Orientaliste, vol.III.

Law, Bimala C. (tr.), 1922: *Designation of Human Types*, Oxford: PTS.

Law, Bimala C., 1979 (1932): *Geography of Early Buddhism*, Delhi: Oriental Books.

Ledi Sayadaw (n.d.): *Treatise on Meditation*, unpublished manuscript, U Hla Maung (tr.), Myanmar: Burma Pitaka Association.

Ledi Sayadaw, 1983 (1971): *The Requisites of Enlightenment*, Ñāṇapoṇika (tr.), Kandy: BPS.

Ledi Sayadaw, 1985 (1977): *The Noble Eightfold Path and its Factors Explained*, U Saw Tun Teik (tr.), Kandy: BPS.

Ledi Sayadaw, 1986a: *The Buddhist Philosophy of Relations*, U Ñāṇa (tr.), Kandy: BPS.

Ledi Sayadaw, 1986b (1961): *The Manual of Insight*, U Ñāṇa (tr.), Kandy: BPS.

Ledi Sayadaw, 1999a: "The Manual of the Four Noble Truths", in *Manuals of Dhamma*, India, Igatpuri: VRI, pp.133–51.

Ledi Sayadaw, 1999b: "The Manual of Law", Barua et al (tr.), in *Manuals of Dhamma*, India, Igatpuri: VRI, pp.93–131.

Ledi Sayadaw, 1999c: *Manual of Mindfulness of Breathing*, U Sein Nyo Tun (tr.), Kandy: BPS.

Ledi Sayadaw, 1999d: "The Manual of Right Views", U Maung Gyi (et al, tr.), in *Manuals of Dhamma*, India, Igatpuri: VRI, pp.63–91.

Levine, Stephen, 1989 (1979): *A Gradual Awakening*, New York: Anchor Books.

Lin Li-Kouang, 1949: *L'Aide Mémoire de la Vraie Loi (Saddharma-Smṛtyupasthāna-Sūtra)*, Paris: Adrien-Maisonneuve.

Ling, Trevor, 1967: "Mysticism and Nibbāna", in *Middle Way*, London, vol.41, no.4, pp.163–8.
Lopez, Donald S., 1992: "Memories of the Buddha", in *In the Mirror of Memory*, Gyatso (ed.), New York: State University Press, pp.21–45.
Maha Boowa, Phra Ajahn, 1983: *Wisdom Develops Samādhi*, Bangkok: Pow Bhavana Foundation, Wave.
Maha Boowa, Phra Ajahn, 1994: *Kammatthāna, the Basis of Practice*, Malaysia: Wave.
Maha Boowa, Phra Ajahn, 1997: *Patipadā or the Mode of Practice of Ven. Acharn Mun,* Thailand, Wat Pa Baan Taad: Ruen Kaew Press.
Mahasi Sayadaw, 1981: *The Wheel of Dhamma*, U Ko Lay (tr.), Myanmar, Rangoon: Buddhasāsana Nuggaha Organization.
Mahasi Sayadaw, 1990: *Satipatthāna Vipassanā: Insight through Mindfulness*, Kandy: BPS.
Mahasi Sayadaw, 1991 (1971): *Practical Insight Meditation: Basic and Progressive Stages*, U Pe Thin (et al, tr.), Kandy: BPS.
Mahasi Sayadaw, 1992 (1981): *A Discourse on the Mālukyaputta Sutta*, U Htin Fatt (tr.), Malaysia: Selangor Buddhist Vipassanā Meditation Society.
Mahasi Sayadaw, 1994 (1965): *The Progress of Insight: A Treatise on Buddhist Satipatthāna Meditation*, Ñāṇapoṇika (tr.), Kandy: BPS.
Mahasi Sayadaw, 1996: *The Great Discourse on Not Self*, U Ko Lay (tr.), Bangkok: Buddhadhamma Foundation.
Malalasekera, G.P., 1965: "Anattā", in *Encyclopaedia of Buddhism*, Sri Lanka, vol.1, pp.567–76.
Malalasekera, G.P., 1995 (1937): *Dictionary of Pāli Proper Names*, 2 vols., Delhi: Munshiram Manoharlal.
Mangalo, Bhikkhu, 1988 (1970): *The Practice of Recollection*, London: Buddhist Society.
Mann, Robert (et al), 1992: *Buddhist Character Analysis*, Bradford on Avon: Aukana.
Manné, Joy, 1990: "Categories of Sutta in the Pāli Nikāyas", in *Journal of the Pāli Text Society*, vol.15, pp.30–87.
Marasinghe, M.M.J., 1974: *Gods in Early Buddhism*, University of Sri Lanka.
Masefield, Peter, 1979: "The Nibbāna-Parinibbāna Controversy", in *Religion*, vol.9, pp.215–30.
Masefield, Peter, 1987: *Divine Revelation in Buddhism*, Colombo: Sri Lanka Institute of Traditional Studies.
Matthews, B., 1975: "Notes on the Concept of the Will in Early Buddhism", in *Sri Lanka Journal of the Humanities*, no.12, pp.152–60.
McGovern, William Montgomery, 1979 (1872): *A Manual of Buddhist Philosophy*, Delhi: Nag Publications.
Meier, Gerhard, 1978: *Heutige Formen von Satipatthāna Meditationen*, Ph.D. diss., University of Hamburg.
Mendis, N.K.G., 1985: *The Abhidhamma in Practice*, Kandy: BPS.

Mills, L.C.R., 1992: "The Case of the Murdered Monks", in *Journal of the Pāli Text Society*, vol.16, pp.71–5.
Minh Chau, Bhikṣu Thich, 1991: *The Chinese Madhyama Āgama and the Pāli Majjhima Nikāya*, Delhi: Motilal Banarsidass.
Monier-Williams, 1995 (1899): *A Sanskrit-English Dictionary*, Delhi: Motilal Banarsidass.
Naeb, Ajahn, 1993 (1977): "The Development of Insight", in Kornfield: *Living Buddhist Masters*, Kandy: BPS, pp.133–58.
Namto, Bhikkhu, 1984 (1979): *Wayfaring – a Manual for Insight Meditation*, Kandy: BPS.
Ñāṇamoli, Bhikkhu (tr.), 1962: *The Guide (Netti)*, London: PTS.
Ñāṇamoli, Bhikkhu (tr.), 1978 (1960): *The Minor Readings and the Illustrator of Ultimate Meaning*, Oxford: PTS.
Ñāṇamoli, Bhikkhu, 1980 (1971): *A Thinker's Note Book*, Kandy: BPS.
Ñāṇamoli, Bhikkhu (tr.), 1982a (1952): *Mindfulness of Breathing*, Kandy: BPS.
Ñāṇamoli, Bhikkhu (tr.), 1982b: *The Path of Discrimination (Paṭisambhidāmagga)*, London: PTS.
Ñāṇamoli, Bhikkhu (tr.), 1991 (1956): *The Path of Purification (Visuddhimagga)*, Kandy: BPS.
Ñāṇamoli, Bhikkhu, 1994: *A Pāli-English Glossary of Buddhist Technical Terms*, Kandy: BPS.
Ñāṇamoli, Bhikkhu, (et al, tr.), 1995: *The Middle Length Discourses of the Buddha*, Kandy: BPS.
Ñāṇananda, Bhikkhu, 1984 (1973): *Ideal Solitude*, Kandy: BPS.
Ñāṇananda, Bhikkhu, 1985 (1974): *The Magic of the Mind in Buddhist Perspective*, Kandy: BPS.
Ñāṇananda, Bhikkhu, 1986 (1971): *Concept and Reality in Early Buddhist Thought*, Kandy: BPS.
Ñāṇananda, Bhikkhu, 1993: *Towards Calm and Insight: Some Practical Hints*, Sri Lanka, Meetirigala: Nissarana Vanaya.
Ñāṇananda, Bhikkhu, 1999: *Seeing Through, a Guide to Insight Meditation*, Sri Lanka, Devalegama: Pothgulgala Arañya.
Ñāṇapoṇika Thera, 1950: "Satipaṭṭhāna: Die Botschaft an den Westen", in *Studia Pāli Buddhistica*, Hamburg, pp.1–27.
Ñāṇapoṇika Thera, 1951: "Satipaṭṭhāna als ein Weg der Charakter Harmonisierung", in *Einsicht*, pp.34–8.
Ñāṇapoṇika Thera, 1973 (1951): *Kommentar zur Lehrrede von den Grundlagen der Achtsamkeit*, Konstanz: Christiani.
Ñāṇapoṇika Thera (tr.), 1977 (1949): *Sutta Nipāta*, Konstanz: Christiani.
Ñāṇapoṇika Thera, 1978: *The Roots of Good and Evil*, Kandy: BPS.
Ñāṇapoṇika Thera, 1983: *Contemplation of Feeling*, Kandy: BPS.
Ñāṇapoṇika Thera, 1985 (1949): *Abhidhamma Studies: Researches in Buddhist Psychology*, Kandy: BPS.
Ñāṇapoṇika Thera, 1986a (1959): *Anatta and Nibbāna*, Kandy: BPS.
Ñāṇapoṇika Thera, 1986b (1968): *The Power of Mindfulness*, Kandy: BPS.

Ñāṇaponika Thera, 1988 (1964): *The Simile of the Cloth*, Kandy: BPS.
Ñāṇaponika Thera, 1990 (1967): *Protection through Satipaṭṭhāna*, Kandy: BPS.
Ñāṇaponika Thera, 1992 (1962): *The Heart of Buddhist Meditation*, Kandy: BPS.
Ñāṇaponika Thera, 1993 (1958): *The Four Sublime States*, Kandy: BPS.
Ñāṇārāma, Mātara Srī, 1990: *Ānāpānāsati Bhāvanā*, Wettimuny (tr.), Colombo.
Ñāṇārāma, Mātara Srī, 1993 (1983): *The Seven Stages of Purification and the Insight Knowledges*, Kandy: BPS.
Ñāṇārāma, Mātara Srī, 1997: *The Seven Contemplations of Insight*, Kandy: BPS.
Ñāṇasaṃvara, Somdet Phra, 1961: *A Guide to Awareness, Dhamma Talks on the Foundations of Mindfulness*, USA: Buddhadharma Meditation Centre.
Ñāṇasaṃvara, Somdet Phra, 1974: *Contemplation of the Body*, Bangkok: Mahamakut.
Ñāṇatiloka Thera, 1910: *Kleine Systematische Pāli Grammatik*, München: Oskar Schloss.
Ñāṇatiloka Thera, 1983 (1938): *Guide through the Abhidhamma Pitaka*, Kandy: BPS.
Ñāṇatiloka Thera, 1988 (1952): *Buddhist Dictionary*, Kandy: BPS.
Ñāṇuttara Thera, 1990 (1979): *Satipatthāna Vipassanā Meditation: Criticism and Replies*, Malaysia: Selangor Buddhist Vipassanā Meditation Society.
Ñāṇavīra Thera, 1987: *Clearing the Path*, Colombo: Path Press.
Nanayakkara, S.K., 1989: "Dukkha", in *Encyclopaedia of Buddhism*, Sri Lanka, vol.4, pp.696–702.
Nanayakkara, S.K., 1993a: "Impermanence", in *Encyclopaedia of Buddhism*, Sri Lanka, vol.5, pp.537–9.
Nanayakkara, S.K., 1993b: "Insight", in *Encyclopaedia of Buddhism*, Sri Lanka, vol.5, pp.580–4.
Nanayakkara, S.K., 1999: "Kusala", in *Encyclopaedia of Buddhism*, Sri Lanka, vol.6, pp.258–9.
Naranjo, Claudio (et al), 1971: *On the Psychology of Meditation*, London: Allen and Unwin.
Newman, John W., 1996: *Disciplines of Attention: Buddhist Insight Meditation, the Ignatian Spiritual Exercises and Classical Psycho-analysis*, New York: Peter Lang.
Nhat Hanh, Thich, 1990: *Transformation & Healing: The Sutra on the Four Establishments of Mindfulness*, California, Berkeley: Parallax Press.
Norman, K.R., 1984 (1982): "The Four Noble Truths: A Problem of Pāli Syntax", in *Indological and Buddhist Studies*, Hercus (ed.), Delhi: Sri Satguru, pp.377–91.
Norman, K.R., 1991–3: "Mistaken Ideas about Nibbāna", in *The Buddhist Forum*, Skorupski (ed.), University of London, School of Oriental and African Studies, vol.III, pp.211–25.
Norman, K.R., 1997: *A Philological Approach to Buddhism*, University of London, School of Oriental and African Studies.

Ott, Julius von, 1912: "Das Satipaṭṭhāna Suttaṃ", in *Buddhistische Welt*, vol.6, nos.9/10, pp.346–80.
Pa Auk Sayadaw, 1995: *Mindfulness of Breathing and Four Elements Meditation*, Malaysia: Wave.
Pa Auk Sayadaw, 1996: *Light of Wisdom*, Malaysia: Wave.
Pa Auk Sayadaw, 1999: *Knowing and Seeing*, Malaysia (no publ.).
Panabokke, Gunaratne, 1993: *History of the Buddhist Saṅgha in India and Sri Lanka*, Sri Lanka: University of Kelaniya.
Pande, Govind Chandra, 1957: *Studies in the Origins of Buddhism*, India: University of Allahabad.
Pandey, Krishna Kumari, 1988: *Dhammānupassanā: A Psycho-Historicity of Mindfulness*, M.phil. diss., Buddhist Department, Delhi University.
Paṇḍita, U (n.d.): *The Meaning of Satipaṭṭhāna*, Malaysia (no publ.).
Paṇḍita, U, 1993 (1992): *In this Very Life*, U Aggacitta (tr.), Kandy: BPS.
Pensa, Corrado, 1977: "Notes on Meditational States in Buddhism and Yoga", in *East and West*, Rome, no.27, pp.335–44.
Perera, T.H., 1968: "The Seven Stages of Purity", in *Maha Bodhi*, vol.76, no.7, pp.208–11.
Piatigorsky, Alexander, 1984: *The Buddhist Philosophy of Thought*, London: Curzon.
Piyadassi Thera, 1972: "Mindfulness – a Requisite for Mental Hygiene", in *Maha Bodhi*, Calcutta, vol.80, nos.10/11, pp.474–6.
Piyadassi Thera, 1998: *Satta Bojjhaṅgā*, Malaysia, Penang: Inward Path.
Pradhan, Ayodhya Prasad, 1986: *The Buddha's System of Meditation*, 4 vols., Delhi: Sterling.
Premasiri, P.D., 1972: *The Philosophy of the Aṭṭhakavagga*, Kandy: BPS.
Premasiri, P.D., 1976: "Interpretation of Two Principal Ethical Terms in Early Buddhism", in *Sri Lanka Journal of the Humanities*, vol.2, no.1, pp.63–74.
Premasiri, P.D., 1981: "The Role of the Concept of Happiness in the Early Buddhist Ethical System", in *Sri Lanka Journal of the Humanities*, vol.7, pp.61–81.
Premasiri, P.D., 1987a: "Early Buddhist Analysis of Varieties of Cognition", in *Sri Lanka Journal of Buddhist Studies*, vol.1, pp.51–69.
Premasiri, P.D., 1987b: "Early Buddhism and the Philosophy of Religion", in *Sri Lanka Journal of the Humanities*, vol.13, nos.1/2, pp.163–84.
Premasiri, P.D., 1989: "Dogmatism", in *Encyclopaedia of Buddhism*, Sri Lanka, vol.4, pp.655–62.
Premasiri, P.D., 1990a: "Emotion", in *Encyclopaedia of Buddhism*, Sri Lanka, vol.5, pp.57–64.
Premasiri, P.D., 1990b: "Epistemology", in *Encyclopaedia of Buddhism*, Sri Lanka, vol.5, pp.95–112.
Premasiri, P.D., 1990c: "Ethics", in *Encyclopaedia of Buddhism*, Sri Lanka, vol.5, pp.144–65.

Premasiri, P.D., 1991: "The Social Relevance of the Buddhist Nibbāna Ideal", in *Buddhist Thought and Ritual*, Kalupahana (ed.), New York: Paragon House, pp.45–56.

Pruden, Leo M. (tr.), 1988–90: *Abhidharmakośabhāṣyam by Louis de la Vallée Poussin*, 4 vols., Berkeley: Asian Humanities Press.

Rahula, Walpola, 1962: "A Comparative Study of Dhyānas According to Theravāda, Sarvāstivāda and Mahāyāna", in *Maha Bodhi*, Calcutta, vol.70, no.6, pp. 190–9.

Rahula, Walpola, 1997: *Humour in Pāli Literature*, Sri Lanka, Kotte: Buddhist Study & Research Institute.

Ray, Reginald A., 1994: *Buddhist Saints in India*, New York: Oxford University Press.

Reat, N. Ross, 1987: "Some Fundamental Concepts of Buddhist Psychology", in *Religion*, no.17, pp.15–28.

Rhys Davids, C.A.F., 1898: "On the Will in Buddhism", in *Journal of the Royal Asiatic Society*, January, pp.47–59.

Rhys Davids, C.A.F. (tr.), 1922 (1900): *A Buddhist Manual of Psychological Ethics*, Oxford: PTS.

Rhys Davids, C.A.F., 1927a: "Dhyāna in Early Buddhism", in *Indian Historical Quarterly*, no.3, pp.689–715.

Rhys Davids, C.A.F., 1927b: "The Unknown Co-Founders of Buddhism", in *Journal of the Royal Asiatic Society*, part II, pp.193–208.

Rhys Davids, C.A.F., 1937: "Towards a History of the Skandha-Doctrine", in *Indian Culture*, vol.3, pp.405–11, 653–62.

Rhys Davids, C.A.F., 1978 (1936): *The Birth of Indian Psychology and its Development in Buddhism*, Delhi: Oriental Books.

Rhys Davids, C.A.F., 1979 (1930): Introduction to Woodward (tr.): *The Book of the Kindred Sayings*, vol.V, London: PTS.

Rhys Davids, T.W. (et al), 1966 (1910): *Dialogues of the Buddha*, vol.II, London: PTS.

Rhys Davids, T.W. (et al), 1993 (1921–5): *Pāli-English Dictionary*, Delhi: Motilal Banarsidass.

Rhys Davids, T.W., 1997 (1903): *Buddhist India*, Delhi: Motilal Banarsidass.

Rockhill, W. Woodville, 1907: *The Life of the Buddha and the Early History of his Order*, London: Trübner's Oriental Series.

Samararatne, Godwin, 1997: "Watching Thoughts and Emotions", in *The Meditative Way – Contemporary Masters*, Bucknell (ed.), England, Richmond: Curzon Press, pp.136–145.

Santucci, James A., 1979: "Transpersonal Psychological Observations on Theravāda Buddhist Meditation Practices", in *Journal of the International Association for Buddhist Studies*, vol.2, no.2, pp.66–78.

Sarachchandra, Ediriwira, 1994 (1958): *Buddhist Psychology of Perception*, Sri Lanka, Dehiwala: Buddhist Cultural Centre.

Sasaki, Genjun H., 1992 (1986): *Linguistic Approach to Buddhist Thought*, Delhi: Motilal Banarsidass.

Schlingloff, Dieter (ed. and tr.), 1964: *Ein Buddhistisches Yogalehrbuch (Sanskrittexte aus den Turfanfunden)*, Berlin: Akademie Verlag.
Schmidt, Kurt (tr.), 1989: *Buddhas Reden*, Germany, Leimen: Kristkeitz.
Schmithausen, Lambert, 1973: "Spirituelle Praxis und Philosophische Theorie im Buddhismus", in *Zeitschrift für Missionswissenschaft und Religionswissenschaft*, vol.57, no.3, pp.161–86.
Schmithausen, Lambert, 1976: "Die Vier Konzentrationen der Aufmerksamkeit", in *Zeitschrift für Missionswissenschaft und Religionswissenschaft*, no.60, pp.241–66.
Schmithausen, Lambert, 1981: "On some Aspects of Descriptions or Theories of 'Liberating Insight' and 'Enlightenment' in Early Buddhism", in *Studien zum Jainismus und Buddhismus*, Bruhn (et al, ed.), Wiesbaden, pp.199–250.
Schönwerth, Sigurd, 1968: "Los vom Selbst oder Los von den Beilegungen auf dem Wege der Satipaṭṭhāna", in *Yāna, Zeitschrift für Buddhismus und Religiöse Kultur auf Buddhistischer Grundlage*, Germany, Utting a.A., Jahrgang 21, pp.105–12, 152–60, 188–95.
Schrader, F. Otto, 1905: "On the Problem of Nirvāna", in *Journal of the Pāli Text Society*, vol.5, pp.157–70.
Schumann, Hans Wolfgang, 1957: *Bedeutung und Bedeutungsentwicklung des Terminus Saṅkhāra im frühen Buddhismus*, Ph.D. diss., Germany: University of Bonn.
Sekhera, Kalalelle, 1995: *The Path to Enlightenment*, Colombo: Godage & Brothers.
Shapiro, Deane H., 1980: *Meditation: Self-Regulation Strategy & Altered State of Consciousness*, New York: Aldine.
Shapiro, Deane H. (et al), 1984: "Zen Meditation and Behavioral Self-Control", in *Meditation: Classic and Contemporary Perspectives*, Shapiro (ed.), New York: Aldine, pp.585–98.
Shattock, Ernest Henry, 1970 (1958): *An Experiment in Mindfulness*, London: Rider & Co.
Shwe Zan Aung (et al, tr.), 1979: *Points of Controversy*, London: PTS.
Sīlananda, U, 1990: *The Four Foundations of Mindfulness*, Boston: Wisdom.
Sīlananda, U, 1995: *The Benefits of Walking Meditation*, Kandy: BPS.
Singh, Madan Mohan, 1967: *Life in North-Eastern India in Pre-Mauryan Times*, Delhi: Motilal Banarsidass.
Smith, Huston, 1959: *The Religions of Man*, New York: Mentor Books.
Sobti, H.S., 1985: *Nibbāna in Early Buddhism*, Delhi: Eastern Books.
Solé-Leris, Amadeo, 1992 (1986): *Tranquility & Insight: An Introduction to the Oldest Form of Buddhist Meditation*, Kandy: BPS.
Solé-Leris, Amadeo (et al, tr.), 1999: *Majjhima Nikāya*, Barcelona: Kairos.
Soma Thera (tr.), 1981 (1941): *The Way of Mindfulness*, Kandy: BPS.
Soma Thera, 1995 (1961): "Contemplation in the Dhamma", in *The Path of Freedom*, Ehara (tr.), Kandy: BPS, pp.353–62.

Soni, R.L., 1980: *The Only Way to Deliverance; The Buddhist Practice of Mindfulness*, Boulder: Prajñā Press.

Speeth, Kathleen Riordan, 1982: "On Psychotherapeutic Attention", in *Journal of Transpersonal Psychology*, vol.14, no.2, pp.141–60.

Stcherbatsky, Theodor, 1994 (1922): *The Central Conception of Buddhism*, Delhi: Motilal Banarsidass.

Story, Francis, 1965: "Buddhist Meditation and the Layman", in *Middle Way*, London, vol.39, no.4, pp.166–72.

Story, Francis, 1975 (1962): Introduction to Vajirañāṇa: *Buddhist Meditation in Theory and Practice*, Malaysia, Kuala Lumpur.

Story, Francis, 1984 (1971): "Nibbāna", in *The Buddhist Doctrine of Nibbāna*, Kandy: BPS.

Strensky, Ivan, 1980: "Gradual Enlightenment, Sudden Enlightenment and Empiricism", in *Philosophy East and West*, Honolulu, pp.3–20.

Stuart-Fox, Martin, 1989: "Jhāna and Buddhist Scholasticism", in *Journal of the International Association of Buddhist Studies*, vol.12, no.2, pp.79–110.

Sujīva, Ven., 1996: "Access & Fixed Concentration", in *Vipassanā Tribune*, Malaysia, vol.4, no.2, pp.6–11.

Sujīva, Ven., 2000: *Essentials of Insight Meditation Practice: a Pragmatic Approach to Vipassana*, Malaysia, Petaling Jaya: Buddhist Wisdom Centre.

Sunlun Sayadaw, 1993 (1977): "The Yogi and Insight Meditation", in Kornfield: *Living Buddhist Masters*, Kandy: BPS, pp.88–115.

Swearer, Daniel K., 1967: *Knowledge as Salvation: A Study in Early Buddhism*, Ph.D. diss., Princeton University.

Swearer, Daniel K., 1971: *Secrets of the Lotus; Studies in Buddhist Meditation*, New York: Macmillan.

Swearer, Daniel K., 1972: "Two Types of Saving Knowledges in the Pāli Suttas", in *Philosophy East and West*, Honolulu, vol.22, no.4, pp.355–71.

Talamo, Vincenzo (tr.), 1998: *Saṃyutta Nikāya*, Roma: Ubaldini Editore.

Tart, Charles T., 1994: *Living the Mindful Life*, Boston: Shambhala.

Tatia, Nathmal, 1951: *Studies in Jaina Philosophy*, India, Banares: Jain Cultural Research Society.

Tatia, Nathmal, 1992: "Samatha and Vipassanā", in *Vipassanā – the Buddhist Way*, Sobti (ed.), Delhi: Eastern Book, pp.84–92.

Taungpulu Sayadaw, 1993 (1977): "The Methodical Practice of Mindfulness Based on the Thirty-Two Constituent Parts of the Body", in Kornfield: *Living Buddhist Masters*, Kandy: BPS, pp.186–91.

Than Daing, U, 1970: *Cittānupassanā & Vedanānupassanā*, Myanmar, Rangoon: Society for the Propagation of Vipassanā (Mogok Sayadaw).

Ṭhānissaro, Bhikkhu, 1993: *The Mind like Fire Unbound*, Massachusetts, Barre: Dhamma Dana.

Ṭhānissaro, Bhikkhu, 1994: *The Buddhist Monastic Code*, California: Mettā Forest Monastery.

Ṭhānissaro, Bhikkhu, 1996: *The Wings to Awakening*, Massachusetts, Barre: Dhamma Dana.

Thate, Phra Ajahn, 1996: *Meditation in Words*, Thailand, Nongkhai, Wat Hin Mark Pen: Wave.

Thate, Phra Ajahn, 1997 (1991): *Steps along the Path*, Ṭhānissaro (tr.), Thailand, Nongkhai, Wat Hin Mark Pen: Wave.

Ṭhitavaṇṇo, Bhikkhu, 1988: *Mind Development*, Buddhasukha (tr.), Bangkok: Mahamakut Buddhist University.

Thiṭṭila, Ashin (tr.), 1969: *The Book of Analysis*, London: PTS.

Tilakaratne, Asanga, 1993: *Nirvana and Ineffability*, Sri Lanka: Kelaniya University.

Tiwari, Mahesh, 1992: "Vedanānupassanā", in *Vipassanā – the Buddhist Way*, Sobti (ed.), Delhi: Eastern Book, pp.76–83.

Vajirañāṇa, Paravahera Mahāthera, 1946: "Bodhipakkhiya Bhāvanā", in *Maha Bodhi*, Calcutta, vol.54, nos.5/6, pp.45–52.

Vajirañāṇa, Paravahera Mahāthera, 1975 (1962): *Buddhist Meditation in Theory and Practice*, Malaysia, Kuala Lumpur: Buddhist Missionary Society.

Vajirañāṇa, Paravahera Mahāthera (et al), 1984 (1971): *The Buddhist Doctrine of Nibbāna*, Kandy: BPS.

Van Nuys, David, 1971: "A Novel Technique for Studying Attention During Meditation", in *Journal of Transpersonal Psychology*, no.2, pp.125–33.

Van Zeyst, Henri, 1961a: "Abandonment", in *Encyclopaedia of Buddhism*, Sri Lanka, vol.1, pp.2–4.

Van Zeyst, Henri, 1961b: "Abhijjhā", in *Encyclopaedia of Buddhism*, Sri Lanka, vol.1, pp.90–2.

Van Zeyst, Henri, 1961c: "Absolute", in *Encyclopaedia of Buddhism*, Sri Lanka, vol.1, pp.140–4.

Van Zeyst, Henri, 1967a: "Attention", in *Encyclopaedia of Buddhism*, Sri Lanka, vol.2, p.331.

Van Zeyst, Henri, 1967b: "Āyatana", in *Encyclopaedia of Buddhism*, Sri Lanka, vol.2, pp.469–71.

Van Zeyst, Henri, 1970: "Concentration and Meditation", in *Problems Bared*, Colombo: Buddhist Information Centre.

Van Zeyst, Henri, ?1981: *In Search of Truth*, Colombo: Vajra Bodhi.

Van Zeyst, Henri, 1982: *Meditation, Concentration & Contemplation*, Kandy: Vajra Bodhi.

Van Zeyst, Henri, 1989: *Awareness in Buddhist Meditation*, Colombo: Public Trustee.

Vetter, Tilman, 1988: *The Ideas and Meditative Practices of Early Buddhism*, Leiden: Brill.

Vimalaraṃsi, U, 1997: *The Ānāpānasati Sutta*, Taipei: Buddha Educational Foundation.

Vimalo, Bhikkhu, 1959: "Awareness and Investigation", in *Middle Way*, vol.34, no.1, pp.26–9.

Vimalo, Bhikkhu, 1974: "Awakening to the Truth", in *Visakha Puja* (annual publ. of the Buddhist Association of Thailand), Bangkok, pp.53–79.

Vimalo, Bhikkhu, 1987: "The Contemplation of Breathing (Ānāpāna-sati)", in *Middle Way*, London, vol.62, no.3, pp.157–60.
Visuddhacara, Bhikkhu, 1996, 1997: "Vipassanā & Jhāna: What the Masters Say", in *Vipassana Tribune*, Malaysia, vol.4, no.2, pp.14–17; vol.5, no.1, pp.12–16.
Walsh, Roger, 1981: "Speedy Western Minds Slow Slowly", in *ReVision*, no.4, pp.75–7.
Walsh, Roger, 1984: "Initial Meditative Experiences", in *Meditation: Classic and Contemporary Perspectives*, Shapiro (ed.), New York: Aldine, pp.265–70.
Walshe, Maurice (tr.), 1987: *Thus Have I Heard: the Long Discourses of the Buddha*, London: Wisdom.
Walshe, Ruth, 1971: "Buddhist Meditation", in *Middle Way*, London, vol.46, no.3, pp.102–4.
Warder, A.K., 1956: "On the Relationship between Early Buddhism and Other Contemporary Systems", in *Bulletin of the School of Oriental and African Studies*, London, no.18, pp.43–63.
Warder, A.K., 1982: Introduction to Ñāṇamoli: *The Path of Discrimination*, London: PTS, pp.1–64.
Warder, A.K., 1991 (1970): *Indian Buddhism*, Delhi: Motilal Banarsidass.
Watanabe, Fumimaro, 1983: *Philosophy and its Development in the Nikāyas and Abhidhamma*, Delhi: Motilal Banarsidass.
Wayman, Alex, 1976: "Regarding the translations of the Buddhist Terms saññā/saṃjñā, viññāṇa/vijñāna", in *Malalasekera Commemoration Volume*, Wijesekera (ed.), Colombo, pp.325–35.
Wayman, Alex., 1984 (1982): "A Study of the Vedāntic and Buddhist Theory of Nāma-rūpa", in *Indological and Buddhist Studies*, Hercus (ed.), Delhi: Sri Satguru, pp.617–42.
Weeraratne, W.G., 1990: "Eight-fold-Path, Noble", in *Encyclopaedia of Buddhism*, Sri Lanka, vol.5, pp.44–6.
Werner, Karel, 1991: "Enlightenment and Arahantship", in *Middle Way*, May 1991, vol.66, pp.13–18.
West, M.A., 1991 (1978): "Meditation: Magic, Myth and Mystery", in *The Psychology of Meditation*, West (ed.), Oxford: Clarendon Press, pp.192–210.
Wezler, A., 1984: "On the Quadruple Division of the Yogaṣāstra, the Caturvyūhatva of the Cikitsāṣāstra and the 'Four Noble Truths' of the Buddha", in *Indologia Taurinensia*, vol.12, pp.289–337.
Wijebandara, Chandima, 1993: *Early Buddhism: Its Religious and Intellectual Milieu*, Sri Lanka: Kelaniya University.
Wijesekera, O.H. de A., 1976: "Canonical Reference to Bhavaṅga", in *Malalasekera Commemoration Volume*, Wijesekera (ed.), Colombo, pp.348–52.
Wijesekera, O.H. de A., 1994: *Buddhist and Vedic Studies*, Delhi: Motilal Banarsidass.
Woodward, F.L. (tr.), 1980 (1927) & 1979 (1930): *The Book of the Kindred Sayings*, vols. IV & V, London: PTS.

Woolfolk, Robert L., 1984: "Self-Control Meditation and the Treatment of Chronic Anger", in *Meditation: Classic and Contemporary Perspectives*, Shapiro (ed.), New York: Aldine, pp.550–4.

Yubodh, Dhanit, 1985: "What is Sati?", in Sujīva: *Hop on Board the Ship of Mindfulness*, Singapore Kowah Printing, pp.12–16.

LIST OF ABBREVIATIONS

SOURCES

A	*Aṅguttara Nikāya*
Abhidh-s	*Abhidhammatthasaṅgaha*
As	*Atthasālinī* (comy to Dhs)
D	*Dīgha Nikāya*
Dhp	*Dhammapada*
Dhp-a	*Dhammapadaṭṭhakathā* (comy to Dhp)
Dhs	*Dhammasaṅgaṇī*
It	*Itivuttaka*
Ja	*Jātaka*
Kv	*Kathāvatthu*
M	*Majjhima Nikāya*
Mil	*Milindapañhā*
Mp	*Manorathapūraṇī* (comy to A)
Nett	*Nettippakaraṇa*
Nid I	*Mahāniddesa*
Nid II	*Cūḷaniddesa*
Paṭis	*Paṭisambhidāmagga*
Pj II	*Paramatthajotikā* (comy to Sn)
Pp	*Puggalapaññatti*
Ps	*Papañcasūdanī* (comy to M)
Ps-pṭ	*Ps-purāṇaṭīkā* (subcomy to M)
S	*Saṃyutta Nikāya*
Sn	*Sutta Nipāta*
Sp	*Samantapāsādikā* (comy to Vin)
Spk	*Sāratthappakāsinī* (comy to S)
Sv	*Sumaṅgalavilāsinī* (comy to D)
Sv-pṭ	*Sv-purāṇaṭīkā* (subcomy to D)

Th	*Theragāthā*
Th-a	*Theragāthāṭṭhakathā* (comy to Th)
Thī	*Therīgāthā*
Ud	*Udāna*
Ud-a	*Paramatthadīpanī* (comy to Ud)
Vibh	*Vibhaṅga*
Vibh-a	*Sammohavinodanī* (comy to Vibh)
Vin	*Vinayapiṭaka*
Vism	*Visuddhimagga*
Vism-mhṭ	*Paramatthamañjūsā* (subcomy to Vism)

OTHER ABBREVIATIONS

BPS	Buddhist Publication Society
comy	commentary (*aṭṭhakathā*)
diss.	dissertation
ed.	edition/editor
PTS	Pāli Text Society
publ.	publisher/publication
sing.	singular
subcomy	subcommentary (*ṭīkā*)
tr.	translated/translation
VRI	Vipassanā Research Institute

GLOSSARY

A

abhijjhā: covetousness, desires
abhijjhādomanassa: desires and discontent
absorption: *jhāna*
adherence: *abhinivesa*
advantage: *assāda*
agreeable: *appaṭikkūla*
aggregate: *khandha*
ajjhatta: internal
akusala: unwholesome
ālokasaññā: clarity of cognition
ānāpānasati: mindfulness of breathing
anattā: not-self
anger: *dosa*
angry despair: *kodhupāyāsa*
anicca: impermanent
anupassanā: contemplation
anusaya: latent tendency
anussati: recollection
anuttara: unsurpassable
anuvyañjana: detail, secondary characteristic
arising: *samudaya*
ariyasacca: noble truth
arrogance: *atimāna*
arūpa: immaterial
āsava: influx
asubha: unattractive
asuci: impure
ātāpī: diligent
attention: *manasikāra*
austerity: *tapa*
avarice: *macchariya*
aversion: *byāpāda*
avijjā: ignorance
awakening factor: *bojjhaṅga*
awareness: *sati*
āyatana: (sense-)sphere

B

bahiddhā: external
bala: power
bhāvanā: development
body contemplation: *kāyānupassanā*
bojjhaṅga: awakening factor
brahmavihāra: divine abode
byāpāda: aversion

C

calm: *samatha*
cessation: *nirodha*
cetovimutti: freedom of the mind
chanda: desire
citta: mind, state of mind
cittassekaggatā: unification of the mind
clarity of cognition: *ālokasaññā*
clearly knowing: *sampajāna*

clinging: *upādāna*
clinging to particular rules and observances: *sīlabbataparāmāsa*
cognition: *saññā*
compassion: *karuṇā*
complaisance: *anunaya*
conceit: *māna*
concentration: *samādhi*
conceptual proliferation: *papañca*
confidence: *saddhā*
consciousness: *viññāṇa*
consternation: *chambhitatta*
contact: *phassa*
contemplation: *anupassanā*
contracted: *saṅkhitta*
counterpart: *paṭibhāga*
covetousness: *abhijjhā*
craving: *taṇhā*

D

delight: *pāmojja*
delusion: *moha*
dependent co-arising: *paṭicca samuppāda*
desire: *chanda*
desires: *abhijjhā*
desires and discontent: *abhijjhādomanassa*
Dhamma: the teaching of the Buddha
dhamma: mental object, factor for, nature of
dhammānupassanā: contemplation of dhammas
dhammavicaya: investigation-of-*dhammas*
diligent: *ātāpī*
direct intuition: *abhiññā*
direct path: *ekāyano*
disadvantage: *ādīnava*
disagreeable: *paṭikkūla*
discontent: *domanassa*
discrimination: *paṭisambhidā*
disenchantment: *anabhirati*
dispassion: *virāga*
dissatisfaction: *arati*
distortion: *vipallāsa*
distracted: *vikkhitta*
diṭṭhi: view
divine abode: *brahmavihāra*
domanassa: discontent
dosa: anger
doubt: *vicikicchā*
dukkha: unsatisfactory

E

effort: *vāyāma*
ekāyano: direct path
elation: *uppila*
element: *dhātu*
emptiness: *suññatā*
energy: *viriya*
envy: *issā*
equanimity: *upekkhā*
ethical conduct: *sīla*
evil: *pāpa*
existence: *bhava*
external: *bahiddhā, bāhira*

F

faculty: *indriya*
fading away: *virāga*
false speech: *musāvāda*
feeling: *vedanā*
fetter: *saṃyojana*
form: *rūpa*
formation: *saṅkhāra*
freedom by wisdom: *paññāvimutti*
freedom of the mind: *cetovimutti*

G

good: *puñña/kusala*
great: *mahaggata*
greed: *lobha*

H

happiness: *sukha*
hindrance: *nīvaraṇa*
honest: *asaṭha*

I

idappaccayatā: specific conditionality
iddhipāda: road to power
ignorance: *avijjā*
immaterial: *arūpa*
impermanent: *anicca*
impure: *asuci*
inattention: *amanasikāra*

indriya: faculty
indriya saṃvara: sense-restraint
influx: *āsava*
in front: *parimukhaṃ*
insight: *vipassanā*
intention: *saṅkappa*
internal: *ajjhatta*
investigation-of-*dhammas*: *dhammavicaya*
irritation: *paṭigha*

J
jhāna: absorption
jhāna-aṅga: factor of absorption
joy: *pīti, somanassa*

K
kāmacchanda: sensual desire
kāyagatāsati: mindfulness directed to the body
kāyānupassanā: body contemplation
khandha: aggregate
knowledge: *ñāṇa*
kukkucca: worry
kusala: wholesome, skilful, good

L
latent tendency: *anusaya*
letting go: *paṭinissagga, vossagga*
liberated: *vimutta*
liberation: *vimokkha*
lobha: greed
logical reasoning: *ākāraparivitakka*
longing: *abhijappā*
loving kindness: *mettā*
luminous mind: *pabhassara citta*
lust: *rāga*

M
magga: path
mahaggata: great
malicious speech: *pisuṇavāca*
manasikāra: attention
material form: *rūpa*
mano: mind
mental application, initial: *vitakka*
mental application, sustained: *vicāra*
mental object: *dhamma*
meritorious: *puñña*
method: *ñāya*
mettā: loving kindness
micchā sati: wrong mindfulness
middha: torpor
mind: *citta* or *mano*
mindfulness: *sati*
mindfulness directed to the body: *kāyagatāsati*
mindfulness of breathing: *ānāpānasati*
moha: delusion

N
nāmarūpa: name-and-form
name: *nāma*
name-and-form: *nāmarūpa*
ñāya: method
neutral: *adukkhamasukha*
nimitta: sign, cause
nirāmisa: unworldly
nīvaraṇa: hindrance
noble: *ariya*
noble truth: *ariyasacca*
non-returner: *anāgāmi*
not-self: *anattā*
nutriment: *āhāra*

O
once-returner: *sakadāgāmi*
oral tradition: *anussava*

P
pabhassara citta: luminous mind
pajānāti: he knows
paññā: wisdom
paññāvimutti: freedom by wisdom
pāpa: evil
papañca: conceptual proliferation
parimukhaṃ: in front
passaddhi: tranquillity
passing away: *atthagama, vaya*
pasture: *gocara*
path: *magga*
paṭicca samuppāda: dependent co-arising
patience: *khanti*
paṭṭhāna: foundation, cause
paṭigha: irritation

paṭikkūla: disagreeable
paṭinissagga: letting go
pīti: joy
phassa: contact
pleasant: *sukha*
power: *bala*
presence: *upaṭṭhāna*
puñña: good, meritorious
purification: *visuddhi*

R

rāga: lust
rapacious greed: *giddhilobha*
recollection: *anussati*
repulsive: *paṭikkūla*
restlessness: *uddhacca*
right: *sammā*
right action: *sammā kammanta*
right concentration: *sammā samādhi*
right effort: *sammā vāyāma*
right livelihood: *sammā ājīva*
right mindfulness: *sammā sati*
right speech: *sammā vācā*
right thought: *sammā saṅkappa*
right view: *sammā diṭṭhi*
road to power: *iddhipāda*
rūpa: form

S

saddhā: confidence
samādhi: concentration
samatha: calm
sāmisa: worldly
sammā: right
sammā ājīva: right livelihood
sammā diṭṭhi: right view
sammā kammanta: right action
sammā samādhi: right concentration
sammā saṅkappa: right thought
sammā sati: right mindfulness
sammā vāca: right speech
sammā vāyāma: right effort
sampajañña: clear knowledge
sampajāna: clearly knowing
samudaya: arising
saṃyojana: fetter
saṅkhāra: volition, formation
saṅkhitta: contracted
saññā: cognition
saññāvedayitanirodha: cessation of cognition and feeling
sappurisa: worthy person
sati: awareness, mindfulness
satipaṭṭhāna: presence of mindfulness
sa-uttara: surpassable
seclusion: *viveka*
sense-restraint: *indriya saṃvara*
sense-sphere: *āyatana*
sensual desire: *kāmacchanda*
sign: *nimitta*
signless: *animitta*
sīla: ethical conduct
sīlabbataparāmāsa: clinging to particular rules and observances
skilful: *kusala*
sloth: *thīna*
specific conditionality: *idappaccayatā*
spiteful scolding: *nindārosa*
standpoint: *adhiṭṭhāna*
state of mind: *citta*
stream-enterer: *sotāpanna*
suññatā: emptiness
sukha: happiness
supatiṭṭhita: well established
surpassable: *sa-uttara*

T

taṇhā: craving
tevijjā: threefold higher knowledge
thīna: sloth
thought: *vitakka*
torpor: *middha*
train: *sikkhati*
tranquillity: *passaddhi*
truth: *sacca*

U

uddhacca: restlessness
unattractive: *asubha*
unease: *duṭṭhulla*
unification of the mind: *cittassekaggatā*
unity: *ekatta*
unpleasant: *dukkha*
unsatisfactory: *dukkha*
unsurpassable: *anuttara*

unwholesome: *akusala*
unworldly: *nirāmisa*
upaṭṭhāna: presence
upekkhā: equanimity

V
vaya: passing away
vāyāma: effort
vedanā: feeling
vicāra: sustained mental application
vicikicchā: doubt
view: *diṭṭhi*
vikkhitta: distracted
vimutta: liberated
viññāṇa: consciousness
vipallāsa: distortion
vipassanā: insight
virāga: fading away, dispassion
viriya: energy
vision: *dassana*
vitakka: initial mental application
volition: *saṅkhāra*

W
way out: *nissaraṇa*
well established: *supatiṭṭhita*
wholesome: *kusala*
wisdom: *paññā*
wise attention: *yoniso manasikāra*
worldling: *puthujjana*
worldly: *sāmisa*
worry: *kukkucca*
worthy person: *sappurisa*
wrong mindfulness: *micchā sati*

Y
yoniso manasikāra: wise attention

INDEX

WINDHORSE PUBLICATIONS

Windhorse Publications is a Buddhist charitable company based in the UK. We place great emphasis on producing books of high quality that are accessible and relevant to those interested in Buddhism at whatever level. We are the main publisher of the works of Sangharakshita, the founder of the Triratna Buddhist Order and Community. Our books draw on the whole range of the Buddhist tradition, including translations of traditional texts, commentaries, books that make links with contemporary culture and ways of life, biographies of Buddhists, and works on meditation.

As a not-for-profit enterprise, we ensure that all surplus income is invested in new books and improved production methods, to better communicate Buddhism in the 21st century. We welcome donations to help us continue our work – to find out more, go to windhorsepublications.com.

The Windhorse is a mythical animal that flies over the earth carrying on its back three precious jewels, bringing these invaluable gifts to all humanity: the Buddha (the 'awakened one'), his teaching, and the community of all his followers.

Windhorse Publications
169 Mill Road
Cambridge CB1 3AN UK
info@windhorsepublications.com

Perseus Distribution
210 American Drive
Jackson TN 38301
USA

Windhorse Books
PO Box 574
Newtown NSW 2042
Australia

TRIRATNA BUDDHIST COMMUNITY

Windhorse Publications is a part of the Triratna Buddhist Community, which has more than sixty centres on five continents. Through these centres, members of the Triratna Buddhist Order offer classes in meditation and Buddhism, from an introductory to a deeper level of commitment. Members of the Triratna community run retreat centres around the world, and the Karuna Trust, a UK fundraising charity that supports social welfare projects in the slums and villages of South Asia.

Many Triratna centres have residential spiritual communities and ethical Right Livelihood businesses associated with them. Arts activities and body awareness disciplines are encouraged also, as is the development of strong bonds of friendship between people who share the same ideals. In this way Triratna is developing a unique approach to Buddhism, not simply as a set of techniques, but as a creatively directed way of life for people living in the modern world.

If you would like more information about Triratna please visit thebuddhistcentre.com or write to:

London Buddhist Centre
51 Roman Road
London E2 0HU
UK

Aryaloka
14 Heartwood Circle
Newmarket NH 03857
USA

Sydney Buddhist Centre
24 Enmore Road
Sydney NSW 2042
Australia

ALSO FROM WINDHORSE PUBLICATIONS

Perspectives on Satipaṭṭhāna

By Anālayo

As mindfulness is increasingly embraced in the contemporary world as a practice that brings peace and self-awareness, Bhikkhu Anālayo casts fresh light on the earliest sources of mindfulness in the Buddhist tradition.

The Satipaṭṭhāna Sutta is well known as the main source for Buddhist teachings on mindfulness and its place in the Buddhist path. Ten years after Anālayo's acclaimed study of the Sutta, his current work, *Perspectives on Satipaṭṭhāna*, brings a new dimension to our understanding by comparing the Pali text with versions that have survived in Chinese. Anālayo also draws on the presentation of mindfulness in a number of other discourses as they survive in Chinese and Tibetan translations as well as in Pali.

The result is a wide-ranging exploration of what mindfulness meant in early Buddhism. Informed by Anālayo's outstanding scholarship, depth of understanding and experience as a practitioner, this book sheds fresh light on material that is central to our understanding of Buddhist practice, bringing us as close as we can come to the mindfulness teachings of the Buddha himself.

'Anālayo builds on his earlier ground-breaking work, *Satipaṭṭhāna: The Direct Path to Realization*. The brilliance of his scholarly research, combined with the depth of his meditative understanding, provides an invaluable guide to these liberating practices.'

Joseph Goldstein

'He offers us a work of great scholarship and wisdom that will be of immense benefit to anyone who wants to seriously study or to establish a practice of mindfulness.'

Sharon Salzberg

'A treasury of impeccable scholarship and practice, offering a wise, open-minded and deep understanding of the Buddha's original teaching.'

Jack Kornfield

1SBN: 9781 909314 03 0
£15.99 / $24.95 / €19.95
336 pages

The Buddha's Noble Eightfold Path

by Sangharakshita

The Noble Eightfold Path is the most widely known of the Buddha's teachings. It is ancient, extending back to the Buddha's first discourse and is highly valued as a unique treasury of wisdom and practical guidance on how to live our lives.

This introduction takes the reader deeper while always remaining practical, inspiring and accessible. Sangharakshita translates ancient teachings and makes them relevant to the way we live our lives today.

Probably the best 'life coaching' manual you'll ever read, the key to living with clarity and awareness. – Karen Robinson, *The Sunday Times*

ISBN 9781 899579 81 5
£9.99 / $16.95 / €16.95
176 pages

Great Faith, Great Wisdom

Practice and Awakening in the Pure Land Sutras of Mahayana Buddhism

by Ratnaguna and Śraddhāpa

The three Pure Land sutras are a body of Mahayana scriptures that for centuries have played an important part in the spiritual life of East Asian Buddhists. These Buddhist texts – both ancient and perennial – communicate a path of faith and grace, as well as effort and practice. Using a practical and imaginative approach, Ratnaguna explores their main themes, which are expressed through myth and magical imagery. This book will appeal to all Buddhists – whether from the East Asian Pure Land traditions or not – as well as anyone interested in Buddhism from a practical point of view. Includes new translations of the three Pure Land sutras by Śraddhāpa.

ISBN 9781 909314 56 6
£13.99 / $21.95 / €17.95
392 pages

Living Ethically

Advice from Nagarjuna's Precious Garland

by Sangharakshita

In a world of increasingly confused ethics, *Living Ethically* looks back over the centuries for guidance from Nagarjuna, one of the greatest teachers of the Mahayana tradition. Drawing on the themes of Nagarjuna's famous scripture, *Precious Garland of Advice for a King*, this book explores the relationship between an ethical lifestyle and the development of wisdom. Covering both personal and collective ethics, Sangharakshita considers such enduring themes as pride, power and business, as well as friendship, love and generosity.

Sangharakshita is the founder of the Triratna Buddhist Community, a worldwide Buddhist movement. He has a lifetime of teaching experience and is the author of over 40 books.

ISBN 9781 899579 86 0
£10.99 / $17.95 / €13.95
216 pages

Living Wisely

Further Advice from Nagarjuna's Precious Garland

by Sangharakshita

How do we live wisely? This is the burning question that Sangharakshita seeks to answer in this companion volume of commentary on a famous text, *Precious Garland of Advice for a King*, the advice being that of the great Indian Buddhist teacher Nagarjuna. In the companion volume, *Living Ethically*, Sangharakshita showed us that to live a Buddhist life we need to develop an ethical foundation, living in a way that is motivated increasingly by love, contentment and awareness. However, from a Buddhist viewpoint, 'being good' is not good enough. We need to use our positive ethical position, our momentum in goodness, to develop wisdom, a deep understanding of the true nature of existence. We become good in order to learn to be wise.

Sangharakshita is the founder of the Triratna Buddhist Community, a worldwide Buddhist movement. He has a lifetime of teaching experience and is the author of over 40 books.

ISBN 9781 907314 93 3
£10.99 / $16.95 / €13.95
152 pages

The Art of Reflection

by Ratnaguna

It is all too easy either to think obsessively, or to not think enough. But how do we think usefully? How do we reflect? Like any art, reflection can be learnt and developed, leading to a deeper understanding of life and to the fullness of wisdom. *The Art of Reflection* is a practical guide to reflection as a spiritual practice, about 'what we think and how we think about it'. It is a book about contemplation and insight, and reflection as a way to discover the truth.

No-one who takes seriously the study and practice of the Dharma should fail to read this ground-breaking book. – Sangharakshita, founder of the Triratna Buddhist Community

The Art of Reflection *will give teachers insight into Buddhist practice. Even more importantly, it may help to develop the ability to engage in deeper personal and professional reflection.* – Joyce Miller, *REtoday*

ISBN 9781 899579 89 1
£9.99 / $16.95 / €12.95
160 pages

This Being, That Becomes

by Dhivan Thomas Jones

Dhivan Thomas Jones takes us into the heart of the Buddha's insight that everything arises in dependence on conditions. With the aid of lucid reflections and exercises he prompts us to explore how conditionality works in our own lives, and provides a sure guide to the most essential teaching of Buddhism.

Clearly and intelligently written, this book carries a lot of good advice. – Prof Richard Gombrich, author of *What the Buddha Thought*

ISBN 9781 899579 90 7
£10.99 / $15.95 / €13.95
216 pages

Meeting the Buddhas series

by Vessantara

This set of three informative guides, by one of our best-selling authors, introduces the historical and archetypal figures from within the Tibetan Buddhist tradition. Each book focuses on a different set of figures and features full-colour illustrations.

A Guide to the Buddhas

ISBN 9781 899579 83 9
£11.99 / $18.95 / €18.95
176 pages

A Guide to the Bodhisattvas

ISBN 9781 899579 84 6
£11.99 / $18.95 / €18.95
128 pages

A Guide to the Deities of the Tantra

ISBN 9781 899579 85 3
£11.99 / $18.95 / €18.95
192 pages

Buddhist Meditation

Tranquillity, Imagination & Insight

by Kamalashila

First published in 1991, this book is a comprehensive and practical guide to Buddhist meditation, providing a complete introduction for beginners, as well as detailed advice for experienced meditators seeking to deepen their practice. Kamalashila explores the primary aims of Buddhist meditation: enhanced awareness, true happiness, and – ultimately – liberating insight into the nature of reality. This third edition includes new sections on the importance of the imagination, on Just Sitting, and on reflection on the Buddha. Kamalashila has been teaching meditation since becoming a member of the Triratna Buddhist Order in 1974. He has developed approaches to meditation practice that are accessible to people in the contemporary world, whilst being firmly grounded in the Buddhist tradition.

A wonderfully practical and accessible introduction to the important forms of Buddhist meditation. From his years of meditation practice, Kamalashila has written a book useful for both beginners and longtime practitioners. – Gil Fronsdal, author of *A Monastery Within*, founder of the Insight Meditation Center, California, USA.

This enhanced new edition guides readers more clearly into the meditations and draws out their significance more fully, now explicitly oriented around the 'system of meditation'. This system provides a fine framework both for understanding where various practices fit in and for reflecting on the nature of our own spiritual experiences. Kamalashila has also woven in an appreciation of a view of the nature of mind that in the Western tradition is known as the imagination, helping make an accessible link to our own philosophical and cultural traditions. – Lama Surya Das, author of *Awakening the Buddha Within*, founder of Dzogchen Center and Dzogchen Meditation Retreats, USA

His approach is a clear, thorough, honest, and, above all, open-ended exploration of the practical problems for those new to and even quite experienced in meditation. – Lama Shenpen Hookham, author of *There's More to Dying Than Death*, founder of the Awakened Heart Sangha, UK

ISBN 9781 907314 09 4
£14.99 / $27.95 / €19.95
272 pages